DEVELOPING TALENT ACROSS THE LIFE SPAN

Developing talent across the life span

edited by

Cornelis F.M. van Lieshout
University of Nijmegen, The Netherlands

Peter G. Heymans
Utrecht University, The Netherlands

Psychology Press
Taylor & Francis Group
HOVE AND NEW YORK

First published 2000 by Psychology Press
27 Church Road, Hove, East Sussex, BN3 2FA

Simultaneously published in the USA and Canada
by Psychology Press
711 Third Avenue, New York, NY 10017

Psychology Press is an imprint of the Taylor and Francis Group, an informa business

© 2000 by Psychology Press

All rights reserved. No part of this book may be reprinted or
reproduced or utilised in any form or by any electronic,
mechanical, or other means, now known or hereafter invented,
including photocopying and recording, or in any information
storage or retrieval system, without permission in writing from
the publishers.

British Library Cataloguing in Publication Data

A catalogue record for this book is available from the British Library

ISBN 13: 978-1-138-88303-1 (pbk)
ISBN 13: 978-0-86377-556-7 (hbk)

Front cover artwork by Jan Gowert Masche and Vanessa Halim, see chapter 9.
Typeset by DP Photosetting, Aylesbury, Bucks.

Publisher's Note
The publisher has gone to great lengths to ensure the quality of this reprint
but points out that some imperfections in the original may be apparent.

Liber Amicorum
in tribute to Franz J. Mönks

Contents

List of Contributors xi
Acknowledgement xiii
Introduction xiv

Part One: Conceptual perspectives on the development of talent

1. Developmental theory and the expression of gifts and talents 3
 David Henry Feldman
  Introduction 3
  The need for a framework to guide research and practice 6
  Towards a framework for the study of giftedness and talent 7
  The universal to unique continuum 8
  The development of gifts and talents 10
  The evolution of gifts and talents 12
  Conclusion 14

2. Slumbering talents: Where do they reside? 17
 Ad W. Smitsman
  Introduction 17
  Talents as hidden core: Preformism and unwanted dichotomies 20
  Development and the organism—environment system 23
  The significance of the environment for an organism's developing capabilities 28
  Enhancement of capabilities to act by tool use 32
  Conclusion 38

Part Two: Intellectual giftedness

3. Successful intelligence: A unified view of giftedness   43
Robert J. Sternberg
    The concept of successful intelligence   44
    Components of successful intelligence   47
    Putting together the three aspects of successful intelligence   58
    Acknowledgement   62

4. The role of intelligence as a major determinant of a successful occupational life   67
Franz E. Weinert and Ernst A. Hany
    Introduction   67
    The GOLD study: Method   76
    Results   82
    General discussion and concluding remarks   92

Part Three: Specific talents: Personality, morality, emotionality, academic achievement, and art

5. The gifted personality: Resilient children and adolescents, their adjustment and their relationships   103
Cornelis F.M. van Lieshout, Ron H.J. Scholte, Marcel A.G. van Aken, Gerbert J.T. Haselager, and J. Marianne Riksen-Walraven
    Different approaches to personality   104
    Resilience across the primary school years   106
    Resilient adolescents   108
    Subtypes of resilient children and adolescents   109
    Agentic and communal resilients, perceived support, and sociometric status   115
    Boys versus girls   119
    Conclusions   121

6. The morality paradox: Choosing not to be moral as a component of moral excellence   125
Tjeert Olthof
    Introduction   125
    The nature of morality   126
    Moral excellence   127
    The case of R   133
    The hazards of untamed moral commitment   140
    In search of moral excellence: Beyond the fusion of goals   142
    Acknowledgements   147

7. Talent for development: Responding to contextual promises   151
Peter Heymans
    Introduction   151

The developmental nexus and its dependence on symbolic structures   154
The developmental nexus   154
Young Marc making a developmental opportunity come true   158
Concluding observations   164

8. Successful achievement in mathematics: China and the United States   167
Harold W. Stevenson, Shinying Lee, and Xiaotong Mu
Introduction   167
Academic achievement in China   168
High achievers in China and the United States   172
Conclusions   181

9. It's (im)possible to become a genius! The development of drawing   185
Werner Deutsch
Introduction   185
A short survey about drawing   185
The documentation of children's drawings   186
The development of drawing: Three individual case studies   188
Development and talent   198
Acknowledgements   198

Part Four: Supporting the development of talent

10. Gifted infants: What kinds of support do they need?   203
J. Marianne Riksen-Walraven and Jolien Zevalkink
The role of experience in the development of talents   203
A supportive environment for gifted infants is one that fosters competence motivation   205
Quality of support provided by parents   209
Quality of parental support and achievement of excellence in Surinamese-Dutch infants   211
Conclusions: Back to the beginning   224

11. Teaching for talent: Lessons from the research   231
Joan Freeman
Problems of definitions   231
Some specific research concerns   233
How the talented are different   236
Educating for the development of talent   238
Current trends in developing talent   241
Conclusions   244

12. The Juilliard model for developing young adolescent performers: An educational prototype   249
Rena F. Subotnik
Introduction: The Juilliard School   249
Structure of the study   251

Explicit talent-development variables   252
More implicit talent-development variables   260
Conclusions   273
Note   275

13. Talent and self-narrative: The survival of an underachieving adolescent   277
Hubert J.M. Hermans and Margreet F. Poulie
The temporal organisation of self-narrative   278
Valuation theory: Self as an organised process   280
The self-confrontation method: Affective organisation of meaning units   282
Leo's story: From the cold road to the road of fire   287
The relevance of becoming aware of one's talent   294
Acknowledgement   296

14. Support for university students: Individual and social factors   299
Kurt A. Heller and Petra Viek
Introduction   299
Current findings on research into talent and excellent performance in higher education   300
The programme evaluation study: Method   306
Results   311
Discussion   315

Author Index   **323**
Subject Index   **329**

List of contributors

Werner Deutsch, TU Braunschweig, Institute for Psychology, Spielmannstrasse 19, 38104 Braunschweig, Germany.
David Henry Feldman, Eliot-Pearson Department of Child Development, Tufts University, 105 College Avenue, Medford, MA 02155, USA.
Joan Freeman, Middlesex University, School of Lifelong Learning and Education, Trent Park, Bramley Road, London, N14 4YZ.
Ernst A. Hany, University of Erfurt, Nordhäuser Str. 63, D-99089 Erfurt, Germany.
Gerbert J.T. Haselager, Department of Developmental Psychology, University of Nijmegen, PO Box 9104, 6500 HE Nijmegen, The Netherlands.
Kurt A. Heller, Department of Psychology, University of Munich, Leopoldstrasse 13, D-80802 Munich, Germany.
Hubert J.M. Hermans, University of Nijmegen, PO Box 9104, 6500 HE Nijmegen, The Netherlands.
Peter G. Heymans, Department of Developmental Psychology, Faculty of Social Sciences, Utrecht University, PO Box 80140, 3584 CS Utrecht, The Netherlands.
Shinying Lee, Center for Human Growth and Development, University of Michigan, 300 North Ingalls, 10th Floor, Ann Arbor, MI 48109, USA.
Xiaotong Mu, Center for Human Growth and Development, University of Michigan, 300 North Ingalls, 10th Floor, Ann Arbor, MI 48109, USA.
Tjeert Olthof, Department of Developing Psychology, Free University Amsterdam, Van der Boechorststraat 1, 1081 BT Amsterdam, The Netherlands.
Margreet F. Poulie, Reflection & Action, Weezenhof 84-09, 6536 BT Nijmegen, The Netherlands.
J. Marianne Riksen-Walraven, Department of Developmental Psychology, University of Nijmegen, PO Box 9104, 6500 HE Nijmegen, The Netherlands.

Ron H.J. Scholte, Department of Developmental Psychology, University of Nijmegen, PO Box 9104, 6500 HE Nijmegen, The Netherlands.

Ad W. Smitsman, Department of Psychology, University of Nijmegen, PO Box 9104, 6500 HE Nijmegen, The Netherlands.

Robert J. Sternberg, Department of Psychology, Yale University, Box 208205, New Haven, CT 06520-8205, USA.

Harold W. Stevenson, Center for Human Growth and Development, University of Michigan, 300 North Ingalls, 10th Floor, Ann Arbor, MI 48109, USA.

Rena F. Subotnik, Educational Foundations, Hunter College, 695 Park Avenue, New York, NY 10021, USA.

Marcel A.G. van Aken, Department of Developmental Psychology, University of Nijmegen, PO Box 9104, 6500 HE Nijmegen, The Netherlands.

Cornelis F.M. van Lieshout, Department of Developmental Psychology, University of Nijmegen, PO Box 9104, 6500 HE Nijmegen, The Netherlands.

Petra Viek, Department of Psychology, University of Munich, Leopoldstrasse 13, D-80802 Munich, Germany.

Franz E. Weinert, Max Planck Institute for Psychological Research, Amalienstrasse 33, D-80799 Munich, Germany.

Jolien Zevalkink, Department of Developmental Psychology, University of Nijmegen, PO Box 9104, 6500 HE Nijmegen, The Netherlands.

Acknowledgement

The publication of this volume was supported by a grant from the Stifterverband für die Deutsche Wissenschaft (Donors Association for the Promotion of Science in Germany) through Bildung und Begabung e.V., Bonn.

Introduction

In recent years, fascinating new theoretical perspectives and decisive empirical findings have been presented on the life-span development of talent. Recent research has examined how talent in general and talent within specific domains can be the result of the acquisition of a sequence of skills and how the acquisition of these skills may be facilitated by changes in the individual's environment. Just which aptitudes and environmental features are involved in the acquisition of these skills and how do these fit in with the individual's development? To what degree are particular aptitudes innate and stable across the life span? And what changes in the physical and social context contribute to the growth or decline of talent? Is the development of talent for general top achievement similar to the development of specific talents in the domains of literature, painting, sculpture, dance, playing chess, sports, or professional skills? Is the development of talent observed for specific groups of people similar to individual cases? How should the different numbers of top talented women and men in several domains be explained? In the chapters in this volume, these and a number of related questions will be investigated.

The contributions in this volume reveal important shifts away from traditional perspectives on giftedness and talent. First, talent and giftedness are no longer viewed as just a matter of rather stable individual differences in potential or performance. Instead, developmental changes in talents are currently examined in close relation to changing contextual support, changing constraints, and changing tasks. Second, giftedness is no longer defined as advanced maturity or achievement beyond certain social comparison groups or age standards. Instead, talented developmental pathways are assumed to be the result of goal-oriented individuals reciprocally and successfully interacting with changing contextual opportunities and constraints. Third, considerable efforts have been made to overcome the classical nature–nurture dichotomy. Across the life course, a continuous interaction is now assumed to occur among various behaviour-regulating systems. Fourth, the study of talent and giftedness is no longer restricted to childhood and adolescence. In several challenging, sometimes paradoxical and sometimes controversial contributions, the study of talent and giftedness is extended across the entire life course. Fifth, giftedness is sometimes described as the development of small privileged groups and sometimes as a unique individual life course in the present volume. And sixth, cultural differences and differences among minority groups in the development of giftedness are also examined.

The book is divided into four parts. Part 1 concerns the changing theoretical perspectives on the development of talent and giftedness. Part 2 addresses the reformulation of the traditional domain of intellectual giftedness. Part 3 extends the intellectual domain of giftedness into a variety of both more general and more specific domains of giftedness. Finally, various forms of support for giftedness across the life span are discussed in Part 4. In the following, we will present a brief overview of the contributions in each part of the volume.

Part 1 consists of two chapters on current theoretical orientations on the development of talent. The basic tenet of Feldman's chapter is that research on exceptional talents and abilities can benefit from a more appropriate theoretical framework. Although psychometric theory has been useful for more than a century, considerable limitations and constraints have become apparent and the need for an alternative framework has become acute. Feldman thus proposes what he calls Non-universal Theory, which places questions of nature/nurture, universal/unique, average/exceptional and the like within the broader context of development and thereby provides a more flexible framework for the study of talent and its development. Smitsman argues that the development of capabilities and talent across the life course rests on the resources provided by an agent's body and brain and the opportunities and constraints furnished by the environment. He emphasises how various resources become available during the life course via tools created by the agent and tools provided by society. Such tools allow an agent to produce new resources and extend existing resources to create new environmental opportunities.

The two chapters in Part 2 offer somewhat contradictory views on the role of intelligence and intellectual giftedness in professional careers. Sternberg vividly argues that intelligence as measured by traditional intelligence tests has only a limited value for the prediction of professional success. Successful intelligence assumes as essential components analytical abilities, creative abilities, and practical abilities, including tacit knowledge. Adding tacit knowledge in particular markedly increases prediction of professional success. Weinert and Hany report on a unique longitudinal study of twins spanning a period of almost 60 years in the life courses of their subjects, encompassing a world war and both the rise and fall of a political–socio-economic system in a country divided for many decades. Their data show the strong genetic contribution of IQ, and also the influential roles of the educational and professional levels of the parents in the prediction of occupational success. In a later chapter in Part 4, Subotnik suggests that successful musicians as mentors provide necessary tacit knowledge for adolescent future performers. In turn, this raises the possibility of parents with high-level education and professions providing necessary tacit knowledge, as assumed by Sternberg, in a manner similar to mentors for adolescent musicians.

Part 3 is devoted to the development of talents outside the traditional field of intelligence. Although Weinert and Hany complained about the generality of the concepts of intelligence and occupational success in their study of the professional life courses of German twins, they nevertheless demonstrated the specific prediction of occupational success by intelligence. Occupational satisfaction, in contrast, was either negatively predicted or not predicted at all by intelligence. Van Lieshout et al. adopt the broader concept of personality to identify talented functioning in the context of children's and adolescents' relationships and groups. In their view, intellect is part of an individual's personality and, indeed, a number of the children, and especially the girls with a gifted personality profile in their sample, are found to develop high-level social competence. Such high-level social competence is found to be most specifically related to the personality dimension of agreeableness. In the next chapter, Olthof focuses on a domain closely related to social competence, namely moral excellence. Olthof proposes a solution to the problem of moral excellence by definition leading to moral tyranny. After reading his chapter, however, one may still ask just how far a person should or may deviate from absolute morality to reach optimal morality or meta-moral excellence. In a related chapter, Heymans explores how the continuous joint commitment to the goal orientations of a target individual and of key individuals in his or her social network is reflected in the emotional development of the target individual. More specifically, Heymans proposes a theory and methodology to study the development of talent in connection with the continuous reciprocal interaction between the individual and the environment. In their chapter, Stevenson and his colleagues add to their earlier comparative studies providing a clear picture of the many ways in which beliefs, attitudes, and everyday practices support the consistently higher academic achievement of East Asian primary and secondary school students when compared to their Western counterparts. They address the question of whether the beliefs, attitudes, and practices of the most academically successful students in East Asia and the West are comparable or different. Finally, in a chapter reporting on a longitudinal comparison of individuals who have failed versus succeeded in the development of drawing and painting skills, Deutsch illustrates and discusses how early children's qualities in drawing can be kept alive at later periods of development.

Part 4 of this volume is devoted to the support of talent development at various points in development, from various theoretical perspectives, for both groups and individuals and in a number of different domains. Riksen-Walraven and Zevalkink raise the question of whether infants need support to develop their talents and what sequences in various kinds of support appear to foster the development of talents across infancy and early childhood. Observational and intervention studies with infants in the Netherlands, Japan, and Indonesia and with Surinam-Dutch minority infants have already shown competence motivation as the impetus for the development of talents to require a supportive environment. In this chapter, the critical aspects of parental support and the conditions impairing parents' ability to provide adequate support are elaborated on and empirically demonstrated for samples of normal and gifted infants and for individual infants as well.

In primary school years, the quality of the school teaching is also found to be essential for the talented. Freeman surveys research on school-based programmes and argues that every school should have a clear policy for the encouragement of high-level performance in both pupils and teachers. More specifically, she proposes the "sports approach" in which those who are particularly talented and motivated can put themselves forward for extra tuition and practice but in the area of foreign languages or physics, for example. Subotnik explores the model of America's most prestigious Juilliard Conservatory of Music, as an educational prototype for talent development in the arts and sciences. In her study, she distinguishes the "explicit" and "implicit" aspects of the programme. The explicit aspects include open and easily accessible programme descriptions, descriptions of standardised practice, explicit statement of philosophy and goals, the recruitment of applicants, available resources, the audition process, and the curriculum. The more implicit aspects include the tacit beliefs, attitudes, and everyday practices of the director, staff, teachers, present students, and former students as they are put forward in interviews.

In a very different chapter, Hermans and Poulie describe and empirically evaluate a support system based on the individual's self-narrative as embodied in a particular research method, the self-confrontation method.

The self-confrontation method allows people to tell and retell significant events from their life-stories as part of an extensive self-investigation. The narrative approach on which this method is based is considered particularly appropriate for the investigation and counselling of talented individuals. A case study of an underachieving adolescent boy is then reported as an illustration of this approach.

Finally, Heller and Viek evaluate the short- and long-term effects of scholarship support for gifted university students using a number of standards of academic excellence and societal participation. Excellence is seen to be the product of internal cognitive and motivational dispositions and socially stimulating conditions in the learning environment. In this evaluation, present and former scholarship holders are compared to present and former university students who did not apply for or receive a scholarship, although they were considered extremely talented by their professors.

This volume is dedicated to an extraordinary scholar and was initiated on the occasion of his 65th birthday. Franz J. Mönks (1932) was trained as a developmental psychologist at the Universities of Munster and Bonn, Germany. In 1963, he was appointed to a position at the University of Nijmegen, The Netherlands, where he held a full Professorship in Developmental Psychology from 1967 to 1988. In 1988, he was awarded a Professorship at the newly established Chair for the Study of the Development of the Gifted Child and became Director of the newly founded Center for the Study of Giftedness. Since the early 1980s, his research and teaching concentrated increasingly on the development and education of the gifted and talented. In 1987, Franz Mönks became a member and later Vice President of the Executive Committee of the World Council for Gifted and Talented Children (WCGT). In 1992, he was elected President of the European Council for High Ability (ECHA). He has directed and organised several European and World conferences and workshops and has also been involved as a consultant in the organisation of several others. He initiated and guides co-operation programmes between the University of Nijmegen and several universities in Indonesia and Peru as well as several European and Latin-American universities. He is one of the editors of the *International Handbook of Research and Development of Giftedness and Talent* and has published numerous articles and books related to the development of giftedness and talent.

C.F.M. VAN LIESHOUT
P.G. HEYMANS

PART ONE
CONCEPTUAL PERSPECTIVES ON THE DEVELOPMENT OF TALENT

CHAPTER ONE

Developmental theory and the expression of gifts and talents

David Henry Feldman
Eliot-Pearson Department of Child Development, Tufts University, USA

> *To his 'dying day' ... Terman believed that every individual has a genetically determined intelligence which is stable over time. However, by the time he was 77, the empirical data of his genetic studies convinced him that many of his 1500 subjects had never made use of their superior ability.*
> —(Mönks, 1992, p. 193)

INTRODUCTION

The field that focuses on exceptional abilities and their development has undergone significant changes during the past decade, especially changes in the basic assumptions about what its purposes should be and how to best pursue those purposes during the decades to come. At issue is nothing less than the identity, the heart, and the soul of a field that now has almost a century of history behind it (Mönks, 1992; Mönks & Mason, 1993).

As Morelock (1996) has recently discussed, there are at least two competing perspectives that seem to have reached something of an impasse: one of these points of view has been part of the field from the beginning: the other, although it came a bit later, has taken an increasing share of the spotlight over time. It now threatens to reduce the other perspective to insignificance unless an appropriate balance between them is restored.

The first perspective, which Morelock calls the "gifted child" point of view, is concerned with the *special qualities* of children whose extremely rapid development (especially in the linguistic area) outpaces other areas. Typically, children who score very high on IQ tests such as the Stanford-Binet (140 IQ, at least) are identified as presenting the qualities of the "gifted child".

The second stream of activity in the field has been more concerned with *achievement* and the attainment of more advanced levels of mastery within various fields than with IQ. Morelock refers to this line of work in two ways: as "talent development" and as "gifted achievement". The two terms are intended to capture the emphasis on the accomplishments in real-world domains that children achieve. Morelock's fear is that the "gifted child" who has traditionally been the primary concern within the field may lose its special place.

Morelock (1996) tries to "put the gifted child back together again" by showing that the focus on internal experience of one group of scholars and educators, as well as the externally oriented achievement orientation of the other group, are both important to the field as it begins its second century. There is value to both perspectives and they should be integrated into a more complete and comprehensive framework rather than seen as competing theories of giftedness or competing world views.

Yet there is a sense in which the preoccupations and concerns of those who wish to preserve the place of the extremely high-IQ, verbally precocious child at the centre of the field have taken their case too far. Even within the traditional field of gifted education, it is not the extreme case that has defined the field in recent years (cf. Feldman, 1979, 1991); it is rather the child who scores two or three deviations above the mean in IQ who has been focus of the field's research and practice. One could argue that it was the *moderately* gifted child who drove the more extreme cases of verbal precocity from centre stage as much as the more recent interest in diversity and domain-specific gifts and talents. Giftedness became "democratised" (if that meaning is possible), such that a more modest degree of precocity became the basis on which the field moved into the mainstream of educational practice (Morelock, 1996).

And so it might be said that in the battle between the "gifted child movement" and the "talent development" movement, both groups *were really on the same side*. The real enemy of both groups was the field itself and its watering down of the meaning of giftedness that had taken place during the last 50 years. Recent activity has aimed at "shifting paradigms" away from such an emphasis (Feldman, 1991; Morelock, 1996, Treffinger, 1991), but not necessarily back to the rarified levels of IQ of Hollingworth's era.

Both groups wanted to bring back to the centre of attention in the gifted education children who have been neglected by the field. Perhaps they would both have also wished to *exclude* the more modestly academically talented children who now hold the official title, perhaps not. But it is clear that a more inclusive field would require that different definitions of giftedness and different criteria for what is called giftedness would be necessary for the field to do its work. That means a major shift of some kind, if not quite the "paradigm shift" imagined in the early 1990s by some in the field (Feldman, 1992; Frasier & Passow, 1994; Treffinger, 1991).

At the very minimum, it would be necessary for the field to accept a more differentiated set of definitions of what giftedness is. Similarly, those who want to see the range and variety of gifts and talents expanded to include a much more diverse set of possibilities fear that, unless a new conception of giftedness is embraced, the field will continue to give little more than lip service to serving anyone other than a child with a moderately high IQ (see Ross, 1993).

Also of great importance is the issue of the term "giftedness" itself. In a sense, whichever group captures this term captures the field. If extreme verbal ability or some other variation of IQ is called giftedness, then other possible uses of the term are curtailed. If general academic talent of the IQ sort continues to hold the field's allegiance for what it means by giftedness, then this constrains other possible meanings of the term. Thus a great deal is at stake when a decision is made about how to use the term "gifted" (Gagné, 1993).

We should not gloss over the fact that the stakes are very high for the field, nor should we fail to recognise that each group's claim has legitimacy. To place the label "gifted" on children with certain defining qualities means to single out such children for special attention and/or treatment and to exclude others, for better and sometimes for worse.

No mere semantic preference, the definition of the term "gifted" is perhaps the most important theoretical task faced by the field as it enters the next century (Mönks & Mason, 1993). As a member of the group that drafted the national report in the US for the Javits Program (Ross, 1993), I know how difficult, divisive, and contentious an issue it can be to try to define or redefine giftedness. That group, which included some of the field's most prominent scholars and leaders (e.g. Mary Frasier, Jim Gallagher, Joe Renzulli, Stuart Tonemeh), argued long and hard to reach consensus on its definition. Here is what the Javits group came up with (Ross, 1993, p. 3):

> Children and youth with outstanding talent perform or show the potential for performing at remarkably high levels of accomplishment when compared with others of their age, experience, or environment. These children and youth exhibit high performance capability in intellectual, creative, and/or artistic areas, possess an unusual leadership capacity, or excel in specific academic fields. They require services or activities not ordinarily provided by the schools. Outstanding talents are present in children from all cultural groups, across all economic strata, and in all areas of human endeavor.

This definition tries to be inclusive and diverse to such a degree that its focus is lost. Yet it reflects the tensions and shifts that have been occurring in the field. After the clean precision of IQ, and even after the 1972 expanded version usually called the "Marland" definition (after the head of the US Office of Education), the 1993 definition must have struck the field as difficult to comprehend and even more difficult to implement in practice.

THE NEED FOR A FRAMEWORK TO GUIDE RESEARCH AND PRACTICE

Clearly there are good reasons to argue for one or another definition of giftedness. Each definition tends to bring certain children to the centre of the field, while tending to move others out towards the periphery. For most of its history, the field of gifted education has been linked with the measurement of intelligence as IQ, and giftedness has been assumed to be measured through intelligence tests (Mönks & Mason, 1993; Morelock, 1996). This has meant that the only real question to be answered was how high a test score is high enough to be considered gifted?

The "talent development" tradition can also be divided into the more moderate versus the more extreme talent focus. Beginning with the aforementioned Marland Report (1978) in the US, talents beyond the academic, such as artistic and leadership abilities, were included in the official definition of gifted/talented students in the US. But as with IQ, the focus was on high but not extreme capabilities.

It was only in the late 1970s that a US Social Science Research Council Committee on Giftedness and Creativity pushed for studies of *extreme* creativity, giftedness, and talent (Csikszentmihalyi, 1996; Feldman, 1982; Feldman, Csikszentmihalyi, & Gardner, 1994; Gardner, 1993, 1995, 1997; Morelock, 1996). Although the motivation behind the Committee's recommendation was primarily to rejuvenate the research field, implications for policy and practice were soon to follow, as for example in the US definition quoted earlier (Ross, 1993).

Therefore, at the very least, the field has to find ways to incorporate *four* different categories of giftedness and talent. These may be summarised as in Table 1.1. All four of these forms of exceptional capability have legitimacy and have reason to be included in the field of gifted and talented education. However, ideological, practical, and theoretical commitments of one sort or another prevent the several kinds of giftedness/talent from being integrated into a common endeavour (although see Feldhusen, 1995; Morelock, 1996, for suggestions about how to do this). There is no coherent framework within which to organise and pursue the several distinct but presumably related areas of endeavour presented in Table 1.1.

TABLE 1.1
Four Categories of Giftedness/Talent

	Gifts	Talents
Moderate	Moderate gifts	Moderate talents*
Extreme	Extreme gifts*	Extreme talents

*Contrasted in Morelock, 1996.

TOWARDS A FRAMEWORK FOR THE STUDY OF GIFTEDNESS AND TALENT

Is it necessary for the field to be guided by theory? One might argue that the study of giftedness, creativity, talent and the like has proceeded for the better part of a century without being greatly concerned about theory. Why is it necessary now? Or is it?

The position taken here is that it is important for the field to be guided by a theory (or theories) if it is to fulfil its promise (Cohen, 1988). It may have been acceptable for the field to have been atheoretical during its first century, but it has become too large, diverse, and complex to continue to bumble along without a star to follow. In this respect Morelock (1996) and LeoNora Cohen before her (Cohen, 1988; Cohen & Ambrose, 1993) should be praised for their foresight, as should other leaders in the field who have tried to provide integrative frameworks along the way (cf. Gagné, 1993; Mönks, 1992; Renzulli, 1992; Tannenbaum, 1983), as well as to build organisational structures and opportunities for theory to have a continuing role.

All of these efforts (and of course many others) have had value and have made important contributions to the field. Each perspective has something important to offer by way of clarifying issues and framing the discussion. Yet it can be fairly said that none of them is sufficiently comprehensive, powerful, heuristically rich, or integrative to serve as a lodestone towards which our collective efforts can be attracted or a Rosetta stone to which they can be compared in orderly fashion.

The theory that I am proposing to guide and help direct the field is called *Non-universal Theory* (Feldman, 1980, 1986, 1994, 1995). Non-universal theory is broader and more inclusive than the study of giftedness (however defined); it is a theory of development that was designed to complement existing theories (e.g. Freud, Erikson, Piaget, Vygotsky, Bruner) by extending the boundaries of developmental theory beyond the universal changes that have been the focus of developmental psychology: thus, *non-universal*. Non-universal theory is therefore more than a theory of giftedness or talent; it is a general theory of development that integrates individual variation and normative patterns of development by focusing on domains of knowledge and experience and the qualities and conditions necessary for mastering them.

Non-universal theory proposes that there are many domains of development beyond the universals of traditional developmental psychology. It also proposes that individuals vary in their natural proclivities for these diverse domains. The theory organises its many developmental domains into developmental "regions" that vary in a number of ways, ranging from the traditional universals of developmental psychology to domains that are unique extensions or transformations of existing domains (Feldman, 1994). The regions of the "universal to unique" continuum of non-universal theory are presented in Fig. 1.1.

THE UNIVERSAL TO UNIQUE CONTINUUM

The central image of the theory is of a continuum of domains ranging from *universal* to *unique* (see Fig. 1.1). For example at the universal end of the continuum are found only domains that are achieved by all people in all cultures over all periods of human history. They also require that all individuals (other than those with significant physical impairments or who are subjected to extreme abuse) achieve full mastery of the knowledge of the domain in question (Feldman, 1994). For such universal domains, variations in natural proclivities for achieving mastery are mostly irrelevant, except for profound deficits that interfere with the natural developmental trajectory.

Other regions of the continuum are specified in other ways; for example, in terms of larger or smaller numbers of people who master them; or the extent to which they require formal or informal instruction; or the range of variation in proclivity for achievement. Once an analysis of a domain has been done, it can be provisionally placed within a region. As

---

Universal to Unique continuum:

UNIVERSAL

    PANCULTURAL

        CULTURAL

            DISCIPLINE BASED

                IDIOSYNCRATIC

                    UNIQUE

FIG. 1.1 Kinds of developmental change. (Based on the Universal to Unique Continuum from Feldman, 1994.)

more data are gathered about the domain, or as the domain evolves, it may be moved from region to region of the universal to unique continuum. Only a small number of non-universal developmental domains have been analysed to date, but the techniques for doing so are fairly well developed and available to other researchers (Feldman, 1994).

Another feature of the universal to unique continuum is that it permits description of domains in terms that lend themselves to systematic comparison. Patterns of similarities and differences may be identified, and prerequisite capabilities for mastery within and across domains can be explored. The taxonomic effort to analyse and then classify the most important domains (judged by explicit criteria) will be a considerable one, but when it is completed it will provide something akin to the periodic table in chemistry, a classification system that will facilitate understanding, analysis, and comparison among the domains that have been constructed, preserved, valued, and transformed in human cultures by human beings (Feldman, 1994; Gardner, 1997). But in contrast with the periodic table, developmental domains continue to evolve over time as they are extended, reorganised, and transformed by those who master them.

The domains of the universal to unique continuum are all assumed to be *developmental*, and this term has special meaning within the theory. Consistent with many traditional developmental theories, developmental domains are assumed to have a sequence or sequences of stages or stage-like levels as part of their core structure. Identifying such a sequence or sequences is one of the first steps to analysing or mapping a domain. Many domains can be thought of as being composed of *levels of expertise* ranging from a beginning or *novice* level to higher levels such as *master*.

What makes most of the domains in the continuum *non-universal* is the fact that they are not mastered by all individuals in all cultures under nearly all conditions. At each region of the continuum beyond universal, fewer and fewer people master the domains of that region. At the unique end of the continuum, a developmental level identified may be achieved by only a single individual; indeed, the most distinctive feature of a unique domain is that it has become unique through the sustained efforts of individuals to extend and/or transform it. Once transformed, it is no longer the same domain as it was prior to the successful effort at transformation, which is the definition of *creativity* in non-universal theory.

Other criteria for judging the degree to which a non-universal domain has evolved its structure include such things as: the existence of special terminology that pertains uniquely to the domain (e.g. "gambit" in chess; "pas de deux" in ballet); the existence of established and accepted pedagogical techniques, institutions, or technologies (see Feldman, 1994, for a fuller discussion); and recognition of exceptional potential for mastery of particular domains such as prodigies, "gifted children", and the like (Feldman, 1991). In essence, it is possible to estimate how well articulated the unique knowledge structures and distinctive practices of a non-universal domain are at a given moment within a given cultural context, using a set of criteria for judging non-universal developmental domains, somewhat like Howard Gardner's criteria for determining the eight intelligences that make up his Multiple Intelligences theory (Gardner, 1993). Knowing which domains are valued and to what degree is a good indicator of the range of gifts and talents valued in that culture.

From the point of view of the study of the extraordinary (Gardner, 1997), the universal to unique continuum has several advantages over other theories. The range and variety of domains of the continuum far exceed those of any other theory, yet these domains are not simply a list of possibilities. Domains are categorised as having certain key features and certain commonalities that can be identified and studied in relation to those of other domains, including the "talents" and "gifts" that individuals must possess in order to master them.

Although domains are not abilities or intelligences *per se*, they have been built over time by individuals who have used their special talents and abilities to construct and contribute to them. Therefore domains serve as repositories of information about the kinds of capabilities necessary for participation, mastery, and transformation of knowledge and experience. Domains are in a sense crystallised and preserved artefacts of various developed human potentials (Cole, 1996). A decision to incorporate a contribution to a domain (or to deny it) is taken by people who know and care about the domain and its development; therefore, when we behold a developmental domain, we see the distilled and preserved traces of those who were judged to have made contributions by those whose role has been to help construct, preserve, protect, and extend the domain (Csikszentmihalyi, 1990; Feldman et al., 1994).

Developmental domains, as conceptualised in non-universal theory, are made by human beings, transformed by human beings, preserved by human beings, transmitted by human beings, given status by human beings, promoted by human beings, and occasionally deconstructed or abandoned by human beings. All of this activity has the potential to reveal the nature, diversity, quality, and distinctiveness of the talents and gifts involved in mastering and extending valued domains. *If dreams are the royal road to the unconscious, as Freud claimed, non-universal theory claims that developmental domains are the superhighway to giftedness and creativity.*

THE DEVELOPMENT OF GIFTS AND TALENTS

Perhaps the most important feature of non-universal theory as a framework for the study of giftedness is the fact that it is at once a *developmental* theory as well as a theory that places the expression of *individuality* at the heart of its theoretical architecture. Although developmental theorists are beginning to recognise that they must somehow deal with individual differences and variability (e.g. Siegler, 1996), non-universal theory was built from the outset to address both developmental sequences common to all individuals, as well as individual expressions that confirm order and unique expressions that create new order (Feldman, 1980, 1994, 1995).

Non-universal theory can be shown to have a number of features that make it especially well suited to serve as a general guide to the field of inquiry that seeks to understand extraordinary human capabilities and how they are expressed. Here are a few of them:

(1) The theory is *exceptionally broad*. Recently, Paul Van Geert (1998) suggested that non-universal theory be labelled a "portfolio" theory; a framework so commodious that it can accommodate the best insights of Piaget, Vygotsky, and many others within its superstructure.

(2) However, it also has remarkable *detail* about two key aspects of intellectual development: the specific *domains* that are mastered and extended by human effort; and, the ways in which one moves from level to level, or *transitions* towards mastery within these domains. In other words, the theory says more about *developmental levels and transitions* than other theories tend to do.

(3) Non-universal theory has *definitions* for most of the major concepts in the field of giftedness/talent, and these definitions are coherent, consistent with the rest of the theory, and have clear relationships to each other. For example, words like "talent", "giftedness", "creativity", "genius", "prodigy", and "savant" are defined in operational or near operational terms within the theory.

(4) The theory is stated with sufficient precision that a number of its most important claims are both *empirically testable* and *falsifiable*. That is, the theory lends itself to empirical research and meets some of the most important criteria of scientific inquiry: its claims can be shown to be false (or supported, of course) by the gathering of data.

(5) The theory is for the most part *neutral* with respect to the various forms and varieties of giftedness and talent that have been studied, analysed, promoted, and supported during the past century. The theory is useful in sorting out the special features of the various forms of giftedness as well as features held in common with other forms, but the theory does not value one kind of giftedness over another

(6) Non-universal theory assumes that there have been two complementary tendencies in the evolution of the human mind and central nervous system (Feldman, 1986; Gagné, 1993). One tendency has led to variations in general adaptiveness (i.e. to "gifts") while the other has led to variations in specific skills or capabilities (i.e. "talents"). These contrasting

yet complementary tendencies are more fully described in the paragraphs to follow.

THE EVOLUTION OF GIFTS AND TALENTS

Measures of "general intelligence" or IQ are rough estimates of the fitness of individuals to thrive in a wide variety of environmental circumstances, at least within a Western industrialised context. Traditional measures of IQ reflect the variations found in our population with respect to this aspect of general adaptiveness. It is likely that, to a significant degree, variability in general adaptive talents is natural, and were there a practical way to detect them, they would reveal themselves at the earliest age (Bornstein & Krasnegor, 1989; Gardner, 1993). Academic talent or IQ is not all there is to general adaptiveness, and several recent theories—most notably that of Sternberg (1993; Sternberg & Wagner, 1996)—have tried to broaden the notion of general intelligence to include practical and creative aspects.

Still, there is a sense that these kinds of intelligences have evolved to make human beings as generally adaptable a species as possible. The success of this evolutionary line is unmistakable: human beings have held dominion over the earth for many centuries. This kind of intellectual prowess, which gives a selective advantage in general terms, has traditionally been what is meant by "giftedness" in the professional field, and IQ has been the index of general intellectual adaptability in Western culture (Feldman et al., 1994; Renzulli, 1992).

Complementing these general adaptive qualities, according to nonuniversal theory, are numerous more specific kinds of talents and skills, evolved, it seems, to provide optimal adaptiveness within *very specific* environmental constraints. As much as general adaptiveness can provide the basis for survival (or even success) across a wide variety of environmental circumstances, specific talents and capabilities may be key to deriving full benefit from a specific situation, or may be necessary for achieving the most advanced levels of mastery of a given developmental domain (Feldman, 1986; Feldman et al., 1994). You can only go so far with *g*; talent for mastering the skills of a specific domain seems equally crucial.

There are of course limitations as well as advantages to each form of adaptation to habitat: the more general adaptive capability one has available, the more likely one will tend to be resourceful, flexible, and capable of thriving under a wide variety of circumstances. The more focused one is on a particular area of strength, and the more that single strength exists in the absence of other specific and general strengths, the greater is the need to be placed in just the right environment where the singular specific talent can best be exploited (Bruner, 1986).

The world's champion in chess from the 1960s, Bobby Fischer, is often cited as a person whose talent was limited to chess; not supported by general adaptiveness or even other specific talents, Mr Fischer seemed unable to do anything very well except play chess, which he was fortunate enough to have encountered when he was 6 (Collins, 1974). But in the absence of general adaptive resources of his own, when his outside support system broke down after he won the championship in 1963, Fischer found himself unable to sustain a viable career as a chess player. He remained in obscurity until recently when he tried (unsuccessfully) to re-establish himself in chess (for a similar case study of the domain of morality, see Olthof, this volume).

It is through the combined resources of whatever general *and* specific talents and abilities each person brings to his or her efforts to engage, pursue, and perhaps master various universal and non-universal developmental domains that achievements occur at the highest levels. These talents and abilities, which no doubt begin as natural biological potentials to a certain degree, are utilised well or less well depending on many factors, some of which are individual, others social, still others cultural, historical, and even evolutionary (Feldman, 1986; Gardner, 1993, 1995, 1997; Mönks, 1992; see also Smitsman, this volume).

How the general and specific potentials (the "gifts" and "talents") of individuals tend to play themselves out over time, and under what conditions such potentials manifest themselves optimally, is a good way to describe the general field of human development (Feldman, 1991, 1994; Mönks, 1992). To the extent that exceptional gifts and talents are part of the story, we have moved into that specific aspect of the broader field of the study of development we call "giftedness".

In this sense, then, the study of giftedness is a special subfield of the study of development. It follows that *development* is the central issue to be explicated in the study of giftedness, but development in non-universal theory is neither inevitable nor limited to universal areas of human experience. Development includes all of the ways in which general and specific potentials may be brought to expression through conditions and contexts evolved and utilised by cultures. Some of these conditions simply exist in a given culture at a given moment in time and will be absorbed and used without special effort. Others require special introduction, tutelage, perhaps apprenticeship, or even unique arrangements for talent to be brought to life, used fully and well (Cole, 1996; Mönks, 1992). For wisdom about how such resources may be used, Franz Mönks (1992; Mönks & Mason, 1993) suggests that Montessori's educational practices may be useful. So might the ideas of Bruner, Vygotsky, Dewey, and other educational psychologists and philosophers (Cole, 1996).

In sum, the following matters should be the main topics of research for the field that studies the development of *talents* and *gifts*: what kinds of general gifts and specific talents, in what combinations, seem to be necessary for mastery of various developmental domains? What kinds of conditions (external and internal) seem to be necessary for extraordinary mastery to occur? What are the requirements, specific as well as general, in addition to those required for initial mastery, that seem to be involved when domains are more and more fully mastered and then *creatively* transformed (Gardner, 1993, 1995, 1997)? How do we characterise those extremely rare events when a well established and cherished developmental domain is transformed so fundamentally that its principles and psychological organisation are irreversibly altered, i.e. when contributions of *genius* have occurred (Feldman, 1986, 1991, 1994; Simonton, 1994, 1997).

CONCLUSION

As should be clear, the scope of the field that concerns itself with the study of "giftedness" is broad, almost as broad as the study of development itself. Its range of topics includes a coherent account of the kinds of natural talents and abilities, both general and specific, that may be found in human newborns as they enter the world. It also includes an effort to rigorously specify the important features of developmental domains, from universal to unique, that engage the capabilities of growing individuals and provide opportunities for expression of these talents and abilities.

The processes involved in fostering the expression of talent also need to be understood (Mönks, 1992). Individual development, assisted and unassisted by others, needs to be studied in relation to non-universal domains, their history, and their evolution in cultures. Extreme cases such as prodigies, savants, high-IQ cases, cases of extraordinary achievements, and the like are particularly helpful in revealing how talents and abilities play themselves out over a life span (Csikszentmihalyi, 1996; Feldman, 1991, 1994; Gardner, 1997; Morelock & Feldman, 1993, 1997), showing how synchronies and asynchronies, opportunities, challenges, frustrations, and chance events are involved in developing talents and abilities to their farthest reaches (Gardner, 1993; Simonton, 1991).

Non-universal theory provides a broad, integrative framework within which to pursue the challenging goals of a field that has as its purpose to better understand and better develop the diverse and highly variable array of talents and abilities that can be found in human populations (Ross, 1993). As our conceptions of giftedness, talent, ability, creativity, and genius have expanded and evolved, have become deeper, more diverse, and more humane, so too must the theories that we use to give direction to the enterprise do so. It will take the best of both theory *and* research to move forward in this noble quest. The argument of this chapter is that we must have one before we can have the other—and of course vice versa.

REFERENCES

Bornstein, M., & Krasnegor, N. (Eds.) (1989). *Stability and continuity in mental development: Behavioral and biological perspectives*. Mahwah, NJ: Lawrence Erlbaum Associates Inc.

Bruner, J.S. (1986). *Actual minds, possible worlds*. Cambridge, MA: Harvard University Press.

Cohen, L.M. (1988). "To get ahead, get a theory": Criteria for evaluating theories of giftedness and creativity applied to education. *Roeper Review, 11*, 95–100.

Cohen, L.M., & Ambrose, D. (1993). Theories and practices for differentiated education for the gifted and talented. In K. Heller, F. Mönks, & A.H. Passow (Eds.), *International handbook of research and development of giftedness and talent* (pp. 339–363). Oxford, UK: Pergamon.

Cole, M. (1996). *Cultural psychology: A once and future discipline*. Cambridge, MA: Harvard University Press.

Collins, J. (1974). *My seven chess prodigies*. New York: Simon & Schuster.

Csikszentmihalyi, M. (1990). The domain of creativity. In M. Runco & R. Albert (Eds.), *Theories of creativity* (pp. 190–212). Newbury Park, CA: Sage.

Csikszentmihalyi, M. (1996). *Creativity*. New York: Harper-Collins Publishers.

Feldhusen, J. (1995). Talent development: The new direction in gifted education. *Roeper Review*, 18, 92.

Feldman, D.H. (1979). The mysterious case of extreme giftedness. In H. Passow (Ed.), *The gifted and the talented: 78th Yearbook of the National Society for the Study of Education* (pp. 335–351). Chicago: University of Chicago Press.

Feldman, D.H. (1980). *Beyond universals in cognitive development*. Norwood, NJ: Ablex.

Feldman, D.H. (1982). A developmental framework for research with gifted children. In D.H. Feldman (Ed.), Developmental approaches to giftedness and creativity (pp. 31–45). San-Francisco: Jossey-Bass.

Feldman, D.H. & Benjamin, A. (1986). Giftedness as a developmentalist sees it. In R. Sternberg & J. Davidson (Eds.), *Conceptions of giftedness* (pp. 285–305). New York: Cambridge University Press.

Feldman, D.H. (1989). Creativity: Proof that development occurs. In W. Damon (Ed.), *Child development today and tomorrow* (pp. 240–260). San Francisco, CA: Jossey-Bass.

Feldman, D.H. (1991). *Nature's gambit: Child prodigies and the development of human potential*. New York: Teachers College Press (with L.T. Goldsmith).

Feldman, D.H. (1992). Has there been a paradigm shift in gifted education? In N. Colangelo, S. Assouline, & D. Ambroson (Eds.), *Talent development: Proceedings from the 1991 Henry B. and Jocelyn Wallace National Research Symposium on Talent Development* (pp. 89–94). Unionville, NY: Trillium Press.

Feldman, D.H. (1994). *Beyond universals in cognitive development* (2nd ed.). Norwood, NJ: Ablex.

Feldman, D.H. (1995). Learning and development in nonuniversal theory. *Human Development, 38*, 315–321.

Feldman, D.H., Csikszentmihalyi, M., & Gardner, H. (1994). *Changing the world: A framework for the study of creativity*. Westport, CT: Greenwood Press.

Frasier, M., & Passow. A.H. (1994). *Toward a new paradigm for identifying talent potential*. Storrs, CT: National Research on the Gifted and Talented, University of Connecticut.

Gagné, F. (1993). Constructs and models pertaining to exceptional human abilities. In K. Heller, F. Mönks, & A.H. Passow (Eds.), *International handbook of research and development of giftedness and talent* (pp. 69–87). Oxford, UK: Pergamon.

Gardner, H. (1993). *Creating minds.* New York: Basic Books.

Gardner, H. (1995). *Leading minds.* New York: Basic Books.

Gardner, H. (1997). *Extraordinary minds.* New York: Basic Books.

Mönks, F. (1992). Development of gifted children: The issue of programming. In F. Mönks & W. Peters (Eds.), *Talent for the future* (pp. 191–202). Assen, The Netherlands: Van Gorcum.

Mönks, F., & Mason, E.J. (1993). Developmental theories and giftedness. In K. Heller, F. Mönks, & A.H. Passow (Eds.), *International handbook of research and development of giftedness and talent* (pp. 89–101). Oxford, UK: Pergamon.

Morelock. M.J. (1996). On the nature of giftedness and talent: Imposing order on chaos. *Roeper Review, 19,* 4–12.

Morelock, M.J. & Feldman, D.H. (1993). Prodigies and savants: What can they teach us about cognitive development? In K. Heller, F. Mönks, & A.H. Passow (Eds.), *International handbook of research and development of giftedness and talent* (pp. 161–181). Oxford, UK: Pergamon Press.

Morelock, M.J., & Feldman, D.H. (1997). High IQ children, extreme precocity, and savant syndrome. In N. Colangelo & G. Davis (Eds.), *Handbook of gifted education (2nd ed.)* (pp. 439-459). Boston: Allyn & Bacon.

Renzulli, J. (1992). A general theory for the development of creative productivity in young people. In F. Mönks and W. Peters (Eds.), *Talent for the future* (pp. 51–72). Assen, The Netherlands: Van Gorcum.

Ross, P.O. (Ed.) (1993). *National excellence: A case for developing America's talent.* Washington, DC: US Government Printing Office.

Siegler, R.S. (1996). *Emerging minds.* New York: Oxford University Press.

Simonton, D.K. (1991). Emergence and realization of genius: The lives and works of 120 classical composers. *Journal of Personality and Social Psychology, 61,* 829–840.

Simonton, D.K. (1994). *Greatness: Who makes history and why.* New York: Guilford Press.

Simonton, D.K. (1997). When giftedness becomes genius: How does talent achieve eminence? In N. Colangelo & G. Davis (Eds.), *Handbook of gifted education* (2nd ed.) (pp. 335–349). Boston: Allyn & Bacon.

Sternberg, R.J. (1993). Procedures for identifying intellectual potential in the gifted: A perspective on alternative "metaphors of mind". In K. Heller, F. Mönks, & A.H. Passow (Eds.), *International handbook of research and development of giftedness and talent* (pp. 185–207). Oxford, UK: Pergamon.

Sternberg, R.J., & Wagner, R.K. (Eds.) (1996). *Mind in context.* New York: Cambridge University Press.

Tannenbaum. A. (1983). *Gifted children: Psychological and educational perspectives.* New York: Macmillan.

Treffinger, D. (1991). Future goals and directions. In N. Colangelo & G. Davis (Eds.), *Handbook of gifted education* (pp. 441–449). Needham Heights, MA: Allyn & Bacon.

Van Geert, P. (1998). The draftman's contract. *New Ideas in Psychology, 15,* 227–234.

CHAPTER TWO

Slumbering talents: Where do they reside?

Ad W. Smitsman
University of Nijmegen, The Netherlands

INTRODUCTION

Biographies of successful people provide interesting vistas on the development of psychological characteristics, including talents. A remarkable phenomenon is that outstanding qualities of people may remain hidden for a rather long period of time before they become apparent. Mediocre students may, for instance, at a much later point turn out to be brilliant scientists, artists, or sportsmen (Kalinowski, 1985; Schneider, 1993; Sloane & Sosniak, 1985; Sosniak, 1985). Nice illustrations of such developmental trajectories can be found in Sosniak's (1985) study of the life history of 21 of the most successful young American pianists. At the time Sosniak studied their history, the pianists were all in their early thirties and highly successful. However, reports by their teachers and parents revealed that the majority hardly showed any sign of giftedness during the first years of their music training. Only after several years of training, around adolescence for some and even later for others, did their performance start to excel compared to other children. Why did their giftedness not appear at an earlier stage? Why were their teachers and parents unable to discover their giftedness earlier? Were they insufficiently attentive or skilled to discover the slumbering talents of their youngsters? Or, was the later occurring talent not slumbering at all, but absent in the beginning, requiring for its creation a lengthy period of nurturing and education? Are talents hidden properties within a person waiting to be awakened by particular circumstances? Or are they properties that are created by continuous nurturing? These questions are important as their answers not only reveal important features of the ways in which talents emerge, but also provide insight into the type of characteristics that comprise a talent.

Talents and their temporal and spatial context

One often conceives of talent as some innate capability to excel in a particular domain. This view, however, should be challenged and is doubtful both from a theoretical as well as an empirical perspective (Howe, Davidson, & Sloboda, 1998). It is important to realise, therefore, that talented behaviour, and also the properties that form the basis for such behaviour, emerges over time. In order to find out the kinds of properties that comprise talents, we first need to look at and be aware of the individual's developmental history. It is, therefore, of particular significance to take notice of the developmental processes and resources that are part of these processes as they shape not only particular characteristics of the person (needed for giftedness), but rather the person him or herself and their physical and socio-cultural environment (which also contribute to giftedness). Complex organisms such as human beings develop many properties, but none of these can emerge and persist in isolation from other properties. They do not all arise simultaneously. Some properties emerge at an early stage, whereas others appear later. However, the emergence of later-occurring properties has been made possible by and is embedded in the history of those that occurred earlier. Some properties relate to the developmental history from birth, while others can relate to the history from conception. For properties such as the genome, the genetic resources of a person, the history begins even earlier. Evolution is part of the developmental history of the individual. The genetic resources of a person, created by experiences of the species over evolutionary time, and possibly modified by experiences of the individual over ontogenetic time (Gottlieb, 1991, 1992), are just as indispensably a part of an individual's later-occurring talent as the later-formed body, brain, and behavioural skills. Finally, characteristics not only vary in time of appearance, but their emergence also depends on the place members of a species inhabit. Environmental resources needed to let particular characteristics arise in individuals are not evenly distributed over the different places in which individuals may live. Therefore new characteristics may emerge when an individual moves from one place to another.

Properties may also vary in whether they are shared by all members of a species or differ among those members. Some of the human properties, such as a body and brain, erect locomotion, and the use of language, are shared by all members of the species. However, there are many properties on which individuals can differ. Talents, as the potential to excel over others in performance, obviously belong to the kinds of properties that are not commonly shared. They emerge within a minority of the members of the species. Most children in the Western hemisphere go to school for a rather extended period of time. Many receive at least some kind of music training and nearly all have been enrolled in physical training. Nevertheless, only a few become great scientists, businessmen, artists, or sportsmen later in life. Although talents may reveal themselves only in a few people, their creation is embedded in a rather long history, which involves the individual as well as the social and physical surroundings of the individual. In the end, all are needed for the emergence of the talent.

Given that some properties are unequally distributed among individuals, one may question whether principles underlying the development of those properties are any different from principles underlying the development of characteristics that typically emerge for every person during life. The answer to this question can hardly be affirmative. Even though some properties may differ and even be rare among people this does not imply different developmental principles for those characteristics. For any answer, we should realise that we cannot separate the question of individual differences from the more general question of ontogenesis. It is more parsimonious to assume that the same principles that govern similarities in the development of characteristics that individuals share, such as erect locomotion and the use of language, also bring about differences in the development of individuals in terms of those characteristics. The development of the individual must underlie the development of differences among individuals—the individual needs to develop for differences to arise. Principles that govern the development of psychological properties that are widespread or common will, therefore, at the same time provide us with a deeper insight into characteristics that are rare.

In sum, we cannot separate the question of what a property entails from the question of how it develops. We also cannot sensibly disconnect the question of the development of the individual from the question of the development of differences among individuals. The study of development of the individual not only reveals processes and principles that enable properties to arise and persist, but also reveals differences that emerge with respect to individuals.

The significance of the question of development for the scientific understanding of psychological characteristics has recently been re-addressed by researchers using insights coming from ecological psychology (Fogel, 1993; E.J. Gibson, 1988, 1997), dynamic systems theory (Smith & Thelen, 1993; Thelen & Smith, 1994; Van Geert, 1995), and epigenetic systems (Gottlieb, 1991, 1992). (See also Dent-Read & Zukow-Goldring, 1997 for a series of publications on this topic.) These new insights have inspired the issues that are raised by the present article. However, the discussion will not focus narrowly on the issue of talents but instead will address more general questions of development that may be useful for our understanding of how particular qualities such as talents may emerge and persist. These qualities are related to an organism's capabilities in general in relation to the organism's environment, what they entail, and how they emerge and may persist. It will be argued that a capability to perform a task, and a talent as the outstanding quality by which one performs the task, are *relational* properties that rest on organism and environment rather than on some hidden core inside the organism or the environment. The developmental perspective of this chapter focuses on the resources in organism and environment that exist and become available over time by development, and that are needed to sustain capabilities and talents. These resources emerge from exchange between organism and environment, and include the evolutionary as well as the ontogenetic and social-cultural history of the organism and, hence, form the basis for education and learning. It will be argued that the study of development involves the study of the emergence of those resources and, therefore, needs to address the individual as well as the environment. Finally, I end the chapter with the example of tool use, illustrating how environment and organism evolve together, and how both environmental and a person's physical and mental properties become modified to create the person's capabilities and talents.

TALENTS AS HIDDEN CORE: PREFORMISM AND UNWANTED DICHOTOMIES

The developmental history of talented behaviour, as reported by Sosniak (1985) shows remarkable similarities with the developmental history of any other psychological characteristic. It often takes a rather long period of time for a quality to finally settle down into a stable form, even though a first appearance of components of that quality often occurs far ahead of time. In discussing cognitive development, Flavell, Miller, and Miller (1993) point to the near impossibility of making any definitive statements about when a cognitive capability develops. For instance, the age at which capabilities such as the Piagetian cognitive skills become apparent varies considerably and depends heavily on the type of tasks used to measure them. For nearly every Piagetian concept, a task has been developed that has indicated some of its presence at a much younger age than it was originally supposed to occur. In discussing the heterochronicity of development, Thelen and Smith (1994, p. xvii) conclude: 'when we experimentally dissect an ontogenetic phenomenon, we often discover that elements of a seemingly integrated behavioral performance can be detected long in advance of the fully functional behavior.' A similar story can presumably be told about the appearance of talents. The ages at which we observe elements of the later talent of a child may vary considerably among individual children and conditions, as supported by the findings of Sosniak (1985).

Talents as hidden core

The task and situation dependency of developing abilities has strengthened optimistic beliefs that the age at which the first presence of a capability can be shown could be lowered. Improved assessment techniques should suit young children's weakly developed abilities to demonstrate their capabilities. However, empirical findings have hardly led to serious debates about the challenges they impose on current theorising about the capabilities themselves, except for some researchers who embrace a dynamic systems approach (Thelen & Smith, 1994). It is of course completely appropriate to search for the earliest presence of developing capabilities and to improve diagnostic techniques that enhance the likelihood of assessing them. However, the theoretical inspiration behind the enterprise may be highly flawed. This enterprise is often accompanied by the assumption of a privileged component, a central core that contains the essence of a task performance (e.g. Baillargeon 1994, 1995; Spelke, 1994). The core would remain hidden inside the person unless one uses a task that is particularly suited to the individual. To understand what this means one should realise that connected to the hypothesis of a central core there is another hypothesis implied by information processing theories and cognitive structuralism (see Thelen & Smith, 1994, ch. 2 for a critical discussion). This associated hypothesis entails that task performance can be split into two types of components: *competence*, the components that are central to achieving the task, and *performance*, the components that are peripheral. To measure the core, therefore, one needs to minimise the contribution of the peripheral performance aspects of a task. Moreover, because the core would mostly concern inference processes that occur inside the brain, tasks are presented that require minimal demands for acting, especially in young children whose physical skills are not yet well developed. For example, to assess object knowledge in young infants, Spelke and her colleagues (e.g. Spelke, Breilinger, Macomber, & Jacobson, 1992), and Baillargeon (1993) presented object events that provided infants with minimal opportunity to actively explore the displacement of an object. Infants had to infer the possible trajectory of the object from seeing only the beginning and outcome of the event.

The hidden core hypothesis easily fits with the idea of talents as slumbering entities. At first sight, it may suggest an appealing explanation for the slumbering, and motivates the search for methods to enhance discovery of their presence. However, it also suggests that a single property finally determines whether or not a person will excel in performing a task. Late occurrence of the talent might then indicate that the required opportunities to reveal the hidden quality were not available to the person thus far. What would such a hypothesis mean for our understanding of the talent to become an outstanding musician? It would indicate that insufficiently developed physical skills for singing or piano playing, which are needed to show the musical talent in the process of exchange between performer and audience, may hinder discovery of the talent in unskilled persons such as young children. In this view, the physical activities of performing are peripheral to the musical talent. However, one may wonder about the nature of musicality, when it can exist without the physical activities that are needed to expose it. Are the actions that underlie talented behaviour and the resources that are needed for these actions really peripheral to the talent? An affirmative answer to this question can hardly be taken seriously. For instance, humans have extremely well evolved talents for reaching, grasping, and manipulation of objects compared to other animals. These talents are also part of the performance of pianists. Moreover, the dexterity of humans rests not on a particular property of the prehensile system, but on the functional organisational capacity that allows the system to adapt to a huge variety of task demands. This potentiality *is* the hidden core, and it involves the whole system including the objects that will be grasped. It does indeed remain hidden as long as there are no tasks that actualise the potentiality.

Preformistic assumptions and unwanted dichotomies

The belief in a hidden core may stem from various sources, but basically rests on a misunderstanding of what development entails, what the resources for actions are, and how capabilities to act develop, including capabilities to act outstandingly. One source is the seventeenth-century preformistic belief of a small-scale man hidden in the fertilised egg cell of a woman. Although nobody today believes in an homunculus in the form of hidden "straw man" of adult form in germ cells, preformistic ideas still survive. Inspired by the biology of population genetics, the psychology of information processing, and cognitive structuralism, the modern versions entail that later physical and psychological phenotypes are already present as blueprints or prescriptions before they arise. As blueprints, they would be available in the genetic material of a person and in the architecture or neuronal nets of the brain, as some modern connectionist versions of this hypothesis might argue. Although preformistic hypotheses often focus on the organism, it is not necessary to conceive of an organism as the locus of the pre-existing form. One may also consider the physical environment or the social environment as the place where the form is located. The behaviourist's tradition, for example, conceived of the environment as pre-structured, and the person as the "tabula rasa" on which environmental structures were written. Comparable ideas can be found in some socialisation theories (e.g. Elias, 1991; see e.g. Wertsch, 1995, for a discussion).

The preformistic way of thinking may take several forms, but the fundamental problem with all of these inspirations is that they create an untenable dichotomy between organism and environment (J.J. Gibson, 1979; Gottlieb, 1992; Johnston, 1987; Sameroff, 1983). By creating such a dichotomy one basically misunderstands what organisms are, and what the driving forces behind an organism's continuity and change are; what development in fact entails. In addition, one also fails to do justice to the experiences organisms need for their continuity and change. Finally, these inspirations overlook the resources that are needed to allow these experiences to happen. These resources are partly available in the genetic material of the individual and the structures that surround the material, partly they become available over time in the developing body and brain and in the co-changing structures that surround the developing body and brain.

DEVELOPMENT AND THE ORGANISM–ENVIRONMENT SYSTEM

Educated within the Cartesian tradition, we tend to think of organisms and environment as distinct entities, although in fact they form a unified system. They presuppose one another—an organism cannot persist without an environment, and an environment can only be defined in relation to the organism it surrounds. The environment is literally that which surrounds the organism. The organism–environment system of complex organisms, such as humans, is in fact composed of many nested systems at several interacting levels (Gottlieb, 1992). These levels include the cellular level but also the higher social-cultural level of persons. For the living cells that form the body and the brain, the environment consists of surrounding cells, tissues, and organs. For the body and the brain as a whole, the environment consists of the surfaces of substances, objects and places that surround the agent, the many artefacts of the culture in which he or she lives, and surrounding creatures of the same and other species (J.J. Gibson, 1979). There is a continuous exchange between organism and environment. Exchange processes take place at all levels of the system, from the cellular to the social-cultural level. The exchange at different levels of the system forms the basis for both changes and persistence or continuity within the system, and of the system as a whole. Therefore, a static view on the organism and the environment, which is related to the dualistic perspective, fundamentally ignores the dynamic relationship that exists between organism and environment (Valsiner, 1987; Valsiner & Benigni, 1986). A dynamic relationship implies change as the fundamental characteristic of organism and environment system (Thelen & Smith, 1994). There is, however, also persistence. Whether one will find persistence or change depends on the time-scale at which one studies the relationship. Structures that do not evolve on a shorter time-scale may give way to new structures emerging for both organism and environment on a longer time-scale.

Persistence and change

The task for developmental psychology consists of explaining both persistence and change for the organism–environment system. Because persistence as well as change result from the relationship between the two, explanations have to be searched for in the exchanges that take place over time, and in the resources that are and become available to the individual to regulate these exchanges. To survive, the organism needs to be able to regulate the exchanges with the environment. Regulation requires resources from both organism and environment that fit one another. These resources are partly available at conception, for example, in the DNA that contains the genetic material, and the cytoplasm that surrounds the core of the fertilised egg cell. However, many more resources evolve over time as a result of the exchange process itself. Resources that develop include the growing body and brain and the structures of which these are composed, and modifications of the natural and social-cultural environment that become available to the agent.

Discontinuities in the exchange process

Exchanges form the basis for both persistence and change. Therefore, neither persistence nor change can solely be attributed to either the organism or the environment, but they follow from the relationship between them and the way it evolves over time. Structures persist as long as exchanges between organism and environment stay the same. Exchange, however, forms a dynamic process, as the ongoing exchange process is also the result of earlier exchanges fed back into the system. Due to this, the organism grows and the environment is modified. However, changes within systems may destabilise relations between systems, thereby creating discontinuities in their mutual relationship. When changes make it impossible to maintain present relations, new structures can emerge. So, growth *per se* does not cause development to take place, but rather discontinuities in the relationship that may emerge as a result of growth.

Discontinuities may result from growth, but they may also have other origins, such as accidents, or changes in environmental resources. The following two examples may highlight the significance for development of emerging discontinuities within the organism–environment system. In both examples, growth forms the cause of the discontinuity.

The first example concerns the disappearance of the stepping reflex after birth and is based on findings of Thelen and her colleagues. The stepping reflex that a healthy infant shows the first week after birth disappears after a couple of weeks. Thelen et al.'s research showed that the main reason for this change is rapid growth of the tissues of muscles and limbs (Thelen, Fisher, Ridley-Johnson, & Griffin, 1982). After birth the weight of muscles and limbs, such as the legs, increases faster than the strength of the leg muscles to lift the legs against gravity. As a consequence, the early relation of the infant's lifted feet to a supporting surface that is seen in stepping can no longer be maintained. However, the reflex does not disappear in every situation. Gravity as a property of the environment forms an intrinsic part of the capability to step. The environment for stepping may be altered by changing the forces that operate on an infant's limbs. Thelen and her colleagues showed that stepping is no longer possible as long as gravity acts on the infant's legs. However, in water (Thelen, Fisher, & Ridley-Johnson, 1984) or on a moving belt (Thelen & Ulrich, 1991) infants continue to show the stepping reflex.

The second example, which highlights the significance of discontinuities in the relation between one part of a system due to growth in the other part, concerns the development of the embryo, especially the process of cell differentiation in the early phase of embryological development. The transition to the process of cell differentiation begins at the end of the blastula stage, at which point the embryo is entirely composed of similar cells. For the formation of this body of similar cells, called blastula, the DNA replicates, but genes are hardly expressed. For cell differentiation, however, different genes need to be expressed in different parts of the embryo. What causes this transition of cell formation to cell differentiation? Again, a discontinuity in the relationship, in this case between cells and the intercellular environment, causes the transition to a new stage. The increasing number of cells of the blastula fosters inequalities in biochemical concentration between cells. At a certain point, the biochemical intracellular environment becomes sufficiently differentially structured to set the stage for the production of specialised cells instead of similar cells.

Both of these examples show that organism and environment form a unified system and that therefore changes in one of the components may cause discontinuities in the relationship between other components, and set the stage for transitions to take place.

Development involves the whole system

Development does not just take place on top of some non-developing hidden core. Development is fundamental to the whole organism–environment system. The entire system is involved in the exchanges that take place over time and that are responsible for both continuity and change. These exchanges are never determined solely by one part of the system, be it DNA or the brain, but involve all parts (Gottlieb, 1992). This is contrary to deterministic views on development, for example, brain determinism or genetic determinism that is often suggested by population geneticists (e.g. Scarr & McCartney, 1983). Although genes or the brain contribute to later-occurring psychological characteristics, they never determine these. There is no unidirectional relationship between genes and psychological behaviour (Gottlieb, 1992; Johnston, 1987). Population geneticists have studied the distribution of genetic material over species and correlated gene differences with behavioural differences within that population. Little is known about the processes that bring about these differences and correlations between phenotypes and genotypes. These include the processes that take place in the transcription of DNA into RNA, and the processes that regulate the expression of the genetic material. However, when processes of cell formation are studied it turns out that environmental processes at the cellular and supra-cellular level co-regulate which genes are transcribed and thus which proteins are made. Also during the development of the embryo, surrounding tissues and local biochemical processes of the inter- and intra-cellular environment heavily constrain the type of cells that are formed and tissues that are made, and consequently the architecture of body and brain. Correlations between genetic properties and later biological and psychological properties of a developing organism always presuppose a particular environment. When the environment changes these relations will also change.

The genome never prescribes the phenotypes that will be formed. The plasticity of the genome in the expression of phenotypes, known as the reaction norm, is often underestimated (Gottlieb, 1992). At each stage of an organism's development, the environment significantly contributes to the persistence as well as the change of the organism. Edelman (1992) argued that body and brain could not possibly be genetically prescribed, but must be developed by time- and place-dependent self-organising processes. The information for the required cells, tissues, and organs does not pre-exist, but arises over time on the basis of constraints provided by the genome and growing body and brain as well as the environment (Oyama, 1985). In fact, the genome itself was not prescribed, but has evolved from exchanges over evolutionary time, and its structure carries these experiences. In the same vein, body and brain carry the experiences over the shorter time-scale that started with conception. History is part and parcel of the present in the way that earlier experiences, distilled in structures formed over time, constrain the formation of current and future structures. The structures that were formed over time concern the organism and the environment—the environment carries a history too and environments and organisms evolve together. The environment is modified due to interactions with members of the species that populate this environment. So, the fruits of earlier exchanges are not only carried by the organism, but also by the environment. For humans, the natural environment has been considerably modified by the joint labours of their ancestors. Both the modified natural environment, and the cultural heritage that evolved from interactions with the natural environment, provides resources to the skills and knowledge that are available today. This heritage is part and parcel of the skills and knowledge of the offspring (Rogoff, 1990; Vygotsky & Luria, 1994).

Constraints on the exchange process

Processes of exchange are markedly different from the processes psychologists commonly study, influenced by information processing theories and cognitive structuralism. Piaget (1970) described these exchange processes in terms of assimilation and accommodation. He was right to conceive of metabolism, in his example of plants, as the root metaphor to describe these processes. Unfortunately, he was never very explicit in further clarifying what these processes involve. Metabolic processes are responsible for the persistence and growth of organisms, for instance, plants. But neither the growth in complexity that results from their metabolism nor the metabolic processes themselves are prescribed by structures inside or outside the plant. Local environmental circumstances heavily constrain the exchange process that takes place over time and the complexity that emerges from their metabolism. However, the information processing that psychologists mostly intend to study has little resemblance to those metabolic processes. It involves processes that are prescribed and that follow from structures psychologists tend to take for granted: cognitive representational capabilities or knowledge structures that together with general-purpose devices, such as attention and memory, are supposed to determine the internal and external activities of the agent. On the other hand, processes that involve an organism's exchanges with the environment are not prescribed. They do not follow from structures, but generate and sustain structures. There are no blueprints for these processes. Organisms stay in open relationship with the environment. This means that their exchanges are co-regulated by the environment, and are consequently creative (Fogel, 1993). The exchanges are creative as they foster new structures. The principles that underlie the emergence and maintenance of structures are more akin to principles that underlie the thermodynamics of cloud formation than to algorithms that underlie the computations within a computer (Kelso, 1995; Thelen & Smith, 1994; van Gelder and Port, 1995).

To conceive of structures of body and brain and environment as constraints on ongoing activities is rather different from conceiving of them as prescriptions for behaviour. Constrained behaviour may look regular and rule-like without applying rules to explain the behaviour. There is no need for an homunculus. Regularities arise from the interactions between heterogeneous components, none of which has a special privilege as to what will happen (Thelen & Smith, 1994). It is more akin to cloud formation or to the way landscape crevices and beds formed over time by rainfall regulate future flows of water towards lower places. It cannot be denied, of course, that people develop and execute programs from time to time, but even then, we need to explain where these programs come from and we should describe the processes that underlie their emergence and maintenance.

THE SIGNIFICANCE OF THE ENVIRONMENT FOR AN ORGANISM'S DEVELOPING CAPABILITIES

To survive, an organism needs to regulate the exchange process with its environment. To negotiate the interaction with the environment, the organism needs resources from itself and the environment that fit one another. Body and brain that evolved from exchanges with the environment provide resources to the activities for further regulating the relationship. Their resources fit the environmental resources, because they were moulded in relation to them and vice versa. Some of the environmental resources were available before the organism began to grow, such as oxygen, gravity, and media that allow the transmission of reflected energy to developing senses, such as reflected light and sound to the visual and auditory senses respectively. Other properties become available by the organism's growth. Examples of later resources are the unequal biochemical composition of cells at the end of the blastula stage that was needed to regulate the process of cell differentiation during the development of the embryo. After birth, caregivers' behaviour, for instance, provides resources to the activities of the offspring (Fogel, 1993). Environmental resources fit the organism because the organism evolved according to what the environment furnished the organism to evolve. On the other hand, the environment is changeable and is modified according to what becomes available to the organism. Over evolution and ontogenesis, the environment is continuously modified to fit the demands of the growing organism.

Capabilities as relational properties of organism and environment

Capabilities rest on the resources that are and become available in both developing body and brain, and in environmental properties that fit the organism. They entail a person's ability to regulate the relationship with the environment. A capability is, therefore, neither solely a property of the organism nor the environment, but of the relation between the two. It involves the actions a person is able to achieve, and especially the fit between a person's activities and environmental resources available to perform an action. A gifted or talented person is someone whose own resources particularly suit the environmental resources, and therefore may become very skilful in making use of what the environment furnishes. Environmental properties are part and parcel of the actions of a person. Therefore, it makes little sense to talk about a capability, for example the capability to perceive, to walk, or to write, without taking into account the environmental properties that sustain the actions of perceiving, walking, and writing. For perceiving, the environmental property consists of the way energy is structured by surrounding surfaces and transmitted through a medium such as air to the receptor surfaces of the senses. For movement, it consists of the media that are available for displacement: surfaces of support to pedestrians, airflow to birds. For writing, the environmental properties consist partly of the writing systems and tools that form part of the cultural heritage of a person.

Plasticity in the formation of capabilities

Environmental properties are not only part of a person's capabilities, they also co-regulate which capabilities are selected, and can persist in development. On the other hand, there is also a lot of plasticity in the way the environment may contribute to development. The environment can and is continuously modified to fit capabilities that emerge. The plasticity of the organism for adaptation is continuously exploited but also the plasticity of the environment. This means that changes of environment and organism often go together. There are many other examples of the co-evolution of organisms and the environment. A nice example of the narrow relation between both involves the emergence of life itself (Sameroff, 1983). It also illustrates the capricious way in which both co-evolve and how one part of the organism–environment system takes advantage of changes in the other part. Plants produce oxygen by photosynthesis, the capacity of using sunlight for metabolism. However the production of oxygen was not the goal for the development of photosynthesis to take place in cells. To get rid of the waste of internal acids that arises in changing inorganic material into organic material, a system was developed which made it possible for photosynthesis to evolve. The production of oxygen that started in the evolution of photosynthesis modified the environment. It slowly changed the atmosphere, and made life possible. For humans, the cultural heritage most clearly indicates how the natural environment needed to be modified to fit capabilities that emerged. This heritage includes tools that extend the capability of humans to act. But the new capabilities that emerged due to those tools required the natural environment to be modified. Man's invention of vehicles of all kind that roll rather than jump, walk, or crawl motivated a dramatic change in landscape. Highways were built to support new forms of transport. During evolution, no other species has evolved the capability to displace themselves by using wheels, which would make little sense given the uneven and bumpy terrain on which each had to find food and escape from predators.

As capabilities emerge and can only exist in relation to an environment, we need to know the environmental resources that sustain the activities of the person, in order to understand what a capability entails. The performance of any task presupposes a fit between the activities a person brings to the task and what the environment affords the person. Correct activities do not make a person capable if the environmental properties to sustain the activities are missing. Humans can spread their arms, just as birds do when flying, they can even flap their arms, but their activities will not take them from the ground (unless a medium other than air was available that movements could exploit—only then, would they be capable of flying). Activities can only become successful actions, if they are grounded in the environment. This is true for all physical activities, but also for mental activities. Even our thinking is and needs to be grounded in the environment. The regulation of the relationship with the environment distinguishes actions from activities (Reed, 1982, 1996). Actions allow a person to regulate the relationship, whereas activities will not do so unless they can take advantage of environmental resources. Therefore, activities may vary for the same action. When flying, for instance, birds regulate their flight sometimes by wing movements, sometimes by keeping their wings spread out and motionless. The activities vary to keep the relation to the air and the ground constant.

The underlying dynamics of capabilities

The major question for understanding what capabilities and talents entail and how they emerge and persist, concerns the relation of an agent's activities and the environmental resources to sustain these activities. Several scholars have addressed this question in the past (Bronfenbrenner, 1979; Bronfenbrenner & Ceci, 1994; Fogel, 1993; J. J. Gibson, 1979; Reed,

1996; Rogoff, 1990). For the present discussion, James Gibson's work is most relevant. Gibson clearly paved the way for understanding how environmental resources may become intrinsically related to the agent's actions and thus sustain time-dependent organisations of activities that compose those actions. To understand the relevance of Gibson's ecological approach to perception and action one needs to realise that the success of physical actions such as grasping, walking, and talking does not depend on the movements and gestures that are made but on properties that emerge from these movements. These properties are time-dependent as the organisation of the activities themselves that compose the action; that is, they will exist as long as the activities take place. For example, for any physical action a pattern of forces is needed that displaces a person's limbs and body and at the same time provides stability to the person's posture. When another person is involved, as in talking to someone, forces are not only created to make the gestures and vocalisations, but the gestures and vocalisations also create information for both the speaker and the listener. The information as well as the force field involve properties that emerge in time from the way activities exploit resources of the body and environment. For example, resources for grasping and walking include the inertial and gravity forces that operate on limbs and body as well as the muscle forces to move the limbs. For communicating, resources are also provided by the listener. They include the listener's attentiveness and ability to comprehend the pattern of vocalisations and gestures. Therefore, vocalisations and gestures are different depending on who is listening: a young child or an adult, another human being or a domestic animal. In any case the final success of an action does not depend on the activities that compose the action but on the time-dependent properties those activities create and the resources that are available to create those properties.

Acknowledgement of the aforementioned resources and time-dependent energetic properties that make activities successful implies a conception of action that differs from the mentalistic conception that characterises cognitive structuralism and information processing views. The latter views relate action to the manipulation of symbols. Material, energetic, and informational properties of body, brain, and environment are indeed insignificant to action from such a perspective. However, for actions such as walking, reaching, and grasping, or more complex actions such as talking to someone or playing a music instrument, material and energetic properties of both person and environment are highly significant. The movements *per se* do not determine the success of an action but rather the energetic and informational properties those movements create over time from resources provided by agent and environment. To act, resources need to be available to the agent and movements need to exploit these resources. For this reason, birds can fly by flapping wings, whereas humans will stay on the ground although they can easily imitate the birds' wing movements. Talents rest on the capability of exploiting these resources. A talented pianist, for instance, is someone who among other things can exploit the mass-spring resources of arms, hands, and fingers in relation to the mechanical characteristics of the keyboard for making limb movements efficient. Furthermore, attentiveness to the audience in combination with communicative skills are part of the talent.

What are the environmental resources for action and how may they become part of the agent's actions? James Gibson called the environmental resources "affordances". In Gibson's terms (J.J. Gibson, 1979, p. 127): "The affordances of the environment are what it *offers* the animal, what it *provides* or *furnishes*, either for good or ill." Affordances entail the environmental contribution to the relation between the agent and the environment. The agent's activities of body and brain build on those affordances to regulate the relation. Affordances are *not* imagined properties, or mental constructions of the agent, but *real* potentialities for action. They do form an *intrinsic* part of any action just as do the activities of the agent. To guide action, the agent needs to be continuously aware of what the environment affords. Therefore, Gibson argued that affordances need to be perceivable. In addition, because action connects affordances and activities, Gibson also argued that perception and action have to form one system. Action without perception is blind, and perception without action drifts away because it misses the information for staying in touch with the environment. Elaborating on Gibson's affordance concept, Heft (1989) argued that the direction of a child's development will be constrained by the affordances available to the child. Affordances may be discovered by the child being active itself, but also by observing others being active. Heft conceived of a child's intentionality as emerging from and fed by the affordances the child perceives, and the potential fit the child discovers between the growing capacity for action and the affordances that are available for action. According to Heft, the discovery of affordances motivates the child to express and optimise this growing capacity.

ENHANCEMENT OF CAPABILITIES TO ACT BY TOOL USE

With age, the potentiality for action grows, but this growth is limited due to constraints of body and brain. We cannot carry objects that cause too much torque on shoulder, elbow, and wrist, and we cannot remember long lists of names. Neither can we perceive details of objects at distances too far away for the resolution of our eyes. To solve this problem, our ancestors discovered a long time ago that the environment provides actors not only with affordances to act and explore, but also with opportunities to alter the resources provided by their bodies and brains. Their own resources can be enhanced by using environmental entities as implements to their own action systems (Smitsman, 1997). Such is the case in tool use. Tool use rests on the capacity of tools to modify and extend one's resources, provided one is able to manipulate the tool. Previously, the capability of tool use has often been attributed solely to the human brain. Tools, however, are extensions of body and brain. The body itself is also important, and not just the brain. For instance, human hand function differs considerably from that of other primates. This hand function together with the ability of bipedal locomotion that freed the hands enabled our ancestors to explore and use the resources for reaching and piercing that resulted from holding a stick.

Tool use has often been described as mediated action (see e.g. Smitsman, 1997; van Leeuwen, Smitsman & van Leeuwen 1994; Wertsch, 1995). The secret of tool use was supposed to be the agent's ability to conceive of an action, such as grasping a stick, as a means to another action, for instance, obtaining an object beyond reach. Of course, one can conceive of one activity as a means to another activity. However, the description of the means–end relationship does not distinguish, in a principled way, activities of tool use from activities that go on without the use of tools. The view of tool use as a means–end problem fundamentally ignores what happens, for instance, to an arm's resources for reaching when a stick is held in the hand (Smitsman, 1997). There are many actions that consist of a sequence of nested activities without the use of a tool. To grasp, one often needs to bend the trunk forward or to step forward to reach the target. The activities of bending and stepping forward can also be conceived of as means to an end. What distinguishes tool use from other nested sequences of activities? The key to a solution is not the organisation of the activities, but the resources that are involved, and especially the instantaneous changes in resources that occur in the case of tool use. The change in resources does not depend on how the action will be organised. Neither does it depend on how the agent conceives the implement, or the goal for which it is grasped, or more generally, on the meaning one imposes on the object. The change follows from the object itself that is grasped and the way it is held. A stick instantaneously changes the prehensile system's resources for reaching by virtue of the act of grasping and the object that is grasped. Attached to the system, the object alters the length of the arm, and the torque and inertial forces on shoulder, elbow, and wrist, irrespective of how the agent conceives the object. These metric and dynamic properties of the prehensile system are all resources for action on which capabilities such as reaching and grasping or piano playing rest. New capabilities and talents emerge and existing ones may disappear due to the change in resources the implement provides to the system to which it belongs. The power of tools to enhance the agent's capabilities rests, in the first place, not on the brain or a particular capability of the brain, but on the new resources for action a tool provides the agent. Tool use in humans often involves the execution of lengthy sequences of nested activities and planning. The brain is needed to regulate such sequences, but such sequences are not typical only of tool use. In this respect, it is interesting to note that Vygotsky and Luria (1994) conceived of the acquisition of speech as an important resource to regulate the stream of activities in tool use. They distinguished tool use in humans from tool use in apes on the basis of the resource of speech that is available to humans.

Tools as sources of development

Although instantaneous, the change in resources of the agent that results from the ability to use tools sets the stage for development. Development involves changes of a person's resources. Resources may change due to growth. However, in tool use, a similar thing happens as in growth of the body, but at a faster pace. Change of resources opens up possibilities for exploration and learning, the acquisition of new capabilities and talents by discovery and practice of the new activities that are possible, and exploration of the opportunities for action or affordances the environment furnishes the changed system. As with body growth, tools generate *discontinuity* in the relationship of the system to the environment and so set the stage for development. Discontinuity exists in the activities that are possible and in the affordances the environment furnishes to the agent. Due to the change in resources, the possibility of some earlier activities and affordances may disappear, whereas new activities and affordances become available for discovery and exploitation. Of course new affordances are available depending on the way the implement alters prior resources. Implements may also eliminate most of the important resources. For instance, a hand-held stick that generates forces on wrist, elbow, and shoulder joints that prohibit the arm from moving, renders the prehensile instrument useless and therefore cannot function as a tool. Use of a tool requires discovery of what the change means for action, and in particular for the relationship of the system to the environment. Exploration of the relationship, and more specifically of the affordances, of the environmental part of the relationship, allows children to discover and develop the new capabilities and talents that may emerge from tool use. Smitsman and Bosman (1985) investigated whether young children perceive the changed relation to environmental objects that arises from implements even when this requires them to act in unusual ways. In their study, Smitsman and Bosman gave 3–5-year-old children, for example, a nylon string to stretch between both of the children's hands. When asked to slice a piece of cake, the children immediately perceived that the string "afforded" cutting, whereas a flexible knife did not. In addition, increase of mass at the tip of a hand-held stick provoked hammering and a search for objects that "afforded" to be hit. These results indicate that young children's attention continues to be directed to the relationship between their own potentiality for action and the environment, even when this potentiality has been changed temporarily in some unusual ways, as is the case with the nylon string.

Over the history of mankind, tool use has grown considerably. Hand-held tools were presumably the first objects humans used to modify their action potentiality. Tools are certainly the first instruments to which young children are exposed. Today, tools form a substantial part of the human resources for action and cognition, which also involves action. Tool use has grown and differentiated in several directions. One can hardly think of an action that does not take advantage of tools in some way. Hand-held tools form just a part of the tools that are available to children as they grow up. The cultural heritage they share includes other tools that are more complex than the medium-sized hand-held objects of our ancestors, and the utensils young children first meet. The more complex tools include symbols and symbol systems of all kinds, such as the number system, the drawing system, taxonomies to categorise objects and events, and a variety of technological artefacts, such as computers and information systems. Symbolic knowledge, such as in physics and mathematics, could develop and persist because of the symbolic and technological tools that became available over time. Much of today's so-called "intelligence" stems from tool-use, and would no longer exist if the tools that sustain the mental capabilities disappeared.

Symbolic media as tools

Symbolic media differ in many respects from the traditional hand-held tools. They, nevertheless, are similar in the sense that their contribution to the development of children's capabilities also rests on the powerful way they modify children's resources for action, and consequently the child's relationship to the environment. Their use entails a change in possible activities and a change in opportunities for action, and consequently in what the environment and the "self" mean. The new meaning becomes available to a person by actually using the tool. The knowledge and skills that form part of the cultural heritage of children becomes part of themselves when they start to use the tools from which the knowledge emerged for their ancestors. For instance, by 5 months of age, infants visually perceive the number of objects that are available in a collection if the collection remains small (Starkey, Spelke, Gelman, 1990; Van Loosbroek & Smitsman, 1990). At about that age, they also perceive when this number changes (Wynn, 1992). However, tools to extend this early capability to larger and different quantities fail during the first year of life. The tool provided by the symbolic system of numerals is not yet part of a child's activities in exploring quantities. Use of this symbolic system happens by the end of the second year of age, when number-words become part of a child's vocabulary and counting activities go along with the recitation of numerals. By assigning numerals to collections, the relation to the quantitative world changes. A new mode of discovering quantities becomes available that extends the earlier mode. Use of the symbolic system of numerals will finally allow the child to assess quantities far beyond the scope of the earlier mode. In addition, it also provides a means to communicate the assessed quantities to other persons. However, although the symbolic system changes the child's own perceptual resources for dealing with the quantitative world as soon as it is used, discovery of the power of the expanded range of resources may take time. At first, the new mode may lead to confusion, especially if the child is not yet very skilful in using the system, and perception of number may become very unstable for some period. The number a child perceives for the same collection will vary on different occasions. The first stage of using a new tool may perhaps best be compared with what happens to someone who tries to eat with chopsticks for the first time. The resources chopsticks entail for grasping food are not immediately discovered. To begin with, it may seem as if all control is lost in relation to the food to be grasped. In handling a tool, one gradually discovers the new resources that become available by means of the tool. Presumably, the difficulties children experience in solving Piagetian problems arise not from a misunderstanding of their surroundings as such, but result from the loss of contact that arises when they have to apprehend them by symbolic means. The symbolic systems of their culture entail a different mode of knowing, but not necessarily higher rationality.

In sum, tool use highlights how the cultural heritage becomes part of a child. It does so by altering the resources to perceive and act that were available in body and brain. By extending those resources tool use also opens up possibilities for discovery of new affordances furnished by the environment. The immediate change of resources that results from implements does not imply that the actor has also changed immediately into a skilful user of the implements. It often takes a rather extended period of exploration and practice, aided by nurturing of the social surroundings, before one becomes skilful. The new resources are discovered in concrete tasks, just as a child discovers the resources of the body by acting. But discovery can take place and new skills arise only after the resources of body and brain for acting have been changed.

Pressure to modify the environment

Tools extend capabilities only as far as the environment still provides affordances to the modified action system of the tool user. Because the affordances may fail, creation of artefacts and technologies also motivates creation of the affordances that are needed to use the new products as tools. All animals modify the environment. Birds build nests, spiders make webs, and other animals dig holes. Humans, however, build houses, cities, and roads not just for their living, but also to use the artefacts that are available to them as tools. The example given before of highways and vehicles for transport that require wheels highlights the narrow relation between tool development and environmental modification. Tool development within a society leads to artificial or created capabilities and talents, but also to artificial environments to furnish affordances to use the artefacts.

Although tools have extended human capabilities beyond imagination, the relation between tool development and environmental change is not uncomplicated. It may also have negative consequences. Environmental modifications may take away important affordances for living that were available before, and surroundings may emerge that are threatening for agents who for some reason are unable to use the new artefacts. This happens today for other species who share the environment with humans, and also for humans who for some reason are unable to keep pace with the ever-increasing rate at which new artefacts become available. Rapid changes of tools and environment easily transform capable and gifted persons of today into incapable and untalented persons of tomorrow, and vice versa. For instance, elderly persons constitute a group of people who face a high risk of loss of talents. The risk does not just exist because of deterioration of physical and mental resources, but also because they may be unable to keep pace with the rate at which new technologies appear (Baltes, 1997). Moreover, deterioration of resources and adaptation to new technologies may be related problems. New technologies may make the elderly feel disabled, and make them painfully aware of a lack of talent compared to young children who grow up amid those innovations and apparently deal with them easily. Capabilities and talents rest in the relationship between organism and environment. Tool use reveals how this relationship can be exploited to create capabilities and talents. In this way tool use is as important to development as growth of the body and brain. By altering resources, it creates discontinuities in the relationship between agent and environment that set the stage for development of new capabilities.

CONCLUSION

In sum, the view presented here entails that capabilities and talents rest on resources provided by the agent's body and brain, and the affordances the environment furnishes the agent. Resources are available on conception in the genome of the organism and the environment that surrounds the genetic material, and many more become available during ontogenesis by growth of the body and brain. During ontogenesis, resources also become available via the tools a society provides the agent to extend resources of body and brain, and the affordances humans create to fit the modified capabilities and talents that emerge from tool use. Developmental processes produce new, and modify existing, resources. Capabilities and talents emerge from exploring and learning to exploit the multiple resources that are and become available over time to perform a task. The quality of performance does not rest on one single component but arises from fusion of the multiple components that are available to a person for the task. Variability in performance between and within individuals arises from the variable resources that are available over time and the variable way they may act together to induce the behavioural pattern to perform the task. One missing component may be sufficient to finally transform an untalented performance into a talented one. The components that are missing may vary over time between and within individuals.

REFERENCES

Baillargeon, R. (1993). The object concept revisited: New directions in the investigation of infants' physical knowledge. In C.E. Granrud (Ed.), *Visual Perception and Cognition in Infancy* (pp. 265–315). Carnegie Mellon Symposia on Cognition. Hillside, NJ: Erlbaum.

Baillargeon, R. (1994). How do infants learn about the physical world? *Current Directions in Psychological Science, 3*, 133–140.

Baillargeon, R. (1995). A model of physical reasoning in infancy. In C. Rovee-Collier & L.P. Lipsitt (Eds.), *Advances in Infancy Research*, 9. Norwood, NJ: Ablex.

Baltes, P.B. (1997). On the incomplete architecture of human ontogeny: Selection, optimization, and compensation as foundation of developmental theory. *American Psychologist, 52*, 366–380.

Bronfenbrenner, U. (1979). *The ecology of human development.* Cambridge, MA: Harvard University Press.

Bronfenbrenner, U., & Ceci. S.J. (1994). Nature–nurture reconceptualized in developmental perspective: A bioecological model. *Psychological Review, 101*, 568-586.

Dent-Read, C., & Zukow-Goldring, P. (1997). Introduction: Ecological realism, dynamic systems, and epigenetic systems approaches to development. In C. Dent-Read & P. Zukow-Goldring (Eds.), *Evolving explanations of development: Ecological approaches to organism–environment systems* (pp. 1–22). Washington, DC: American Psychological Association.

Edelman, G.M. (1992). *Bright air, brilliant fire. On the matter of mind.* New York: Basic Books.

Elias, N. (1991). *The society of individuals* (M. Schrober, Ed., E. Jephcott, trans.). Oxford: Blackwell.

Flavell, J., Miller, P.A., & Miller, S. (1993). *Cognitive development.* Englewood Cliffs, NJ: Prentice-Hall
Fogel, A. (1993). *Developing through relationships: Origins of communication, self, and culture.* New York: Harvester Wheatsheaf.
Gibson, E.J. (1988). Exploratory behavior in the development of perceiving, acting, and the acquiring of knowledge. *Annual Review of Psychology, 39,* 1—41.
Gibson, E.J. (1997). An ecological psychologist's prolegomena for perceptual development: A functional approach. In C. Dent-Read & P. Zukow-Goldring (Eds.), *Evolving explanations of development: Ecological approaches to organism–environment systems* (pp. 23–45). Washington, DC: American Psychological Association.
Gibson, J.J. (1979). *The ecological approach to visual perception.* Boston: Houghton-Mifflin.
Gottlieb, G. (1991). Experiental canalization of behavioral development: Theory. *Developmental Psychology, 27,* 4–13.
Gottlieb, G. (1992). *Individual development and evolution: The genesis of novel behavior.* New York: Oxford University Press.
Heft, H. (1989). Affordances and the body: An intentional analysis of Gibson's ecological approach to visual perception. *Journal for the Theory of Social Behavior, 19,* 1–30.
Howe, M.J.A., Davidson, J.W., & Sloboda, J.A. (1998). Innate talents: Reality or myth? *Behavioral and Brain Sciences, 21,* 399-442.
Johnston, T.D. (1987). The persistence of dichotomies in the study of behavioral development. *Developmental Review, 7,* 149-182.
Kalinowski, A.G. (1985). The development of Olympic swimmers. In B.S. Bloom (Ed.), *Developing talent in young people.* New York: Ballantine.
Kelso, J.A.S. (1995). *The self-organization of brain and behavior.* Cambridge, MA: MIT Press.
Oyama, S. (1985). *The ontogeny of information.* Cambridge MA: Cambridge University Press.
Piaget, J. (1970). Piaget's Theory. In P.H. Mussen (Ed.) *Carmichael's Manual of Child Psychology* (3rd edition, vol. 1, pp. 730–733).
Reed, E.S. (1982). An outline of a theory of action systems. *Journal of Motor Behavior, 14,* 97-134.
Reed, E.S. (1996). *Encountering the world: Toward an ecological psychology.* Oxford: Oxford University Press.
Rogoff, B. (1990). *Apprenticeship in thinking: Cognitive development in social context.* New York: Oxford University Press.
Sameroff, A.J. (1983). Developmental systems: Contexts and evolution. In P.H. Mussen (Ed.), *Handbook of child psychology (vol. 1): W. Kessen (Ed.), History, theory, and methods* (pp. 237–294). New York; Wiley.
Scarr, S., & McCartney, K. (1983). How people make their own environments: A theory of genotype environments effects. *Child Development, 54,* 424–435.
Schneider, W. (1993). Acquiring expertise: Determinants of exceptional performance. In K.A. Heller, F.J. Mönks, & A.H. Passow (Eds.), *International handbook of research and development of giftedness and talent.* Oxford: Pergamon Press.
Sloane, K.D., & Sosniak, L.A. (1985). The development of accomplished sculptors. In B.S. Bloom (Ed.), *Developing talent in young people.* New York: Ballantine.
Smith, L.B., & Thelen, E. (1993). *A dynamic systems approach to development: Applications.* Cambridge, MA: MIT Press.
Smitsman, A.W. (1997). The development of tool use: Changing boundaries between organism and environment. In C. Dent-Read & P. Zukow-Goldring (Eds.), *Evolving explanations of development: Ecological approaches to organism–environment systems* (pp. 301–329). Washington, DC: American Psychological Association.
Smitsman, A.W., & Bosman, A.M.Th. (1985). *Some consequences of Gibson's affordance concept to the study of meaning and its development in children.* Paper presented at the Third International Conference on Event Perception and Action, Uppsala, June.

Sosniak, L.A. (1985). Learning to be a concert pianist. In B.S. Bloom (Ed.), *Developing talent in young people*. New York: Ballantine.

Spelke, E.S. (1994). Initial knowledge: Six suggestions. *Cognition, 50*, 431–445.

Spelke, E.S., Breilinger, K., Macomber, J., & Jacobson, K. (1992). Origins of knowledge. *Psychological Review, 99*, 605–632.

Starkey, P., Spelke, E.S., & Gelman, R. (1990). Numerical abstraction by human infants. *Cognition, 36*, 97–127.

Thelen, E., Fisher, D.M., Ridley-Johnson, R., & Griffin, N. (1982). The effects of body build and arousal on newborn infant stepping. *Developmental Psychobiology, 15*, 447–453.

Thelen, E., Fisher, D.M., & Ridley-Johnson, R. (1984). The relationship between physical growth and a newborn reflex. *Infant Behavior and Development, 7*, 479–493.

Thelen, E., & Smith, L.B. (1994). *A dynamic systems approach to the development of cognition and action*. Cambridge, MA: MIT Press.

Thelen, E., & Ulrich, B.D. (1991). Hidden skills: A dynamic systems analysis of treadmill stepping during the first year. *Monographs of the Society for Research in Child Development*, Serial No. 223, *56* (1).

Valsiner, J. (1987). *Culture and the development of children's action: A cultural-historical theory of developmental psychology*. Chichester, UK: Wiley.

Valsiner, J., & Benigni, L. (1986). Naturalistic research and ecological thinking in the study of child development. *Developmental Review, 6*, 203–223.

Van Geert, P. (1995). Growth dynamics in development. In R.F. Port & T. van Gelder (Eds.), *Mind as motion: Exploration in the dynamics of cognition*. Cambridge, MA: MIT Press.

Van Gelder, T., & Port, R.F. (1995). It's about time: An overview of the dynamical approach to cognition. In R.F. Port & T. van Gelder, *Mind as motion: Exploration in the dynamics of cognition*. Cambridge, MA: MIT Press.

Van Leeuwen, L., Smitsman, A.W., & van Leeuwen, C. (1994). Affordances, perceptual complexity, and the development of tool use. *Journal of Experimental Psychology: Human Perception and Performance, 20*, 174–191.

Van Loosbroek, E., & Smitsman, A.W. (1990). Visual perception of numerosity in infancy. *Developmental Psychology, 50*, 916–922.

Vygotsky, L., & Luria, A. (1994). Tool and symbol in child development. In R. van der Veer & J. Valsiner (Eds.), *The Vygotsky reader*. Oxford: Blackwell publishers.

Wertsch, J.V. (1995). Sociocultural research in the copyright age. *Culture & Psychology, 1*, 81–102.

Wynn, K. (1992). Addition and subtraction by human infants. *Nature, 358*, 749–750.

PART TWO
INTELLECTUAL GIFTEDNESS

CHAPTER THREE

Successful intelligence: A unified view of giftedness

Robert J. Sternberg
Yale University, USA

Every society wants to identify its gifted—those who potentially have the most to contribute to that society, and in many ways, may demand the least from it in terms of resources. For this reason, societies devise a variety of ways to identify their gifted. What would happen if a society devised means of identifying the gifted that identified only a small proportion of those who were really gifted, or worse, identified the wrong people? We would then have a society that, at best, failed to utilise its human resources in an optimal way, and worse, misutilised these resources to the detriment of the society, as well as to the individuals who constitute that society.

To the extent that societies rely heavily on conventional tests of intelligence in the tradition of Binet and Simon (1916), whatever particular tests they may be, I will argue in this chapter that they are committing—in the language of signal-detection theory—serious "misses" as well as "false alarms". In other words, they are missing large proportions of their talent, and are identifying as gifted some who will probably turn out to be relatively undistinguished in any significant way with regard either to the goals of the society or even to the goals of these individuals. The basis of this argument will be a theory of successful intelligence (Sternberg, 1996).

In this chapter, I will first describe what successful intelligence is and why it is important. Next I will describe the elements of successful intelligence. Finally, I will discuss the interaction of these elements.

THE CONCEPT OF SUCCESSFUL INTELLIGENCE

What is successful intelligence?

Successful intelligence is one's ability purposively to adapt to, shape, and select environments so as to accomplish one's goals and those of one's society and culture (Sternberg, 1996).

Successful intelligence involves an individual's discerning his or her pattern of strengths and weaknesses, and then figuring out ways to capitalise on the strengths and at the same time to compensate for or correct the weaknesses. According to this view, the traits associated with successful intelligence are partially idiographic rather than fully nomothetic. There is no one set of abilities along which all people could be measured that would completely characterise their successful intelligence: People attain success, in part, in idiosyncratic ways that involve their finding how best to exploit their own patterns of strengths and weaknesses.

Intelligence versus successful intelligence

Successful intelligence differs from conventional, more academic notions of intelligence in several ways. Consider some of the main differences.

Adaptation versus shaping and selection as well. Conventional definitions of intelligence stress adaptation to existing environments (see e.g. "Intelligence and its measurement," 1921; Sternberg & Detterman, 1986). According to this view, a person is intelligent to the extent that he or she adapts to already existing environments. The problem with this definition is that it puts the individual into a relatively passive role with regard to the environmental context: The context demands; the individual responds. Although this passive role may adequately describe intelligence in many school settings and even in lower-level job settings, it does not describe the role taken by people who actively set goals and meet them over the course of their lives.

For example, in our current research on leadership (e.g. Sternberg et al., in press), we are devising a model and a test of tacit knowledge for leadership—what leaders need to know in order to lead that they typically are not explicitly taught and that often is not even verbalised. Leaders are active shapers of their environment: They try to mould the environment and to convince others to follow their lead (see also Gardner, 1995). Only weak and unsuccessful leaders accept the environment totally as a given, and try to convince people to adapt to this environment, as they have as leaders. A notion of intelligence as the ability to adapt to the environment could not possibly capture what successful leaders know and do, because leaders shape rather than adapt to environments.

Criteria relevant for assessing predictive validity. Conventional conceptions of intelligence have often been devised in relation to fairly abstract and academic kinds of tasks (e.g. Binet & Simon, 1916; Piaget, 1972). Conventional tests have stressed such tasks, and validation of these conceptions and the tests deriving from them has then often been in terms of school performance or performance on standardised achievement tests measuring scholastic performance. Successful intelligence, in contrast, cannot adequately be measured solely by abstract, academic kinds of tasks, nor could it be adequately validated by school grades.

For example, we investigated the predictive validity of a test that is commonly and almost routinely used for admission to graduate programmes in the United States: the Graduate Record Examination, known as the GRE (Sternberg & Williams, 1997). This multiple-choice test yields four scores: verbal, quantitative, analytical, and subject-matter achievement. This test is used in almost every field of graduate study, and weighs heavily in many admissions decisions. But what, exactly, does the test predict?

Our review of the literature showed that the overwhelming number of research studies that had been done to validate the test had used what we considered to be relatively uninteresting criteria against which to validate the test, such as first- or second-year grades in a graduate programme. But professionals are not judged by their grades. So in our study, we asked the advisors of all matriculants to the Yale University graduate programme in psychology over a 12-year period to rate their advisees for (a) analytical ability, (b) creative ability, (c) practical ability, (d) teaching ability, and (e) research ability. We also asked readers of the students' doctoral dissertations (not including the main advisor) to rate the quality of the dissertations.

We found the test to be a fine predictor of first-year grades in our graduate programme, especially after various corrections for restriction of range. But the test was a poor predictor of almost everything else, regardless of whether the data were corrected for restriction of range or not. None of the four subtests significantly predicted any of the ratings of women's performance. Only the analytical test significantly (but weakly) predicted ratings of men's performance. Thus, a conventional ability test that is widely used in the US was a good predictor of grades, but beyond that, its predictive validity was practically nonexistent. Yet users of the test simply assume that it is valid.

Life Performance. Conventional notions of intelligence seem to emphasise skills that are extremely relevant in school, but that perhaps become relatively less important later on. Thus, memory and analytical skills—the kinds emphasised by traditional theories of intelligence (see

Carroll, 1993; Gardner, Kornhaber, & Wake, 1996; Sternberg, 1990)—are very important in school, and although they continue to be important later on, they are arguably less so, as other skills come into play. It is thus unsurprising, perhaps, that conventional tests of intelligence predict school grades quite a bit better than they predict job performance (Wagner, 1997). Interestingly, these tests may not even be the best predictors of all aspects of school performance.

For example, we devised a test for college students that was quite different in kind from the Scholastic Assessment Test (SAT) widely used to predict college success in the US. Our test asked students practical questions, such as about what teachers expect in essays, how to study effectively, and how to perform effectively in a small recitation class accompanying a large lecture course (see Sternberg, Wagner, & Okagaki, 1993). We found that scores on this test predicted college academic success at Yale as well as did the SAT, and predicted personal adjustment to the college environment much better than did the SAT.

Personal, societal, and cultural values. The concept of successful intelligence explicitly acknowledges personal, societal, and cultural values (Sternberg, 1988b), as well as their interaction. Truly, one cannot talk about adaptation, selection, or shaping outside a cultural context, any more than one can talk completely about any kind of intelligence outside a cultural context (Berry, 1974; Cole, 1996; Laboratory of Comparative Human Cognition, 1982; Sternberg, 1984). Intelligence cannot be measured in a culture-free way, because intelligence occurs and is evaluated in the context of a culture. Cultures and even subcultures may differ in their concepts even of what is intelligent (Cole, Gay, Glick, & Sharp, 1971; Greenfield, 1997; Wober, 1974).

For example, in our own research, we found that US implicit theories or conceptions of intelligence yielded three main factors: practical problem solving, verbal ability, and social competence (Sternberg, Conway, Ketron, & Bernstein, 1981). But these conceptions may differ even from one occupation to another: We found that professors of art, business, philosophy, and physics had different conceptions of what would constitute an "intelligent" student, and that their conceptions fit the adaptive requirements of their respective fields (Sternberg, 1985b).

Even within a given country, conceptions of intelligence may differ. In a study in the culturally diverse community of San Jose, California, we found that Latino, Asian, and Anglo parents had rather different conceptions of what it means for their children to be intelligent (Okagaki & Sternberg, 1993). In particular, Asian parents heavily emphasised cognitive skills, Latino parents heavily emphasised social skills, and Anglo parents came in between, although closer to the Asian than to the Latino conception. More to the point, the school performance of the children in each group could be predicted from the match between the parental conception of intelligence and that of the teachers in school, who more emphasised cognitive competencies.

Once we go outside a given country, conceptions can become even more diverse. For example, in a recent study of Taiwanese Chinese conceptions of intelligence (Yang & Sternberg, 1997), we found five factors underlying individuals' implicit theories of intelligence: general cognitive ability, interpersonal ability, intrapersonal ability, intellectual assertiveness, and intellectual circumspection or modesty. Conventional tests of intelligence do not fully or even well capture any of the implicit theories of intelligence that we have studied.

It is also important to take into account personal goals. In schooling, it is often assumed that the ultimate goal is to obtain the best grades possible, and grade-point-averages (GPAs) are often used as criteria of success. But even in a school environment, practically anyone would agree that leadership roles, musical accomplishments, dramatic performances, and other forms of activities and good citizenship are part of individual success. Different students may weigh various criteria differently, much as would different individuals later in their lives. The money that is so important to one person might mean little to another, whereas the fame that one person strives for might actively be shunned by another. In measuring life success, therefore, we need to take into account not only what the society or culture values, but what the individual values as well.

In sum, successful intelligence is a broader construct than is traditional, academically defined intelligence. What are the components of successful intelligence?

COMPONENTS OF SUCCESSFUL INTELLIGENCE

Although successful intelligence is partially idiographic, there are certain broad nomothetic abilities that are relevant to the successful intelligence of virtually anyone. These are analytical, creative, and practical abilities (Sternberg, 1985a, 1988a, 1996). Analytical abilities are required to analyse and evaluate the options available to oneself in life. Creative abilities are required to generate these options in the first place. And practical abilities are required to implement the options and to make them work.

Analytical Abilities

Analytical abilities are involved in analysing, judging, evaluating, and comparing and contrasting. When, for example, a student is asked to write an essay comparing two different forms of government, or to solve a mathematical word problem, the student is being asked to employ his or her analytical skills.

In our research, we have studied analytical abilities largely through methods of componential analysis (see Sternberg, 1977), whereby information processing on cognitive tasks is decomposed into its elementary components. According to the theory, there are three main kinds of components (Sternberg, 1985a, 1988a). Metacomponents are used to plan, monitor, and evaluate problem solving and decision making. Performance components are used to implement the instructions of the metacomponents. Knowledge-acquisition components are used to learn how to solve the problems or make the decisions in the first place.

Metacomponents are particularly important to successful intelligence. They include (a) identifying the existence of a problem; (b) defining the nature of the problem; (c) mentally representing the problem; (d) planning a strategy for solving the problem; (e) allocating resources to solving the problem; (f) monitoring one's problem solving while it is ongoing; and (f) evaluating one's problem solving after it is done.

In our research, we have found that more intelligent individuals differ in their metacomponential functioning from less intelligent individuals (as measured by tests of fluid abilities). For example, we found that on complex analogy tasks, the more intelligent individuals distributed their time differently from the less intelligent ones: More intelligent individuals spent relatively more time on global planning, or deciding where they were going to go before they started; less intelligent individuals spent relatively more time on local planning, or deciding what to do in the course of solving problems (Sternberg, 1981). The advantage of putting more time up front is that one is less susceptible to false paths and detours, thereby reducing overall problem-solving time. In another study (Wagner & Sternberg, 1987), we found that better readers distributed their time differently in reading multiple passages than did poorer readers. In particular, the better readers adjusted their reading speed to take into account the purpose for which they were reading, whereas the poorer readers did not.

Results such as these suggest to us that the traditional view of intelligence as quick thinking (Jensen, 1982; Sternberg et al., 1981; Vernon & Mori, 1992) is an oversimplification of what is really involved in high-quality intellectual functioning. Successfully intelligent people are not necessarily faster than other people; rather, they are more effective at deciding when to be fast and when to be slow. They allocate their time more effectively.

Using componential analysis, one can take a task, such as an inductive-reasoning problem—analogy, classification, or series-completion problem—and decompose performance on this problem into its elementary performance components, such as encoding the terms of the problem, inferring relations between the terms of the problem, and applying the inferred relation to generate a response (Sternberg & Gardner, 1982). Our models of task performance have generally accounted for 80–95% of the variation in latency data for solutions to the various kinds of induction problems. Correlations of components of reasoning with scores on psychometric inductive-reasoning tests have generally been in the −.3 to −.6 range (negative because latencies are being correlated with percentages correct). In our work, we have isolated component latencies and difficulties for individual participants, as well as the strategies they used in solving the problem. Percentages of variation accounted for in response time data of individuals are, of course, considerably lower than those for averaged data. We have used similar techniques for studying various kinds of deductive-reasoning problems (e.g. Guyote & Sternberg, 1981; Sternberg, 1980; Sternberg & Turner, 1981; Sternberg & Weil, 1980) and verbal-comprehension problems (Sternberg, 1987a,b; Sternberg & Powell, 1983). Task models have typically accounted for over 80% of the variation in latency and response-choice data for the deduction tasks.

In our verbal-comprehension work, we formulated a cognitive model of how people figure out meanings of words in natural contexts (see Sternberg, 1987b). The model had three major elements: contextual cues, processes of decontextualisation, and textual variables that facilitate or impede decontextualisation. This model accounted both for which words were easier and more difficult to learn, and for which individuals were better in decontextualisation than others. We also showed that the ability to figure out meanings of words from context could be taught (Sternberg, 1987a).

Creative abilities

Creative abilities are involved in creating, inventing, discovering, imagining, and going beyond the information given. A creative individual is one who generates ideas that are novel, high in quality, and task-appropriate (Sternberg & Lubart, 1991).

According to our investment theory of creativity, creative individuals are ones who "buy low and sell high" in the world of ideas: They are willing to generate ideas that, like stocks with low price–earnings ratios, are unpopular and perhaps even deprecated. Creative individuals try to convince other people of the worth of these ideas. Having convinced at least some people of the value of these ideas, they then sell high, meaning that they move on to the next unpopular idea. According to this theory, creativity requires a confluence of six resources: certain cognitive processes (redefining problems, and selectively encoding, combining, and comparing information), knowledge, thinking styles, personality, motivation, and the environment.

We have used a variety of kinds of problems to assess various aspects of creative thinking. One kind of problem is convergent, requiring a keyed answer.

In one convergent type of problem (Sternberg, 1982; Tetewsky & Sternberg, 1986), called a conceptual-project problem, participants are presented with novel kinds of concepts, such as *grue* (meaning green until the year 2000 and blue thereafter) and *bleen* (meaning blue until the year 2000 and green thereafter) (Goodman, 1955). Or participants might be told that there is a planet, Kyron, where there are four kinds of people: plins, who are born young and die young; kwefs, who are born young and die old; balts, who are born old and die young; and prosses, who are born old and die old. Participants then have to solve induction problems, based on incomplete information. Information-processing models of task performance generally accounted for over 90% of the variation in response-latency data. The critical finding was that creative individuals are those who are more efficiently able to switch between conceptual systems, say, green–blue, on the one hand, and grue–bleen, on the other. In other words, they have the flexibility to alter their system of thinking without being hesitant or troubled by the switch.

Another type of item (Sternberg & Gastel, 1989a,b) required participants to solve analogies and other kinds of induction problems, but with either factual premises (e.g. "Birds can fly") or counterfactual premises (e.g. "Sparrows can play hopscotch"). Scores on the counterfactual items were moderately related to scores on conventional fluid-intelligence tests, and the counterfactual items seemed to be the better measures of the ability to redefine conventional ways of thinking.

The creative part of intelligence as applied to creativity also involves three knowledge-acquisition components, or processes used in learning. These three processes, in the context of creativity, are bases of insightful thinking. They are called selective encoding, which involves distinguishing relevant from irrelevant information; selective combination, which involves combining bits of relevant information in novel ways; and selective comparison, which involves relating new information to old information in novel ways. For example, Bohr's model of the atom as a miniature "solar system" was a selective comparison insight, relating the atom to the solar system, as was Freud's hydraulic model of the mind.

Sternberg and Davidson (1982; see also Davidson, 1986, 1995; Davidson & Sternberg, 1984) tested this theory of insight in a variety of studies, using mathematical insight problems (e.g. "If you have blue socks and brown socks in drawer mixed in a ratio of 4 to 5, how many socks do you have to take out of the drawer in order to be assured of having a pair of the same colour?"). They found that the three kinds of insights could be separated via different kinds of problems, and that correlations between the insight problems and tests of fluid intelligence were moderate. In particular, the insight problems correlated .56 with a test of solving mystery problems, .53 with a classification test (letter sets), and .43 with nonsense syllogisms (a test of deductive reasoning included for discriminant-validation purposes). They also found that it was possible to teach elementary students to improve their insightful thinking. In one study (Davidson & Sternberg, 1984), fourth-grade students (roughly 9 years old) who were labelled either as gifted or nongifted were either given training in solving insight problems or were given irrelevant training (control group). All students were given a pre-test and a post-test. Experimental students improved significantly more than did controls. The training also showed transfer from the kinds of problems that were explicitly taught to related kinds of problems.

Gifted students started out at a higher level than did nongifted students, and ended up at a higher level as well. Thus, although all students improved, on average, group differences were maintained. Training typically does not remove individual differences. But it can place everyone at a higher level of functioning, and sometimes change rank orders of individuals.

Sternberg and Lubart (1995) tested the investment theory as a whole using divergent rather than convergent test items (see also Lubart & Sternberg, 1995; Sternberg & Lubart, 1996). They asked people to generate creative products in four domains, choosing two from among a variety of topics they were given: writing (e.g. "The Keyhole", "2983"), art (e.g. "Earth from an Insect's Point of View", "Beginning of Time"), advertising (e.g. "Brussels sprouts", "Cuff links"), and science (e.g. "How could we know if there were extraterrestrial aliens hidden among us?").

All products were rated by multiple raters. Interrater reliabilities for the four domains ranged from .81 to .89, with a median of .86. Averaging over domains, mean interrater reliability was .92. Correlations between the two products in the same domains were .63 for writing, .37 for art, .65 for advertisements, .52 for science, and .67 overall, averaging across domains.

Sternberg and Lubart found only weak to moderate correlations across the four domains. In particular, correlations across domains ranged from .23 to .62, with a median of .36.

Practical abilities

Practical abilities are involved when intelligence is applied to real-world contexts. Our notion of practical abilities hinges largely, although certainly not exclusively, on the construct of tacit knowledge.

The nature of tacit knowledge. Whereas an academically intelligent individual is someone who is characterised by facile acquisition and use of *formal academic knowledge*, the kind of knowledge sampled by IQ tests and other tests of their ilk, conversely, the hallmark of the practically intelligent individual is facile acquisition and use of *tacit knowledge*. Tacit knowledge refers to action-oriented knowledge, which is typically acquired without direct help from others and which allows individuals to achieve goals they personally value (Horvath et al., 1994; Sternberg & Wagner, 1993; Sternberg, Wagner, Williams, & Horvath, 1995). The acquisition and use of such knowledge appears to be uniquely important to competent performance in real-world endeavours.

What, exactly, is tacit knowledge? There are three characteristic features of tacit knowledge. First, tacit knowledge is about "knowing how"—about doing. It is procedural in nature. Second, tacit knowledge is relevant to the attainment of goals people value. It is not the kind of academic information that teachers sometimes try to stuff in students' heads, where neither the students nor the teachers sometimes have the slightest idea of why the information is being imparted. Third, tacit knowledge is typically acquired with little help from others.

Knowledge with these three properties is called tacit because it often needs to be inferred from actions or statements. But although the term tacit is used to refer to this type of knowledge, the knowledge can be, and sometimes is, brought out into the open, although usually with difficulty and often with resistance. For example, there may be a big difference between what gets one a promotion according to a rule book and what gets one a promotion in reality. A company may not be eager for the true criteria—the tacit ones—to emerge, but these criteria can, and sometimes do come to light.

Promotions are, in fact, a particularly good example of the importance of tacit knowledge to practical intelligence. When one looks at the people who get promoted within an organisation, they are usually the people who have figured out how the system they are in really works, regardless of what anyone may say about how the system is supposed to work. Lawyers, for example, quickly figure out that billable hours are the key to success in a law firm; but they may also need to figure out that not all billable hours are equal—that some cases may be far better as career-builders than are others. In many fields, what matters even more than the work one does is the reputation one builds for that work, and reputation is not always tantamount to the quality of the work. People are often promoted more on the grounds of the reputation they have built than for the quality of the work, resulting in some people being promoted whose work is not, in fact, as good as that of other people who are left behind. The winners figured out what would lead to their advancement, and it was more than just the quality of the work they did.

What does tacit knowledge actually look like? Usually, it is expressed in the form of a sequence of if-then conditionals, which can be rather complex. For example:

If [you need to deliver bad news to your boss]
and
If [it is Monday morning]
and
If [the boss' golf game was rained out the day before]
and
If [the staff seems to be "walking on eggs"]
Then [wait until later to deliver the news.]

What one can see from this example is that tacit knowledge is always wedded to particular uses in particular kinds of situations. People who are asked about their knowledge in practical situations will often begin by articulating general rules in roughly declarative form (e.g. "a good leader needs to know what people are like"). When such generalisations are probed, however, they often reveal themselves to be summaries of much more specific, and more useful, tacit knowledge.

Indeed, tacit knowledge is practically useful—it is knowledge that is instrumental to the goals people want to attain, such as how to lead, how to get promoted, or whatever. For example, knowledge about how to make subordinates feel valued is practically useful for managers or leaders who value that outcome, but is not practically useful for those who are unconcerned about making their subordinates feel valued. Thus, tacit knowledge is distinguished from knowledge, even "how to" knowledge, that is irrelevant to goals that people care about personally.

An important feature of tacit knowledge is that it is usually acquired without direct help from others, and may even be acquired despite barriers to its acquisition. This feature of tacit knowledge may make it sound somehow sleazy or even illegitimate in some sense. But there is a reason why the environment does not support its acquisition: If everyone knew it, it would be useless. Consider, for example, how to get the next promotion. In a typical company, not everyone can get that promotion. There is knowledge about what matters to the higher-ups that distinguishes those who are more likely to get that promotion from those who are not. But suppose everyone had the knowledge. Then it would not distinguish among people, and it would be useless in determining who got the promotion. Very quickly, some other piece of information that some people know and others do not would become the inside information that distinguishes people who forge ahead from those who get left behind.

The implication of all this is that practically intelligent people are not ones who simply try to acquire as much knowledge as they can about the system in which they are working—they are people who know that they need to acquire the information that is not readily accessible to everyone. This fact applies at any level.

Testing tacit knowledge. The tacit-knowledge aspect of practical intelligence can be effectively measured (see Sternberg et al., 1993; Sternberg et al., 1995). The measurement instruments used consist of a set of work-related situations, each with between 15 and 20 response items. Each situation poses a problem for the participant to solve, and the participant indicates how he or she would solve the problem by rating the various response items. For example, in a hypothetical situation presented to a business manager, a subordinate whom the manager does not know well has come to him for advice on how to succeed in business. The manager is asked to rate each of several factors (usually on a 1 = low to 9 = high scale), according to the importance of each for succeeding in the given situation.

Some findings about tacit knowledge. One of the first questions we asked was whether tacit knowledge predicts performance of managers. We were particularly interested in managers because they are people who are judged on their practical, not their academic, intelligence. No one cares about their IQ scores, SATs (college admission test scores in the US), or college grades. Their superiors do care, however, about their ability to generate bottom-line revenue for the company, and to enhance the company's reputation.

Does performance on measures of tacit knowledge actually predict performance in management? We found that it does. For example, in two studies (Wagner, 1987; Wagner & Sternberg, 1985), we found correlations of .2 to .4 between tacit-knowledge scores and criteria such as salary, years of management experience, and whether the manager worked for a company at the top of the Fortune 500 (a list of top US companies in terms of revenues). In another study, tacit knowledge was significantly correlated with managerial compensation (.39) and level within the company (.36). Tacit knowledge was also correlated, although more weakly, with job satisfaction (.23). These correlations were as good as or better than the .2 correlations typically found when IQ tests are used to predict managerial performance (Wigdor & Garner, 1982).

When more precise criteria were used to assess managerial performance, the tests of tacit knowledge looked even better. In a study of bank managers, for example (Wagner & Sternberg, 1985), we found correlations between tacit knowledge and average percentage of merit-based salary increase of .48 and between tacit knowledge and "generating new business for the bank" of .56.

Further support for the tacit-knowledge approach came out of a study done at a leading management training centre, the Center for Creative Leadership in Greensboro, North Carolina, USA (Wagner & Sternberg, 1990). In this study, we were able to examine correlations among a variety of measures, including an intelligence test, a well known personality test, several tests of cognitive styles, a test of preference for innovation, a test of job satisfaction, and a test of orientation in interpersonal relations. We found the test of tacit knowledge to be the single best predictor of performance on two managerial simulations, called Earth II and Energy International. The correlation was .61. In contrast, IQ correlated only .38 with performance.

One might wonder whether that aspect of practical intelligence measured by tests of tacit knowledge is itself related to IQ. The answer, as far as we can tell, is no. We typically get correlations at the level of .1, which are not even statistically significant. In other words, contrary to the claims of Herrnstein and Murray (1994), IQ is not the only, and probably not even the best, measure of practical performance, in organisations or elsewhere. In fact, we used hierarchical regression to look at the correlation of tacit knowledge with managerial performance, even after taking into account every other measure the Center for Creative Leadership used. The result: Tacit knowledge was still a significant predictor of performance, even after taking everything else into account.

The lesson of these studies is that tacit knowledge often matters as much or more than does academic intelligence for job success. It seems not to matter what the job is. Even in ivory-tower academic jobs, tacit knowledge is key. Knowing the ropes is more important than knowing the syllabus one learns in school.

Tacit knowledge comes from effective utilisation of experience. In a study of 54 business managers, 51 business school students, and 22 undergraduates, we found, as one would predict, that tacit knowledge for management increases, on the average, with business experience. But IQ does not increase. So tacit knowledge is like other aspects of practical intelligence in that it increases over the course of the life span, in contrast to academic intelligence, which decreases. It is important to keep one additional finding in mind, however: People with more business experience did not score uniformly higher than did those with less such experience. In fact, some people with many years of business experience performed quite poorly. The point here is that what matters most is not how much experience one has had, but rather, how much one has profited from the experience one has had. Some people can be in a situation for years, and they just do not get much out of it, because they don't learn from their mistakes, or from other people's.

In a later unpublished study that focused on the development of tacit knowledge over the managerial career, Wendy Williams and I used extensive interviews and observations to construct measures of tacit knowledge for different levels of management. We administered this measure to all executives in four high-technology manufacturing companies. We also obtained nominations from managers' superiors for "outstanding" and "underperforming" managers at the lower, middle, and upper levels. This approach enabled us to delineate the specific contents of tacit knowledge for each level of management (lower, middle, upper) by examining what experts at each level knew that their poorly performing colleagues did not.

Our results showed that there was indeed specialised tacit knowledge for each of the three management levels and that this knowledge was differentially related to success. We derived these results by comparing outstanding and underperforming managers within each management level on inventories specific for the various levels of management. For example, within the domain of knowledge about oneself, knowing how to seek out, create, and enjoy challenges is substantially more important to upper-level executives than to middle- or lower-level executives. Knowledge about maintaining appropriate levels of control becomes progressively more significant at higher levels of management. Knowledge about self-motivation, self-direction, self-awareness, and personal organisation is roughly comparable in importance at the lower and middle levels, and becomes somewhat more important at the upper level. Finally, knowledge about completing tasks and working effectively within the business environment is substantially more important at high levels. In general, the lower the level of management, the more important it is to know how to get day-to-day, operational tasks accomplished, whereas the higher the level of management, the more important it is to know how to set a vision for the company to follow.

As mentioned earlier, some psychologists believe in the importance of a general ability, roughly IQ, which they believe explains almost everything involving intelligence that you can explain about job performance (Jensen, 1993; Ree & Earles, 1993; Schmidt & Hunter, 1993). These individuals have criticised our work as ignoring this general ability. In fact, we have not ignored it, as we showed when we discussed our studies at the Center for Creative Leadership, where our measures outpredict IQ-type tests in predicting managerial skill. But it turns out that managerial ability itself shows some "g-like" qualities.

We analysed scores from our tacit-knowledge tests and found that, in fact, people who tend to be knowledgeable about some aspects of tacit knowledge also tend to be knowledgeable about others. In other words, there was something like a general factor. Moreover, when people were tested for their tacit knowledge in two domains–business management and a field that is practically as different as one could find, academic psychology–the correlation between scores in the two domains was .58. Thus, people who are good at acquiring and using tacit knowledge do appear to have a generalisable skill. In everyday parlance, they are high in common sense. But common sense is *not* academic intelligence. In study after study, as mentioned earlier, we have found only trivial correlations between tacit knowledge and IQ (e.g. Wagner & Sternberg, 1985, 1990).

Our belief that tacit knowledge is not IQ was put to a rather severe test by a researcher who correlated scores on a tacit-knowledge test with scores on the Armed Services Vocational Aptitude Battery (Eddy, 1988), which is essentially a very sophisticated and relatively broad-ranging IQ test. In a sample of 631 air force recruits, of whom 29% were women and 19% members of minority groups, the median correlation between tacit knowledge scores and *ASVAB* scores, on the 0–1 scale, was a mere .07. Statistical analysis revealed that when scores were grouped according to the underlying constructs they measured, all the *ASVAB* tests tended to cluster together, but separately from tests of tacit knowledge. Quite simply, practical and academic intelligence are not the same, never have been, and in the foreseeable future, never will be.

Interestingly, both IQ and tacit knowledge are related to education. We have found correlations with both years of higher education (.37) and with self-reported school performance (.26). We have even found correlations with quality of college (.34). The fact that IQ also correlates with these measures tells us that tacit knowledge is predicted by educational variables, but by those aspects of education that are not correlated with IQ. In other words, what one gains in college that is not straight academic information matters for tacit knowledge! Thus, from our point of view, what students learn in courses truly is only a minor part of the college or any other educational experience.

One other result stands out from the Eddy (1988) study. Scores on the *ASVAB* were significantly related to both sex and race, such that women and minority-group members performed more poorly than did men and majority-group members. However, tacit-knowledge scores were unrelated to either sex (correlation of .02) or race (correlation of .03). In other words, tacit knowledge, unlike IQ, is not sex- or race-loaded.

Beyond business. Although our focus has been on business management, tacit knowledge is related to success in other domains as well. For example, in two studies of the tacit knowledge of academic psychology professors, we found correlations in the .4 to .5 range between tacit knowledge and various criteria, such as number of citations to the professors' work reported in the *Social Science Citation Index* (a measure of impact on the field) and the rated scholarly quality of an individual's departmental faculty (see Wagner, 1987; Wagner & Sternberg, 1985).

More recently, we have studied the role of tacit knowledge in the domain of sales (see Sternberg et al., 1993). We have found correlations in the .3 to .4 range between measures of tacit knowledge for sales and criterion measures such as sales volume and sales awards received for a sample of life insurance salespersons. In this work, we have been able to express the tacit knowledge of sales people in terms of sets of *rules of thumb*—rough guides to action in sales situations. Not only does knowing the rules of thumb for sales help us to assess sales tacit knowledge, it also potentially could help us in terms of devising a training programme for more effective sales work.

We have also studied the role of tacit knowledge for children quite a bit younger than college students. Why? Because tacit knowledge is important at all ages. Students, as much as anyone else, need to learn about tacit knowledge as it applies in school.

Together with a team at Harvard headed by Howard Gardner, we instituted a six-year programme of research, called the Practical Intelligence for Schools programme (Williams et al., 1996), which involved intensive observations and interviews of students and teachers in order to determine the tacit knowledge necessary for success in school. Curricula designed to teach the essential tacit knowledge were developed and evaluated both in Connecticut and in Massachusetts, in a variety of school districts. The curriculum has been sent to hundreds of schools, and is now being widely used.

The results of the curriculum evaluations have been uniformly positive. For example, students receiving PIFS showed significantly greater increases in reading, writing, homework, and test-taking ability over the school year, compared with students in the same schools not receiving the curriculum. Furthermore, teachers, students, and administrators reported fewer behavioural problems in classes using the programme (see Gardner et al., 1994; Sternberg, Okagaki, & Jackson, 1990; Williams et al., 1996). In other words, children can not only be assessed for tacit knowledge; they can also be taught it.

PUTTING TOGETHER THE THREE ASPECTS OF SUCCESSFUL INTELLIGENCE

How do all of the aspects of successful intelligence fit together? And how do they matter in the school? We decided a few years ago to do a study to check out our views on the three aspects of successful intelligence, and further to test out the notion that students can succeed if they are able to capitalise on any of the three nomothetic aspects of successful intelligence, so long as they are taught and assessed in a way that enables them to capitalise on their strengths.

The goal of the study was simple. It was to see whether students would perform better in the classroom if they were taught in a way that allowed them to make use of their natural patterns of abilities. In other words, if one teaches children in a way that fits them, rather than in a one-size fits all way, will children learn and perform better? Here's what we did (Sternberg, 1994, 1997; Sternberg & Clinkenbeard, 1995; Sternberg, Ferrari, Clinkenbeard, & Grigorenko, 1996).

We sent a test based on the theory of successful intelligence to students all around the country. The test contained analytical, creative, and practical items, in the verbal, quantitative, figural, and essay domains. The idea was to look in a wide variety of ways for students' patterns of abilities. We didn't want to limit ourselves to the analytical kinds of items found on IQ tests; nor did we want to limit ourselves just to, say, the verbal domain, or just to multiple-choice items. But testing the three aspects of the theory of successful intelligence in four different domains, we were greatly increasing the chances that, if a student had high intellectual abilities of some kind, we would be able to detect them.

What were some examples of the kinds of items that appeared on the test? In the analytical domain, for example, students had to figure out meanings of words from natural contexts, just as they did when they first learned vocabulary. In the creative domain, for example, students had to work with novel (newly invented) number operations that they had never used before. In the practical domain, students had to use maps to plan routes and schedules to compute times and distances, much as they do in everyday life. The practical essay required students to describe a life problem they were facing, and propose practical solutions to it.

The students taking the test were high-school students from all around the US and some from abroad who had been identified by their teachers or schools as potential candidates for the programme. They were not necessarily identified as conventionally gifted. We then chose students for the programme who met one of five types of criterion. Either they were very high in analytical abilities, very high in creative abilities, very high in practical abilities, high but not necessarily very high in all three kinds of abilities, or relatively low in all three kinds of abilities. This gave us five different ability groupings.

It is worth saying from the start that the groups differed from each other not only in abilities, but in some other fairly obvious ways. For example, the high analytic group was most notable for its traditional composition in terms of the usual "gifted" students in the US: It was mostly white, middle- to upper-middle class, and composed of students who had been identified many times in the past as gifted in their schools. The high-creative and high-practical groups, in contrast, were much more diverse, ethnically, racially, and with respect to socio-economic class. Many of the students in these groups had never been identified as gifted before, and they were generally not the highest achievers in their schools. The high-balanced group (who did well on all the tests) again looked more like a typical gifted group, presumably because they were high in the more conventional analytical abilities. The low-balanced group was diverse.

The students were brought to Yale to take an advanced-placement course in introductory psychology. In other words, it was a college-level course being taught to high-school students. All students received the same basic introductory psychology text (Sternberg, 1995), which is based on the three-part theory of intelligence. Students all also received identical lectures in the mornings from a star teacher at Yale who had won a teaching award.

The critical treatment distinguishing the groups occurred in the afternoons. There were four different types of afternoon instruction. One kind emphasised analytical thinking: comparing and contrasting, judging, evaluating, analysing. A second kind of instruction emphasised creative thinking: discovering, inventing, imagining, supposing. A third kind of instruction emphasised practical thinking: using, utilising, and applying. And the fourth kind of instruction—the so-called control group—emphasised memory, as do most introductory courses, in psychology or in other areas. Of course, these techniques are applicable not just to psychology, but to other fields as well.

In science, analytical thinking is involved in, say, comparing one theory to another; creative thinking is involved in formulating a theory or designing an experiment; practical thinking is involved in applying scientific principles to everyday life. In literature, analytical thinking is involved in analysing plots, themes, or characters; creative thinking in writing a poem or a short story; practical thinking in applying lessons learned from literature to everyday life. In history, analytical thinking is involved in thinking about how two countries or cultures are similar and different; creative thinking in placing oneself in the positions of other people of other times and places; practical thinking in applying the lessons of history to the present. In art, analytical thinking is involved in analysing an artist's style or message; creative thinking in producing art; practical thinking in deciding what will sell, and why, in the art world. Even in sports, all three kinds of thinking are needed: analytical thinking in analysing an opponent's strategy, creative thinking in coming up with one's own strategy, and practical thinking in "psyching out" the opponent.

It is important to realise one thing about the instruction we gave. Because we were doing an experiment, we assigned students to sections that emphasised only one of analytical, creative, or practical thinking, or memory. A good course, however, will be a balanced combination of all of these different types of thinking. The reason is that you want to help students both to learn in ways that are comfortable to them, and to learn in ways that are not. We don't produce successfully intelligent people by coddling them—by always making things easy for them. We produce successfully intelligent people by making some things easy and others hard—by allowing students both to capitalise on strengths and to compensate for or remediate weakness.

In our summer course, we evaluated all students for four kinds of achievements: memory, analytical, creative, and practical. Thus, students could not just succeed by showing that they had memorised the book. They had to show different kinds of proficiencies. Teaching in analytical, creative, and practical ways is important, because it actually enhances learning of material rather than detracting from it. Everyone knows that memorising a book results in very short-term learning. Most students forget the material as soon as they take the exam, or, unfortunately, sometimes before. By thinking about the material in different ways, students are forced to process it more deeply, and thus to learn it better. By thinking to learn, they learn to think.

When we looked at the results, they were strong and clear. Students who were placed in afternoon sections that matched their pattern of abilities performed better than did students who were placed in afternoon sections that mismatched. For example, if a creative student was given at least some chance to exercise his or her creative abilities in the course, the student's performance would be better than if not given such a chance. The same was true for analytical and practical students.

There were other results of note as well. Although overall correlations between analytical, creative, and practical scores ranged from .38 to .49, the correlations were quite a bit lower (around .1 to .2) when LISREL analysis controlled for mode of testing (multiple choice versus essay). Furthermore, factor analysis revealed no strong general factor, confirming the view of the theory of successful intelligence that the general factor of intelligence is largely an artefact of using principal-components of principal-factor analysis (which maximises the size of the general factor) on a narrow range of tests rather than the broader range we used.

Correlations were also computed between our abilities test and more conventional tests of abilities, including the *Concept Mastery Test* (largely a test of crystallised abilities), the *Watson–Glaser Critical Thinking Appraisal*, the *Cattell Culture-Fair Test of g* (Scale 3), and a homemade test consisting of insight problems. The analytical tests on our own measure correlated about .5 with these tests, as did the creative tests, but the practical tests correlated only about .3, on average. We also found, when we used stepwise multiple regression, that prediction of grades in the college-level psychology course was significantly improved by using creative and practical as well as analytical measures of abilities.

In a way, the results are not surprising. It makes sense that students would do better if allowed to show their strengths. But the way we teach in school, students are rarely given such a chance. We value the students with strong memory and perhaps analytical abilities, and practically write off those with strong creative and practical abilities. If we want to capitalise on the gifts of our students, at any level, we need to change, and teach and assess students in ways that recognise their strengths, not just their weaknesses. One-size-fits-all teaching is a poor fit to most students. A study like this shows that we have come a long way from IQ to successful intelligence. If we want to understand human abilities and giftedness in them in all their diversity, then we may wish to think in terms not just of IQ, but of successful intelligence.

ACKNOWLEDGEMENT

The work reported herein was supported under the Javits Act programme (Grant #R206R950001) as administered by the Office of Educational Research and Improvement, US Department of Education. The findings and opinions expressed in this report do not reflect the positions or policies of the Office of Educational Research and Improvement or the US Department of Education.

REFERENCES

Berry, J.W. (1974). Radical cultural relativism and the concept of intelligence. In J.W. Berry & P.R. Dasen (Eds.), *Culture and cognition: Readings in cross-cultural psychology* (pp. 225–229). London: Methuen.

Binet, A., & Simon, T. (1916). *The development of intelligence in children*. Baltimore: Williams & Wilkins. (Originally published in 1905.)

Carroll, J.B. (1993). *Human cognitive abilities: A survey of factor-analytic studies*. New York: Cambridge University Press.

Cole, M. (1996). *Cultural psychology*. Cambridge, MA: Harvard University Press.

Cole, M., Gay, J., Glick, J., & Sharp, D.W. (1971). *The cultural context of learning and thinking*. New York: Basic Books.

Davidson, J.E. (1986). The role of insight in giftedness. In R.J. Sternberg & J.E. Davidson (Eds.), *Conceptions of giftedness* (pp. 201–222). New York: Cambridge University Press.

Davidson, J.E. (1995). The suddenness of insight. In R.J. Sternberg & J.E. Davidson (Eds.), *The nature of insight*. Cambridge, MA: MIT Press.

Davidson, J.E., & Sternberg, R.J. (1984). The role of insight in intellectual giftedness. *Gifted Child Quarterly, 28*, 58–64.

Eddy, A.S. (1988). *The relationship between the Tacit Knowledge Inventory for Managers and the Armed Services Vocational Aptitude Battery*. Unpublished master's thesis, St. Mary's University, San Antonio, TX.

Gardner, H. (1995). *Leading minds*. New York: Basic Books.

Gardner, H., Kornhaber, M.L., & Wake W.K. (1996). *Intelligence: Multiple perspectives.* Fort Worth, TX: Harcourt Brace College Publishers.

Gardner, H., Krechevsky, M., Sternberg, R.J., & Okagaki, L. (1994). Intelligence in context: Enhancing students' practical intelligence for school. In K. McGilly (Ed.), *Classroom lessons: Integrating cognitive theory and classroom practice* (pp. 105–127). Cambridge, MA: Bradford Books.

Goodman, N. (1955). *Fact, fiction, and forecast.* Cambridge, MA: Harvard University Press.

Greenfield, P.M. (1997). You can't take it with you: Why assessments of abilities don't cross cultures. *American Psychologist, 52,* 1115–1124.

Guyote, M.J., & Sternberg, R.J. (1981). A transitive-chain theory of syllogistic reasoning. *Cognitive Psychology, 13,* 461–525.

Herrnstein, R.J, & Murray, C. (1994). *The bell curve.* New York: Free Press.

Horvath, J.A., Forsythe, G.B., Sweeney, P., McNally, J., Wattendorf, J., Williams, W.M., & Sternberg, R.J. (1994). *Tacit knowledge and military leadership: Evidence from officer interviews. ARI Technical Report.* Alexandria, VA: US Army Research Institute for the Behavioral and Social Sciences.

"Intelligence and its measurement": A symposium (1921). *Journal of Educational Psychology, 12,* 123–147, 195–216, 271–275.

Jensen, A.R. (1982). The chronometry of intelligence. In R.J. Sternberg (Ed.), *Advances in the psychology of human intelligence* (Vol. 1, pp. 255–310). Hillsdale, NJ: Lawrence Erlbaum Associates Inc.

Jensen, A.R. (1993). Test validity: g versus "tacit knowledge". *Current Directions in Psychological Science, 1,* 9–10.

Laboratory of Comparative Human Cognition (1982). Culture and intelligence. In R.J. Sternberg (Ed.), *Handbook of human intelligence* (pp. 642–719). New York: Cambridge University Press.

Lubart, T.I., & Sternberg, R.J. (1995). An investment approach to creativity: Theory and data. In S.M. Smith, T.B. Ward, & R.A. Finke (Eds.), *The creative cognition approach* (pp. 269–302). Cambridge, MA: MIT Press.

Okagaki, L., & Sternberg, R.J. (1993). Parental beliefs and children's school performance. *Child Development, 64,* 36–56.

Piaget, J. (1972). *The psychology of intelligence.* Totowa, NJ: Littlefield Adams.

Ree, M.J. & Earles, J.A. (1993). g is to psychology what carbon is to chemistry: A reply to Sternberg and Wagner, McClelland, and Calfee. *Current Directions in Psychological Science, 1,* 11–12.

Schmidt, F.L., & Hunter, J.E. (1993). Tacit knowledge, practical intelligence, general mental ability, and job knowledge. *Current Directions in Psychological Science, 1,* 8–9.

Sternberg, R.J. (1977). Component processes in analogical reasoning. *Psychological Review, 84,* 353–378.

Sternberg, R.J. (1980). The development of linear syllogistic reasoning. *Journal of Experimental Child Psychology, 29,* 340–356.

Sternberg, R.J. (1981). Intelligence and nonentrenchment. *Journal of Educational Psychology, 73,* 1–16.

Sternberg, R.J. (1982). Nonentrenchment in the assessment of intellectual giftedness. *Gifted Child Quarterly, 26,* 63–67.

Sternberg, R.J. (1984). What should intelligence tests test? Implications of a triarchic theory of intelligence for intelligence testing. *Educational Researcher, 13,* 5–15.

Sternberg, R.J. (1985a). *Beyond IQ: A triarchic theory of human intelligence.* New York: Cambridge University Press.

Sternberg, R.J. (1985b). Implicit theories of intelligence, creativity, and wisdom. *Journal of Personality and Social Psychology, 49,* 607–627.

Sternberg, R.J. (1987a). Most vocabulary is learned from context. In M.G. McKeown & M.E. Curtis (Eds.), *The nature of vocabulary acquisition* (pp. 89–105). Hillsdale, NJ: Lawrence Erlbaum Associates Inc.
Sternberg, R.J. (1987b). The psychology of verbal comprehension. In R. Glaser (Ed.), *Advances in instructional psychology* (Vol. 3, pp. 97–151). Hillsdale, NJ: Lawrence Erlbaum Associates Inc.
Sternberg, R.J. (1988a). *The triarchic mind: A new theory of human intelligence.* New York: Viking.
Sternberg, R.J. (1988b). A triarchic view of intelligence in cross-cultural perspective. In S.H. Irvine, & J.W. Berry (Eds.), *Human abilities in cultural context* (pp. 60–85). New York: Cambridge University Press.
Sternberg, R.J. (1990). *Metaphors of mind.* New York: Cambridge University Press.
Sternberg, R.J. (1994). Diversifying instruction and assessment. *The Educational Forum, 59,* 47–53.
Sternberg, R.J. (1995). *In search of the human mind.* Orlando, FL: Harcourt Brace College Publishers.
Sternberg, R.J. (1996). *Successful intelligence.* New York: Simon & Schuster.
Sternberg, R.J. (1997). What does it mean to be smart? *Educational Leadership, 54,* 20–24.
Sternberg, R.J., & Clinkenbeard, P. (1995). A triarchic view of identifying, teaching, and assessing gifted children. *Roeper Review, 17,* 255–260.
Sternberg, R.J., Conway, B.E., Ketron, J.L., & Bernstein, M. (1981). People's conceptions of intelligence. *Journal of Personality and Social Psychology, 41,* 37–55.
Sternberg, R.J., & Davidson, J.E. (1982). The mind of the puzzler. *Psychology Today, 16,* 37–44.
Sternberg, R.J., & Detterman D.K. (Eds.). (1986) *What is intelligence? Contemporary viewpoints on its nature and definition.* Norwood, NJ: Ablex.
Sternberg, R.J., Ferrari, M., Clinkenbeard, P., & Grigorenko, E.L. (1996). Identification, instruction, and assessment of gifted children: A construct validation of a triarchic model. *Gifted Child Quarterly, 40,* 129–137.
Sternberg, R.J., Forsythe, G.B., Hedlund, J., Horvath, J., Snook, S., Williams, W.M., Wagner, R.K., & Grigorenko, E.L. (in press). *Practical intelligence in everyday life.* New York: Cambridge University Press.
Sternberg, R.J., & Gardner, M.K. (1982). A componential interpretation of the general factor in human intelligence. In H.J. Eysenck (Ed.), *A model for intelligence* (pp. 231–254). Berlin: Springer-Verlag.
Sternberg, R.J., & Gastel, J. (1989a). Coping with novelty in human intelligence: An empirical investigation. *Intelligence, 13,* 187–197.
Sternberg, R.J., & Gastel, J. (1989b). If dancers ate their shoes: Inductive reasoning with factual and counterfactual premises. *Memory and Cognition, 17,* 1–10.
Sternberg, R.J., & Lubart, T.I. (1991). Creating creative minds. *Phi Delta Kappan, 8,* 608–614.
Sternberg, R.J., & Lubart, T.I. (1995). *Defying the crowd: Cultivating creativity in a culture of conformity.* New York: Free Press.
Sternberg, R.J., & Lubart, T.I. (1996). Investing in creativity. *American Psychologist, 51,* 677–688.
Sternberg, R.J., Okagaki, L., & Jackson, A. (1990). Practical intelligence for success in school. *Educational Leadership, 48,* 35–39.
Sternberg, R.J., & Powell, J.S. (1983). Comprehending verbal comprehension. *American Psychologist, 38,* 878–893.
Sternberg, R.J., & Turner, M.E. (1981). Components of syllogistic reasoning. *Acta Psychologica , 47,* 245–265.

Sternberg, R.J., & Wagner, R.K. (1993). The geocentric view of intelligence and job performance is wrong. *Current Directions in Psychological Science, 2,* 1–5.

Sternberg, R.J., & Wagner, R.K., & Okagaki, L. (1993). Practical intelligence: The nature and role of tacit knowledge in work and at school. In H. Reese & J. Puckett (Eds.), *Advances in life-span development* (pp. 205–227). Hillsdale, NJ: Lawrence Erlbaum Associates Inc.

Sternberg, R.J., Wagner, R.K., Williams, W.M., & Horvath, J.A. (1995). Testing common sense. *American Psychologist, 50,* 912–927.

Sternberg, R.J., & Weil, E.M. (1980). An aptitude–strategy interaction in linear syllogistic reasoning. *Journal of Education Psychology, 72,* 226–234.

Sternberg, R.J. & Williams, W.M. (1997). Does the *Graduate Record Examination* predict meaningful success in psychology graduate school? A case study. *American Psychologist, 52,* 630–641.

Tetewsky, S.J., & Sternberg, R.J. (1986). Conceptual and lexical determinants of non-entrenched thinking. *Journal of Memory and Language, 25,* 202–225.

Vernon, P.A., & Mori, M. (1992). Intelligence, reaction times, and peripheral nerve conduction velocity. *Intelligence, 8,* 273–288.

Wagner, R.K. (1987). Tacit knowledge in everyday intelligent behavior. *Journal of Personality and Social Psychology, 52,* 1236–1247.

Wagner, R.K. (1997). Intelligence, employment and training. *American Psychologist, 52,* 1059–1069.

Wagner, R.K., & Sternberg, R.J. (1985). Practical intelligence in real-world pursuits: The role of tacit knowledge. *Journal of Personality and Social Psychology, 49,* 436–458.

Wagner, R.K., & Sternberg, R.J. (1987). Executive control in reading comprehension. In B.K. Britton & S.M. Glynn (Eds.), *Executive control processes in reading* (pp. 1–21). Hillsdale, NJ: Lawrence Erlbaum Associates Inc.

Wagner, R.K., & Sternberg, R.J. (1990). Street smarts. In K.E. Clark & M.B. Clark (Eds.), *Measures of leadership* (pp. 493–504). West Orange, NJ: Leadership Library of America.

Wigdor, A.K. & Garner, W.R. (Eds.) (1982). *Ability testing: Uses, consequences, and controversies.* Washington, DC: National Academy Press.

Williams, W.M., Blythe, T., White, N., Li, J., Sternberg, R.J., & Gardner, H.I. (1996). *Practical intelligence for school: A handbook for teachers of grades 5–8.* New York: HarperCollins.

Wober, M. (1974). Towards an understanding of the Kiganda concept of intelligence. In J.W. Berry & P.R. Dasen (Eds.), *Culture and cognition: Readings in cross-cultural psychology* (pp. 261–280). London: Methuen.

Yang, S.Y. & Sternberg, R.J. (1997). *Taiwanese conceptions of intelligence.* Unpublished manuscript.

CHAPTER FOUR

The role of intelligence as a major determinant of a successful occupational life

Franz E. Weinert and Ernst A. Hany
Max Planck Institute for Psychological Research, Munich, Germany

INTRODUCTION

This chapter provides an overview of the relevance of intelligence for occupational development. After describing some psychological literature on both concepts, data from a longitudinal twin study are presented, which demonstrate the long-lasting influences of cognitive and educational factors on occupational attainment. Models of occupational development—even as crude and incomplete as they are today—are regarded as the theoretical starting-point from which studies on unusual life achievement have to start. Careers of excellence often arise out of the context of a regular occupation. However, even in individual cases where the general pattern of career choice and development seems not to apply, models of regular development provide the theoretical background against which models of qualitatively different development have to be designed and tested.

The attractiveness of the concept of intelligence

Individuals who are able to judge effectively, to understand quickly, and to think rationally are called intelligent. Nearly 100 years ago Binet and Simon (1905) used such a characterisation of intelligence to begin to describe individual differences between more and less intelligent people, and to measure these differences in children with a method of testing that they had invented. On the basis of the test they had designed, they made predictions both for the future mental development of the children and for their future failure or success at school. Binet and Simon's work was a significant starting point, for the study of individual differences in cognitive development and for the psychometric approach in intelligence research as well as for the practical use of psychological findings. The scientific programme that followed from that was and still is one of the most fertile fields in modern psychology.

The original concept of intelligent behaviour and of intelligence as a personal trait that had been used by Simon and Binet has been changing gradually since that time; it has been defined more broadly, theoretically more elaborated, and measured with more sophisticated instruments, and it has been adapted to the requirements of psychological diagnosis as well as for those of educational and professional guidance, by means of a net of empirical findings. All this happened in spite of criticism of intelligence research for theoretical deficiencies and for the preferential use of global measures, e.g. the intelligence quotient (IQ; Siegel, 1995). However, recently IQ was compared with the Rock of Gibraltar, which has continuously been attacked by the tides, has always been a bone of contention between different interests, and has long been predicted to be likely to disappear soon—and yet is still an isle of prosperity. What is it, then, that makes intelligence research and in particular the IQ so attractive both for psychological science and for practical application? By presenting the six main reasons for this attractiveness, we also establish the theoretical framework of the current chapter.

(1) The concept of intelligence as a cluster of abilities to think rationally was enlarged by David Wechsler (1944). He added cognitive capacity to act, and defined intelligence (1944, p. 3) as "the aggregate or global capacity of the individual to act purposefully, to think rationally, and to deal effectively with his environment." If one looks for the common constituents of the three components of this definition, one could characterise intelligence as the individual capacity to uncover and to invent regularities or redundancies when processing external and internal stimuli, from inside or outside. With this broadening of the term, intelligence not only means the individual, variable capacity to solve academic problems in a psychological laboratory but also the sum of cognitive capacities one needs to master different tasks in real life.

(2) Intelligence is a positively biased trait both for lay people and for scientists, although the concept of intelligence and the technology for measuring intelligence was originally developed by Binet and Simon in order to identify mentally retarded children, who needed special education, and although it is assumed for all intelligence tests that the scores are symmetrically distributed within the population. Persons are labelled intelligent if they are able to process new information quickly and cor-

rectly, produce original ideas, appropriately and usefully represent many phenomena in situational models, and if they are able to learn effectively, to solve hard problems efficiently, and to control their thinking and acting purposively with the help of meta-cognitive strategies (Sternberg, 1985). Unintelligent persons are often described as not showing or only rarely showing these (positive) cognitive indicators. Therefore it is not surprising that measures of intelligence have always been relevant in research on highly gifted persons (Mönks, 1963). Similarly, lay persons believe in an immediate correlation between outstanding intelligence and excellent achievement, which is determined through the criteria of excellence, rarity, productivity, demonstrability, and the social value of products (Sternberg, 1993). In scientific models too, a person's high intelligence is supposed to be a necessary but not sufficient prerequisite for outstanding mental achievement (Mönks, 1992b).

(3) With such a broad definition of the construct of intelligence and its indicators it is plausible that intelligence cannot consist only of one single mental capacity. For theoretical reasons, it has rather to be a complex system of more or less independent abilities for abstract, concrete, verbal, numerical, spatial, and practical reasoning. Nevertheless, intelligence research has again and again succeeded in integrating the great variety of process-specific and content-specific aspects, of global and specific factors—both by empirical studies and with the help of comprehensive theoretical models.

(4) Individual differences in general intelligence prove to be extremely stable during the lifetime, although in childhood the intellectual competencies develop in a universal way and change dramatically, and although grown-ups still acquire a variety of cognitive competencies. Thus, for children aged between 4 and 12, coefficients of stability for measures of general, fluid, and crystallised intelligence are about .7 (Weinert & Schneider, 1999). In adulthood, the long-term stability of individual differences in IQ (about .9) approaches the coefficients of reliability of the intelligence tests applied (Dörfert, 1996). This indicates that the rank order of the individual test scores remains nearly the same over many years. Individual differences in intelligence when observed early in childhood therefore allow for valid long-term predictions.

(5) The stability of individual differences in intelligence during the lifetime undoubtedly depends on the relatively strong heredity of the intelligence quotient (see Plomin, 1988). In addition, genetic and environmental effects do not vary independently, but covary considerably. This covariation results first from the fact that the biological parents also design the environment of the child; second that nearly all human beings react in a specific way to the different genotype, which is expressed by the phenotype; and finally that older children, adolescents, and adults are

increasingly able to select and organise their environment according to their inherited dispositions (Scarr & McCartney, 1983). Individual differences are further intensified by the actual effectiveness of the so-called "Matthew principle" which states that only those who already have will receive more (Walberg & Tsai, 1983). In other words, children with favourable genetic predispositions and with a home that supplies lots of stimuli will acquire helpful capacities and intelligent knowledge quite early in life. Thus their possibilities of learning successfully improve a great deal in the long run. Lack of such conditions will produce the opposite effect (see Herrnstein & Murray, 1994).

(6) The facts described so far make it plausible that general intelligence is the only psychological variable that is correlated to *all* critical experimental, scholastic, and professional indicators of learning, achievement, and success (Fraser, Walberg, Welch, & Hattie, 1987). The empirical correlation coefficients are all positive but they vary between .1 and .9. This gives a reason to accept that intelligence is actually a necessary prerequisite for cognitive performance, but that the magnitude of the correlation depends on the chosen sample of subjects (selection bias, restriction of variance), on the specific tasks used, their demands, and the situational contexts. The functional impact of intelligence and at the same time its restricted situational effectiveness is particularly valid for occupational achievement and success during the lifetime of an individual.

Intelligence and occupational development

As many empirical studies (e.g. Sears, 1984) and meta-analytical evaluations of research (e.g. Ree & Earles, 1996) show, multi-factor models of determination and prediction are nearly always used to describe and explain professional development. In addition to general abilities, the parental social status—often indicated by the profession of the father—and the education of the individual play a central role in such models (cf. Blau & Duncan, 1967). Intelligence has a significant influence on different criteria of professional success but the intensity of this influence is limited (Schmitt, Gooding, Noe, & Kirsch, 1984; however, cf. the more optimistic view of the significance of intelligence for professional achievement in Schmidt & Hunter, 1981). With such a limited set of variables it is normally not possible to explain more than 50% of the variance of professional success (cf. e.g. Sewell & Hauser, 1972). Furthermore, the validity of explanatory patterns of variables for professional success is cohort-specific, as Mayer found when he compared the German cohorts of births for 1929–31, 1939–41, and 1949–51. The path model Mayer (1991) reported for the eldest cohort he examined (Fig. 4.1) shows an interesting pattern of path coefficients. When interpreting this predictive model (based on data assessed in retrospect),

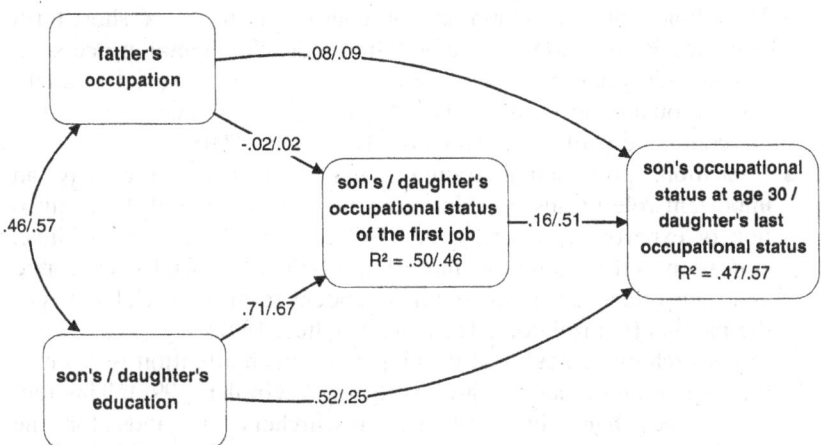

FIG. 4.1 Path model of occupational status attainment for men (first coefficient) and women (second coefficient, after the slash), born between 1929 and 1931 (from Mayer, 1991, p. 322).

one has to keep in mind that the individuals who were born between 1929 and 1931 in Germany chose their occupation immediately after World War II. Compared to the cohorts of individuals born later, the great poverty, the lack of jobs, and the uncertainty concerning further economic development may have influenced the correlation between the father's occupation and the first occupation of his child (in younger cohorts .14 to .19) as well as the correlation between the status of men's first and last jobs (younger cohorts .41 to .60). The difference between the cohorts considered seems to be plausible because their environment changed dramatically in 50 years, and the economic situation improved substantially.

However, Mayer's results (1991) confirm the expected correlation between father's occupation and child's education as well as the correlation between individual education and status of first job. The variability of the occupational status in adulthood proves to be relatively high. Much attention is nowadays given to this fact because occupational development is more and more supposed to be a lifelong process (Vondracek, Lerner, & Schulenberg, 1986) and because for a large number of people living in industrial countries, "work is the most salient life role" (Brown, 1990b, p. 508).

Characteristics of modern theories of occupational development

With regard to the classic theories concerning choice of occupation and professional success, modern models could be characterised as follows:

- The choice of occupation is not considered to be a short-term sequence of decisions but a long-term developmental process, in which individual capacities, socialisation effects, social models, occupational opportunities, and professional experience made earlier are combined (Miller-Tiedeman & Tiedeman, 1990).
- Education, professional training, and lifelong learning play an important role in this process. Individual education and the acquisition of expertise (see Ericsson, 1996) take on the role of a hinge; education and training are more important than social background and their effects are relatively independent from the social status of the parents (Ganzeboom, Treiman, & Ultee, 1991).
- In research on professional development, much attention is given to the middle and older age groups (Stroh & Greller, 1995). This tendency goes hand in hand with researchers' demands for the development of "multidisciplinary system views of career behavior" (Osipow, 1983), for more contextuality and research (Vondracek et al., 1986), and for "comprehensive life span—life space approaches to career development" (Super, 1990). Currently, it cannot be said to what extent the accuracy of prediction will increase with the complex models of these theoretical approaches compared with the previous rather economical models (see Brooks, 1990, p. 394).
- Apart from general intelligence, which is still considered, stable personal traits have lost scientific attractiveness with regard to the prediction of professional development. Dynamic constructs that are supposed to change during a professional career are taking their place. Among many others, personal self-concepts (Super, 1990), self-efficacy models (Bandura, 1997), occupational aspirations (Gottfredson, 1983), need-based social psychological models (Astin, 1984), and different concepts of personal identity (Gilligan, 1982) are some of these dynamic constructs.

By including this type of variables, researchers attempt to consider the continuous interactions between personal development and changing professional circumstances. Once more it must be said that at the moment this is more a theoretical programme than an integrated bundle of valid empirical results. Accordingly, Brooks (1990, p. 394) gives at least a sceptical survey for the recent theoretical developments:

On the one hand, comprehensiveness is a seemingly worthwhile goal for theory, on the other hand, the ultimate pay-off may be slim, since all-encompassing theories pose barriers to research.

From a scientific point of view (but perhaps not from an applied perspective) it therefore may be effective to go back to one of the central propositions of Super's theory about occupational development. During 40 years he adhered to this central point in spite of several revisions of his theory (see Super, 1953, 1990): and stated (1990, p. 207):

> The nature of the career pattern—that is, the occupational level attained and the sequence, frequency and duration of trial and stable jobs—is determined by the individual's parental socioeconomic level, mental ability, education, skills, personality characteristics (...) and by the opportunities to which he or she is exposed.

Models of occupational satisfaction

While occupational success manifests in social categories, in standards that are valid for many individuals, and partly in normative criteria, and can therefore be measured objectively, occupational satisfaction—by definition—is experienced subjectively. It depends on many individual factors, i.e. personal expectations, individual groups of reference, and subjective perceptions and causal attributions of occupational success and failure. This is why the results of many studies concerning occupational satisfaction are disappointing compared to studies on occupational success. For instance, in Meulemann's study (1991) only 16% of the variance of occupational satisfaction can be explained through 39 predictor variables. In this study, occupational achievement—especially if it is measured through income—and belief in the effectiveness of active self-control correlate with occupational satisfaction with a positive coefficient whereas life stress correlates with a negative coefficient. Personal factors, even intelligence, scholastic achievement, and occupational aspirations in school age, have no or even a *negative* effect on future occupational satisfaction. Occupational satisfaction as an individual judgement is less dependent on occupational success, the more successful the person was at young age and the more skilled they believe themselves to be. Therefore, quantitative studies of occupational satisfaction can only contribute in a limited way to theoretical progress because the results described probably do not reflect a generally valid pattern of the determining factors. It is not wrong to assume that these studies only refer to typical constellations of variables which at an individual level freely combine to produce cumulative, compensatory, or trade-off effects.

Evaluation of recent models of occupational development

If one evaluates the available theoretical models and empirical studies on the explanation and prediction of professional attainment and satisfaction, one reaches contradictory conclusions. On the one hand, there is an impressive sample of interesting studies, various—not mutually exclusive—theoretical attempts, and many scientific findings which are not at least useful in applied settings (e.g. for occupational counselling). On the other hand, all authors of newer state-of-the-art reviews agree with Brown (1990a, p. 363) that "theories of career development are at a relatively low level of development." The empirical results of the studies often are vague, differ from each other, are of unknown validity, and therefore without sufficient theoretical relevance. What are the reasons for this?

The issue of occupational development is of course a complex, heterogeneous set of phenomena. To arrive at an adequate theoretical understanding, we need to develop and integrate different theories of "middle range" for various criteria of occupational careers and perhaps also for definite types of professions (e.g. for blue-collar workers or for academics). However, few confine their research aspirations, so that we frequently find overgeneralisations of empirical findings which are misinterpreted as theoretical statements. This process is facilitated by the fact that theoretically comprehensive taxonomies of processes of occupational development are missing. Finally, many research programmes suffer from methodological weaknesses and problems. This is the case with the often used "samples of convenience" which are representative only for ill-defined populations. Further, frequently only short-term studies with not more than two points of measurement are realised (but cf. Schmitt et al., 1984); longitudinal studies are always designed with retrospective measurements; and the most relevant predictor variables covary so that their effects cannot be separated by means of an analysis of variance (for instance, as a rule father's occupation represents genetic factors, socialisation effects, educational aspirations, and direct influences on their children's occupational choice).

It is therefore nearly impossible to get detailed answers to the central questions of research on social mobility which were formulated by Jencks (1979, p. 213) as follows: "To what extent do the most desirable jobs go to the brightest, to the most educated, to the most ambitious, or to the sons and daughters of the rich?" In his own studies, Jencks used data from pairs of brothers, which at least allowed him to demonstrate that the social status of the family of origin explains no more than 50% of the variance of the occupational attainment, and no more than 35% of the variance of the children's later income. However, genetically sensible designs, which include persons of different biological relationships, are necessary to identify the additional "genetic transmission" within the family. Such studies allow the variance of a characteristic to be split into parts which are determined either by genetic factors, by the environment shared by biologically related individuals (such as siblings in the same family), or by the individually experienced, non-shared environment (Plomin, DeFries, & McClearn, 1990).

With such a behavioural genetic study comprising data from more than 8000 families, Heath et al. (1985) were able to show that 60% of the variance of the *educational attainment* of persons born between 1915 and 1939 was of genetic origin (or the result of gene–environment interactions). Only 28% could be attributed to familial sources. A genetic influence of 74% for males and 45% for females, and an environmental influence of 8% and 41% respectively was found with individuals born between 1940 and 1949. If a person was born after 1949, the genetic influence was somewhat lower. Thus the influence of the parental level of education and the resources of the family (transmitted via the shared environment) could only be substantiated for women. Other studies that particularly include other forms of biological relationships beside twins have found a somewhat weaker genetic and a somewhat stronger environmental determination of the individual differences in education (Behrman & Taubman, 1995; Vogler & Fulker, 1983).

A significant genetic influence can also be demonstrated for *occupational attainment* (Lichtenstein, Hershberger, & Pedersen, 1995), at least for men in whom the genetic influence is stronger for older cohorts (60–80%) than for younger cohorts (around 50%). In contrast, for women the genetic influence is quite weak, particularly for the oldest cohorts (born around 1920). The shared environment (i.e. the family background and the ecological differences between families and individual developments) is a substantial source of variance only for the oldest cohorts of women.

Tambs, Sundet, Magnus, and Berg (1989) investigated whether shared environment was the common source of covariance of intelligence, educational attainment, and occupational status. They were able to confirm the common source for the cohort of people born between 1931 and 1935, but only for the correlation between IQ and educational attainment. Occupational status proved to be influenced mainly by the individual environment. The shared environment did not play a significant role either in this cohort or in the other cohorts (born between 1944 and 1960). However, occupational status in younger cohorts proved to depend on genetic factors.

Aims of the GOLD study

Although the methodological problems of many studies are well known (often to the authors, too), it is hard to solve them in research. In the rest of this chapter, a research project is presented that at least claims to avoid some of the problems described. A prerequisite for this project was what one can call "good luck", even in science. In 1990 the first author of this chapter was offered the opportunity to continue a study that was started in 1937 by Kurt Gottschaldt with a random sample of 11-year-old identical and fraternal twins. Gottschaldt himself had run this study until 1967, and in 1992 the study was continued under the name GOLD (Genetic Oriented Life-span study on differential Development) when the subjects were about 65 years old. Data collected in 1937, 1965–67, and from 1992 onwards allowed the following research questions to be answered (among other questions which are not considered in this chapter):

(1) How stable and predictive are individual differences of intelligence over a time interval of nearly 60 years?
(2) How precisely can the occupational attainment in young, middle, and later adulthood be predicted by intelligence measures collected in childhood? How consistent are the effects of high and low intellectual abilities?
(3) Beside intelligence, what are the long-term effects of several other traits and environmental influences—and their patterns of combination—on occupational attainment and satisfaction? Can a parsimonious model of determinants of occupational development be accepted as adequately valid?
(4) Despite the small sample of identical and fraternal twins, can we find at least some tentative clues for the relevance of genetic factors and environmental influences for occupational development?

THE GOLD STUDY: METHOD

Design

The empirical data reported here have been collected in a longitudinal twin study designed and started by Kurt Gottschaldt as early as 1937 (Gottschaldt, 1939). Identical and fraternal twins were intended to be observed and compared in a complex and long-term setting which allowed naturalistic observations. Hours or a few days of observation did not satisfy Gottschaldt's demands for a comprehensive judgement of the "whole personality". Therefore he invited his school-aged twins to a summer camp which lasted for some six weeks. During this time Gottschaldt, his co-workers, and trained observers watched the twins at their daily routines and performing special tests of cognitive abilities and of facets of personality that had been carefully selected and designed by the investigators. With this procedure, Gottschaldt attempted to combine the biographical–characterological approach to personality with the experimental method, to investigate the genetic basis of personality.

The original twin study from 1937 was never intended to support Nazi ideology. American and German authors who researched the history of Gottschaldt's work testified to his work being free from any attitudes favouring eugenics or justifying the Nazi regime's brutalities towards minorities or the handicapped (Ash, 1992; Stadler, 1985). Therefore, Gottschaldt was able to continue his twin study during the 1950s after he had been appointed professor at the Humboldt University in Berlin. In the years 1949 to 1951, he and his co-workers visited as many as possible of the twins in the original sample—about 70 pairs—and collected biographical data as well as standardised ratings. After he had moved from East Berlin to Göttingen, Gottschaldt further continued his study in 1967 and invited the twins—now 53 pairs—to the Psychological Institute where standardised tests were applied, questionnaires were given, comprehensive interviews were recorded, and the ratings already applied in 1937 and for 1951–54 were carried out for a third time (Gottschaldt, 1968).

A fourth wave of data collection was planned for the 1990s but was delayed by Gottschaldt's death. It was started in 1992 by the Max Planck Institute for Psychological Research in Munich which received Gottschaldt's data in a bequest in his Will. In 1992–93, and again in 1995–97, the "Gottschaldt twins" were invited to the Munich institute or visited at home if they preferred. Some 87 persons from the original sample could be tested and interviewed (see Weinert, Geppert, Dörfert, & Viek, 1994, and Dörfert, 1996, for a more detailed description). An additional sample of aged twins was included in the data collection but this sample will not be considered in this paper.

At the first time of measurement, the subjects were about 11 years old. In 1993, they had reached an age of about 66 years. Therefore, data are available for an age span of 55 years which comprises youth and adulthood, and in particular both entrance into and exit from the occupational career.

Sample

The original sample consisted of 47 pairs of identical (monozygotic: MZ) twins and 43 pairs of same-sex fraternal (dizygotic: DZ) twins. A total of 31 MZ pairs (18 female and 13 male pairs) and 16 DZ pairs (8 male, 8 female) came from an urban environment; 16 MZ pairs (15 female, 1 male) and 24 DZ pairs (11 female, 13 male) were of rural origin. About half of the sample came from the south of Germany, the other half from the northern part. Gottschaldt had asked local welfare authorities to recruit the twins. He only insisted that every school-aged twin pair from the local districts selected had to be included and none should be excluded. The 180 children were on average 10.7 years old (range 9–13 years).

Biographical data and rating scales are available for all 180 subjects. However, not all subjects performed the cognitive tests applied in 1937. For some scales, data of no more than 50 persons are available.

The reduced sample tested in the 1950s comprised 148 subjects. Several twins had died during the war or moved to unknown places of residence. This second wave of data collection will not be considered in this paper because mainly qualitative data were collected.

A total of 119 subjects, among them 32 MZ and 21 DZ pairs, could be interviewed and tested for the third time in 1965–68. In 1992–93, 87 participants of the original study (among them 23 intact MZ and 10 DZ pairs) could be contacted and provided additional data (fourth point of measurement); 42 participants were deceased, 8 had emigrated, 4 could not be located, and 39 were not willing to participate further in the study.

Comparison of the participating and non-participating sub-samples in each of the follow-up points of measurement (1949–51, 1965–67, 1992–93) revealed a small "selective survival" effect: Continuing subjects were on the average more intelligent than the individuals who left the study. The IQ differences were, however, not significant.

Instruments

For the first point of measurement in 1937, several test scores and rating scales were selected for assessing intelligence and cognitive competence. Five tests measured logical, verbal, and arithmetic skills. The *verbal comprehension test* consisted of a text (five sentences from the beginning of a German fairytale) in which 43 words or parts of words were replaced by dashes. Subjects had to complete the text by writing down the missing syllables. The *conceptual relations test* consisted of a list of 10 objects (e.g. car, hammer, anxiety) and a separate list of 10 higher-level concepts in mixed order (e.g. vehicle, tool, and emotion, as the corresponding concepts). Subjects had to assign the object names to the higher-level concepts. A third test measuring *comparative reasoning in a spatial context* provided information on four families residing in a house with four floors. From some relational information about which family lived above or below another family, the subjects had to arrange the four family names into the correct order of floors. A similar test for *comparative reasoning* consisted of three items. Each item introduced three persons (e.g. Paul, Fritz, Hans) and stated two rank-order relations between pairs of them (e.g. Paul runs slower than Fritz; Hans runs slower than Paul). A final question (e.g. Who is the slowest?) required the subjects to fully reconstruct the rank order between the elements. A fifth test for *arithmetic skills* stated 14 arithmetic problems in text form, in ascending order of difficulty (e.g. If 7 bottles of wine cost 21 marks, what do you have to pay for 10 bottles?).

The raw scores of these five tests were first subjected to a regression analysis, with gender and age as independent variables. After eliminating the effects of age and gender, the residual values of the five tests were summed up and averaged for a total score of *General intelligence*. In order to reduce the number of missing values, this sum score was calculated even for subjects who had less than five but at least three valid test scores. Besides this general score, a score for *Comprehension* was computed by averaging the conceptual relations and the arithmetic skills test scores, and a score for *Reasoning* was computed by averaging the scores of the two deductive reasoning tests.

In addition, Gottschaldt assessed a huge variety of cognitive and personality aspects through rating scales. In 1937 and the later data collections, more than 200 characteristics were rated on a 10-point scale. About 50 items on aspects of intelligence were factor analysed. One of the emerging scales—with ten items; Cronbach's $\alpha = .96$—were used for this study. According to Gottschaldt's original labels, the scale measured capacity of thinking, with items on comprehension, insight, flexibility, and speed of thinking, and was labelled *rating of intelligence*. Table 4.1 gives the basic statistical information on the indicators of intelligence.

At the third and the fourth point of measurement, the non-revised version of the German WAIS (Wechsler, 1964) was applied for assessing intelligence. The total IQ was used in addition to verbal IQ and performance IQ, as indicator of general intelligence. In 1992, a computerised test was also applied. The test battery named *BaseCog* was intended to measure five dimensions of intelligence: fluid intelligence, crystallised intelligence, speed, fluency, and memory (Lindenberger, Mayr, & Kliegl, 1993). This test was developed at the Max Planck Institute for Human Development in Berlin for a comprehensive ageing study. In this paper, only the dimensions of fluid and crystallised intelligence will be considered. Both dimensions are measured through three subtests, by averaging the standardised scores received for each subtest.

Information on *occupational status* was collected in 1992 (Table 4.2). The subjects retrospectively provided data on their occupations in 1950, 1965, and 1990. This information was coded in terms of occupational status, using Scheuch's (1961) index which provided quantitative rank data ranging from 1 (lowest: unskilled worker) to 30 (highest: entrepreneur in a leading position). If a subject was married to a partner with a higher status, the partner's score was used. This was particularly relevant for unem-

TABLE 4.1
Descriptive data of the intelligence scales in this study

	Scale	N	Mean	SD	Minimum	Maximum
1937 data	Rating of intelligence	144	5.08	1.39	2.20	8.60
	Text Completion	100	2.25	0.78	0	3
	Deductive Reasoning	51	16.14	8.51	1	27
	Arithmetic Skills	62	2.84	1.44	0	4
	Conceptual Knowledge	120	6.65	3.23	0	10
	Syllogistic Reasoning	96	0.57	0.25	0	1.00
	Comprehension Tests	88	0.02	1.75	−4.17	3.58
	Reasoning Tests	62	0.02	1.67	−3.78	2.22
	All Tests	95	0.03	0.74	−2.12	1.63
1965–67 data	German WAIS Verbal IQ	99	97.44	13.05	69	127
	German WAIS Performance IQ	99	98.45	14.55	57	122
	German WAIS Total IQ	99	97.52	13.87	65	122
1992 data	German WAIS Verbal IQ	86	102.44	10.76	75	127
	German WAIS Performance IQ	86	105.80	12.65	66	129
	German WAIS Total IQ	86	104.34	11.59	69	126
	BaseCog: Fluid tests	85	50.00	10.00	29.9	67.9
	BaseCog: Crystallised tests	85	50.00	10.00	24.6	67.7

TABLE 4.2
Descriptive data of other scales used in this study

Scale	N	Mean	SD	Minimum	Maximum
Occupational status 1950[a]	81	11.14	5.79	1	30
Occupational status 1965[a]	81	12.79	7.45	1	30
Occupational status 1990[a]	81	13.51	8.05	1	30
Occupational satisfaction (1992)[b]	84	1.93	0.88	1	4
Educational level[c]	89	5.55	4.88	0	20
Father's educational level[c]	88	5.55	5.24	0	20
Mother's educational level[c]	89	3.72	3.15	0	12
Combined educational level of the parents[c]	88	9.28	7.49	0	29

[a] These data were retrospectively collected in 1992 and coded according to Scheuch's occupational index (Scheuch, 1961). The scores of this scale begin with 1 (unskilled worker) and end with 30 (businessman in leading position). Husband's occupation was coded in the case of unemployed housewives.

[b] Scale ranges from 1 (very satisfied) to 6 (completely unsatisfied).

[c] These data were retrospectively collected in 1992 and coded according to Scheuch's educational index (Scheuch, 1961). This list begins with 0 (elementary school, not completed) and ends with 20 (university degree).

ployed housewives (about 40% of the sample) who were ascribed to their husband's status because the status of a housewife was coded as "0" in Scheuch's index.[1] Occupational satisfaction was assessed through ratings in 1992 (Table 4.2).

Retrospectively, subjects indicated years of education and their own final educational status as well as that of their parents. Educational status data were coded using Scheuch's index for education (Scheuch, 1961) which resulted in an ordinal scale ranging from 0 (primary school only) to 20 (completed university studies). Again retrospectively for 1937, educational stimulation provided by the parents, parents' economic situation and social prestige, and satisfaction with residence were judged by the subjects using rating scales (see Table 4.2).

---

[1] We assumed that these women would have been able to reach the same occupational status as their husbands if they had continued their career. This assumption was supported by the high correlation of the married persons' and their partners' level of educational attainment ($r = .81$), and by the low correlation between the status of the persons' learned occupation and the status of their practised occupation (.18), in contrast to the higher correlation between their learned occupation and the occupational status score we used (.52). Thus, our score represents the individuals' occupational potential better than the score for their actual occupation does, and in this way we were able to include the housewives in the statistical models. By omitting the housewives, the status of the actual occupation and our score representing the maximum status of the couple correlated to .69 for 1950, .94 for 1965, and .80 for 1990. These numbers demonstrate that our score may not severely bias the status of the employed subjects but adjusted the housewives' status to a more adequate level.

At each point of measurement, several other instruments were used which are not reported here (including computerised and paper-and-pencil tests, questionnaires, biographical and in-depth interviews, and behavioural observations).

For about half of the sample, twin zygosity was determined by DNA fingerprinting in 1995, with assistance provided by the Department of Pediatric Genetics at the University of Munich. The other half of the sample was not available for blood taking in 1995. For these cases, zygosity was determined by Gottschaldt in 1937 through extensive comparison of some 80 physical characteristics because this procedure had been found to be 100% reliable.

Procedure

In 1937, data were collected in the ecological setting of a summer camp. The children were grouped in several "house communities" as they slept in different bungalows of the youth camp "Seehospiz" on the island of Norderney. The children enjoyed playing on the shore and participating in group activities. The subjects were continuously observed and daily protocols were written by the observers and the group supervisors. On several days, groups of twins were invited to participate in psychological tests which were introduced to them as "writing games". On the basis of many different observations, Gottschaldt and his co-workers filled out the rating forms for each subject.

In 1965–67 and 1992–93, interviews and tests were given individually. All subjects participated voluntarily and were informed about the purpose and preliminary results of the study. Instruments were administrated by psychologists or well trained psychological staff.

RESULTS

In the following sections we present four related lines of results from the multitude of data available from the GOLD longitudinal study. The question of how stable individual differences in general intellectual abilities are through the life span is our starting point. Then intelligence as a predictor of individual differences of occupational success is investigated. Next, we focus on the question of whether occupational attainment (and occupational satisfaction) can be predicted better if other personal characteristics are considered in addition to intelligence. Finally, we investigate genetic and environmental factors that determine individual differences in occupational careers.

The stability of individual differences in general intellectual abilities

Before starting to study the role of intelligence as a determining factor (and statistical predictor) of occupational development, it is necessary to check the ontogenetic changes in this variable. Two quite different questions have to be answered here: (a) How does the level of cognitive performance change over the course of occupational life? (b) How stable or variable are individual differences in cognitive abilities that may be varying at different ages?

The first question can be answered by comparing the average level of intellectual performance from various points of the life span. In our GOLD study, longitudinal data from a sample of N=72 individuals are available for the years 1967 and 1992; that is, for an interval of 25 years (from the 41st to the 66th year of life and later).

When comparing the means of the subscales of the WAIS, we find remarkable similarities and changes between middle adulthood and retirement. The results shown in Table 4.3 parallel data reported by other authors: Performance at the scales representing *crystallised intelligence* (Horn & Donaldson, 1980) remains constant or even shows a small rise (particularly at Similarities, Vocabulary, and Knowledge). In contrast, performance at tasks requiring *fluid intelligence* (especially Block Design, Digit–Symbol, Digit Span, and Arithmetic Skills) drops substantially.

TABLE 4.3
Mean changes of the WAIS subscale scores 1967–92

	German WAIS scales	1967 Mean	SD	1992 Mean	SD	t test
Verbal Scales	Knowledge	9.51	2.80	9.92	2.76	−2.64
	Comprehension	10.10	2.94	9.26	2.55	3.34*
	Similarities	9.81	2.75	10.60	2.26	−3.52*
	Arithmetic Skills	9.64	2.68	8.40	2.72	4.69*
	Digit Span	9.74	2.26	8.53	2.19	4.89*
	Vocabulary	9.51	2.48	9.85	2.16	−2.57
Performance Scales	Digit–Symbol	9.51	2.39	8.38	2.61	5.56*
	Picture Arrangement	9.56	2.97	8.51	2.85	3.02*
	Picture Completion	9.24	2.98	9.19	2.57	0.160
	Block Design	9.94	2.80	8.17	2.56	7.21*
	Puzzles	9.79	3.13	8.60	3.21	2.95*

$N = 72$
*$p < .01$

These significant changes in individual abilities during the life span (ability-specific drops of performance from middle to later adulthood—cf. Table 4.3—and strong gains of all cognitive abilities during childhood) urged us to test whether the individual differences in the abilities studied are stable or variable over the life span. We did this by using the GOLD data set which comprised nearly 60 years of individual life (1937, 1967, and 1992 as points of measurement). Table 4.4 gives a summary of some coefficients of stability. It is obvious from Table 4.4 that individual differences in cognitive abilities are extremely stable. This is particularly true for the time interval between middle and late adulthood. Correcting the coefficients of stability for the scale reliabilities, we get correlation coefficients of .92. This means that between 1967 and 1992, we can observe a nearly perfect identity of the individual rank order (Dörfert, 1996, p. 134).

Furthermore, the average scores of intelligence are also highly stable between 1937 and 1967. Interpretation of these coefficients depends on the fact that in 1937, assessment of intelligence was based on a different theory and method (reasoning tasks in the tradition of Gestalt theory) than in 1965 or 1992 (intelligence scales from the psychometric tradition). Therefore, the "true" stability of the individual differences in ability may be somewhat underestimated. The results of longitudinal studies of childhood support this assumption. Between the seventh and twelfth year of age, coefficients of stability reach values of .7 or .8 (Weinert & Stefanek, 1997). In other words, early *differences* between individuals remain almost constant even in phases of development where the average *level* of abilities changes substantially (as is the case with childhood and later adulthood). As a rule, very intelligent children become very intelligent adults, and frequently, less intelligent adults already performed below average when they were children.

TABLE 4.4
Coefficients of correlation of the indicators of intelligence, measured 1937, 1967, and 1992

		WAIS 1967			WAIS 1992			BaseCog 1992	
		V-IQ	P-IQ	IQ	V-IQ	P-IQ	IQ	Fluid	Cryst.
Scales 1937	Rating: Int.	.51	.41	.48	.60	.41	.54	.41	.62
	All Tests	.52	.56	.57	.61	.51	.60	.63	.56
German WAIS 1967	V-IQ	—	.79	.94	.88	.65	.81	.77	.84
	P-IQ		—	.95	.73	.79	.82	.74	.74
	Total IQ			—	.87	.77	.88	.82	.85

$N = \sim 70$; V-IQ = Verbal IQ; P-IQ = Performance IQ; Int. = Intelligence; Cryst. = Crystallised.

Intelligence as a significant predictor of occupational development and attainment

Occupational development and the associated success manifest themselves in the social status of the selected and practised occupation on one hand and in the careers within these occupations on the other hand. Most instruments for the assessment of occupational attainment—for example the Scheuch index (Scheuch, 1961) which was used in the GOLD study—focus on objective criteria which include both of those aspects (e.g. by considering income; the social prestige of the occupation; responsibility and independence at work; or workplace safety, among others). However, severe disadvantages contrast with the advantage of such a comprehensive, mixed index if individual differences in career development are theoretically modelled. For the career development in most occupations, general abilities are probably a causal factor that is necessary but rarely sufficient, and its varying relevance depends on the permanent or temporary demands of work. Therefore, correlation coefficients of only medium value can be expected for the relationship between general intelligence and occupational attainment. This expectation is even more justified by the fact that their husband's score was used for the index of occupational attainment for all non-working women, who are a substantial part of the individuals born in the 1920s. In contrast, the correlation between cognitive abilities and occupational satisfaction should be completely insignificant or even negative, according to the results reported in the research literature. Our empirical results largely confirm these expectations (Table 4.5).

TABLE 4.5
Correlations between measures of intelligence and criteria of occupational success/satisfaction at various points of occupational life

Measures of intelligence		N	Occupational Status			Satisfaction with occupation
			1950	1965	1990	
1937	Rating of intelligence	65–68	.35*	.43*	.49*	−.19
	All Tests	40–41	.13	.28	.33	−.37
1967 WAIS	Verbal IQ	65–66	.36*	.52*	.53*	−.01
	Performance IQ	65–66	.28	.39*	.41*	−.26
	Total IQ	65–66	.34*	.50*	.52*	−.15
1992 WAIS	Verbal IQ	79–80	.35*	.54*	.59*	−.06
	Performance IQ	79–80	.23	.31*	.34*	−.18
	Total IQ	79–80	.31*	.46*	.49*	−.13
1992 BaseCog	Fluid tests	78–79	.31*	.45*	.43*	−.16
	Crystallised tests	78–79	.31*	.53*	.57*	−.01
1990	Occupational status	76				.05

*$p < .01$

The results reported in Table 4.5 correspond to the expectations drawn from the research literature. For instance, the scores of intelligence and occupational attainment correlate between .3 and .6, on the average. However, some patterns of results should be emphasised: The correlation coefficients between all measures of intelligence—no matter if they were collected in 1937, 1967, or 1992—with the criteria for occupational attainment rise from 1950 to 1965 and finally to 1990.

This empirical fact can have different reasons: On the one hand, occupational status data for different phases of life were obtained in retrospect in 1992, so that judgement errors due to the temporal distance could occur. On the other hand, it is well known that the concurrent validity of variables is always higher than their predictive validity. By considering our different points of measurement, intelligence and (self-rated) occupational status were concurrently assessed only in 1992. For 1950, early measurements of intelligence (1937) and late measures of the occupational status (1992) were separated by a long distance in time. A third possible explanation could be that the numerically mostly low or medium coefficients of correlation obtained for 1950 result from the fact that after the end of World War II, many young adults accepted a job that corresponded neither to their abilities nor to their interests, because it was accepted only for "surviving" in a challenging historical period. When circumstances normalised, many individuals may have improved their occupational level in accordance with their cognitive abilities, while others may have pursued a successful career in the job they originally chose. In both types of occupational life course we expect that the correlation coefficients between intelligence and occupational status would rise later in life—and that actually happens according to our empirical results.

Finally, the numerically low correlation coefficients between measures of intelligence and indicators of occupational satisfaction are particularly remarkable. The possible reasons for this result have already been discussed in the introductory section of this chapter.

Multiple models for the prediction of individual differences in occupational attainment

Occupational success in various contexts of work depends on many and different personal factors. The unique effect of some of these factors may be very small, and presumably some of the small factors may (at least partially) be substituted or compensated by other factors. After thorough inspection of the GOLD data set we found that from the large number of tentative predictor variables collected (i.e. special parameters of cognitive performance, motivational and personal traits, environmental factors, scores for educational attainment, and others beyond general cognitive abilities), only highly aggregated scores of intelligence (collected at several points in time) and the subjects' and their parents' educational level significantly contributed to the statistical explanation of occupational success. Figure 4.2 shows a path model for the prediction of intellectual and occupational development on the basis of longitudinal data. It is based on the data of 49 individuals and is well supported by the data ($\chi^2 = 21.69$; df = 25; $p > .65$).

The paths depicted in Fig. 4.2 allow for the following characterisation of the cognitive and occupational development over the life span: The development of intelligence and of occupational status between the 41st and the 66th year of life both seem to be highly internally determined and almost totally independent of external influences. The development of intelligence up to the age of 40 years is highly determined by the level of ability acquired in late childhood, but school education has a substantial additional effect. The occupational status in middle adulthood is also multiply determined. According to our expectations, characteristics of the former occupational development but also the intellectual potential available at that time significantly influence occupational status. Obviously in the biographical period around the age of 40, long-lasting decisions on the further occupational career are made.

The level of early occupational status (at the chronological age of 25 years) is mainly determined by individual educational attainment. Obviously during the war and post-war period, individual differences of

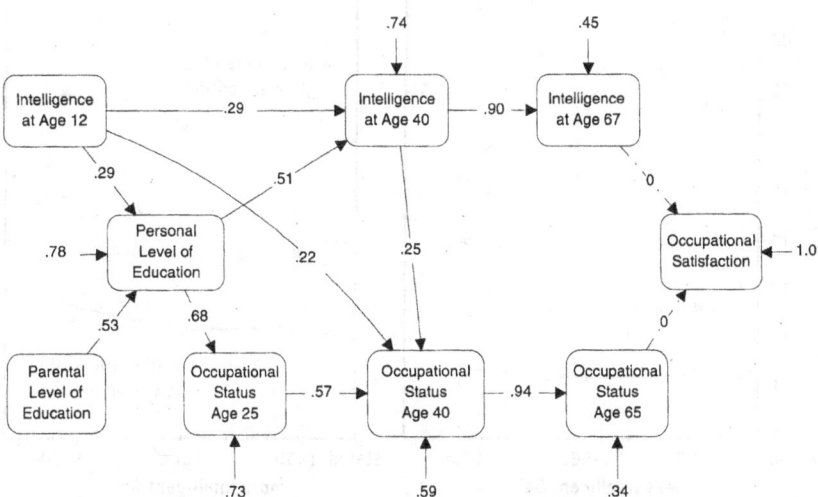

FIG. 4.2 Path model for the prediction of intellectual and occupational development (with longitudinal data).

education were a highly valid indicator both for the intelligence of the young people and for their parents' level of education as well as for the resulting educational and occupational aspirations that the parents developed towards their children.

As expected, occupational satisfaction at the end of working life is influenced neither by the occupational status attained nor by the intelligence level.

The empirically clear and theoretically interesting complex effects of the individual's intelligence and their parents' education are further illuminated by a comparison between individuals of low or high intelligence who had parents of low or high school education, respectively. Figure 4.3 presents the empirical data. The level of the occupational status rises during the work years ($F[2,118] = 6.66; p < .01$). However, this trend is qualified by a significant interaction between the educational level of the parents and the points of measurement ($F[2,118] = 4.68; p < .02$), indicating that children of well educated parents improve their status much more than the other children. There is another significant effect, of the level of intelligence ($F[1,59] = 4.58; p < .05$) indicating that the more intelligent the children are, the higher the status they obtain. Detailed comparison of the group means of our sample shows that in families of low educational status, high intelligence does not improve the chance of occupational development. In this way, highly intelligent children may be strongly dis-

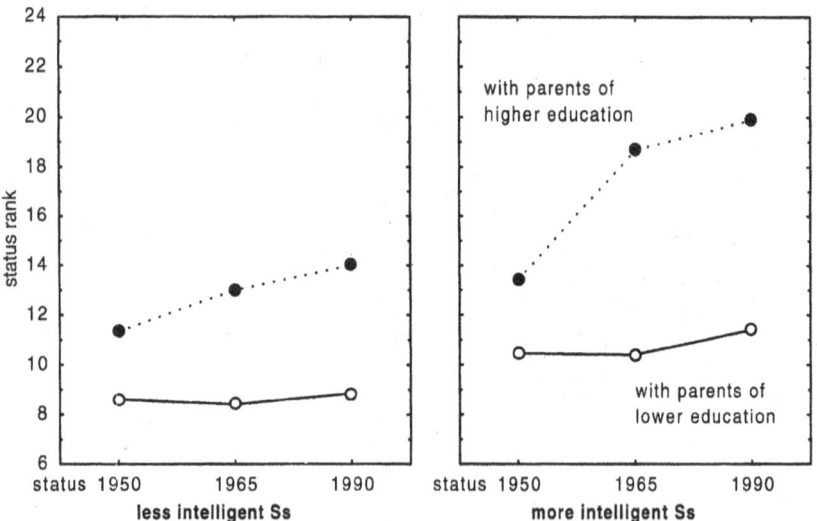

FIG. 4.3 Comparison of the occupational status across life, of children of high and low intelligence (measured at age 11) with parents of either high or low education.

advantaged when they have less educated parents. These results illustrate the asymmetrical causal net of personal abilities and environmental factors, resulting in different levels of occupational success, which at the same time is an essential part of life success for many people.

Behaviour genetic analysis of individual differences in intelligence and occupational status

We might expect a quite strong effect of genetic factors on the between-individuals variance of intelligence, as well as a substantial but more context-dependent heritability of occupational development, considering the relevant literature (which was presented briefly in the introduction). The small sample size of the GOLD longitudinal study allows only an exploratory analysis of the data, and the results gained here must be interpreted with caution.

Intra-pair correlation coefficients of identical and fraternal twins were compared in the behavioural genetic evaluations. Structural equation models with strong assumptions (Neale & Cardon, 1992) were not applied due to the small sample sizes (about 20 pairs of MZ twins and 10 pairs of DZ twins). Instead, estimates of heritability were calculated on the basis of the intra-pair correlation coefficients using Falconer's formula (Falconer, 1982). These estimates can be made not only for a single construct; here the coefficient of heritability equals the proportion of variance of a trait that is caused by genetic factors. Heritability can also be calculated for the correlation of two variables and it then shows the genetically determined proportion of this correlation (Thompson, Detterman, & Plomin, 1991). The coefficients calculated are listed in Tables 4.6–4.8. These coefficients represent the upper limit of the (possible) genetic influence, for as many combinations of variables as possible. For some combinations that are

TABLE 4.6
Intra-pair correlations and heritability estimates for the measures of intelligence

	Intra-pair correlations for MZ twins			Intra-pair correlations for DZ twins			Heritability estimates		
	Tests 1937	IQ 1967	IQ 1992	Tests 1937	IQ 1967	IQ 1992	Tests 1937	IQ 1967	IQ 1992
Tests 1937	.69	.50	.56	.37	.14	.43	.64	.27*	.26
IQ 1967		.92	.82		.80	.42		.23	.80
IQ 1992			.84			.43			.83

*Lower limit of estimation (minimum value).

TABLE 4.7
Intra-pair correlations and heritability estimates for the measures of occupational status

	Intra-pair correlations for MZ twins				Intra-pair correlations for DZ twins				Heritability estimates			
	EL	OS 1950	OS 1965	OS 1990	EL	OS 1950	OS 1965	OS 1990	EL	OS 1950	OS 1965	OS 1990
Educational level (EL)	.44				.50				0			
Occupational status (OS) 1950	.35	.38		.49	.56	.72			0	0		
1965	.19	.34	.65		.38	.69	.22		0	0	.43*	
1990		.43	.66	.73	.35	.62	.17	.12	.27		.34*	.24*

*Lower limit of estimation.

TABLE 4.8
Intra-pair correlations and genetic correlations between measures of intelligence and occupational status

	Intra-pair inter-variable correlations for MZ twins				Intra-pair inter-variable correlations for DZ twins				Estimates of genetic correlation			
	EL	OS 1950	OS 1965	OS 1990	EL	OS 1950	OS 1965	OS 1990	EL	OS 1950	OS 1965	OS 1990
Tests 1937	.39	.31	.36	.39	.24	−.25	−.20	−.05	.30	0*	0*	0*
IQ 1967	.51	.41	.53	.56	.38	.06	.19	.24	.26	.11*	.39*	.48*
IQ 1992	.49	.42	.45	.48	.23	.17	.02	.01	.45*	.35*	.04*	.01*

*Lower limit of estimation.

shown in the tables only the lower limit could be estimated. In this case, the genetic influence could be higher but a more precise quantification would require a larger sample.

The estimates of heritability for the scales of intelligence differ according to the time of measurement. At a young age and at later adulthood, we find a substantial genetic proportion of variance (Table 4.6). However, the WAIS total score assessed in 1967 (at the subjects' age of 41) shows only a small genetic influence. This score rather depends on the twins' shared environment, i.e. on differences of the families and of the educational careers. A close genetic correlation (of .8) can be found between the measures at 41 and 66 years of age which might be responsible for the long-term stability of intelligence. Later measures show only a small genetic correlation with the first measure taken at 1937. The medium-sized intra-pair correlations for MZ and DZ twins speak for a strong influence of the individual (non-shared) environment.

For several variables indicating educational and occupational status, the intra-pair correlation coefficients (Table 4.7) do not fit the classical behavioural genetic model, as DZ twins happened to be more similar than MZ twins. Thus the genetic effects on educational level and occupational status in 1950 can only be estimated as zero. This also happens to most correlations with these variables. Only the status scores for middle and later adulthood show a genetic effect, which is higher at the age of 41 ($h^2 = .43$) than at 66 ($h^2 = .24$). However, due to the small samples these estimates can have a substantial measurement error.

Despite this limitation, the pattern of coefficients seems plausible with regard to the assumption that occupational status shortly after World War II was more dependent on the rare opportunities to work (i.e., on environmental variables) than on individual characteristics (i.e. on genetic factors). Only in the later decades could a job be taken that corresponded to personal abilities and interests. This conclusion implies the assumption that occupational status is not inherited *per se*, but its genetic variance may indicate the influence of some characteristics of the person (such as intelligence) that are substantially inherited. This assumption is corroborated by the genetic correlations between intelligence and occupational status (Table 4.8). For the year 1965, the genetic correlation is .39, and this is close to the coefficient of heritability for occupational status (.43). Intelligence measured in 1967 is also genetically substantially correlated with occupational status in 1990. Therefore, nearly all of the genetic variance of the occupational status stems from its dependence on general intelligence. Intelligence itself is somewhat inherited but its variance, which can be attributed to the shared environment, depends on the parents' genetic endowment, which also determines the parents' educational level, occupational status, and their educational aspirations towards their children. Therefore, part of the correlation between the parents' educational level and their children's occupational level must be explained as mediated through genetics. The small twin sample does not allow for a precise estimation of the percentage of this genetic influence.

GENERAL DISCUSSION AND CONCLUDING REMARKS

The empirical results about the determinants of the occupational development showed that the life course of most individuals may be divided into three different periods (cf. Super's and Levinson's stage models of occupational development; cited in Ornstein & Isabella, 1990).

A first phase up to the middle of the third decade of life is characterised by the choice of occupation and the settling within a definite profession which may be more or less well achieved. The individual level of education best predicts the occupational status that will be reached at the age of about 25. However, this index is also influenced by individual differences in intelligence as well as by the differing educational backgrounds of the parents.

The second phase of occupational development (approximately to the 40th year of life) is characterised by many dynamic changes, a high between-persons variability of occupational progress, and a growing consolidation of the differences in occupational status between individuals. Intellectual abilities—besides level of education of the parents and early personal occupational development—are essential factors in this change. Intelligence and education co-effect in cumulative as well as in compensating ways (see Fig. 4.3). Without a doubt the individual opportunities for such compensations are influenced—i.e. facilitated or impaired—by the type of professional activity. Thus, the amount of compensation for an unfavourable family background by high intelligence may substantially differ for blue-collar and white-collar employees, academicians, and businesspeople. Presumably many personal and social factors are relevant for the acquisition of the professional expertise required and the development of individual differences in professional status. This interaction results in the limited variance of status differences explained by the additive combination of the factors considered.

The third phase of occupational development, between age 40 and the time of retirement within the seventh decade of life, is characterised by substantial continuity of professional career and the stability of the individual differences observed. In other words, further occupational development becomes more and more determined by its previous course.

Such a three-phase life-span model of occupational development cannot be expected to have general validity, that is, to be valid disregarding the respective contexts of society, economy, education, and professions. Studies that include several age cohorts confirm this conclusion (e.g. Mayer, 1991). Thus it is particularly important not to (mis)interpret the empirically found patterns of relationships between independent, dependent, and mediating variables neither as a mechanical mirror of reality nor as a context-independent theory of social psychology. In contrast, it is important to analyse in detail the functional meaning of the conditions, characteristics, and consequences of behaviour, measured through psychological variables (Melamed, 1996).

If we take the influence of intelligence on occupational development as an example, the followings statements result from the empirical evidence:

- If intelligence is defined as a nearly content-free cognitive adaptability towards new situations—that is, the ability of an individual to act purposefully, to solve problems successfully through reasoning—then the effect of intelligence on occupational development is the stronger the more one's occupation or one's professional position requires the mastery of various, new, and demanding tasks (American Psychological Association, 1995).
- The more the occupational tasks require domain-specific expertise for their solution, the more the function of general cognitive abilities is replaced by experience, deliberate practice, training, and the availability of domain-specific knowledge. However, the level of difficulty of the professional domain in which an individual can acquire expertise depends on the intellectual resources available (Sternberg, 1996). Furthermore, the quality of knowledge acquired (i.e. flexible access, transfer to new situations, multiple mental representations etc.) also depends on the level of general intelligence. Thus it is not surprising that intellectual abilities prove to be valid predictors for long periods of occupational development, but they are far from being the only causal determinants. As described, within definite limits deficits of intelligence can be compensated by effort, experience, education, training, and instruction (Ericsson, 1996; Haertel, Walberg, & Weinstein, 1983). These factors are mostly provided by the parents through stimulation, support, and direct (material and psychological) supply, whose educational level may be a useful indicator for the level of their assistance (cf. Fig. 4.3).
- There are many professional careers in which success depends not only on intellectual abilities and domain-specific expertise but also on social competencies (e.g. leadership), motivational tendencies (e.g. achievement motivation), and volitional self-control competencies. On the basis of this plausible assumption one might ask why the effects of such non-intellectual characteristics were not made man-

ifest in our data analysis (a result that mirrors any available statistical meta-analysis; cf. Fraser et al., 1987). In contrast to the general behavioural effectiveness of intelligence, motivational and social variables are highly sensitive to context, and they need to be stimulated and adapted to the situation at hand. Therefore, the relevance of motivation can only be measured in studies that observe internal behavioural tendencies and external conditions of behaviour, allowing for transactional effects. In studies like the GOLD project, which focus on the individual, the influences of motivational and social factors on occupational success are frequently underestimated.

On the other side, the relevance of cognitive abilities might be overestimated (Ree & Earles, 1996) because of three facts: the absolute level of intelligence (particularly of crystallised intelligence) rarely changes during the individual's occupational life span; during young and middle adulthood the individual differences in ability remain highly stable through genetic factors and cumulative effects of learning; and intelligence is substantially correlated with personal attractiveness, social status, education, a positive general self-concept etc. Thus the IQ is not only a measure of general cognitive ability but also indicates the level of many other variables which are related to intelligence and which favour occupational success.

If occupational achievement is in fact determined by multiple causes, it is highly problematic to estimate its heritability. Roubertoux and Capron (1990) used an illustrative analogy for describing the—in their eyes fruitless—approach to estimating the heritability of intelligence, which they regard as a composite of many factors: It might make sense to calculate coefficients of heritability for different kinds of vegetables like onions or tomatoes but it is absolutely meaningless to calculate the heritability of a soup made of an assortment of these vegetables. If we accept this conclusion in regard to occupational status, how could the empirical data on the heritability of occupational development be understood (see Tables 4.7 and 4.8; cf. Lichtenstein et al., 1995)?

Our reply to this question is that we do not regard heritability as that part of the variance of a characteristic that is provided by the ancestors and which will be genetically transmitted to the next generation (intergenerational perspective). We just regard heritability as that part of the variance that could genetically covary with other traits (intra-generational perspective). From the matrix of genetic covariances, factors still have to be determined that have a "true" biological basis and which make other traits appear being biologically determined that actually are not ("indirect heritability" according to Block, 1995). In our study we found the medium heritability of occupational status to be the effect of correlated intelligence. Thus we were able to conclude that occupational development is genetically influenced by intelligence and environmentally influenced both by the parents' educational status and the resulting intellectual and financial resources. In this way, the behavioural genetics methodology allows for a more specific dependency analysis of the causal pathways of within-family relationships.

This chapter has focused on the normal occupational development of an unbiased sample of individuals. Within this regular group, intelligence, level of education, and parental support were the most relevant causal factors for occupational career. Of course, in a sample of individuals who were highly intelligent and highly educated, and who enjoyed their parents' support, other personal and environmental factors would better predict individual differences, for instance: motivation and self-concept; quality of instruction and practice; or a satisfying fit between personality and working environment (Subotnik & Arnold, 1993). Studies on samples with restricted variances on specific characteristics could provide quantitatively different results compared to our study, and this might stimulate researchers to build different models of development for special subgroups of the population (e.g. Scarr & Weinberg, 1994). Scientists who include case studies in their programme of research and who observe the varieties of individual development may sometimes conclude that development is only predictable at the universal and differential level, but not predictable at the level of the individual (Mönks, 1992a).

REFERENCES

American Psychological Association (Ed.) (1995). *Intelligence: Knowns and unknowns. Report of a Task Force established by the Board of Scientific Affairs.* Washington: American Psychological Association.

Ash, M.G. (1992). Die Erbpsychologische Abteilung am Kaiser-Wilhelm-Institut für Anthropologie, menschliche Erblehre und Eugenik 1935–1945 [The Department of Hereditary Psychology at the Kaiser Wilhelm Institute for Anthropology, human genetics and eugenics]. In L. Sprung & W. Schönpflug (Eds.), *Geschichte der Psychologie in Berlin [History of psychology in Berlin]* (pp. 205–222). Frankfurt am Main: Lang.

Astin, H.S. (1984). The meaning of work in women's lives: A sociopsychological model of career choice and work behavior. *Counseling Psychologist, 12*, 117–126.

Bandura, A. (1997). *Self-efficacy: The exercise of control.* New York: Freeman.

Behrman, J.R., & Taubman, P. (1995). Is schooling 'mostly in the genes'? Nature–nurture decomposition using data on relatives. In J.R. Behrman, R.A. Pollak & P. Taubman (Eds.), *From parent to child* (pp. 249–268). Chicago: The University of Chicago Press.

Binet, A., & Simon, T. (1905). Méthodes nouvelles pour le diagnostic du niveau intellectuel des anormaux. *L'année Psychologique, 11*, 191–244.

Blau, P.M., & Duncan, O.D. (1967). *The American occupational structure.* New York: J. Wiley.

Block, N. (1995). How heritability misleads about race. *Cognition, 56*, 99–128.

Brooks, L. (1990). Recent developments in theory building. In D. Brown, L. Brooks (Eds.), *Career choice and development* (pp. 364–394). San Francisco: Jossey-Bass.

Brown, D. (1990a). Summary, comparison, and critique of the major theories. In D. Brown, L. Brooks (Eds.), *Career choice and development* (pp. 338–363). San Francisco: Jossey-Bass.

Brown, D. (1990b). Issues and trends in career development: Theory and practice. In D. Brown, L. Brooks (Eds.), *Career choice and development* (pp. 506–517). San Francisco: Jossey-Bass.

Dörfert, J. (1996). *Dynamik und Genetik der Intelligenz. Ergebnisse einer Längsschnittstudie mit Zwillingen [Dynamics and genetics of intelligence. Results of a longitudinal study with twins]*. Göttingen: Cuvillier.

Ericsson, K.A. (1996). The acquisition of expert performance: An introduction to some of the issues. In K.A. Ericsson (Ed.), *The road to excellence* (pp. 1–50). Mahwah, NJ: Lawrence Erlbaum Associates Inc.

Falconer, D.S. (1982). *Introduction to quantitative genetics* (2nd ed.). London: Longman.

Fraser, B.J., Walberg, H.J., Welch, W.W., & Hattie, J.A. (1987). Syntheses of educational productivity research. *International Journal of Educational Research, 11,* 145–252.

Ganzeboom, H.B.G., Treiman, D.J., & Ultee, W.C. (1991). Comparative intergenerational stratification research: Three generations and beyond. *Annual Review of Sociology, 17,* 277–302.

Gilligan, C. (1982). *In a different voice.* Cambridge, MA: Harvard University Press.

Gottfredson, L.S. (1983). Creating and criticizing theory. *Journal of Vocational Behavior, 23,* 203–212.

Gottschaldt, K. (1939). Erbpsychologie der Elementarfunktionen der Begabung [Hereditary psychology of the basic functions of giftedness]. In G. Just (Ed.), *Handbuch der Erbbiologie des Menschen [Handbook of the human biology of genetics]* (Vol. 5/1, pp. 445–537). Berlin: Springer.

Gottschaldt, K. (1968). Zwillingsuntersuchungen vom zweiten bis zum sechsten Lebensjahrzehnt [Twin studies from second to sixth decade of life]. In R. Schubert (Ed.), *Herz und Atmungsorgane im Alter. Psychologie und Soziologie in der Gerontologie [Aging heart and respiration organs. Psychology and sociology in gerontology]* (Vol. 1, pp. 176–185). Darmstadt, Germany: Steinkopff.

Haertel, G.D., Walberg, H.J., & Weinstein, T. (1983). Psychological models of educational performance: A theoretical synthesis of constructs. *Review of Educational Research, 53,* 75–91.

Heath, A.C., Berg, K., Eaves, L.J., Solaas, M.H., Corey, L.A., Sundet, J., Magnus, P., & Nance, W.E. (1985). Education policy and the heritability of educational attainment. *Nature, 314,* 734–736.

Herrnstein, R.J., & Murray, C. (1994). *The bell curve.* New York: Free Press.

Horn, J.L., & Donaldson, G. (1980). Cognitive development in adulthood. In O.G. Brim Jr., & J. Kagan (Eds.), *Constancy and change in human development* (pp. 445–529). Cambridge, MA: Harvard University Press.

Jencks, C. (1979). *Who gets ahead? The determinants of economic success in America.* New York: Basic Books.

Lichtenstein, P., Hershberger, S.L., & Pedersen, N.L. (1995). Dimensions of occupations: Genetic and environmental influences. *Journal of Biosocial Sciences, 27,* 193–206.

Lindenberger, U., Mayr, U., & Kliegl, R. (1993). Speed and intelligence in old age. *Psychology and Aging, 8,* 207–220.

Mayer, K.U. (1991). Lebenslauf und Bildung. Ergebnisse aus dem Forschungsprojekt "Lebensläufe und gesellschaftlicher Wandel" des Max-Planck-Instituts für Bildungs-

forschung. [Life course and education. Results of the research project "Life courses and societal change" of the Max Planck Institute of Research in Education.] *Unterrichtswissenschaft, 19*, 313–332.
Melamed, T. (1996). Validation of a stage model of career success. *Applied Psychology: An International Review, 45*(1), 35–65.
Meulemann, H. (1991). Lebenszufriedenheit und Lebenserfolg im Übergang vom Jugendlichen zum Erwachsenen [Life satisfaction and life success at the transition from youth to adulthood]. *Kölner Zeitschrift für Soziologie und Sozialpsychologie, 43*, 476–501.
Miller-Tiedeman, A., & Tiedeman, D.V. (1990). Career decision making: An individualistic perspective. In D. Brown, L. Brooks (Eds.), *Career choice and development* (pp. 308–337). San Francisco: Jossey-Bass.
Mönks, F.J. (1963). Beiträge zur Begabtenforschung im Kindes- und Jugendalter [Contributions to the research in giftedness in childhood and adolescence]. *Archiv für die gesamte Psychologie, 115*, 326–382.
Mönks, F.J. (1992a). Development of gifted children: The issue of identification and programming. In F.J. Mönks & W.A.M. Peters (Eds.), *Talent for the future. Social and personality development of gifted children* (pp. 191–202). Assen, The Netherlands: Van Gorcum.
Mönks, F.J. (1992b). Ein interaktionales Modell der Hochbegabung [An interactional model of giftedness]. In E.A. Hany & H. Nickel (Eds.), *Begabung und Hochbegabung [Talent and giftedness]* (pp. 17–22). Bern, Switzerland: Huber.
Neale, M.C., & Cardon, L.R. (1992). *Methodology for genetic studies of twins and families.* Boston: Kluwer Academic Publishers.
Ornstein, S., & Isabella, L. (1990). Age vs stage models of career attitudes of women: A partial replication and extension. *Journal of Vocational Behavior, 36*, 1–19.
Osipow, S.H. (1983). *Theories of career development* (3rd ed.). Englewood Cliffs, NJ: Prentice-Hall.
Plomin, R. (1988). The nature and nurture of cognitive abilities. In R.J. Sternberg (Ed.), *Advances in the psychology of human intelligence* (Vol. 4, pp. 1–33). Hillsdale, NJ.: Lawrence Erlbaum Associates Inc.
Plomin, R., DeFries, J.C., & McClearn, G.E. (1990). *Behavioral genetics: A primer (2nd ed).* New York: Freeman.
Ree, M.J., & Earles, J.A. (1996). Predicting occupational criteria: Not much more than g. In I. Dennis & P. Tapsfield (Eds.), *Human abilities. Their nature and measurement* (pp. 151–165). Mahwah, NJ: Lawrence Erlbaum Associates Inc.
Roubertoux, P.L., & Capron, C. (1990). Are intelligence differences hereditarily transmitted? *Cahiers de Psychologie Cognitive, 10*, 555–594.
Scarr, S., & McCartney, K. (1983). How people make their environment: A theory of genotype–environment effects. *Child Development, 54*, 424–435.
Scarr, S., & Weinberg, R.A. (1994). Educational and occupational achievements of brothers and sisters in adoptive and biologically related families. *Behavior Genetics, 24*, 301–325.
Scheuch, E.K. (1961). Sozialprestige und soziale Schichtung [Social prestige and social stratification]. In D.V. Glass & R. König (Eds.), *Soziale Schichtung und soziale Mobilität [Social stratification and social mobility] Special Issue of Kölner Zeitschrift für Soziologie und Sozialpsychologie, 5*, 65–193.
Schmidt, F.L., & Hunter, J.W. (1981). Employment testing: Old theories and new research findings. *American Psychologist, 36*, 1128–1137.
Schmitt, N., Gooding, R.Z., Noe, R.A., & Kirsch, M. (1984). Meta-analyses of validity studies published between 1964 and 1982 and the investigation of study characteristics. *Personnel Psychology, 37*, 407–422.

Sears, R.R. (1984). The Terman Gifted Children Study (TGC). In S.A. Mednick, M. Harwey, & K.M. Finello (Eds.), *Handbook of longitudinal research. Vol. 1: Birth and childhood cohorts* (pp. 398–414). New York: Praeger.

Sewell, W.H., & Hauser, R.M. (1972). Causes and consequences of higher education: Models of the status attainment process. In W.H. Sewell, R.M. Hauser, & D.L. Featherman (Eds.), *Schooling and achievement in American society* (pp. 9–27). New York: Academic Press.

Siegel, L.S. (1995). Does the IQ god exist? Special Issue: Canadian perspectives on The Bell Curve. *Alberta Journal of Educational Research, 41*, 283–288.

Stadler, M. (1985). Das Schicksal der nichtemigrierten Gestaltpsychologen im Nationalsozialismus [The fate of the Gestalt psychologists who did not emigrate during the time of National Socialism]. In C.F. Graumann (Ed.), *Psychologie im Nationalsozialismus [Psychology during the time of National Socialism]* (pp. 139–164). Berlin: Springer.

Sternberg, R.J. (1985). Implicit theories of intelligence, creativity and wisdom. *Journal of Personality and Social Psychology, 49*, 607–627.

Sternberg, R.J. (1993). Procedures for identifying intellectual potential in the gifted: A perspective on alternative "metaphors of mind". In K.A. Heller, F.J. Mönks, & A.H. Passow (Eds.), *International handbook of research and development of giftedness and talent* (pp. 185–207). Oxford: Pergamon Press.

Sternberg, R.J. (1996). Costs of expertise. In K.A. Ericsson (Ed.), *The road to excellence* (pp. 347–354). Mahwah, NJ: Lawrence Erlbaum Associates Inc.

Stroh, L.K., & Greller, M.M. (1995). Introduction to the Special Issue on careers from midlife. *Journal of Vocational Behavior, 47*, 229–231.

Subotnik, R.F., & Arnold, K.D. (1993). Longitudinal studies of giftedness: Investigating the fulfillment of promise. In K.A. Heller, F.J. Mönks, & A.H. Passow (Eds.), *International handbook of research and development of giftedness and talent* (pp. 149–160). Oxford: Pergamon.

Super, D.E. (1953). A theory of vocational development. *American Psychologist, 8*, 185–190.

Super, D.E. (1990). A life-span, life-space approach to career development. In D. Brown, L. Brooks (Eds.), *Career choice and development* (pp. 197–261). San Francisco: Jossey-Bass.

Tambs, K., Sundet, J.M., Magnus, P., & Berg, K. (1989). Genetic and environmental contributions to the covariance between occupational status, educational attainment, and IQ: A study of twins. *Behavior Genetics, 19*, 209–222.

Thompson, L.A., Detterman, D.K., & Plomin, R. (1991). Associations between cognitive abilities and scholastic achievement: Genetic overlap but environmental differences. *Psychological Science, 2*, 158–165.

Vogler, G.P., & Fulker, D.W. (1983). Familial resemblance for educational attainment. *Behavior Genetics, 13*, 341–354.

Vondracek, F.W., Lerner, R.M., & Schulenberg, J.E. (1986). *Career development: A life-span developmental approach.* Hillsdale, NJ: Lawrence Erlbaum Associates Inc.

Walberg, H.J., & Tsai, S. (1983). Matthew effects in education. *American Educational Research Journal, 20*, 359–373.

Wechsler, D. (1944). *The measurement of adult intelligence.* Baltimore: Williams & Wilkins.

Wechsler, D. (1964). *Die Messung der Intelligenz Erwachsener. Textband zum Hamburg-Wechsler-Intelligenztest für Erwachsene (HAWIE). Dritte Auflage. [The measurement of adult intelligence. Manual for the Hamburg-Wechsler-Test for adult intelligence. German version by A. Hardesty & H. Lauber. Edited by C. Bondy. Third edition.]* Bern, Switzerland: Huber.

Weinert, F.E., Geppert, U., Dörfert, J., & Viek, P. (1994). Aufgaben, Ergebnisse und Probleme der Zwillingsforschung—dargestellt am Beispiel der Gottschaldtschen Längsschnittstudie [Tasks, results and problems of twin research—a description using Gottschaldt's longitudinal study as example]. *Zeitschrift für Pädagogik, 40,* 265–288.

Weinert, F.E., & Schneider, W. (Eds.) (1999). *Individual development from 3 to 12: Findings from the Munich Longitudinal Study.* New York: Cambridge University Press.

Weinert, F.E., & Stefanek, J. (1997). Entwicklung vor, während und nach der Grundschulzeit [Development before, during, and after primary school age]. In F.E. Weinert & A. Helmke (Eds.), *Entwicklung im Grundschulalter [Development during primary school age].* Weinheim, Germany: Psychologie Verlags Union.

PART THREE
SPECIFIC TALENTS: PERSONALITY, MORALITY, EMOTIONALITY, ACADEMIC ACHIEVEMENT, AND ART

CHAPTER FIVE

The gifted personality: Resilient children and adolescents, their adjustment and their relationships

**Cornelis F.M. van Lieshout, Ron H.J. Scholte,
Marcel A.G. van Aken, Gerbert J.T. Haselager, and
J. Marianne Riksen-Walraven**
University of Nijmegen, The Netherlands

Most research on giftedness concerns intellectual giftedness or talents in such specific domains of performance as the school, sports, or arts. In this paper giftedness in the domain of personality is considered because personality development has rarely been studied from such a perspective. Personality is defined here as the genetically influenced behavioural styles that typify individuals across different situations and different points in time, and manifest themselves in the problem solving of the individuals and quality of adjustment across the life span. From such a perspective, facets of an individual's openness to new experience, such as intellect, creativity, imagination, and fantasy, are part of the individual's personality. In other words, intellectual giftedness is part of a gifted personality.

Many of the central issues concerning the development of giftedness are also central for the development of personality. Similar to twin and adoption studies of intelligence, behavioural genetic population studies of twins and adoptees have shown substantial heritability for most broad personality dimensions (estimates between 40% and 60%) (cf. Loehlin, 1992). Similar to studies of intellectual (dis)abilities, molecular-genetic studies have revealed a number of associations between human personality traits and specific polymorphic genetic loci (cf. Cloninger, 1998). Just like the dimensions of intellectual giftedness, moreover, the dimensions of personality reveal remarkable stability across the life span but can also change with changing environmental contexts (Costa & McCrae, 1994). Just like giftedness, personality is also multifaceted (Goldberg, 1993;

Hofstee, de Raad, & Goldberg, 1992), which means that both individuals as well as groups—such as males and females—can be distinguished according to different configurations of personality traits (Caspi, 1997).

The first goal in this chapter is to define the gifted personality for the primary school and adolescent years. Next, we will attempt to establish whether the adaptation and psychosocial functioning of children and adolescents with a gifted personality, their networks of relationships, and their positions and reputations within their school classes differ from those for children and adolescents with a less gifted personality. We will focus in particular on the diversity of the gifted personality profiles for boys and girls in relation to the quality of their relationships and their positions and reputations within their school classes.

DIFFERENT APPROACHES TO PERSONALITY

The first task in this chapter is to distinguish the gifted from the less gifted personality. For the study of personality, variable-centred as well as person-centred approaches have been used. Variable-centred studies investigate the basic dimensions of personality. For example, the Big-Five or Five-Factor personality model (Goldberg, 1993; Hofstee et al., 1992; van Lieshout & Haselager, 1994) is frequently used to distinguish five basic dimensions of personality: *Extraversion* or behavioural activity versus passivity; *Agreeableness* or the tendency to consider one's own interests in relation to the interests of others; *Conscientiousness* or an orientation towards standards of excellence; *Emotional Stability* or the regulation of emotions; and *Openness to New Experiences* or flexibility, creativity, and imagination in the processing of information. Individuals are then characterised according to their scores on each of the five dimensions of personality. Person-centred approaches to personality, in contrast to variable-centred approaches, distinguish individuals according to the profile of scores they attain with regard to personality characteristics—according to the profile of their Big-Five personality scores, for example. In person-centred studies, the aim is to identify prototypical personality profiles and thereby enable the categorisation or classification of people according to personality type. In defining the gifted personality, we combined the dimension- and person-centred approaches. A gifted personality profile should thus manifest itself as favourable scores on all of the personality dimensions characterising the profile.

Other sets of personality dimensions have also been used in different theoretical orientations on personality. For example, Block and Block (1980) have assumed the dimensions of Ego-resilience and Ego-control to clearly distinguish different personalities. *Ego-control* refers to the control of impulses, desires, and emotions. Some people tend to suppress impulses, needs, and feelings (*Overcontrol*) whereas others tend to give free rein to their impulses (*Undercontrol*). *Ego-resilience* refers to the dynamic capacity of individuals to modify their modal level of ego-control as a function of the demand characteristics of the situation. Ego-resilience thus is defined as resourceful, flexible, and persistent adaptation to changing circumstances and environmental contingencies in problem solving. Individuals differ in the degree of ego-resilience, with ego-brittleness indicating little adaptive flexibility, an inability to respond to the dynamic requirements of the situation, and a tendency to become disorganised under stress. According to Block and Block (1980), individuals with average or moderate ego-control tend to have the highest ego-resilience; the ego-resilience of Overcontrollers and Undercontrollers is lower, which implies a curvilinear relation between the dimensions of ego-resilience and ego-control (see Fig. 5.1).

The dimensions of ego-resilience and ego-control actually pertain to the full domain of human problem solving, including the social, personal, and cognitive domains (Block & Block, 1980). High ego-resilience and moderate levels of ego-control enable individuals to adapt optimally to a large

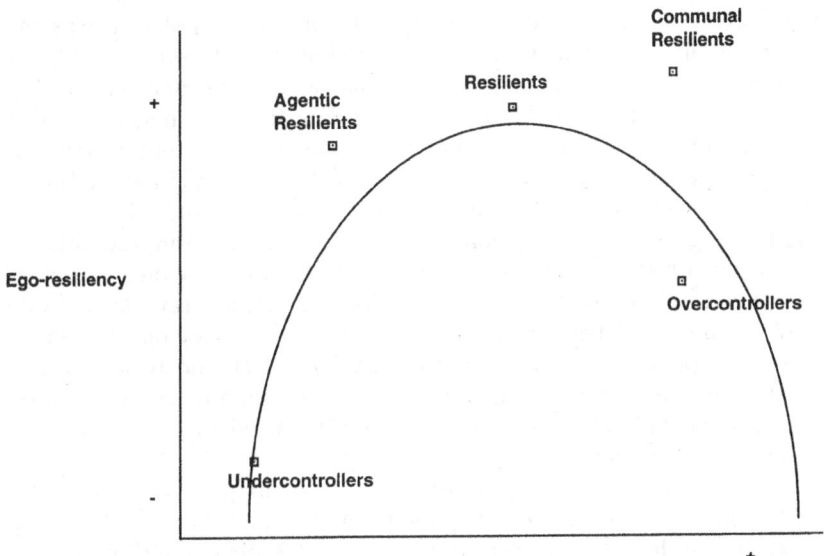

FIG. 5.1 The curvilinear relation between ego-resilience and ego-control. The mean scores for Resilient, Overcontrolled, and Undercontrolled primary school children and for the Communal Resilient and Agentic Resilient subtypes (see later in the text) are plotted in the graph.

variety of problem situations and can, therefore, be considered a characteristic of the gifted personality. Individuals who habitually and unduly suppress impulses or are simply unable to control impulses, have less adapted problem solving and thus a less gifted personality (see also Robins, John, Caspi, & Moffitt, 1996).

In a recent review of personality development, Caspi (1997) reviewed eight studies concerned with personality types. Caspi claimed substantial support for three replicable and generalisable personality types across age levels, birth cohorts, assessment instruments, data sources, geographic regions, and statistical procedures for type derivation. The three personality types also reflect the curvilinear relation between Ego-control and Ego-resilience. The first type of personality consists of well adjusted individuals who are often labelled *Resilients*; the second type consists of less well adjusted overcontrolling individuals or *Overcontrollers*; and the third type consists of less well adjusted undercontrolling individuals or *Undercontrollers*.

RESILIENCE ACROSS THE PRIMARY SCHOOL YEARS

Our longitudinal study of children across the primary school years was one of the studies mentioned by Caspi (van Lieshout, Haselager, Riksen-Walraven, & van Aken, 1995). In this study, repeated personality descriptions were provided by the teachers of 79 primary school children at the ages of 7, 10, and 12 years. For the personality descriptions, the teachers used a Dutch version of the California Child Q-set (Block & Block, 1980). For each child at each of the investigated ages, the scores on the Big-Five personality dimensions were computed (cf. van Lieshout & Haselager, 1994). Cluster analysis of the five Big-Five personality dimensions for the three ages together was performed next and revealed a group of children scoring high on ego-resilience and intermediate on ego-control across the primary school years (Resilients, $n = 27$), and two groups of children scoring lower on ego-resilience but differently on ego-control. One group could indeed be classified as Overcontrollers ($n = 25$) and the other as Undercontrollers ($n = 27$) (see Fig. 5.1).

In Fig. 5.2A, the Big-Five personality profiles are plotted for the three personality types identified among the primary school children. As can be seen, the Resilient type is characterised by high scores on all five dimensions of personality: high Extraversion, high Agreeableness, high Conscientiousness, high Emotional Stability and high Openness. This means that the Resilient children have a favourable or gifted personality profile with respect to the Big-Five personality factors. The other two personality types were not so much characterised by lower scores but rather qualita-

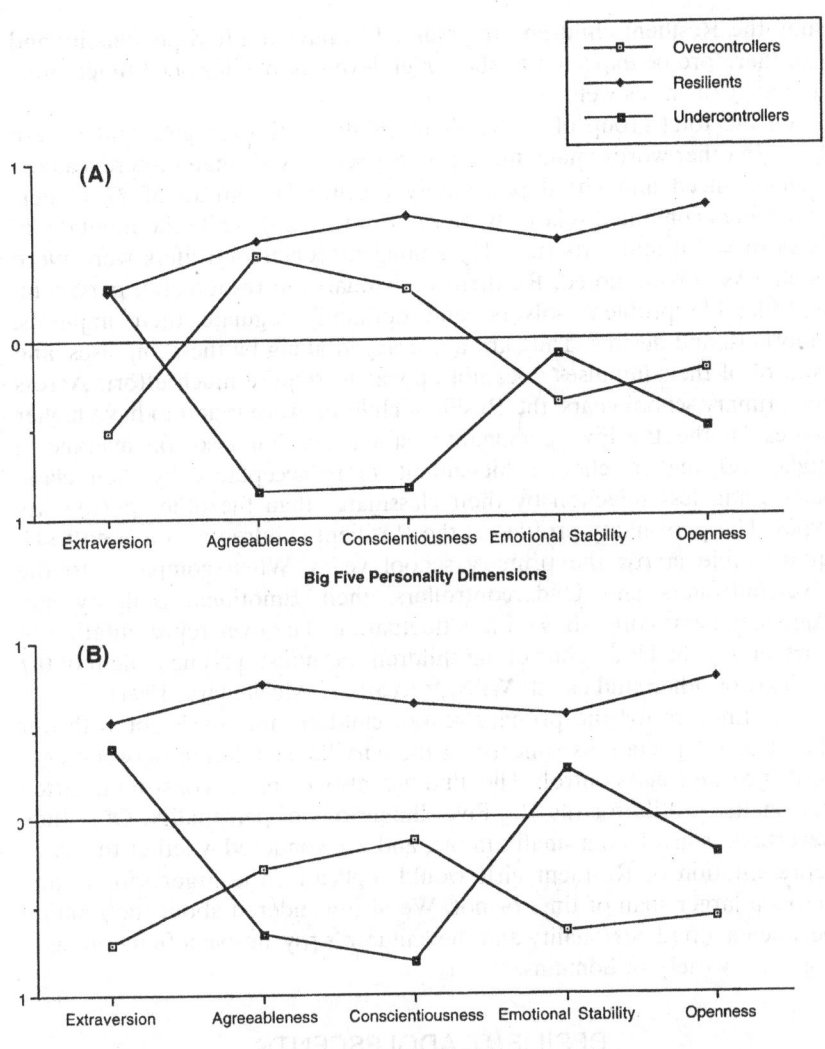

FIG. 5.2 Big-Five personality profiles for Resilients, Overcontrollers, and Undercontrollers. (A) the primary school sample; (B) the adolescent sample.

tively different or mixed profiles. Overcontrollers showed low Extraversion (i.e. Introversion) and Emotional Instability. Undercontrollers revealed high Extraversion, low Agreeableness, and low Conscientiousness. It should be further noted that the Big-Five profiles of the Overcontrollers and Undercontrollers were mirror images of each other. In sum, the Resilient children are assumed to have a gifted personality and can therefore be expected to show high levels of psychosocial functioning and adjustment as well.

Of the total group of 27 Resilient children, 22 were girls and 5 were boys. In other words, many more primary school girls than boys revealed a well balanced and gifted personality profile. The group of 27 Undercontrollers contained relatively more boys (n = 20), while the numbers of boys (n = 10) and girls (n = 15) among the Overcontrollers were more equal. As already noted, Resilient individuals are resourceful, persistent, and flexible problem solvers, and optimally regulate their impulses, emotions, and desires. They are not dragged along by their impulses, and control of their impulses does not appear to require much effort. Across the primary school years, the Resilient children were found to have higher scores on the Big-Five personality dimensions but also, on average, a higher IQ, higher school achievement, more acceptance by their classmates, and less rejection by their classmates than the other personality types. The personality profiles of the Resilient children also tended to be quite stable across the primary school years. When compared to the Overcontrollers and Undercontrollers, their Emotional Stability and Agreeableness scores showed less fluctuation. The over-representation of boys among the Undercontrolling children was not surprising in light of the findings of other studies (cf. Wills, Vaccaro, & McNamara, 1994).

The findings for the primary school children are consistent with our theoretical expectations concerning the curvilinear relation between ego-resilience and ego-control. The findings also reveal a consistent, gifted personality profile for the Big-Five dimensions of personality. Our study nevertheless involved a small sample, and we wondered whether the over-representation of Resilient girls would replicate in a larger sample and across a larger span of time or not. We also wondered about the relation between a gifted personality and the children's psychosocial functioning in a greater variety of domains.

RESILIENT ADOLESCENTS

In a second recent study, the focus has been on a large sample of adolescents (Scholte, 1998; van Aken, van Lieshout, & Scholte, 1998; van Lieshout, van Aken, & Scholte, 1998). In this study, 3284 students (1402 girls and 1882 boys) in the first four grades of secondary school were asked to provide self-descriptions of their personality. Once again, three separate clusters with regard to the Big-Five personality factors were found to represent three different personality profiles (see Fig. 5.2B). The three profiles clearly resembled the profiles found for the primary school children. Again, nearly one third of the adolescents ($n = 1178$) revealed a

Resilient profile, marked by high scores on all of the Big-Five personality factors. The adolescent Undercontrollers ($n = 750$) showed a very similar profile to the Undercontrollers in primary school. However, the adolescent Overcontrollers ($n = 1356$) scored lower on all of the personality dimensions on average than the Overcontrollers in primary school although the profile remained quite similar with the exception of Agreeableness: Adolescent Overcontrollers scored much lower on Agreeableness than their counterparts in primary school. The Agreeableness observed among the overcontrolled primary school children appears to indicate a high degree of social desirability which is clearly lower among the adolescents.

In other domains of adaptation and psychosocial functioning (see Table 5.1, left panel), the Resilient adolescents also scored much higher than the Overcontrollers and Undercontrollers (cf. van Aken et al., 1998). Resilient adolescents reported the highest perceived relational support from key figures in their social network (i.e. parents, siblings, and best friends). On several aspects of psychological well-being such as self-esteem, loneliness, and psychosomatic complaints, the Resilient adolescents scored most favourably. Adolescent Undercontrollers reported higher levels than Resilients and Overcontrollers of various forms of antisocial behaviour and addictive behaviour, such as smoking, gambling, and alcohol and substance use. Undercontrollers were also most often the perpetrators of bullying while Overcontrollers were most frequently the victims, and Resilients were least frequently the victims of direct and indirect bullying.

Not only self-reports but also peer nominations showed Resilient adolescents to be more accepted and Undercontrollers to be more rejected by their peers. Resilient adolescents scored intermediately between Overcontrollers and Undercontrollers with regard to Aggression–Inattentiveness and Achievement–Withdrawal. Resilients scored higher than Overcontrollers with regard to Self-confidence and Sociability, and they scored lower with regard to Emotionality–Nervousness.

In sum, Resilient children and adolescents revealed a relatively gifted personality profile, which is also reflected in their adjustment and psychosocial functioning within the home, the school, and the relational network.

SUBTYPES OF RESILIENT CHILDREN AND ADOLESCENTS

In the present section, we will consider the gifted or resilient personality profile in greater detail. One third of the population categorised as gifted is, after all, a considerable amount. In an earlier study, Robins, John, and Caspi (1998) distinguished two subtypes of resilient boys (as they studied an exclusively male sample) and referred to them as Communal Resilient

TABLE 5.1
Psychosocial adaptation (z-scores) for three personality types and resilient subtypes

	Personality Types				Resilient Subtypes		
	Overcontrollers	Resilients	Undercontrollers	F	Communal	Agentic	t
Relational Support							
Parental Support	-0.13^a	0.30^b	-0.19^a	76.36***	0.28	0.31	-0.66
Friend Support	-0.20^a	0.45^b	-0.15^a	93.83***	0.33	0.36	-0.41
Convergence of Goals	-0.04^a	0.24^c	-0.27^b	62.32***	0.37	0.15	3.52***
Sibling Support	-0.16^a	0.28^b	-0.14^a	59.53***	0.25	0.30	-0.87
Respect for Autonomy	-0.19^a	0.31^b	-0.13^a	86.85***	0.26	0.35	-0.53
Well-being							
Self-esteem	-0.24^a	0.29^c	-0.01^b	82.60***	0.20	0.36	-3.32**
Loneliness	0.18^a	-0.16^b	-0.08^b	35.50***	-0.16	-0.16	0.03
Brooding	0.18^a	-0.15^b	-0.08^b	35.40***	0.02	-0.27	4.73***
Worrying about Home	0.05^a	-0.07^b	0.04^{ab}	4.49*	-0.06	-0.08	0.23
Psychosomatic Complaints	0.14^a	-0.17^c	-0.01^b	26.31***	-0.07	-0.24	2.95**
Antisocial behaviour							
Overt	-0.17^a	-0.02^c	0.29^b	44.81***	-0.23	0.13	-5.95***
Covert	-0.12^a	-0.09^a	0.34^b	48.84***	-0.26	0.02	-5.05***
Authority Conflicts	-0.07^a	-0.14^a	0.33^b	47.52***	-0.22	-0.08	-2.23*
Addictive behaviours							
Cigarette Smoking	-0.12^a	-0.05^a	0.27^b	36.95***	-0.18	0.04	-3.62***
Alcohol use	-0.19^a	0.01^a	0.33^b	60.89***	-0.16	0.14	-4.60***
Drugs use	-0.07^a	-0.06^a	0.24^b	23.38***	-0.19	0.03	-3.92***
Gambling	-0.12^a	-0.01^a	0.23^b	24.85***	-0.17	0.11	-4.76***

Involvement in Bullying						
Perpetrator	-0.20^a	-0.11^a	0.49^b	118.20***	-0.29	0.01	-5.21***
Victim of Direct Bullying	0.18^a	-0.21^c	-0.02^b	42.57***	-0.18	-0.23	0.95
Victim of Indirect Bullying	0.28^a	-0.28^c	-0.09^b	95.33***	-0.16	-0.36	4.04***
Sociometric Status							
Peer Acceptance	-0.10^a	0.15^b	0.06^b	20.58***	0.16	0.14	0.43
Peer rejection	-0.03^a	-0.05^a	0.10^b	6.14**	-0.13	0.00	-2.31*
Peer Group Reputation							
Aggressive–Inattentive	-0.25^a	-0.03^c	0.44^b	123.97***	-0.27	0.15	-7.34***
Achievement–Withdrawal	0.30^a	-0.04^c	-0.42^b	134.25***	0.14	-0.17	5.43***
Self-Confidence	-0.25^a	0.21^b	0.16^b	80.77***	0.14	0.25	-1.90
Sociability	-0.16^a	0.16^b	0.09^b	34.02***	0.21	0.12	1.60
Emotionality–Nervousness	0.17^a	-0.14^b	-0.09^b	35.92***	-0.06	-0.21	2.65**

* $p < .05$; ** $p < .01$; *** $p < .001$

Note: Means in the same row with different superscripts (^a, ^b, ^c) differ at $P < .05$.

and Agentic Resilient. The concepts of agency and communion originate from Bakan (1966). Agency refers to the striving of individuals to separate from others, be autonomous and independent, master the environment, and to assert, protect, and expand the self. Communion refers to the individual's striving to lose one's own individuality by merging with others in social harmony, be interdependent, participate in social networks that are larger than the self, and to relate to others in a warm, close, intimate, and loving manner.

For both primary school children and adolescents, we indeed detected two subtypes of the Resilient personality with remarkably similar Big-Five personality profiles also resembling the profiles found by Robins et al. (see Figs 5.3A and B). The subtypes of Communal and Agentic Resilient children revealed a very favourable personality profile but nevertheless differed. Compared to the Communal Resilients, the Agentic Resilients were more Extraverted, more Emotionally Stable, and more Open. The Communal Resilients, in contrast, scored higher on Agreeableness and Conscientiousness. The Communal Resilients revealed a more prosocial personality profile, were less assertive, and more emotionally involved; the Agentic Resilients were more individualistic and autonomous.

Despite the continuity in the personality profiles of the Agentic Resilient and Communal Resilient children and adolescents, the Communal Resilient primary school children showed lower Extraversion and higher Agreeableness and Conscientiousness than the Communal Resilient adolescents, who also showed lower Emotional Stability. The Agentic Resilient primary school children showed lower Agreeableness than the Agentic Resilient adolescents. It should be noted that these differences may certainly reflect some general differences in the personality profiles of children and adolescents. However, the differences may also reflect the methodological difference between teacher descriptions of the primary school children and self-report on the part of the adolescents.

Resilient adolescent subtypes and perceived relational support

The persons in a relationship provide each other with relational support and can also evaluate the quality of experienced relational support they receive (van Lieshout, Cillessen, & Haselager, 1999; van Lieshout & Doise, 1998). One might expect Resilient adolescents to be particularly capable of maintaining supportive relationships and thereby to experience a high quality of relational support. Communal Resilients with their orientation towards social harmony and participation in social networks may even surpass Agentic Resilients with regard to the quality of experienced support.

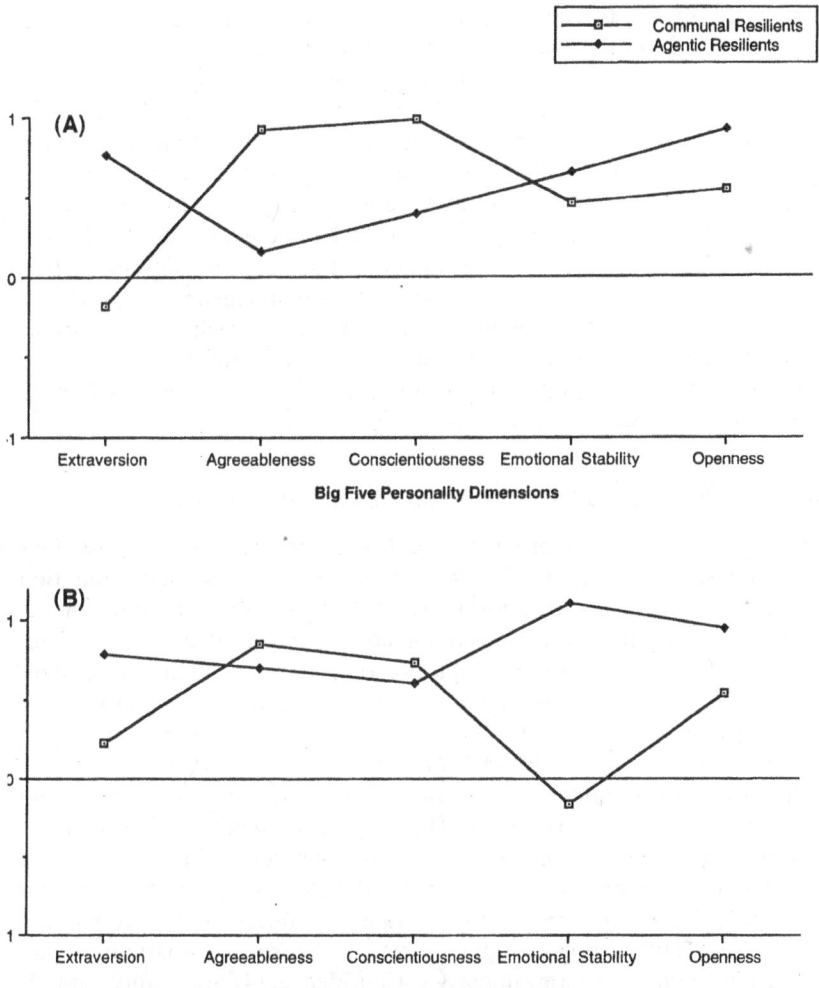

FIG. 5.3 Big-Five personality profiles for the Communal and Agentic Resilient subtypes. (A) the primary school sample; (B) the adolescent sample.

We assessed the adolescents' perceptions of relational support from four key people in their relational network: their father, mother, best friend, and most special sibling. Factor analysis on the four aspects of perceived relational support and perceived acceptance from each of the four key individuals in the relational network (Scholte, 1998) produced five dimensions of perceived relational support: (1) emotional support from parents, (2) emotional support from best friend, (3) emotional support from sibling, (4) convergence versus opposition of goals, and (5) respect for autonomy versus perceived setting of limits. Emotional support in the form of perceived acceptance and informational support appears to be specific to each key person while the more "instrumental" aspects of support, such as the perceived convergence versus opposition of goals and the balance between autonomy and limit setting, were perceived similarly across the different individuals in the adolescent's relational network.

Contrary to our expectation, Communal Resilient adolescents did not experience higher levels of support than Agentic Resilient adolescents (see Table 5.1, right panel). With the exception of one dimension (i.e. perceived respect for autonomy), Communal and Agentic Resilient adolescents perceived similarly high relational support. Agentic Resilients perceived more respect for their autonomy from all people in their network when compared to Communal Resilients.

Resilient adolescent subtypes and peer reputation

The most common peer group for adolescents is their school class. Our 3284 adolescents attended 149 school classes and we took their reputation in the school class to be a major indicator of their peer group functioning. In order to assess the reputations of the adolescents in their school classes, all of the adolescents in our sample were asked to nominate classmates with regard to 20 items concerning peer group functioning. The format of the questions was "Who in your class is most...": quarrelsome and blaming of others, irritable and unfriendly, hard working and precise, withdrawn and inhibited, co-operative and sincere, considerate and friendly, nervous and insecure etc. The number of nominations received in response to each item, corrected for the number of nominating and nominated classmates, was taken to be the item score for a particular individual. Factor analysis on the 20 items produced 5 peer reputation factors (see Table 1, bottom-right panel): (1) Aggression–Inattentiveness, (2) Achievement–Withdrawal, (3) Self-Confidence, (4) Sociability, and (5) Emotionality–Nervousness (see Scholte, van Aken, & van Lieshout, 1997). These factors resemble the peer reputation factors found in other studies (cf. Masten, Morison, & Pellegrini, 1985) and show that classmates also distinguish the two subtypes of Resilient adolescents. Agentic Resilients were scored higher for Aggression–Inattentiveness and thus experienced as more aggressive and inattentive in the peer group than the Communal Resilients. The Communal Resilient adolescents were given higher scores for Achievement–Withdrawal and Emotionality–Nervousness. Compared to the Agentic Resilient adolescents, the Communal Resilients appeared to be more oriented towards group goals, less assertive, and more open about emotional insecurity and vulnerability. According to their classmates, the two subtypes of Resilients did not differ with regard to Self-Confidence and Sociability. They also showed no differences with regard to acceptance by classmates, although the Communal Resilients were found to be less rejected than the Agentic Resilients.

Resilient adolescent subtypes and other domains of psychosocial functioning

Both subtypes of Resilient adolescents can be expected to be fairly well adapted in numerous psychosocial domains. Differences between the two subtypes can nevertheless be expected with regard to adaptation. When compared to Communal Resilient adolescents, for example, Agentic Resilients more frequently reported such addictive behaviours as cigarette smoking, gambling, and use of alcohol and drugs. Agentic Resilient adolescents were also more frequently involved in a variety of antisocial behaviours including open and covert antisocial behaviours, authority conflicts, and the bullying of other children. With regard to the different facets of well-being, however, the Agentic Resilient adolescents also tended to score higher than the Communal Resilient adolescents. The Agentic Resilients had higher self-esteem, brooded less, reported fewer psychosomatic complaints, and were less often the victim of bullying than the Communal Resilients. The two subtypes did not differ with regard to worrying about home or loneliness, however.

In sum, the two subtypes of adolescent Resilients both appear to be very well adjusted. When compared to the Communal Resilients, however, the Agentic Resilients present themselves as more autonomous, independent, risk-taking, and experimenting in a number of domains, perceive more respect for their autonomy from key people in their relational network, and are also perceived by their classmates as more autonomous and less conforming. In contrast, Communal Resilients tend to be more prosocial, more socially and emotionally involved, and have more concerns than Agentic Resilients.

AGENTIC AND COMMUNAL RESILIENTS, PERCEIVED SUPPORT, AND SOCIOMETRIC STATUS

Our subtyping of Resilient adolescents as Agentic or Communal was based on their personality profile alone. One can nevertheless expect such gifted adolescents to demonstrate special talents in various other domains pertaining to relationships and group functioning as well. In order to explore this possibility, we further qualified the subtypes of Communal and Agentic Resilient adolescents, first, in terms of high versus low experienced support from their relational network and, second, in terms of popular versus non-popular sociometric status within the school class (Haselager, 1997; Scholte, 1998; van Lieshout et al., 1999; see Fig. 5.4).

First, using cluster analysis on our sample of adolescents (Scholte, van Lieshout, & van Aken, 1999), we were able to distinguish five groups of adolescents clearly differing on the four aforementioned dimensions of experienced relational support and acceptance from four key people in their relational network. In other words, we found five groups of adolescents with different profiles of experienced support. One group (35%) was marked by high levels of experienced support on all five dimensions from all four people. These adolescents thus revealed high competence in dealing with key people in their relational network. Two more groups perceived generally average (27%) or low (22%) support from all key people. A fourth group received mixed support (9%) from the different people in their network (i.e. low support from parents and high support from friends and siblings). Finally, we found a fifth group of adolescents who did not have a mutual friend (7%). We then split our sample of adolescents into two groups consisting of the 35% with an overall high level of experienced support, on the one hand, and those with less optimal patterns of perceived support, on the other hand. Next, we examined the two new groups for the two subtypes of Resilient adolescents and found nearly half of the Communal Resilient and half of the Agentic Resilient adolescents to experience high relational support. Both Communal Resilient and Agentic Resilient adolescents were also found to report less optimal levels of perceived support, which surprised us for two reasons. First, we had expected the majority of the resilient adolescents no matter what subtype to perceive high levels of support. That is, only half of the adolescents with a gifted personality demonstrated the excellent social competencies that attract high relational support and allow them to function effectively in key relationships. Second, it was surprising that the proportion of adolescents reporting high levels of relational support was the same for the Agentic Resilient adolescents as for the more socially oriented Communal Resilient adolescents, considering that Agentic Resilient adolescents tend to be more independent, individualised, and autonomous

Second, in subsequent analyses, we further considered the four subgroups of Communal Resilient and Agentic Resilient adolescents with high versus non-high relational support with respect to a popular versus non-popular sociometric status within the school class. We considered popularity to indicate excellent functioning in the group. A popular sociometric status implies that the adolescent is liked by a significant number of classmates and disliked by few. Studies have shown children with a popular sociometric status type to indeed have high social

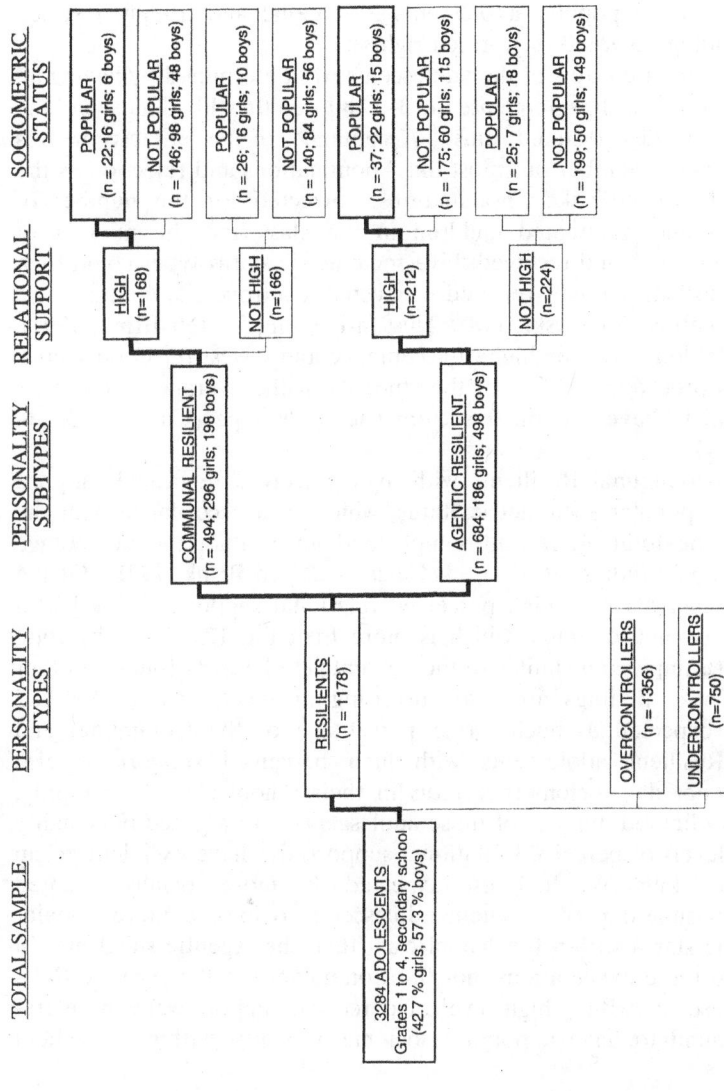

FIG. 5.4 Resilient adolescents, their perceived relational support, and their sociometric status. (The numbers in the two right columns do not correspond to the numbers for the Communal and Agentic Resilient subtypes because the adolescents without a sibling and a best friend and without a sociometric status classification were omitted.)

competence (Newcomb, Bukowski, & Pattee, 1993). In their class groups, popular adolescents are found to respect the interests of their classmates. Their class interactions and relationships are also marked by high levels of social responsibility and prosocial behaviour. Aggressive behaviour among popular adolescents is minimal and usually justified (e.g. defending accepted or justified rights).

The sociometric status of the adolescents was determined by having all of the children in a class nominate the 3–5 children they liked most and the 3–5 children they disliked most. Acceptance of an adolescent was measured as the number of "most-like" nominations and rejection as the number of "most-dislike" nominations, corrected for the number of nominating and nominated children in the class and the number of nominations given and received. Five sociometric status types could then be distinguished: popular, rejected, neglected, controversial, and average (cf. Newcomb & Bukowski, 1983; Thissen-Pennings & ten Brink, 1994). Popular children have the highest acceptance and lowest rejection scores. Using this procedure, 16.7% of the students in the average school class were found to have a popular sociometric status type (Cillessen & ten Brink, 1991).

Of the Communal Resilients with high perceived relational support, 13% had a popular sociometric status, which is in accordance with the 12.6% of the total adolescent sample and lower than the percentage found in other studies (16.7%) (cf. Cillessen & ten Brink, 1991). Of the Agentic Resilients with high perceived relational support, 17.5% had a popular sociometric status, which is more than the 12.6% of the total adolescent sample and similar to the percentage of 16.7% found in other studies. These findings are also surprising in several ways. We had originally expected a much larger percentage of the Communal and Agentic Resilient adolescents with high perceived support to also achieve a popular sociometric status in their school class. Apparently, only a very limited number of those adolescents with a gifted personality and high levels of perceived relational support also have excellent group functioning skills. We had also expected the more socially oriented Communal subgroup of Resilient adolescents to have a more popular sociometric status within the school class than the Agentic subgroup. In contrast to these expectations, not the Communal but the Agentic Resilient adolescents with a high level of perceived support were more frequently found to have a popular sociometric status within the school class.

Next, we compared these two extremely well adapted subgroups of Communal and Agentic Resilient adolescents on the earlier measures of psychosocial functioning. The largest differences were observed for their personality profiles. The Agentic Resilient subgroup of adolescents with high relational support and a popular class status were found to be more extraverted, emotionally stable, and open to new experiences than their Communal Resilient counterparts. The Agentic Resilient adolescents drank more alcohol and less often felt themselves to be socially excluded than their Communal Resilient counterparts. In sum, the already established differences between the Communal and Agentic Resilient adolescents simply were confirmed by these extreme subgroups.

BOYS VERSUS GIRLS

Finally, in our analyses of the adolescent sample, we further examined the gender differences that stood out so markedly in the primary school sample. As already mentioned, many more Resilient girls than boys were encountered in the primary school sample. In the adolescent sample, this gender difference was not found. The number of Resilient boys and girls simply reflected the distribution of boys and girls within the total sample. In the primary school sample, more girls than boys were observed among both the Communal and Agentic Resilient children. In the adolescent sample, 60% of the Communal Resilients were girls and 40% were boys, while only 27% of the Agentic Resilients were girls and 73% were boys. Among the very well functioning adolescent subgroups (i.e. those Communal and Agentic Resilient adolescents experiencing high levels of perceived support and popularity within the school class), the number of girls was much larger than the number of boys; 38 versus 21.

What can be said about these gender differences? Our findings are in agreement with those of Gilligan (1982) who suggests that primary school girls tend to have a more balanced personality profile than primary school boys and that this gender difference gradually disappears during adolescence. The higher proportion of Resilient girls in our primary school sample and smaller proportion in our adolescent sample confirm this suggestion. But there are nevertheless other explanations for the observed gender difference. First, the higher proportion of Resilient girls observed in primary school may be due to the tendency of teachers to evaluate well adapted, well balanced, achievement-oriented, and overcontrolled girls as well as highly sociable and agreeable girls as resilient. Second, the evaluations of the adolescents were based on self-descriptions which may be coloured by images of their ideal self or gender stereotypes. Third, the onset of puberty in girls, on average, is two years earlier than in boys and this early onset of puberty in girls is more often related with emotional turmoil and social turbulence than in boys (Simmons & Blythe, 1987). Boys frequently welcome the increased maturity, physical growth, and strength associated with the early onset of puberty and this may promote a more balanced and autonomous personality profile.

Gilligan (1982) uses the distinction between Communal and Agentic to characterise the personality differences between girls and boys and women and men. Males are more oriented towards autonomy, separation, and independence, which characterise the agentic personality. Females are more oriented towards close bonds, interdependence, and social harmony, which characterise the communal personality. In the domain of moral development, moreover, Gilligan suggests that males may be more oriented towards rules of justice and fairness while females are more oriented towards empathy, sympathy, and offering care to those in need. Empirical evidence to support this distinction, however, is either absent or highly controversial (cf. Turiel, 1997). Our findings are also not consistent with such a distinction. In primary school, the girls outnumbered the boys within the Agentic and Communal Resilient subtypes. On the basis of the self-descriptions of the adolescents, however, more boys fell into the Agentic Resilient group and more girls in the Communal Resilient group. This shift in the personality profiles of boys and girls may indeed reflect the increasing attachment of girls to social interaction and social networks, and the increasing detachment of boys from such social networks. The stronger interpersonal orientation of females compared to males has also been observed in studies of both prosocial and antisocial human interactions and relationships (Crick, 1995; Crick & Grotpeter, 1995) and the social relationships and coalitions of both humans and primates (de Waal, 1996). Adolescent girls may thus become more proficient in such interpersonal skills.

It should be emphasised that Agentic and Communal Resilience are not mutually exclusive personality profiles strictly associated with boys, on the one hand, and girls, on the other. A large number of boys fall within the Communal Resilient subgroup and numerous girls within the Agentic Resilient subgroup. Moreover, in both the Communal and Agentic subgroups of adolescents with high levels of perceived support and a popular sociometric status, boys and girls are encountered, although the girls tend to outnumber the boys. Compared to adolescent boys, a larger number of adolescent girls appear to combine a gifted personality with excellent relational and group skills.

In contrast to the personality descriptions and measures of perceived relational support, the sociometric status of the Communal and Agentic Resilient adolescents was not determined using self-descriptions. Evaluation by classmates, rather, showed advanced interpersonal skills for the maintenance of social relationships and group cohesion among the Agentic and Communal Resilient subgroups of adolescents. The sociometric data also show these skills to be well appreciated by the classmates of the adolescents.

CONCLUSIONS

Some of the questions raised in the introduction to this chapter can now be answered. Personality appears to be important for the study of giftedness. Among primary school children and adolescents, a group of highly resilient individuals can be distinguished from groups of less resilient under-controlled and less resilient overcontrolled individuals. Resilient children and adolescents can be considered gifted because they reveal a highly favourable Big-Five personality profile. Resilient children and also adolescents also show considerable agreeableness and emotional stability across age and high levels of adaptation in a number of other domains. Within the larger group of children and adolescents with a Resilient personality, specific subgroups with more prosocial or individualistic personality profiles could also be distinguished. Such distinctive profiles were found in teacher reports on primary school children and the self-reports of adolescents. Both the Communal and the Agentic Resilient personality profiles were also associated with higher IQ and school achievement, higher levels of perceived support, more adapted psychosocial functioning, and more positive evaluations by classmates. Compared to the Communal Resilient adolescents, the Agentic Resilient adolescents showed more autonomous and independent adjustment with greater risk-taking and experimentation in various domains. Having a resilient or gifted personality, however, does not appear to always predispose adolescents towards a particularly supportive relational network or class popularity. Only a small percentage of both the Communal Resilient and Agentic Resilient adolescents experience high-quality interpersonal relationships and a popular sociometric status. In other words, these gifted individuals proficiently employ their gifted personality in the social contexts of relationships and groups.

Across the primary school and adolescent years, the personality profiles of boys and girls appear to shift. The agentic, autonomous personality profiles of primary school girls become more communal in adolescence. Boys, in contrast, tend to become more individualistic, experiment more, take more risks, and develop a more agentic personality profile. Among the small group of children and adolescents with a gifted personality profile, whether Communal or Agentic, and a high quality of perceived support and class popularity, girls predominate.

REFERENCES

Bakan, D. (1966). *The duality of human existence: Isolation and communion in Western man.* Boston: Beacon Press.
Block, J.H., & Block, J. (1980). The role of ego-control and ego-resiliency in the organisation of behaviour. In W.A. Collins (Ed.), *The Minnesota Symposia on Child Psychology (Vol. 13,* pp. 39–101). Hillsdale, NJ: Lawrence Erlbaum Associates Inc.
Caspi, A. (1997). Personality development across the life course. In W. Damon (Ed.), *Handbook of child psychology* [N. Eisenberg (Vol. Ed.), *Social, emotional, and personality development, Vol 3* (pp. 311–388)]. New York: Wiley.
Cillessen, A.H.N., & ten Brink, P.W.M. (1991). Vaststelling van relaties met leeftijdgenoten [Assessment of children's peer relationships]. *Pedagogische Studiën, 68,* 1–14.
Cloninger, C.R. (1998). The genetics and psychobiology of the seven-factor model of personality. In K.R. Silk (Ed.), *Biology of personality disorders.* Washington, DC: American Psychiatry Press.
Costa, P.T. Jr., & McCrae, R.R. (1994). Stability and change in personality from adolescence through adulthood. In C.F. Halverson, G.A. Kohnstamm, & R.P. Martin (Eds.), *The developing structure of temperament and personality from infancy to adulthood* (pp. 139–150). Hillsdale, NJ: Lawrence Erlbaum Associates Inc.
Crick, N.R. (1995). Relational aggression: The role of intent attributions, feelings of distress, and provocation type. *Development and Psychopathology, 7,* 313–322.
Crick, N.R., & Grotpeter, J.K. (1995). Relational aggression, gender, and psychosocial adjustment. *Child Development, 66,* 710–722.
De Waal, F.B.M. (1996). *Good natured. The origins of right and wrong in humans and other animals.* Cambridge, MA: Harvard University Press.
Gilligan, C. (1982). *In a different voice: Psychological theory and women's development.* Cambridge, MA: Harvard University Press.
Goldberg, L.R. (1993). The structure of phenotypic personality traits. *American Psychologist, 48,* 26–34.
Haselager, G.J.T. (1997). *Classmates. Studies on the development of their relationships and personality in middle childhood.* University of Nijmegen: Unpublished Doctoral Dissertation.
Hofstee, W.K., de Raad, B., & Goldberg, L.R. (1992). Integration of the Big Five and circumplex approaches to trait structure. *Journal of Personality and Social Psychology, 63,* 146–163.
Loehlin, J.C. (1992). *Genes and environment in personality development.* Newbury Park, CA: Sage
Masten, A.S., Morison, P., & Pellegrini, D.S. (1985). A revised class play method of peer assessment. *Developmental Psychology, 21,* 523–533.
Newcomb, A.F., & Bukowski, W.M. (1983). Social impact and social preference as determinants of children's peer group status. *Developmental Psychology, 19,* 856–867.
Newcomb, A.F., Bukowski, W.M., & Pattee, L. (1993). Children's peer relations: A meta-analytic review of popular, rejected, neglected, controversial, and average sociometric status. *Psychological Bulletin, 113,* 99–128.
Robins, R.W., John, O.P., Caspi, A., & Moffitt, T.E. (1996). Resilient, overcontrolled, and undercontrolled boys: Three replicable personality types. *Journal of Personality and Social Psychology, 70,* 157–171.
Robins, R.W., John, O.P., & Caspi, A. (1998). A typological approach to studying personality. In R.B. Cairns, L. Bergman, & J. Kagan (Eds.), *Methods and models for studying the individual: Essays in honor of Marian Radke-Yarrow.* Thousand Oaks, CA: Sage.
Scholte, R.H.J. (1998). *Adolescent relationships.* University of Nijmegen: Unpublished Doctoral Dissertation.

Scholte, R.H.J. van Aken, M.A.G., & van Lieshout, C.F.M. (1997). Adolescent personality factors in self-ratings and peer nominations and their prediction of peer acceptance and peer rejection. *Journal of Personality Assessment, 69*, 534–554.

Scholte, R.H.J., van Lieshout, C.F.M., & van Aken, M.A.G. (1999). *Relational support in adolescence: Factors, types, and adjustment.* Manuscript submitted for publication.

Simmons, R.G., & Blythe, D.A. (1987). *Moving into adolescence: The impact of pubertal change and school context.* New York: Aldine.

Thissen-Pennings, M.C.E., & ten Brink, P.W.M. (1994). *SOCSTAT user manual* (unpublished computer program). Nijmegen: KUN, Groep Rekentechnische Dienstverlening.

Turiel, E. (1997). The development of morality. In W. Damon (Ed.), *Handbook of child psychology* [N. Eisenberg (Vol. Ed.), *Social, emotional, and personality development, Vol 3* (pp. 863–932)]. New York: Wiley.

van Aken, M.A.G., van Lieshout C.F.M., & Scholte, R.H.J. (1998). *The social relationships and adjustment of the various personality types and subtypes.* Paper presented at the VIIth Biennial Meeting of the Society for Research on Adolescence. San Diego, Cal., USA. February 26–March 1.

van Lieshout, C.F.M., Cillessen, A.H.N., & Haselager, G.J.T. (1999). Interpersonal support and individual development. In W.A. Collins & B. Laursen (Eds.). *Relationships as developmental contexts. The Minnesota Symposia on Child Psychology, Vol. 30* (pp. 37–60). Hillsdale, NJ: Lawrence Erlbaum Associates Inc.

van Lieshout, C.F.M., & Doise, W. (1998). Social development. In A. Demetriou, W. Doise, & C.F.M. van Lieshout (Eds.), *Life-span developmental psychology* (pp. 271–316). New York: Wiley.

van Lieshout, C.F.M., & Haselager, G.J.T. (1994). The big-five personality factors in Q-sort descriptions of children and adolescents. In C.F. Halverson, G.A. Kohnstamm, & R.P. Martin (Eds.), *The developing structure of temperament and personality from infancy to adulthood* (pp. 293–318). Hillsdale, NJ: Lawrence Erlbaum Associates Inc.

van Lieshout, C.F.M., Haselager, G.J.T., Riksen-Walraven, J.M., & van Aken, M.A.G. (1995). *Personality development in middle childhood.* Paper presented at the Biennial Meetings of the Society for Research in Child Development, Indianapolis, USA.

van Lieshout, C.F.M., van Aken, M.A.G., & Scholte, R.H.J. (1998). Adolescenten met verschillende persoonlijkheidstypen. Hun sociale relaties en hun psychosociaal functioneren [Adolescents with different personality types. Their social relationships and psychosocial functioning]. *Nederlands Tijdschrift voor Opvoeding, Vorming en Onderwijs, 14*, 114–133.

Wills, T. A., Vaccaro, D., & McNamara, G. (1994). Novelty seeking, risk taking, and related constructs as predictors of adolescent substance use: An application of Cloninger's theory. *Journal of Substance Abuse, 6*, 1–20.

CHAPTER SIX

The morality paradox: Choosing not to be moral as a component of moral excellence

Tjeert Olthof
Utrecht University, The Netherlands

> *Be not righteous over much; neither make thyself over wise: why shouldest thou destroy thyself?*
> —Ecclesiastes 7:16

INTRODUCTION

In a thought-provoking essay, Franz Mönks discussed the issue of what might constitute *moral giftedness* (Mönks, 1996). The general tenet of his contribution is that traditional approaches to moral development, most notably that of Lawrence Kohlberg, are too narrowly focused on moral judgement to provide an adequate basis for defining moral giftedness. Moral giftedness does not, or not only, imply high-level thinking about justice, it also implies a high level of behavioural commitment. However, even consistent enaction of one's moral principles may not be the royal road to moral excellence. Using the morally and religiously motivated cruelties of the Spanish Inquisition as an example, Mönks argued that such a consistency may well lead to practices that are anything but morally praiseworthy.

How then to define moral giftedness? In the present chapter I will first discuss several of the answers to this question that have been given in the literature. These include the answer that is implicit in Kohlbergian theory, the empirically based answer of Colby and Damon (1992, 1993, 1995), and the answer that Mönks eventually gave. Subsequently, a case study will be presented as a means to evaluate the answers that have been given and as the basis for formulating an answer of my own. However, before going into the issue of what might constitute moral excellence, some conceptual groundwork needs to be done.

THE NATURE OF MORALITY

To identify the gifted among a group of persons that differ in terms of a particular dimension of interest, one needs to have an idea about where giftedness is located on the scale corresponding to that dimension. For many dimensions it is quite obvious where the gifted can be found. For example, one way to identify the intellectually gifted is to select the highest-scoring individuals on an IQ test. Similarly, particularly creative individuals can be identified on the basis of their high scores on an instrument measuring creativity. For other dimensions, however, the scores that correspond to optimal performance are not located at the extremes of the dimension. For example, an optimal level of self-control is indicated by scores at the middle of a scale representing that dimension, thus avoiding both undercontrol and overcontrol (see Van Lieshout et al., this volume).

When aiming to identify morally outstanding individuals it would seem natural to treat the dimension of morality as similar to those of intelligence and creativity, i.e. as a dimension where giftedness is located at the high end of the scale. The more a person can be characterised as a "moral" person, the more he or she can considered to be a morally gifted person, or so it would seem. One aim of the present chapter is to cast doubt on this assumption. I will argue that the dimension of morality might rather resemble that of self-control, in that the optimal level characterising the gifted is not located at the high extreme of the scale, but at some other point.

The tendency to equate the morally gifted with those at the high end of some "morality" scale is likely to arise from the implicit assumption that being "moral" is the same as being "good". However, defining morality in terms of goodness is not very helpful, because it does not tell us anything about what kind of entities should rightly be considered as being "moral". For the purpose of this chapter I take it that the concept of morality implies the concept of "ought". If a person A gives an evaluatively negative moral judgement about some state of affairs, she does not so much say "I don't like that state of affairs", but rather "That state of affairs ought not to exist". The ought statement indicates that A feels that there are objective reasons that are independent of her own preferences, for considering the state of affairs to be undesirable. This again implies that A feels that other persons should share her conviction that the state of affairs actually is undesirable. When giving a *moral* judgement rather than any other type of judgement, A thus appeals to the authority of a set of consensual (or presumably consensual) moral principles to add cogency to her evaluation of the state of affairs at hand.

It is useful to examine more closely the nature of those consensual moral principles and the nature of the situations that elicit moral judgements. Although it has been claimed that there exists such a thing as a *victimless morality* (Haidt, Koller, & Dias, 1993), by far the most important category of situations that members of our culture consider to be morally relevant consists of those in which harm is caused to a victim (cf. Olthof & Brugman, 1994). For person A to consider a situation as morally relevant, it is thus required that A considers the following elements to be present in the situation: (a) a *victim*, that is, an entity that A credits with moral status and that A believes to be currently suffering, and (b) a *perpetrator*, that is, a person to whom A attributes responsibility for the victim's suffering *or* a *potential helper*, that is a person who is, again according to A, in the position to do something to alleviate the victim's suffering. This sketch of morally relevant situations implies that there are at least two very general moral principles, i.e. (1) one should avoid making victims, that is, no harm should be caused to any entity that is credited with moral status, and (2) if a victim has nevertheless been made and if one is in the position to alleviate the victim's suffering, then one should do so.

When a person A perceives an event as being morally relevant, A can be expected to give a moral judgement, but A might or might not also experience a moral *emotion*. In line with current thinking on the nature of emotion (e.g. Campos, Campos, & Barrett, 1989; Frijda, 1986), I assume that A will experience a moral emotion when the event is relevant to A's own concerns. That is, to elicit A's emotional reaction, the event should touch on some need or desire of A. As will be pointed out later on in this chapter, the nature of the concern that the event touches upon subsequently determines the nature of the emotion that A experiences.

Finally, having discussed the concepts of moral judgement and moral emotion, the concept of *moral action* can now easily be defined as any action that is motivated by either a moral judgement or a moral emotion or both.

MORAL EXCELLENCE

Moral excellence in Kohlbergian terms

Now we are in the position to ask what moral excellence might be. Before discussing the contributions of the few authors who have explicitly addressed this question, I will discuss the answer that is implicit in Lawrence Kohlberg's theory of the development of moral judgement.

Kohlberg based his theory on the answers that his respondents gave when confronted with his famous moral dilemmas. When described in terms of the aforementioned analysis of morally relevant situations, Kohlberg's dilemmas consist of situations in which the protagonist is placed in two different roles at the same time. For example, the well known Heinz dilemma consists of two morally relevant situations in which Heinz fulfils mutually conflicting roles. In the first situation, Heinz's wife is the victim who suffers from a severe illness and who badly needs an expensive medicine that Heinz cannot afford to buy. Heinz himself is a potential helper who might or might not provide the help that his wife needs by stealing the medicine from a greedy druggist. Considered in isolation, it is obvious what Heinz should do in this situation, i.e. get his wife the medicine that she needs. However, should he try to do so, a different morally relevant situation would arise in which the druggist would be the victim and Heinz the perpetrator responsible for the druggist's loss. If this second situation is considered in isolation, it is again clear what Heinz should do, i.e. not steal the drug. The respondent's problem is what to do when both morally relevant situations are considered simultaneously, rather than in isolation. What would be the ideal solution to that problem, according to Kohlbergian theory?

In the most recent version of the scoring system that is used to categorise the respondents' reactions to the Kohlbergian dilemmas (Colby & Kohlberg, 1987), five stages are distinguished that represent increasingly advanced levels of thinking. One way that Kohlberg himself characterised the theoretically ideal response is that such a response results from *playing moral musical chairs* that is, from taking into account the perspectives of all participants in the situation at hand (Boom & Olthof, 1994). Accordingly, in Kohlbergian theory, moral giftedness is implicitly defined as the ability to take all the relevant perspectives into account.

Of course, as an account of moral giftedness, this definition is limited in the same way as is Kohlberg's account of moral development as a whole. As has been pointed out by Mönks (1996) and by other authors as well (e.g. Flanagan, 1984), the most important limitation of Kohlbergian theory is that it only deals with moral judgements and not with moral behaviour or with moral emotions. This is especially bothersome when aiming to identify the ingredients of moral excellence, as we expect morally outstanding persons not so much to give sophisticated moral judgements as to show extraordinary moral commitment in their behaviour. As the level of moral judgement is at most one of several determinants of moral behaviour (Rest, 1983), a full account of moral giftedness should obviously incorporate moral behaviour. Actually, a good case can be made that it is the *consistency* between verbally expressed moral judgements and moral behaviour that is a critical ingredient of moral excellence. This is precisely the line of reasoning that is followed by Colby and Damon (1992, 1993, 1995), authors of one of the very few empirical studies on moral excellence.

Colby and Damon's empirically-based answer

Colby and Damon asked a panel of experts to nominate persons who could be considered as morally outstanding individuals because of (1) a sustained commitment to moral ideals, (2) a disposition to act in accord with those ideals, (3) a willingness to put their own self-interest at risk, (4) a tendency to inspire others, and (5) a sense of humility about their own importance (Colby & Damon, 1993, p. 155). Colby and Damon subsequently interviewed 23 of the nominated persons with the aim of identifying those characteristics of these persons that made them moral exemplars. Questions were asked about their personal experiences and beliefs, and about important events and crucial decisions that might have shaped their life. In addition, they also carried out the standard Kohlbergian Moral Judgement Interview to assess the moral exemplars' level of moral reasoning.

Results with respect to the latter measure indicated that the moral judgements of about half of the moral exemplars reflected stage 5 reasoning, whereas the judgements of the other respondents represented a lower stage, mostly stage 3. Although the level of moral reasoning in the moral exemplar group might on average exceed that of the population as a whole, these findings indicate that a high level of moral reasoning is not a necessary condition for being a moral exemplar.

Colby and Damon interpreted their respondents' answers to the life history interview as indicating that the moral exemplars were open to moral change and also to social influences that fostered their already existing moral commitments. At the same time they also sought the company of others who would have such beneficial effects on their own morality. Through a process of mutual influence they gradually transformed their goals in such a way that their personal goals eventually became fully united with their moral goals. Colby and Damon see this unity of personal and moral goals as the key characteristic of their sample of moral exemplars.

As an example of this goal transformation process, Colby and Damon (1993) describe in detail the life history of Virginia Foster Durr, who was brought up in the racially segregated southern part of the United States, but who gradually changed her views on the moral acceptability of racial segregation through a succession of personal experiences and social influences. In the course of her life she became ever more deeply involved in the civil rights movement, particularly in the legal struggle that involved challenging the constitutionality of segregation laws. Colby and Damon make a convincing case that for her and the other moral exemplars in their sample, there was no discrepancy whatever between what they considered to be morally appropriate and what they personally preferred to do.

Colby and Damon's results imply that unity of personal and moral goals is likely to be a necessary condition for being a moral exemplar. When discussing their results, Colby and Damon seem to imply that they also consider this unity to be a *sufficient* condition for being a moral exemplar. I think there are important reasons to doubt this latter implication. These are the topic of the following argument.

Reasons for doubting Colby and Damon's answer: Controversial moral heroes

My doubts arise from the suspicion that Colby and Damon's procedure for identifying their moral exemplars may well have introduced a commonality between their respondents that is not likely to emerge from the life history interviews. When asking a panel of experts to decide on who might be a moral exemplar, one is almost guaranteed to get a sample of persons who channelled their moral zeal into a cause that is wholly uncontroversial among the panel of nominators. Although Virginia Foster Durr's activities in the civil rights movement were of course highly controversial in their time, they are now almost universally recognised as serving a praiseworthy goal.

But what about the following hypothetical character? Imagine a young woman named Mrs A, who got a liberal and non-religious upbringing in Western Europe. In the 1980s she moves to the USA to finish her studies. There she gradually changes her views on the moral acceptability of the liberal climate in her homeland through a succession of personal experiences and social influences. She ends up becoming a member of a fundamentalist religious group and she now spends her life as an anti-abortion activist. On the basis of her religious conviction, she credits the human foetus with the same moral status as a full-term neonate, and she consequently rejects abortion as being equivalent to murder. She campaigns against liberal abortion laws and in favour of restrictive legislation. Through personal contacts with other persons working for the same cause and through debates with opponents, she gets ever more deeply involved in the anti-abortion movement, which eventually results in her personal goals being fully united with the moral goal of banning abortion. In short, her life resembles that of Foster Durr in every aspect, except that she fights for a different cause. Would she stand a chance of being included in Colby and Damon's sample?

Or take another—and non-hypothetical—example from the other side of the political spectrum. Consider the case of the Dutch priest and radical pacifist Kees Koning who made a habit of cutting holes in military airport fences and, once inside, used a big hammer to beat as many dents in the available aircraft as he could. He was repeatedly jailed, where he behaved as a model prisoner and made himself popular among other prisoners and guards alike. Once set free again, he immediately continued his anti-military campaign, and resumed his career as a nuisance to both military officials and the non-pacifist majority of the population. Those who are tempted to argue that Koning's activities in a moderate and relatively liberal minded country like the Netherlands did not invoke great personal risks should note that he did take such risks on other occasions. For example, he was among the peace activists who went to Iraq just before the Gulf War broke out, in a desperate attempt to prevent the allied forces from bombing the country.

I do not know whether Mrs A and Kees Koning would be eligible for inclusion among Colby and Damon's sample of moral exemplars, but to me it seems evident that both of them fully satisfy both Colby and Damon's inclusion criteria and their eventual analysis of moral excellence. In my view, the least that these examples show is that Colby and Damon's formal description of moral excellence might very well apply to individuals who direct their moral effort towards causes that are controversial.

Being open-minded liberals, we might, of course, stick to Colby and Damon's analysis and thus grant individuals like Mrs A and Kees Koning their status of moral hero, even if we personally are unsympathetic to the goals that they pursued and to the methods that they used. But as soon as we grant this a further question arises, i.e. would it be wholly unimaginable that the Colby and Damon criterion for moral excellence—unity of personal and moral goals—would also apply to individuals who pursue goals and use means that we consider not just as controversial, but rather as being utterly repugnant? For example, what about the officials of the Spanish Inquisition cited by Mönks in his example? Is it inconceivable that some of them would also satisfy Colby and Damon's criterion of unity of personal and moral goals?

This is an important issue, because if the Colby and Damon criterion also applies to individuals whose actions we can only repudiate, this would indicate that there is something wrong with the criterion.

Mönks' answer: Love as the need to give

On the basis of examples drawn from theological writings and literary fiction, Franz Mönks gave what I take to be a tentative answer to the question of how to define moral giftedness. In this answer, for which Mönks recruited further support from the work of theorists in the *ethic of care* tradition (Gilligan, 1977), much weight is given to the presence of *a need to give*. Mönks referred to this need as a universal form of disinterested love that arises from a positive choice in favour of goodness, rather than from a choice not to do anything morally reprehensible. Without this love, even the most conscientious follower of moral principles would never qualify as a moral hero.

To me it seems that something like Mönks' love for others actually characterises many of Colby and Damon's respondents, without this aspect receiving much attention in the interviews that Colby and Damon had with them. It seems hardly conceivable that someone could be nominated as a moral exemplar, without the nominators having the strong impression that the nominee has a strong prosocial and loving attitude towards others. That such a characteristic was not prominent in the interviews that Colby and Damon conducted with their respondents, might indicate that the respondents themselves did not consider their prosocial attitude as anything special or worth talking about. In sum, it seems highly likely that something like Mönks' criterion of love should be included in the list of characteristics that are essential for the morally gifted.

Nevertheless, even if we grant this, it seems to me that one could still raise similar doubts as those raised against Colby and Damon's criterion. Specifically. to take Mönks' own example, would it be wholly impossible for the inquisitors to claim with some justification, that they acted out of love? Love for the Church, the Holy Virgin, their nation, or even out of love for the immortal souls of their victims? Dostoevsky's character of the Grand-inquisitor actually claimed that he and his colleagues acted out of love for all those simple folks who would be unable to live up to the high ideals that Jesus Christ wanted them to live up to (Dostoevsky, 1969).

Or to take a contemporary example: It may be argued that many of the crimes that were committed in the war in the former Yugoslavia were motivated by a disinterested love for others: love for the Serbian, or Croatian, or Bosnian people; or love for the Orthodox, or Catholic, or Moslem religion; or simply the love for one's relatives who should be protected against a cruel enemy.

One way of solving this problem is to require that the love of a moral hero should be directed equally to all the parties involved. This would make Mönks' answer surprisingly similar to that which I derived from Kohlbergian theory, except that the Kohlbergian cognitive strategy of giving equal weight to the perspectives of all participants changes into the affective strategy of directing one's love to all participants in equal degree.

The use of this restrictive criterion might well imply that some or most of Colby and Damon's moral exemplars would no longer qualify as being morally gifted. Take the example of Virginia Foster Durr. Of course she is likely to have loved the oppressed African Americans for whom she worked in the civil rights movement. She may also have respected the white segregationists who were her opponents, in the sense that she was prepared to listen to their arguments and that she granted them all the rights that citizens have in a democratic society. This would probably be enough for her to satisfy the Kohlbergian criterion for moral excellence.

But is there any reason to believe that Foster Durr also loved the white segregationalists who were her opponents? If not, this would disqualify her as a moral exemplar according to the restrictive version of Mönks' criterion and the same is probably true for many of Colby and Damon's other moral exemplars as well.

In sum, we end up with two versions of Mönks' criterion. The first of these requires that a moral hero is motivated by love for others and in general by strong prosocial feeling. The second is far more restrictive because it requires that this love for others is truly universal in the sense that it is equally directed to all parties involved.

THE CASE OF R

In an attempt to evaluate the four criteria just discussed, I will in the following paragraphs discuss the case of a well known 18th-century politician by presenting some biographical facts about him. For the time being, this individual will be referred to as R. His actual name will be revealed later on in the chapter (together with the sources of the biographical material). The selection of the material is guided by the wish to sketch a rudimentary portrait of R while focusing on those aspects of his ideas and actions that are relevant for a decision about whether he would qualify as a moral exemplar in terms of the criteria discussed earlier. As far as possible this sketch will be built up by citing either R himself, or persons who knew him.

R as a man of high moral standing

R was born in a middle-class family in a provincial town in a rural area. As his father left the family when R was still a child, R grew up under the constant threat of poverty. However, he obtained several scholarships that enabled him to gain an academic education and to qualify as a lawyer. As such he began to practise in his home town, and he soon became renowned for his ability and as someone who was not at all interested in making personal gains. A colleague said about him:

> None of our colleagues has a greater right to be called the defender of the widow and the orphan. R is not interested in making money; he is and will always remain only the lawyer of the poor.

Another contemporary who was hostile towards R for reasons that will become obvious later on, nevertheless felt obliged to describe him as follows:

One must be fair to everyone, even to R; one must admit that he was never motivated by a love of money. On the contrary, he was quite exceptionally disinterested. He gave unpaid consultations for several years and disliked taking fees from his clients even when he had won their cases from them, even though he had no patrimony and was so hard up that he had borrow clothes.

R also was deeply religious (although his beliefs were far from orthodox) and he held well articulated political opinions. Both his religious beliefs and his political convictions had strong moral overtones. On one occasion, when defending an officer who had deserted from the army, he described the tasks of the country's highest government official as follows:

> To lead men to happiness through virtue and to virtue by laws founded on the unshakeable principles of universal morality, designed to restore to human nature all its rights and all its primal dignity; to re-forge the immortal chain that must bind man to God and to his fellow-men by destroying all the forces of oppression and tyranny which fill the earth with fear, suspicion, pride, baseness, egoism, hatred, greed and all the vices that draw men far from the goals assigned to society by the eternal legislator...

R's belief in the moral value of religion is clearly expressed in a treatise that he authored or co-authored later on in his career. The following passage, describing what its authors considered to be the best way to fulfil one's religious duties, captures the flavour of the treatise as a whole quite well:

> to detest bad faith and despotism, to punish tyrants and traitors, to assist the unfortunate, to respect the weak, to defend the oppressed, to do all the good that one can do to one's neighbour, and to behave with justice to all men.

At the age of 30 and after having worked a few years as a lawyer, R became a deputy for his district in what we would now call the national parliament. There he continued his struggle against oppression and poverty. For example, in his second speech as a deputy he addressed a Roman Catholic bishop who appeared at a parliamentary meeting to discuss the issue of the poverty of the lower classes, with the following words:

> All that is necessary is that bishops and dignitaries of the church should renounce that luxury which is an offence to Christian humility that they should give up their coaches and give up their horses; if need be, that they should sell a quarter of the property of the church and give to the poor.

As was the case in his work as a lawyer, R soon earned a reputation as a man of high moral standing. One colleague deputy testified that he was

6. THE MORALITY PARADOX

> ...always steadfast in the austerity of his principles; he never deviated. He was the same at the end as he had been in the beginning, which is a tribute one can pay to very few of his colleagues...

Unlike many of his colleagues, R was utterly insensitive to the temptation of using politics as a vehicle to personal wealth, which yielded him the epithet *the Incorruptible*. As is clear from the following quote from one of his speeches, he not only behaved as a man of high principles, but he also advocated a view of the tasks of government that was thoroughly moral:

> In our country we want to substitute morality for egoism, probity for honour, principles for conventions, duties for social obligations, the empire of reason for the tyranny of fashion, contempt of vice for contempt of misfortune, pride for insolence, greatness of soul for vanity, love of glory for love of money, good people for the right society, merit for intrigue, genius for wit, truth for show, the charms of true happiness for the satiety of lust, the greatness of man for the pettiness of the great, a magnanimous, powerful and happy people for an agreeable, frivolous and miserable one...

During his years as a representative he spoke against many forms of governmental repression including the death penalty, and in favour of liberty of the press, freedom of speech, freedom of worship, civil rights for religious and ethnic minority groups, and clerical marriage.

Despite his public reputation for being a stern and inaccessible man, the little that is known of his private life suggests that in his personal contacts he was a rather affable man who could enjoy the simple pleasures of life. In his years as a lawyer he was a member of a group of educated men who gathered weekly to entertain each other by reciting light-hearted poetry of their own making. Although he is not known to have had any intimate relationships with women, a 19th-century historian later claimed to have talked to the daughter of a woman who had been R's regular dancing partner, which suggests that he must have led a somewhat active social life. According to the daughter, her mother used to say that R "had a serious air but he was a very good man". During his years as a deputy he lived in the house of a skilled craftsman where he was fully accepted and appreciated as a member of the family.

Later in this chapter I will discuss whether R would qualify as being morally gifted when evaluated against each of the criteria that have been proposed in the literature, but thus far I take it that he would certainly be a good candidate. I should now confess, however, that the above account of R's life, although accurate, has been somewhat selective. In the next paragraph a few more facts from his biography will be presented.

R as a bloodthirsty tyrant

Historically interested readers have probably already realised that R was actually one of the great leaders of the French revolution, Maximilien Robespierre. The biographical material that was given earlier can be found in Hampson (1974) and Rudé (1976) and a more general sketch of his person is given by Schama (1989). From 1789 until his death in July 1794, Robespierre was a member of each of the three successive representative bodies of revolutionary France, i.e. the Constituent Assembly, the Legislative Assembly, and the National Convention. From July 1793 until his death in 1794 he was a leading member of the most powerful of the two executive committees of the National Convention that served as a revolutionary government. Under the reign of this committee, also known as the *reign of terror*, thousands of real or supposed enemies of the revolution were decapitated under the guillotine at an ever increasing rate. From figures given by Schama (1989), it can be calculated that, during the last few months that Robespierre was in power, the average number of executions in Paris increased from 5 to 34 *a day*.

During the reign of terror, an atmosphere of increasing mistrust, fear and hatred had developed within the revolutionary movement itself. After making a speech to the National Convention that was somewhat less coherent than usual, Robespierre and his devotees were overthrown by a rival faction and the next day he was sent to the guillotine himself. In the days thereafter it became clear how much hatred he had engendered among the citizens of Paris and he was often depicted as a *buveur de sang*, that is, as a bloodthirsty tyrant (Rudé, 1976, p. 117).

Of course, several factors could be cited that mitigate Robespierre's responsibility for the reign of terror. First, although Robespierre was the unofficial leader of the most powerful executive committee, other members of these committees obviously also had their share in the responsibility. Second, a reasonable argument could be made that at least some of the executions were justified and unavoidable. Third, there is evidence indicating that the massive numbers of executions in Robespierre's last months were partially directed at eliminating those revolutionary factions that were most responsible for the excesses of the months before and that were therefore a hindrance to a transition to a less repressive regime (Hampson, 1974, p. 270).[1]

Nevertheless, regardless of how many mitigating circumstances there may have been, I take it that Robespierre *was* sufficiently responsible for

---

[1] This is supported by the fact that at least one contemporary, the later emperor Napoleon Bonaparte, thought that Robespierre's fall was caused by even more radical colleagues who suspected him of wanting to end the terror.

the atrocities of the reign of terror to prevent us from granting him the status of moral hero. This in turn implies that should he nevertheless satisfy the criteria for moral excellence that have been proposed in the literature, there is something wrong with those criteria. Next, I will therefore examine to what extent Robespierre can reasonably be said to satisfy each of the criteria discussed earlier.

The Kohlbergian criterion: Did Robespierre reach stage 5?

A stage 5 Kohlbergian moral hero takes into account the perspectives of all participants who are involved in the situation at hand. Can Robespierre be said to have satisfied this criterion? If we apply this principle not only to what he thought, but also to his behaviour, the least that can be said is that he certainly did not give sufficient weight to the perspectives of his victims to prevent him from sending them to the guillotine.

Indeed many, if not most, of the victims of the guillotine at the height of the reign of terror did not receive anything like a fair trial in which they had a chance to defend themselves (Hampson, 1974; Rudé, 1976; Schama, 1989). Accordingly, we can conclude that most of the victims' perspectives were *not* taken into account and that this is enough to disqualify Robespierre from being a moral exemplar according to the Kohlbergian criterion. As this is precisely what we want any criterion to do when applied to Robespierre, this implies that the Kohlbergian criterion has proven to be adequate in this particular case.

The Colby and Damon criterion: Was there a unity of personal and moral goals?

To me it seems that the biographical information given earlier, concerning Robespierre's moral and personal goals, provides sufficient justification for characterising him as a man for whom there was very little discrepancy between the two types of goals. He seems to have lived up to his moral ideals. One might even claim that not only were his personal goals indistinguishable from his moral goals, but that the same was true of his religious and political goals as well. When taken together, it does not seem unreasonable to suggest that Colby and Damon's description of moral exemplars in terms of a unity of personal and moral goals might well have applied to Robespierre. This in turn implies that Colby and Damon's criterion is not sufficiently restrictive. If a man like Robespierre satisfies it, the criterion includes individuals who should be excluded.

The Mönks criteria: Was Robespierre motivated by love?

Was Robespierre motivated by a disinterested love for others? From the biographical information that was given earlier, it is clear that he was disinterested. In addition, it seems quite reasonable to argue that he did act out of love. Love for his country, for the French people, perhaps also for the poor and for those who were oppressed under the old regime. All this would qualify him as a moral hero according to the first version of Mönks' love criterion, which, of course, reinforces the criticisms levelled earlier at this criterion. The fact that even Robespierre might well satisfy it is further illustration of the fact that this version of the love criterion is simply too inclusive.

However, matters are different when it comes to the second version of Mönks' love criterion. There are no indications that Robespierre ever felt anything even remotely resembling love for the victims of the revolution. Moreover, the simple fact that he was at least partly responsible for their execution is, of course, very difficult to reconcile with the idea that he loved them. Accordingly, it can safely be concluded that Robespierre fails to satisfy the second and most restrictive version of Mönks' criterion, which is, of course, as things should be.

Preliminary conclusions

Now, what can be learned from confronting the four proposed criteria for moral excellence with the case of Robespierre? Two criteria, Colby and Damon's unity of personal and moral goals, and the least restrictive version of Mönks' love criterion, appeared to be insufficiently restrictive, as even Robespierre might well have satisfied them. The fact that these criteria did not stand the confrontation with Robespierre, does, of course, not make them useless as ways of characterising actual moral exemplars. The problem is merely that individuals who can definitely not be seen as moral exemplars might also satisfy the same criteria.

Two other criteria, the Kohlbergian ideal of giving equal weight to the perspectives of all those involved, and Mönks' ideal of universal love, did stand the confrontation with Robespierre, as he failed on both of them. As has been pointed out earlier, Mönks' criterion can be seen as an affective, but structurally similar, version of the Kohlbergian criterion. Actually, it can be argued that Mönks' criterion implies the Kohlbergian one, because it is difficult to see how one could equally love all participants involved, without also giving equal weight to their perspectives.

Both criteria differ, however, in that Mönks' is far more restrictive than the Kohlbergian criterion. In the Kohlbergian account, it is possible for a moral hero to give full weight to a particular perspective and subsequently to decide that justice requires a decision in favour of another party involved. Being a Kohlbergian moral hero is not necessarily incompatible with delivering punishment to those who deserve it. For a moral hero who satisfies Mönks' criterion of universal love, it would seem scarcely possible to love all parties involved equally and subsequently to do something against the interests of one party. Such a moral hero should refrain from causing harm to any of the parties involved.

Before returning to the issue of which of these criteria actually is most adequate as a criterion for moral excellence, an unresolved question concerning Robespierre needs to be addressed. The question is how to explain that the same individual can be responsible for the execution of thousands of real or supposed opponents, while at the same satisfying a well researched criterion for moral excellence.

Was Robespierre morally inconsistent?

It is quite natural to think that there is something of a discrepancy between Robespierre's apparently high moral standing and his bearing a large share of the responsibility for the murderous practices of the revolutionary government in the years 1793–94. Although some historians have tried to do so (see the overview of Robespierre interpretations by Rudé, 1976), Robespierre's responsibility for the executions cannot easily be dismissed. It is true that he shared the responsibility with others and that he probably had his reservations about a considerable number of the executions, but he was also both an initiator of the reign of terror and one of its most ardent defenders.

It is tempting to think that there were two quite different personalities in this one person, one being the morally minded democratic representative and the other the ruthless dictator of the reign of terror. Alternatively, one might suspect that he was a hypocrite or simply a fraud who used moral talk to hide his abuse of power. Or one might argue, as some historians have done (see again Rudé's overview), that the hardness of life at the top soon made the youthful idealistic democrat of the early 1790s lose his innocence and turned him into the dictator that he was at the end of his career.

However, these solutions to the apparent discrepancy are too facile. For Robespierre himself there was no discrepancy whatever between his moral principles and his political activities, including those during the reign of terror. His speech to the National Convention of 5 February 1794 is illuminating, because it shows how he justified the reign of terror in the same moral terms that he always used to justify his proposals (Rudé, 1976, p. 118):

> If the mainspring of popular government in time of peace is virtue, its mainspring in time of revolution is virtue and terror combined: virtue without which terror is squalidly repressive, terror without which virtue lies disarmed. Terror is nothing other than swift, severe and inflexible justice; it is therefore an emanation of virtue; and it is not so much a principle in itself as a consequence of the general principle of democracy when applied to the most urgent needs of the nation.

Could it then be that there actually is no discrepancy between Robespierre, the morally minded democratic representative and Robespierre, the ruthless dictator of the reign of terror? Could it be that both aspects are two sides of the same coin? It seems to me that the answer might well be: yes, they are. Robespierre's tendency to let moral considerations dominate over all other considerations left him no place for the concept of morally respectable political opponents. His tendency to fuse personal and political goals with moral goals not only led him to use politics as a means to fight immorality, but also to denouncing political opponents as being immoral. Both tendencies are well expressed in the following two citations from speeches made to the National Convention on 5 February, 1794, and 7 May, 1794, respectively (Hampson, 1974, pp. 160 & 183):

> In the system of the French Revolution, whatever is immoral is bad politics, what corrupts is counter-revolutionary.

> The only basis for civil society is morality. All the combinations that make war on us rest on crime.

After citing the last remark, Hampson (1974) further concluded that "for Robespierre all the opposition to the revolution since 1789 had been due to a single conspiracy of the egotistical and the corrupt...". It was this tendency to attribute immorality to anyone who stood in the way of what he considered to be the only morally justified course of action that motivated Robespierre's liberal use of procedures derived from the criminal justice system against such individuals.

THE HAZARDS OF UNTAMED MORAL COMMITMENT

If the above interpretation is correct, it is no arbitrary coincidence that Robespierre both satisfied the Colby and Damon criterion for moral excellence by showing a unity of moral, personal, political, and religious goals, and that he behaved in a way that provoked others to call him a bloodthirsty tyrant. On the contrary, his overwhelming moral commitment can well be seen as the very cause of his behaviour.

It can be concluded that the unity of moral goals and other goals that a person might have is a mixed blessing. It can as well be a recipe for disaster, as was true for Robespierre, as for moral excellence, as was true for Colby and Damon's respondents. Before going into the issue of *when* unity of goals leads to disaster and when to excellence, it is useful to step back for a moment and ask how much weight should be given to this particular interpretation of the life of just one individual, i.e. Robespierre. Two considerations are relevant in this respect.

First, my interpretation of Robespierre as a prime example of the hazards of letting moral considerations dominate above everything else, is not original and neither does it apply only to Robespierre. Writing about 19th-century Russian thinkers, the political philosopher Isaiah Berlin even used Robespierre's name as a general label for all morally motivated radical revolutionaries who aimed to create a new and better world on the ruins of the old (Berlin, 1981, p. 399).

Second, the idea that taking a moral perspective on a particular state of affairs can have less than desirable consequences, is also well known from a very different area of investigation, i.e. that of the social and developmental psychology of anger, aggression, and guilt. This literature is briefly reviewed next.

Excessive moral emotionality: Aggression and guilt-proneness

As pointed out in the introduction, morally relevant situations that touch on an individual A's own concerns not only elicit moral judgements, but moral emotions as well. Which emotion A experiences depends on which concern is touched upon by the morally relevant event, and this in turn depends on the role that A assumes for herself in the morally relevant situation (Olthof, 1994). If A perceives herself as being a victim of a perpetrator's harm-causing behaviour (or if she identifies with another person who is a victim), she can be expected to become angry. If A perceives herself as a perpetrator who is responsible for a victim's suffering or as a potential helper who failed to provide help (or if she identifies with other persons in these roles), she can be expected to feel guilty.

According to this account, both guilt and anger have their origins in a moral evaluation of the situation at hand. As guilt is commonly recognised as the prime example of a moral emotion, this claim is wholly uncontroversial as far as guilt is concerned. The moral origins of anger are less self-evident, but some social psychological and developmental studies have provided supporting evidence. For example, inspired by Ferguson and Rule's (1983) model of anger and aggression, my colleagues and I were able to show that 5–15-year-old children's estimates of how angry a victim would become at a perpetrator who had caused harm to him were closely related to their moral evaluations of the perpetrator's behaviour (Olthof, 1990; Olthof, Ferguson, & Luiten, 1989).

Individuals who are frequently exposed to conditions that elicit a particular emotion are likely to develop an affective style that is dominated by that particular emotion (Malatesta & Wilson, 1988). For such individuals, conditions that most other persons would not even notice are sufficient to elicit the particular emotion dominating their affective style. In the case of guilt, such individuals are usually referred to as being *guilt-prone* (Tangney, 1990). Analogously, persons with a tendency to get angry could be called *anger-prone*. When combined with the claim made earlier that both guilt and anger originate from a moral evaluation of someone's behaviour, it follows that guilt-prone individuals have an excessive tendency to evaluate their own behaviour from a moral perspective, whereas anger-prone individuals tend do the same with the behaviour of others.

In the literature on guilt-proneness it has been claimed that guilt-proneness, unlike shame-proneness, is a desirable trait that helps a person to maintain satisfying personal relationships (Tangney, 1991; Tangney, Burggraf, & Wagner, 1995). However, recent evidence indicates that guilt can also serve the person maladaptively, in that it causes one to ruminate fruitlessly on past events (Ferguson & Stegge, 1998; Ferguson, Stegge, Miller, & Olsen, 1999).

We know, both from daily experience and from the psychological literature, of course, that anger can also have maladaptive and even harmful consequences. On the basis of the social psychological and developmental literature, it can be argued convincingly that a tendency to get angry is related to a tendency to behave aggressively towards other persons (Ferguson & Rule, 1983; Graham, Hudley, & Williams, 1992; Olthof, 1990).

If there exists such a thing as a maladaptive tendency to get angry or to feel guilty, and if these emotions originate from a moral evaluation of a particular state of affairs, it follows that an overly strong tendency to look at things from a moral perspective can have consequences that are quite undesirable. Accordingly, the conclusion that I reached on the basis of studying the case of Robespierre is supported by the social psychological and developmental evidence on guilt and anger.

IN SEARCH OF MORAL EXCELLENCE: BEYOND THE FUSION OF GOALS

The case of Robespierre, and the developmental and social psychological evidence, show that if we differentiate among individuals in terms of the extent to which they tend to look at things from a moral perspective, the morally excellent should not be sought at the high end of such a dimension. Even though the morally excellent have a strong moral commitment to the extent that their personal goals are fused with their moral goals, there apparently is something that keeps them from letting the moral perspective dominate over all other considerations. What might this "something" be? Two candidate answers to this question have already been raised in the discussion of the criteria for moral excellence, i.e. a tendency to give equal weight to the perspectives of all those involved in the situation, and a tendency to love all those involved equally.

When seen from the present perspective, the problem with both criteria is that they only give guidance once a situation is defined as being morally relevant. Although the Robespierre of the reign of terror certainly failed to give equal weight to all perspectives, let alone to love all those involved equally, this account implies that this is not the only, or even the most important, reason for denying him the status of a moral hero. Rather, Robespierre's most fundamental mistake was that he indiscriminately and overwhelmingly applied a moral perspective to all the domains in which he was active. He failed to take a perspective that would have allowed him to escape from the moral absolutism that inspired both his thinking and his behaviour. Such a perspective is described in the next paragraph.

Taking a meta-moral perspective as an antidote against moral absolutism

What kind of perspective would keep the morally excellent from moral absolutism? To me it seems that such a perspective should allow one to realise that looking at things from a moral point of view is one particular way of looking at things, i.e. that it is a perspective in itself. In the remainder of this chapter I will designate the perspective that allows one to think about whether a moral perspective should or should not be used in a particular situation, as a *meta-moral* perspective.

The following example might further clarify the distinction between a moral perspective and a meta-moral perspective. As it has become clear that smoking cigarettes provides a health risk, both for oneself and for those who are exposed to the pollutants that are produced, the situation of a person A smoking a cigarette in the presence of another person B can easily be seen from a moral perspective. Using that perspective, A is a perpetrator who causes harm to a victim B. Such an interpretation would not only entail negative moral judgements about A's behaviour, but it might also encourage B's anger against A, as well as A's feelings of guilt with respect to B. Once A and/or B have accepted that (a) smoking is dangerous and (b) the issue should be looked at from a moral perspective, nothing can prevent them from giving such moral evaluations and from experiencing such emotions.

It would take a meta-moral perspective, however, to question the wisdom of considering this situation from a moral perspective. One reason for *not* applying a moral perspective might be the realisation that cigarette smoking is only one of many human activities that are potentially harmful to other persons and that a moral perspective might as well be applied to such mundane activities as driving a car (dangerous both for oneself and other road users) and travelling by plane (dangerous for life at the planet as a whole due to air pollution).

Is there any evidence that persons who are considered to be morally excellent actually use a meta-moral perspective to evaluate the wisdom of applying a moral perspective to a particular situation? To my knowledge no formal research has been done to investigate this issue, but a very informal pilot study carried out by some of my students did yield some suggestive preliminary results. Eight adult respondents were first asked to think of a person they considered to be a moral exemplar. Subsequently, they were asked why they considered that particular person to be a moral exemplar. As one respondent identified two moral exemplars, this procedure yielded nine descriptions of the ingredients of moral excellence. Most descriptions could easily be interpreted as consistent with Colby and Damon's description of moral exemplars as showing a unity between personal and moral goals.

However, in three cases respondents also spontaneously said that their moral heroes were characterised by things like a "wonderful ability to put things into perspective", "wisdom", "enjoyment of life", and "humour". In one other case a respondent remarked that her admiration for her moral heroes suffered somewhat from the fact that they almost were *too* virtuous and lacked a sense of humour. In my view, these descriptions can well be interpreted as indicating that these respondents felt that one characteristic of a moral hero is a tendency not to let a moral perspective dominate all other perspectives.

Perhaps the clearest example of attributing a meta-moral perspective to a moral hero was provided by another respondent who identified the former South African president Nelson Mandela as a moral hero. It should be noted that on the basis of what was publicly known about Mandela's life history when this study was carried out, he obviously qualified as a moral hero in terms of Colby and Damon's criterion of unity between personal and moral goals. Although information about Mandela's life history will surely have motivated the respondent's answer, he justified his choice in a different way, i.e. by saying that Mandela forgave his former oppressors rather than taking revenge on them. Obviously, to forgive when justice would seem to imply punishment is a prime example of refraining from the use of a moral perspective, and thereby a sign of taking a meta-moral perspective.

Development of a meta-moral perspective

Colby and Damon (1993, 1995) characterised the developmental process leading to moral excellence as a gradual transformation of goals through social influence. If the present account is correct, this development should also be characterised by an increasing awareness that looking at things from a moral point of view is one particular way of looking at things, i.e. that it is a perspective in itself.

In the absence of research, one can only speculate about how a meta-moral perspective might develop. One source of this development might consist of incidents in which children are confronted with the cultural conventions that specify which entities are entitled to play the role of a *victim* in morally relevant situations and which are not. For example, in non-vegetarian families children are bound to discover that the moral rule of not causing harm to others does not protect the life of the animals whose cooked body parts they are supposed to eat. Even though the behaviour of a meat-eater can easily be interpreted as the behaviour of a perpetrator who causes harm to a victim, cultural conventions concerning the (lack of) moral status of farm animals prevent non-vegetarians from considering the consumption of meat as being morally relevant.

Even though religious teachings are often seen as promoting a strong commitment to moral values (e.g. Colby & Damon, 1995), religion might also provide reasons for allowing a moral perspective to be superseded by other considerations. For example, unlike the Dutch essayist who wrote a book entitled *The unbelievable badness of the Divine Being* (my translation) (Van het Reve, 1987), faithful Christians usually refrain from taking a moral perspective when thinking about the behaviour of God as it is conveyed in biblical and theological writings. Using such examples as the case of Abraham who was told to sacrifice his son, Van het Reve argued that—when seen from the moral perspective that we usually apply when evaluating other people's behaviour—the behaviour of God can only be considered as highly immoral.

In Van het Reve's examples, God can be said to deviate on the negative side from what would commonly be considered as morally appropriate. However, deviations on the positive side are also not uncommon in biblical writing. For example, the concept of forgiveness discussed earlier, which entails that the forgiver refrain from using a moral perspective, is valued highly in the Christian faith. Similarly, in several New Testament writings Jesus is portrayed as favouring a course of action that deviates on the positive side from what would be morally justified. One example is the parable of the owner of a vineyard who ignored the principle of equity (Frankena, 1962) by paying all his labourers as if they had worked a whole day, irrespective of whether they had actually worked all day or just one hour. Another case is that of the adulterous woman who should have been stoned to death according to existing law, but who escaped that fate because Jesus suggested that an accuser without sin should be the first to cast a stone at her.

The latter example is interesting because there is no doubt that, given the moral rules of the day, using a moral perspective would be fully appropriate. Nevertheless, Jesus did not use such a perspective and my guess is that most readers today would consider this a wise decision. But why is it in some cases "better" to refrain from using a moral perspective? The following example might clarify this. Imagine the case of an 8-year-old daughter of a mother with a strong morally based anti-smoking attitude. The girl knows her mother as someone who is eager to prevent all visitors from smoking in the house, but to her great surprise her mother does not make any objection when at her birthday party 90-year-old great-grandfather happily lights a huge cigar!

From this incident, the child might not only learn that there is such a thing as a moral perspective that may or may not be applied to a particular case, but she might also learn that there are sometimes good reasons for not taking a moral perspective. One of these is that using a moral perspective in any particular case is not in itself morally neutral. Had the child's mother given a negative moral evaluation of great-grandfather's behaviour, she would not only have deprived him of the enjoyment of his cigar, she might also have harmed him in more subtle ways, for example by implying that she considers him to be an ill-mannered person for not asking permission to smoke.

My general point is that the use of a moral perspective inevitably creates a new morally relevant situation, with the evaluator in the role of the perpetrator and with the evaluated person in the role of the victim. Giving moral evaluations about a perpetrator's behaviour thus creates a moral dilemma in which the original morally relevant situation that motivated the evaluator to give a moral evaluation in the first place is complemented by a second morally relevant situation that arises from the very act of giving a moral judgement.

Of course, in many situations the morally relevant situation that originally motivated the evaluator to give a moral judgement far outweighs the secondary morally relevant situation created by the evaluator's act of giving a moral judgement. However, the previous examples show that this is not necessarily so. In particular cases, one might decide on moral grounds not to use a moral perspective when thinking about someone else's behaviour.

Individuals with an extraordinary commitment to moral values necessarily live among others who do not meet the strict standards that they impose on themselves. Such individuals can easily be tempted to demand the same commitment from others and to consider a lack thereof as a moral transgression in itself. In my view, the case of Robespierre shows that when such individuals lack the meta-moral awareness that is needed to resist this temptation, their extraordinary moral commitment can lead them to become anything but a moral exemplar.

When individuals with an extraordinary moral commitment have enough meta-moral awareness to prevent them from evaluating others against the strict standards that they use for themselves, an asymmetric pattern of judgement results that I consider to be characteristic of real moral exemplars. Such individuals not only show an extraordinary moral commitment, but they are at the same time mild when judging someone else's behaviour. Moral excellence not only implies a strong commitment to moral values, but also an awareness that there are sometimes good reasons not to take a moral perspective.

ACKNOWLEDGEMENTS

I am grateful to Tanja Berenschot, Ellen Bruinsma, Gwendolyn Burgman, Sandra van Egmond, and Ilse Rijpsma for gathering the pilot data that are discussed in this chapter and to Gerard Brugman, Bram Guiljam, and Jan ter Laak for their thoughtful comments on several of the ideas that are presented here.

REFERENCES

Berlin, I. (1981). *Russische denkers*. Amsterdam: Synopsis. [Dutch translation of *Russian thinkers*. London: The Hogarth Press.]

Boom, J., & Olthof, T. (1994). Kohlbergs theorie over de ontogenese van rechtvaardigheidsoordelen. In T. Olthof & D. Brugman (Eds.) *Het ontstaan van moreel besef* [The origins of moral awareness] (pp. 39–65). Lisse, The Netherlands: Swets & Zeitlinger.

Campos, J.J, Campos, R.G., & Barrett, K.C. (1989). Emergent themes in the study of emotional development and emotion regulation. *Developmental Psychology, 25*, 394–402.

Colby, A., & Damon, W. (1992). *Some do care: Contemporary lives of moral commitment*. New York: The Free Press.

Colby, A., & Damon, W. (1993). The uniting of self and morality in the development of extraordinary moral commitment. In G.G. Noam & T.E. Wren (Eds.), *The moral self* (pp. 149–174). Cambridge, MA: MIT Press.

Colby, A., & Damon, W. (1995). The development of extraordinary moral commitment. In M. Killen & D. Hart (Eds.), *Morality in everyday life: Developmental perspectives* (pp. 342–370). Cambridge, UK: Cambridge University Press.

Colby, A., & Kohlberg, L. (1987). *The measurement of moral judgment*. Cambridge, MA: Cambridge University Press.

Dostoevsky, F.M. (1969). De gebroeders Karamazow. Wageningen: Veen. [Translation of *The brothers Karamazov*.]

Ferguson, T.J., & Rule, B.G. (1983). An attributional perspective on anger and aggression. In R.G. Geen & E.I. Donnerstein (Eds.), *Aggression: Theoretical and empirical reviews*, Vol. 1, (pp. 41–74). New York: Academic Press.

Ferguson, T.J., & Stegge, H. (1998). Measuring guilt in children: A rose by any other name still has thorns. In J. Bybee (Ed.), *Guilt and children* (pp. 19–74). San Diego, CA: Academic Press.

Ferguson, T.J., & Stegge, H., Miller, E.R., & Olsen, M.E. (1999). Guilt, shame, and symptoms in children. *Developmental Psychology, 35*, 347–357.

Flanagan, O. (1984). *The science of the mind.* Cambridge MA: MIT/Bradford Press.

Frankena, W.K. (1962). The concept of social justice. In L.R.B. Brand (Ed.), *Social justice* (pp. 1–29). Englewood Cliffs, NY: Prentice Hall.

Frijda, N. (1986). *The emotions.* Cambridge: Cambridge University Press.

Gilligan, C. (1977). In a different voice: Women's conceptions of self and morality. *Harvard Educational Review, 47*, 481–517.

Graham, S., Hudley, C., & Williams, E. (1992). Attributional and emotional determinants of aggression among AfricanAmerican and Latino young adolescents. *Developmental Psychology, 28*, 731–740.

Haidt, J., Koller, S.H., & Dias, M.G. (1993). Affect, culture, and morality, or is it wrong to eat your dog? *Journal of Personality and Social Psychology, 65*, 613–628.

Hampson, N.H. (1974). *The life and opinions of Maximilien Robespierre.* London: Duckworth.

Malatesta, C.Z., & Wilson, A. (1988). Emotion cognition interaction in personality development: A discrete emotions, functionalist analysis. *British Journal of Social Psychology, 27*, 91–112.

Mönks, F.J. (1996). Van moreel oordeel naar morele daad [From moral judgement to moral action]. In G. Hutschemaekers & M. de Winter (Eds.), *De veranderlijke moraal [Variable morality]* (pp. 49–62). Nijmegen, The Netherlands: SUN.

Olthof, T. (1990). *Blame, anger and aggression in children: A social-cognitive approach.* (Dissertation Catholic University Nijmegen.) Groningen: Stichting Kinderstudies.

Olthof, T. (1994). Morele emoties en de morele ontwikkeling van jonge kinderen. [Moral emotions and the moral development of young children]. In T. Olthof & D. Brugman (Eds.), *Het ontstaan van moreel besef [The origins of moral awareness]*, (pp. 67–97). Lisse, The Netherlands: Swets & Zeitlinger.

Olthof, T. & Brugman, D. (1994). Moraliteit in ontwikkeling: Een inleiding [Morality in development: An introduction]. In T. Olthof & D. Brugman (Eds.), *Het ontstaan van moreel besef [The origins of moral awareness]*, (pp. 9–38). Lisse, The Netherlands: Swets & Zeitlinger.

Olthof, T., Ferguson, T.J., & Luiten, A. (1989). Personal responsibility antecedents of anger and blame reactions in children. *Child Development, 60*, 1328–1336.

Rest, J.R. (1983). Morality. In J.H. Flavell & E. Markman (Eds.), *Manual of child psychology: Vol. 3. Cognitive development* (pp. 555–629). New York: Wiley.

Rudé, G. (1976). *Robespierre: Portrait of a revolutionary democrat.* New York: The Viking Press.

Schama, S. (1989). *Citizens: A chronicle of the French Revolution.* New York: Knopf.

Tangney, J.P. (1990). Assessing individual differences in proneness to shame and guilt: Development of the Self-Conscious Affect and Attribution Inventory. *Journal of Personality and Social Psychology, 59*, 102–111.

Tangney, J.P. (1991). Moral affect: The good, the bad, and the ugly. *Journal of Personality and Social Psychology, 61*, 598–607.

Tangney, J.P., Burggraf, S.A., & Wagner, P.E. (1995). Shame-proneness, guilt-proneness, and psychological symptoms. In J.P. Tangney & K.W. Fisher (Eds.), *Self-conscious emotions. The psychology of shame, guilt, embarrassment, and pride* (pp. 343–367). New York: Guilford Press.

Van het Reve, K. (1987). *De ongelooflijke slechtheid van het Opperwezen* [*The unbelievable badness of the Divine Being*]. Amsterdam: Van Oorschot.

CHAPTER SEVEN

Talent for development: Responding to contextual promises

Peter Heymans
Utrecht University, The Netherlands

INTRODUCTION

Outstanding achievements in a specific domain of action are a requirement before the label "talented" is attached to an individual. The excellence of an individual's performance is inferred from a comparison with (a) other individuals considered comparable, or (b) a normative developmental timetable plausible to the judges. Thus, one speaks of a young individual with a "talent for mathematics", "a talent for cooking", or a "talent for music". In one sense the qualification of being talented refers to the past: outstanding performances that became known to a judging audience. In another sense being called "talented" also refers to the future: one may legitimately expect that the talented individual will show more and/or higher-level achievements, assuming a not too unfavourable environment. Calling someone talented is treating such an individual as if he or she had entered a contract to deliver outstanding achievements (in mathematics, cooking, or music) which surpass the previous ones, and which are also due in the near future. As in any contract, commitments are established between at least two parties by sets of conditional promises. But who are the parties with whom the talented individual has to deal? One party is certainly the individual's social environment, which is assumed to be "conducive to or fitting for talent development". In the "talent-contract" the social environment is supposed to promise and provide developmental opportunities, and the individual is supposed to fulfil these promises.

Although talents are usually specified according to a domain of action, they all imply future patterned changes for the better of a type called "development". As there are so many types of talent—all implying development of the individual—it is not unreasonable to assume a *talent for development*. This manifests itself in the way an individual responds to developmental promises offered by the social environment. This chapter explores the theoretical and empirical plausibility of the construct *talent for development* and I will proceed in the following way: first, the construct talent for development is anchored in the context of a developmental theory: Incantation Theory (Heymans, 1994) which allows a role for the individual in shaping his or her own development. According to this theory, development is produced out of observable behavioural changes on the basis of a specific consensus between social context and individual, called "incantation". This incantation procedure feeds on transformational symbols embedded in symbolic structures. Talent for development will be elaborated as the sensitivity of an individual to symbolic structures, which contain transformational symbols.

Second, it will be argued that situations of individual adversity are a good place to look for the surfacing of this talent for development. Many developmental theories state that confrontations with some (mild) form of adversity give rise to situations that are conducive to development. Third, a longitudinal case study of an 11-year old boy is presented, and his talent to detect and take advantage of developmental promises in situations of adversity is empirically demonstrated.

Before continuing, some methodological positions need to be mentioned. Position 1 concerns the use of intensive longitudinal follow-up studies of single or coupled individuals. In the search for developmental processes and their intra-individual interrelations a longitudinal case is considered an invaluable data source. Position 2 consists of the choice of idiographic descriptions of what is going on during an individual's trajectory through specific contexts in order to heighten ecological validity. In conjunction with position 1, attention is focused on the *unique* socialisation environment, which according to a multitude of behaviour-genetic studies is highly important in explaining inter-individual differences in developmental outcomes (Plomin & Daniels, 1987; Scarr, 1997). Position 3 is a focus on what is *common* to developing individuals instead of primarily focusing on inter-individual differences. The "fact" that all people "develop" needs explanation. All things that individuals in a sample have in common (characteristics, experiences, age-graded developmental tasks, and so on) can never be detected to influence developmental progress or outcome on the basis of the usual correlation/regression methodology, which takes individuals as replications to estimate covariances. Socialisation studies on the basis of present-day behaviour-genetic model building cannot find elements, which are commonly implied, in developmental progress. The three positions mentioned together lead to so-called "idiothetic" (Thomae, 1966) studies, in which nomothetic laws are explored on the basis of idiographic descriptions of single lives. Position 4 concerns an extension of the set of factors allowed to explain development. Most developmental theories rest on interpretations in retrospect of sequences of (observed) ordered changes. This fits in with the deterministic causal explanations that make up the "developmental mechanism". In general, explanatory factors are events, which happened before the to-be-explained development. Exceptions are explanatory efforts using non-linear dynamics (van Geert, 1994). However, the resulting patterns of changes will still have to be interpreted by a researcher as "development".

Outside mainstream empirical developmental psychology, philosophers studying human actions have no difficulty in allowing *mental causation* into causally explanatory systems (Heil & Mele, 1995), even when the content of the mind (e.g. a belief or a want) refers to a future state, located in time *after* the explanandum. Efforts are being made to formulate the minimal requirements for an intentional system to work in compatibility with the laws of physics (Kugler, Shaw, Vincente, & Kinsella-Shaw, 1990). Allowing for the possible acceptance of mental causation in explaining human development makes it relevant to look for existing evidence that mental factors (mainly of an intentional nature) influence development. Given that such evidence exists, e.g. from anecdotal observations showing how individuals influence their own development, the need arises for a coherent conceptualisation of the components of the developmental nexus. The idea of a "talent for development" predicates on such a conceptualisation.

To summarise: the question is: "How can individuals through their own creative initiatives contribute to the shaping of their own development?" In this chapter, a special, valued aptitude of a person will be explored: talent for development. Talent for development denotes an aptitude for taking a prospective attitude towards one's own development as expressed in a sensitivity to detect promises of development in the momentary context of one's life and in the capacity to make these promises come true.

The talent-related issue of possible differences between individuals in this creative aptitude or talent-for development will not be treated in this chapter. The exploration of talent for development begins with a description of the characteristics of the contextual arrangements that produce development. Such a contextual arrangement is called the developmental nexus. The talent contract shapes the developmental nexus in a special way.

THE DEVELOPMENTAL NEXUS AND ITS DEPENDENCE ON SYMBOLIC STRUCTURES

Culture-provided symbolic structures are important ingredients in transforming a behaviourally changing individual into a developing person. The contextual arrangement, which allows a developmental transformation, will be described, and the role of symbolic structures herein will be highlighted.

THE DEVELOPMENTAL NEXUS

Development is created when symbolic order is imposed on patterns of co-occurring behavioural changes. This symbolic order is borrowed by the observers from culture-provided frames of interpretations, and re-created by the individual person when accepting observers' interpretation of his or her behavioural changes. Symbolic constructions suitable for the creation of "development" always contain a "time-arrow" and a value-related intentional structure. Development is development for the better. More formally, this can be stated as follows: Development is the by-product resulting from a mapping of observable changes in the past of the individual's life onto a symbolic structure which contains a time-arrow related distribution of a valuation of states. A simple example of such a symbolic structure is the ladder-like ordering of stages in many theories of socio-cognitive development.

The developmental nexus is the situation in which a developmental transformation is going to take place. Participants are a to-be-transformed child (adolescent or adult), an individual (parent/educator) acting as transformator, and individuals acting as an audience. Moreover, at least one symbolic structure and a transformational symbol, valid within that structure, play a role. The dramaturgical scene consists of the six components shown next, together forming the developmental nexus. These components are conceptually distinct, but empirically correlated elements, which are woven into a pattern in real time. Components of the developmental nexus according to Incantation Theory (Heymans, 1994) are:

Component 1. Educator and child are sharing a conceptual/symbolic frame. The educator elaborates parts of this frame, and persuades the child about his/her position according to this frame of reference. Initially the focus is on the child's present position against the background of recent changes, but gradually indications of the child's next position and of the way to get there are given.

Component 2. The child shows signs of acceptance of the alleged power of the educator to transform him/her. This can be shown by many signs, e.g.

submission, deference, willingness to obey prescriptions from the educator, willingness to wait, giving payments, publicly accepting the definition the educator gives of the child's position in the conceptual frame. Other adults acting on behalf of the child can also give these signs.

Component 3. The induction of emotional arousal in the child. This arousal is a state of tension, which should *not* be so intense as to orient the child's attention to him/herself. The educator's definition of the child's present and next position is usually a good place to start arousal induction; it is continued while component 4 is being executed.

Component 4. Choice and execution of transformation ritual. The ritual fits the conceptual frame assumed to be valid (component 1). The ritual always contains one or more transformational symbols. The educator maps the child's present and future position and the associated emotions onto states of this transformational symbol. The symbol is transformed and, through the mapping of subject-states attached to it, the child's identity travels temporarily parallel with the publicly visible changes in the symbol being transformed by the educator.

Component 5. The child imagines his/her present and future position in terms of the conceptual frame assumed to be valid, and—while the transformational symbol is being changed—envisions him/herself as (a) never being the same again as before the ritual started, and (b) as changing along a line isomorphic to the change in the transformational symbol.

Component 6. The public "surrounding" the ritual treats the child—after the ritual is over—"as-if transformed", as having acquired a new identity as a more "developed" individual, i.e. as having extended his or her competence(s). This is shown by allowing the child to enter new areas of action in which the child from now on is held fully accountable for his or her new actions.

Arranging a situation according to this developmental script is to arrange for a developmental *incantation* (Heymans, 1994). Ritual performances with transformational power can be found in the family (e.g. around birthday celebrations, giving of material items to the child such as new clothing/shoes, or specific gear, e.g. sports wear, bicycle, musical instrument, computer, money for driving licence), as well as in school (certain educational sessions), and in the peer group (assignment of specific roles and associated material symbols).

A talent contract shapes the components of the developmental nexus in a special way. The conceptual frame work (c1) consists (besides a developmental "narrative") of a kind of "giftedness" narrative such as the one critically analysed by Howe, Davidson, and Sloboda (1998). The empirical truth of such a narrative does not matter. What matters is the cosmology implied by this narrative, and the possible life courses for a gifted individual. Component 2 can take the form of the child showing a preference for being in the presence of experts in his or her talent area, taking their advice and modelling their actions. Excitement and feeling your identity challenged are aspects of component 3. The rituals (component 4) tend to be the public performances of tasks that are presumed to be mastered only by grown-ups or experts, frequently involving the use of special gear (logic, calculus, ingredients, instruments). The child's mental imagery (component 5) can consist in mappings of his or her own lifeline onto the life course of famous models. The operationalisation of component 6 is not only an applauding audience, but also the pride of the parents and the trust shown when the child exercises his or her new competencies. On the part of the child, flow-experiences in a newly opened up area of action signal that he or she has mastered new skills. Shame and guilt over actions in the new area are indicative of a changed identity, incorporating the new area.

The description of what—according to incantation theory—is going on in the developmental nexus may give the impression of a rather passive child undergoing a certain ritual. Note, however, that the child has to be *mentally* very active in (a) adopting and following the elaborations given of the conceptual/symbolic frame imposed on the situation (component 1), in (b) paying attention to the changes in the transformational symbol (component 4), in (c) mentally imagining a range of time-ordered positions of his or her identity within the conceptual frame given (component 5), and in (d) executing the newly acquired identity as "a more-grown-up" by behaviourally entering areas of action that are opened to him/her on the basis of the newly acquired identity, knowing that he or she is now held fully responsible for his/her actions. Moreover, the child has to be *sensitive* to symbolic frames and their associated transformational symbols that fit his or her present situation. And the child may be *active in drawing attention* of people in the environment to his or her "fitness for becoming transformed", by pointing to his or her behavioural changes in combination with suitable conceptual/symbolic frames.

The individual's sensitivity and attentiveness to symbolic structures with a transformational potential, together with an aptness in having his or her momentary situation being mapped upon such symbolic structures by important others, are the basic ingredients for what can be called "talent for development". In an analogous way the adult can be more or less apt in taking and performing the role of transformator according to the developmental script.

Adversities as catalysts for development

Development is conceptually associated with improvement. Nevertheless, many developmental theories assume that subjectively undesirable experiences or situations are at the root of developmental progress. This concurs with the position of incantation theory that moderate negative arousal is implied in a developmental transformation (component 3 of the developmental script). Many developmental theorists have located the motor of development in efforts to overcome some undesirable state of mind.

In Erikson's life-span theory the individual has to face (and possibly avoid) a looming crisis before attaining a new level. Piaget introduced the idea that the child has to solve a cognitive conflict that threatens to shatter his or her existing cognitive structure. Kohlberg specified this predicament in his theory on the development of moral judgement as a moral-cognitive conflict. Selman, in his theory on the development of role-taking and the concept of friendship, by analogy postulated a socio-cognitive conflict. In the tradition of learning theory Siegler postulated in his theory of cognitive development that the source of development is the accumulation of negative feedback. Even in apparently child-friendly theory, such as the Bowlby–Ainsworth attachment theory, the formation of the "internal working models" arises out of a struggle for meaning, most clearly in the non-secure attached children. In discussing principles of intervention in early childhood Futterweit and Ruff (1993) state that "development requires periods of instability and adaptive reorganisation" (p. 158) and " it may even sometimes be appropriate to cause some instability or disequilibrium to drive the system to a higher level of organisation" (p. 159).

Recently Baltes (1997) gave a meta-theoretical analysis of development over the life span. The hallmark of all development is—according to Baltes—the production of goal-directed, new adaptational capacity by selective optimisation of resources with a compensation for losses that have occurred. Here the emphasis is also on adversities, i.e. situations of loss, as a trigger for development.

Stronger and/or more enduring situations of adversity make people suffer. Intense suffering may preclude participation in developmental transformations, but when suffering has subsided reflections upon one's ordeal may be brought into a developmental ritual, e.g. in discussion-groups of fellow patients. Frank (1993) has categorised the illness narratives of seriously suffering adults who attribute their developmental progress to their suffering. These rhetorics of self-change function as transformational symbols in the sense of incantation theory. In any case, development can occur under seemingly adverse medical conditions. Chronic illness in adolescents, although initially causing a developmental delay, does not prevent the completion of developmental tasks at the same level as healthy adolescents after three years (Roth & Seiffge-Krenke, 1996). Childhood illness may have a beneficial effect on the child's later development (Parmelee, 1986).

In sum: (a) the developmental process may be painful, but the resulting state reduces the discomfort or suffering; (b) situations in which an individual faces adversities are especially suited to the study of the developmental mechanism, as these are the situations in which parts of this mechanism may come close to the observable surface.

YOUNG MARC MAKING A DEVELOPMENTAL OPPORTUNITY COME TRUE

A case study will now be presented in which an 11-year-old boy manages to overcome his childhood fears and his depressive state by aptly using a transformational narrative offered to him by an adult helper in a situation that was puzzling and anxiety provoking. First, the family situation is described, then the data collection and the analysis procedure. The focus of the analysis will be on the effects of a phone conversation between the boy and the adult helper.

Marc's lifeworld

A two-person family consisting of a mother and her son was followed for more than a year. Three persons play a prominent role in the episode to be focused on: mother Mirthe, 11-year-old Marc, and a self-styled therapist or helper, Gee. All names are pseudonyms. The reason for following this family was the unusual percepts reported by son Marc: he regularly sees "dark men" coming to his room and bed, hears voices while there is no one physically speaking, and has other paranormal experiences. This has been going on for some years. Marc shares his percepts with his mother Mirthe, who has a longstanding interest in psychic experiences and attaches much significance to the paranormal experiences of her son, as she is convinced that they are coming from entities out of another world. As validation of her son's report, she states to have seen herself parts (claw-like hands) of the dark men sneaking into her son's room. Mirthe has had a difficult life, and has always seen negative experiences as opportunities for learning and development.

At elementary school Marc is mediocre; often he pays no attention to the teacher or the topic as he is having special visions of non-terrestrial beings and phenomena. Marc is quite frequently involved in fights with other children. Mother and son are concerned about the anxiety caused by the visits of the dark men. Marc regularly consults the female self-styled helper/therapist Gee, sometimes in the company of a group of children with similar experiences. Gee works on the basis of a framework in which experiences as reported by Marc are signs that entities from the Empire of Evil are trying to make Marc dependent on them; Gee teaches children how to defend themselves and how to control these evil forces (see Puyn, 1993). Mother Mirthe explicitly rejected any kind of (psychiatric) "medicalisation" of Marc's plight. She was convinced that Marc's percepts foreshadowed—if properly treated—a bright future for her son.

Data collection

Mirthe and Marc consented to a data collection procedure in which they kept track of their emotions daily (132 emotions for Mirthe, 32 emotions for Marc) and major events of the day (including, of course, the appearance of dark men or other paranormal events or experiences). Moreover, there were extensive interviews (tape-recorded and transcribed), and structured self-judgements in several contexts. The participants' consent was regularly updated, as they got more experiential knowledge of what it meant to participate in the study. It was regularly stressed that each participant could stop her or his participation without giving any reason: the investigator would exert no pressure at all. Finally the data collection lasted for about one year. The analyses that follow for Marc are based on the first 123 days.

A significant part of the lifeworld of Marc (11 years old) consists—in the episode where he informs us about his life—of his dealings with the world of paranormal entities. Marc goes to school with its associated hassle. From Marc's diary notes and from the interviews, which were conducted at about monthly intervals with him and his mother, a list of life events was generated. Events were defined from the point of view of the subject, but their occurrence was validated against a second data source (diary information was validated against the mother's report). Life events were categorised into three types: PARA-events, Liminal events, and Instructional events. The category PARA consists of 14 events relating to Marc's contact with a "paranormal world" of negative energies and entities which "try to drag Marc into their Realm of Darkness, and try to suck positive energy from Marc" [descriptive terms from interviews with Marc]. These PARA-events are conceptualised as stressful. In accordance with the literature on life events their effect is assumed to be cumulative, and the PARA-index is the unweighted sum of having experienced such an event since the beginning of data collection.

The second category of life events consists of two liminal experiences. On day 100 Marc is meditating in a session with his therapist Gee, and

> sees a bird falling from heaven in front of him and die; immediately thereafter a beautiful white horse is seen to fall in an abyss and die. Out of the horse comes a little devil, and people shrank away. In the background of this

scene there is Light; a figure—identified by Marc as "papa"—prevents Marc from going toward the Light. Marc fights and finally comes near the Light.

Gee tells Marc that this vision means "that you have now come into the Light". Marc interprets this as "my accidents will stop now" (Marc had experienced a series of minor strokes of bad luck, which he attributed to hindrances by evil spirits). On day 108 Marc experiences the confirmation of a prediction made by Gee on day 105, when Marc at home "sees" his "guiding spirit" for the first time. This spirit looks like a young man and announces that he will stay with Marc for the coming 10 years. Only the liminal experience on day 108 will be coded as such in the analysis (LIM108); the event on day 100 was considered much more loaded by instructional content given by Gee and is coded as a category-3 event [Gee100]; see later. The third category consists of instructional events in which an experience is given meaning by putting it into a specific conceptual frame. There are five such events; in the analysis each of them is coded as a dichotomous variable and its impact is assessed separately. Event 1 concerns Marc giving explanations to his cousin of nearly his age who complained about similar experiences with "dark men"; this event took place on day 66 during this cousin's overnight stay with the family [NEPHEW66]. On day 79 Marc visited and played at a horse-riding stable (manege) where an instructor explained how animals are perceptive to indicators of (spiritual) "dark and light" [Manege79]. On day 90 in the same stable Marc participated in an "Indian ceremony" where he saw signs of "dark and light" above each participating individual, was told what their meaning was, and "saw" some of these signs being changed or removed [INDIAN90]. On day 100 Marc received the interpretation of the events on that day from Gee [GEE100], as described under category 2. On day 105 our focus event took place. On day 105 Marc was given by telephone—upon his request—an interpretation from Gee for two puzzling happenings in the previous days. On day 104 Marc was alone in his room, when the radio started to make strange noises and the lights began to flicker; Marc perceived that the light-switch was physically being moved to the "off"-position, and the lights went off. Besides Marc, no one was visible in the room. Marc became very anxious. When he reported this to his mother, Mirthe told Marc that in the night from day 102 → 103 she had been woken up by a deep voice, just saying "HELLO". Gee, when asked by telephone for help on day 105, interpreted these events as announcements that both son Marc and mother Mirthe would receive a (new) Guiding Spirit; for Marc this would be the first Guiding Spirit, for Mirthe it would be a replacement [GEE105]. This telephone call to the family helper Gee was made by Marc in a situation where Mirthe and Marc were very anxious about the accumulation of strange events in the past days.

Exploration of the impact of Marc's life events upon the activation of his emotional concerns.

The general strategy is as follows. First dependent variables will be constructed out of the 32 time series of Marc's emotions. It will be shown that these variables can be interpreted as the degree to which—on a certain day—Marc's concerns are activated.

These concern activations serve as the "dependent variables" in a "natural experiment" where the occurrence and/or intensity of certain types of life events are the "independent variables". The following analysis explores what—if any—impact several types of life events have on Marc's concern activations. Technically, an interrupted time series will be analysed with arima-modelling of (a) the internal dependencies in the time series, followed by (b) an estimate of the size of the interruption associated with a life event, after having corrected for internal dependencies in the time series.

Identification of Marc's emotional concerns. Feeling emotions is—according to the emotion theory of Frijda (1986)—the result of an awareness of a change in action tendency. This changed action tendency arises when perceived events activate one or more concerns of an individual, besides the already existing concern to reach a specific goal. Humans share a lot of concerns (e.g. for safety), but may also have specific concerns. Emotions are warning signals, which tell the individual that something important is happening. For the present discussion it is relevant that concerns are a characteristic of the individual person; moreover, the type and degree of concern activation can tell us something about events-as-perceived or their meaning.

The data set includes the intensities of each day's emotions, recorded in the evening. The variation in emotion intensities over time is indicative of differential degrees of concern activation due to the flow of events in which the individual participates. A group of emotions with a similar profile of intensities over time is assumed to refer to a common underlying concern which is activated by the stream of events to varying degrees. So, clustering the emotions on the basis of their varying intensities over time is a way to identify the concerns of an individual. Hierarchical cluster analysis (method Ward) revealed seven clusters or concerns for Marc; their content summary is in the first column of Table 7.1. Note that each concern is indicated by a different number of emotions.

The impact of life events on Marc's concern activations. In the first step of the analysis all internal dynamics in the time series of concern activation is removed by estimating a suitable arima model (the type of model is

TABLE 7.1
Results of intervention analyses

Dependent variable	Results from intervention analysis
Emotional concern son Marc (11 years old)	Predictors: PARA, five instructional experiences, liminal experience on day 108. (Always in that order tested for effect)
S1: feeling safe, open [model: arima(1,0,0)] 6 emotions	PARA-effect: $b = +0.18$ ($p = .00$) Instructional Experiences: –Cousin66 effect: $b = -0.49$ ($p = .10$) Liminal experience: no effect
S2: tense, under strain [model arima(1,1,0)] 3 emotions	PARA-effect: $b = -1.19$ ($p = .08$) Instructional experiences: no effects Liminal experience: no effect
S3: angry [model: arima (0,0,0)] 1 emotion	PARA-effect: no effect Instructional experiences: no effect Liminal experience: no effect
S4: anxious [model: arima(0,1,1)] 7 emotions	PARA-effect: $b = +0.56$ ($p = .01$) Instructional experiences: –GEE105 effect: $b = -2.86$ ($p = .01$) Liminal experience: no effect
S5: over-assertive [model: arima(0,0,0)] 11 emotions	PARA-effect: no effect Instructional experiences: –Gee100 effect: $b = +1.48$ ($p = .00$) –Gee105 effect: $b = -1.33$ ($p = .00$) Liminal experience: no effect
S6: tired & satisfied [model: arima(0,1,1)] 2 emotions	PARA-effect: $b = -0.50$ ($p = .01$) Instructional experiences: –Cousin66 effect: $b = +1.96$ ($p = .00$) –Manege79 effect: $b = +1.63$ ($p = .00$) Liminal experience: no effect
S7: sad, sorrowful [model: arima(1,1,0)] 2 emotions	PARA-effect: $b = +1.69$ ($p = .11$) Instructional experiences: –GEE105 effect: $b = -6.65$ ($p = .03$) Liminal experience: no effect

Overview of the results of intervention analyses of several time series of concern activation interrupted by several life events on the activation of Marc's emotional concerns. Time series length is 123 days. Effects on the activation of Marc's emotional concerns are shown. Effect sizes are reported as unstandardised regression coefficients b; two-sided statistical tests. Positive values of b indicate that the event increases the activation of that concern; negative values of b indicate a decrease.

PARA = the cumulative number of Marc's past contacts with the paranormal world.

indicated in Table 7.1, column 1); in the second step the life events are used as predictors (in a regression-like way) to explain dynamism-free variance in arima-whitened deviation-from-the-model scores. Always the life event groups were entered in the order as presented: paranormal contacts (PARA) first, then the group of five instructional events ordered according to real time, and finally the liminal experience at day 108 (Marc meeting his guiding spirit). The results are summarised in Table 7.1, column 2.

Some effects of contacts with the paranormal world are statistically significant but somewhat paradoxical: on the one hand Marc feels more safe, open (S1) and less tense (S2), while on the other hand more anxious (S4), less content (S6) [= tired & satisfied] and substantially sadder (S7) due to his PARA experiences. The liminal experience at day 108 (Marc meeting his Guiding Spirit) has no impact at all. The effect of Gee's intervention on day 105 is remarkable: it reduces anxiety (S4) and sadness (S7) considerably, even though the phone call took merely five minutes! Also Marc's over-assertiveness, which is especially activated in the school environment and associated with trouble with peers, is reduced.

It is worthwhile to have a closer look at GEE105 in terms of incantation theory. Marc, Mirthe, and Gee had already been communicating about the spirit world and its relation to everyday life for a longer period of time. So they shared a common conceptual framework (component 1) to a large degree. Marc and Mirthe were also showing due reverence to Gee as having more expertise in spirit matters; Marc, in anguish about a possible spirit attack on day 104, called Gee for advice about what to do (component 2). There certainly was a great deal of arousal in Mirthe and Marc because of the events on days 103–104 (component 3). Instead of a behavioural prescription, Gee provided Marc with an interpretation of the situation which has the qualities of a transformational symbol (component 4): Gee stated that Mirthe and Marc were participating in a ritual through which Marc would receive the attention of a Guiding Spirit, and Mirthe's (maybe tired) guiding spirit would be replaced by a fresh one. Switching off the lights in Marc's room on day 104 was a way of drawing Marc's attention to the things to come! The transformational narrative offered by Gee to Marc gives him the opportunity to make sense of a cumulative number of strange experiences. Moreover, this narrative can be shared with an important audience for Marc: mother Mirthe. Most importantly, this narrative has implications for Marc's future: (1) you will not be alone in your struggle: a guiding spirit will be with you for at least 10 years; (2) you are apparently accepted by higher powers as being worthy of protection: "you have definitely come into the Light"; (3) you have got on a more equal footing with adults, as you have now a guiding spirit just as your mother has and has had.

Components 5 and 6 of the incantation script concern the faith of Marc that his transformation will become true. Marc's reporting on day 108 that he saw a white-clothed entity that identified himself as his guiding spirit, testifies to Marc's continuation of the narrative offered to him by Gee. This report also testifies to Marc's faith that the events are unfolding as the narrative prescribes (component 5). Mother Mirthe reports that she believes Marc has suddenly been acting more grown-up, and that she feels more trust in Marc's future (component 6).

From the interview material one can learn that there were ample discussions between Mirthe and Marc regarding the implications of Gee's (day 105) interpretation. Among other things, Marc asked his mother whether the message could be correct as she had never told Marc about her having a guiding spirit: so how could it be replaced? But Mirthe asserted that in earlier years she had felt the presence of her guiding spirit, but not for the last year or so. So Mirthe and Marc jointly concluded that the message delivered through Gee was indeed intended for them. On day 108 Marc reports to Mirthe that he has met his Guiding Spirit. Mirthe and Marc are both relieved: their situation has changed, they see the world with new eyes (components 5 & 6) and act accordingly.

In terms of the proposed construct "talent for development", Marc is the one who on day 105 shows this talent through his sensitivity to the transformational implications of Gee's message. He is able to grab the developmental promise implied in the message: you will no longer be a dependent child! Moreover, having a guiding spirit just like your mother puts you on a more equal footing with adults! (Of course, Gee's message comes from a clever mind.) After this turbulent episode Marc acts more grown-up. In his own terms, he has overcome the Forces of Darkness which wanted to take his soul, and he knows he is accepted in the kingdom of Light, of which the arrival of his white-clothed guiding spirit is clear and final evidence. Pubertal changes can be heard in Marc's voice and his face shows some pubertal hair growth. The solution to a lot of problems (as described earlier) coincides with Marc's transformation from child to adolescent.

CONCLUDING OBSERVATIONS

Marc was able to perceive the promissory character of a short-lived social environmental constellation, and was able to forge a "contract" with the environment out of these promises. Such a contract implies mutual obligations: If I perform certain actions, and change myself, then the other (environmental) party has to treat me "as changed" and to allow me to display a specific new competency. The social environmental element that mediates this promise-perception and this contract-making is the transformational symbol embedded in the associated worldview. In the case of Marc the transformational symbol was the announcement of a "coming Guiding Spirit". Marc was talented enough to map parts of his life up till now and his near future onto this "coming of his Guiding Spirit", and immediately his depressive anxiety was reduced, his Self was changing into a worthwhile person who had "come into the Light", and he became confident of mastering the episode of becoming an adult.

Talent for development is sensitivity to promissory structures in the environment, coupled with a tendency for behavioural engagement, which turns the environmental promise into a contract for Self-redefinition. The promissory structure is extracted by the individual from the discovery of a ritual-embedded transformational symbol against the background of an intentional structure carried by others. The content of this promise refers to a changed self with new, better competencies. Co-individuals participating in the ritual (parent, sibs, peers, models) "seduce" or "encourage" the target individual to dare to make the leap of conceptually mapping his or her present and near-future Self onto the transformational symbol *and showing some behavioural manifestation* of the new Self. After the ritual the child is oriented towards new behavioural domains and makes efforts to execute the newly obtained competency of the Self; doing this the child learns new skills. Then after some time the child–environment system may enter a new transformational episode. In fact this describes a cycle that is superimposed on the usual day-to-day stream of events and behaviours. This sequence of cycles is responsible for long-term development over the life span.

Where does the individual's sensitivity to intentional structures come from? I am tempted to assume that humans are born prewired in this respect. Research has shown that at the age of 12 months, infants already seem capable of attributing some form of goal-directedness or intentionality even to abstract stimuli (Karmiloff-Smith, 1997). Meltzoff (1995) showed that 18-month-olds could infer an adult's intended act by watching failed attempts. Research into the acquisition of a "folk psychology" or "theory of mind" has shown that in their pre-school years, most young children already begin to conceive of others' behaviours as originating from mental/intentional states of mind. Although there seems to be a global, universal core, there certainly are cultural variations in the theories of mind adopted.

Talent for development is only to a limited degree a characteristic of an individual: its manifestation can only be seen in the developmental nexus. This implies that there must be a social environment that is symbolically structured such as to offer a developmental promise. Talent for development is assumed to be present in all healthy humans. However, the talent for development might become blunted because of disuse: growing up in an environment poor in promissory structures leads to blunting of the talent for development.

REFERENCES

Baltes, P. (1997). On the incomplete architecture of human ontogeny. *American Psychologist, 52*, 366–380.
Frank, A. (1993). The rhetoric of self-change: Illness experience as narrative. *The Sociological Quarterly, 34*, 39–52.
Frijda, N. (1986). *The emotions.* Cambridge: Cambridge University Press.
Futterweit, L., & Ruff, H. (1993). Principles of development: Implications for early intervention. *Journal of Applied Developmental Psychology, 14*, 153–173.
Heil, J., & Mele, A. (1993). *Mental causation.* Oxford: Clarendon Press.
Heymans, P. (1994). Developmental tasks: A cultural analysis of human development. In J. ter Laak, A. Podolski, & P. Heymans (Eds.), *Developmental tasks: Towards a cultural analysis of human development.* Dordrecht: Kluwer Academic Publishers.
Howe, M., Davidson, J., & Sloboda, J. (1998). Innate talents: Reality or myth? *Behavioral and Brain Sciences, 21*, 399–442.
Karmiloff-Smith, A. (1997). Promisory notes, genetic clocks and epigenetic outcomes. *Behavioral and Brain Sciences, 20*, 355–360.
Kugler, P., Shaw, R., Vincente, K., & Kinsella-Shaw, J. (1990). Inquiry into intentional systems I: Issues in ecological physics. *Psychological Research, 52*, 98–121.
Meltzoff, A. (1995). Understanding the intentions of others: Re-enactment of intended acts by 18-month-old children. *Developmental Psychology, 31*, 838–850.
Parmelee, I. (1986). Children's illnesses: Their beneficial effects on behavioral development. *Child Development, 57*, 1–10.
Plomin, R., & Daniels, D. (1987). Why are children in the same family so different from each other? *Behavioral and Brain Sciences, 10*, 1–16.
Puyn, R. (1993). *Kinderen van de Duisternis: krankzinnig of bezeten?* [Children of Darkness: Mad or possessed?]. Naarden: Paravisie.
Roth, M., & Seiffge-Krenke, I. (1996). Die Realisierung von Entwicklungsaufgaben: gelingt es chronisch kranken Jugendlichen ihre Defizite aufzuholen? *Zeitschrift für Entwicklungspsychologie und Pedagogische Psychologie, 28*, 108–125.
Scarr, S. (1997). Behavior-genetic and socialization theories of intelligence: Truce and reconciliation. In R. Sternberg & E. Grigorenko (Eds.), *Intelligence, heredity and environment* (pp. 3–41). Cambridge, Cambridge University Press.
Thomae, H. (1966). *Das Individuum und seine Welt* [The individual and his world] . Göttingen: Hogrefe Verlag für Psychologie.
van Geert, P. (1994). *Dynamic systems of development: Change between complexity and chaos.* New York: Harvester Wheatsheaf.

CHAPTER EIGHT

Successful achievement in mathematics: China and the United States

Harold W. Stevenson, Shinying Lee,* and *Xiaotong Mu
University of Michigan, USA

INTRODUCTION

Our research group at the University of Michigan in collaboration with colleagues in other universities and research centres has been conducting a series of comparative studies of students' academic achievement since the early 1980s. In the course of conducting this research we have compared elementary and secondary students of East Asia with their counterparts in the United States. We have been especially interested in these comparisons because, in a barrage of cross-cultural studies, East Asian students have consistently outperformed students in the West in areas such as mathematics and science. For example, in the recent reports of the Third International Mathematics and Science Study of eighth-grade students, the top four of the 41 participating countries in mathematics and three of the top four countries in science were from East Asia (Peak, 1996).

Most of our research efforts have been spent in trying to understand why these remarkable differences should exist. By now, we have a reasonably clear picture of many of the ways in which the beliefs, attitudes, and everyday practices both in and out of school support the generally high academic achievement of East Asian students, but relatively few reports have been published about the top performers within each country. Would it be the case, as some have proposed, that even though average students in the West are behind their counterparts in East Asia, the performance of more highly able students in East Asia and the West would be more comparable? Are the beliefs, attitudes, and practices of highly able students in East Asia similar to those of top performers in the West? Are differences between the top performers and average students similar in East Asia and the West, or is there little generality to the characteristics that distinguish these two groups of students in each country?

This chapter reports the results of some of our exploratory research that has been focused on these questions. The subjects were students attending some of the most elite high schools in China and the United States. For comparative purposes we also included students enrolled in regular high schools. We chose China rather than other East Asian countries for these comparisons because in several studies, Chinese students have been the highest performers among students from East Asian countries.

ACADEMIC ACHIEVEMENT IN CHINA

Because most readers are relatively unfamiliar with the history of academic achievement in China, we begin by presenting a brief overview of Chinese practices and philosophy as they have developed during the twentieth century.

China has a long history of stressing and valuing education. Traditionally, the content of education was mainly based on the philosophy of Confucius and was concerned almost exclusively with moral codes, social order, history, and literature. Embedded within the traditional Confucian philosophy is the belief that education is the path to advancement in social status, intellectual reputation, and material possessions, not only for oneself but also for one's family.

The belief has been weakened during recent years because, with the introduction of the new market economy, a family's material wealth may be less closely related to academic achievement than to other factors. Even so, Chinese parents still consider academic achievement to be the most important goal for their children and adolescents, and they value doing well in school over accomplishments in any other domain, including social skills, sports, personality, and psychological adjustment (*Renmin Ribao*, 1995).

Public education

Education had been the privilege of a very small group of individuals throughout China's history and only in the twentieth century has public education been available for ordinary Chinese citizens. This first occurred during the first decade of the twentieth century, when a national school system was formed under the influence of contemporary Western and

Japanese educators. Following this, education rapidly became a matter of national concern, and in 1925 the Nationalist government began the countrywide implementation of educational reforms formulated by American-trained scholars, including disciples of John Dewey, the American educator and philosopher. American and European influences continued to exert an influence on education in China until the founding of the People's Republic of China in 1949.

Immediately after 1949, education underwent widespread reform. Changes, patterned after the educational system of the Soviet Union, placed increased emphasis on mathematics and the natural sciences. Chinese educators translated high-school mathematics and science textbooks used in the Soviet Union and adapted them for use in the national high-school curriculum. Opportunities for education, primarily at the elementary school level, expanded greatly during the early years of the People's Republic. The expansion continued until the mid-1960s, when the educational system underwent massive disruption during the 10-year period of the Cultural Revolution. From the mid-1960s through the mid-1970s the educational system was in havoc, schools were closed, middle-school students were sent to the countryside, and factories were introduced in elementary schools to emphasise the importance of labour.

Following the recovery from the Cultural Revolution, China began its compulsory education programme in 1986 and mandated that children be in school for nine years, including six years of elementary school and three years of lower middle school (junior high school). Admission to the subsequent three years of senior high school was to depend on the score obtained on an entrance examination. The first goal was realised by the early 1990s, when over 98% of children from 7–11 years of age were enrolled in elementary schools (State Education Commission, 1996). The magnitude of this accomplishment is evident in the fact that the number of students entering school each year in China during that period was over 27,000,000.

The goal of universal middle-school attendance was not reached, but 91% of the graduates of elementary schools in China were enrolled in lower middle schools by 1995. The percentage of students attending lower middle schools is lower in rural than in urban areas, for educational facilities are more limited in rural areas and parents are less enthusiastic about education. However, within the metropolitan area of Beijing, the site for our research, 94% of eligible students were enrolled in lower middle schools in 1995 and 48.3% of the lower middle school graduates went on to upper middle school (senior high school) (State Education Commission, 1996). Among the academic upper middle school students, 41% eventually entered colleges and universities, and of those who graduated from universities, 6% entered postgraduate programmes (State Education Commission, 1996). These are remarkable percentages in view of the fact that within the whole country fewer than 10% of the persons of the eligible ages actually are able to attend a university.

In Chinese schools and universities, a high value is placed on mathematics, physics, and chemistry. As a result, these have become the most sought-after majors by China's university students. Chinese high schools have more teachers of mathematics and more of these teachers have post-high-school training than is the case for any other subject (State Education Commission, 1996).

High achievers

The Chinese are not reluctant to identify and nurture students who are capable of high levels of academic achievement. This was not always the case. During the early years of the People's Republic, as part of the socialist philosophy, individual differences in intellectual abilities and academic achievement were de-emphasised by educators and government officials. It was not until the 1970s, after the disruptive years of the Cultural Revolution ended, that serious attention was paid to the education of gifted and talented students.

Even though the national government currently has no nationwide policies or institutions that are concerned with the education of the gifted, numerous in-school and out-of-school programmes have been organised, such as Olympic Schools that concentrate on mathematics and science, special schools for students talented in athletics and the arts, Children's Palaces that offer a wide array of courses, and summer and winter camps that typically concentrate on topics such as science, foreign languages, and computers.

At present, many of China's most gifted and talented children and youths are found in what are called key schools. These schools were established to educate students who demonstrated superior academic performance and who, after graduation from high school, have a high likelihood of qualifying for admission to the country's most prestigious universities. However, budgetary constraints in the field of education have continually hampered efforts to expand the number of key schools, and the number fluctuates throughout the years. Despite these problems, the general quality of education in large metropolitan areas is high and teachers employ pedagogical techniques that appear to be very effective.

Schools similar to the key schools for high-achieving students are rare in the United States. Although such schools do exist, the major avenue for special treatment of exceptionally able students is through their electing to enrol in advanced placement classes, which are more demanding than the ordinary high-school classes. Advanced placement classes are often used as substitutes for college-level courses. Even if students do not receive college credit for the classes, it is sometimes possible for them to enrol in college-level courses during their last year of high school.

Academic achievement

It has been difficult to assess the level of academic achievement of students in China because the government has chosen not to participate in such studies as the Second International Mathematics Study of the early 1980s or the Third International Mathematics and Science Study of the mid-1990s. However, in the mid-1980s, the Chinese government began to pursue a policy of greater openness to other parts of the world. At that time, it became possible for students from Mainland China to be included in international comparative studies.

Among the studies is one our group conducted of elementary school children in Minneapolis and Beijing (Stevenson et al., 1990). Differences between the Chinese and American students were dramatic. Chinese elementary school children surpassed their American peers as early as the first grade. By the fifth grade, the *highest*-scoring of a representative sample of 40 Minneapolis classrooms obtained an average score only marginally above that of the *lowest*-scoring of 20 representative Beijing classrooms (Stevenson & Stigler, 1992). In another of our studies, high-school students in Beijing surpassed their peers in Canada, Germany, Hungary, and the United States (Chen, Lee, & Stevenson, 1996).

The question is often raised as to why so much attention has been paid to mathematics and science, rather than to reading and other academic subjects. The answer is that it is especially difficult to conduct well designed studies in these areas. Comparative studies of reading, for example, involve different languages, different grammars, and different writing systems. As a consequence, the requirements for learning to read a writing system involving logographs, such as Chinese characters, are very different from those required for learning to read a language represented by an alphabetic writing system. Nevertheless, in reading and comprehending words that have appeared in their textbooks, Chinese elementary school students received higher scores than did their American counterparts (Stevenson & Stigler, 1992).

It is hard to imagine how reliable, culturally appropriate, and comparable materials could be constructed for subjects such as social studies or history, where the content and goals of the curricula differ so greatly among countries. To our knowledge there have been no other comparative studies dealing with such subjects and involving students from mainland China.

HIGH ACHIEVERS IN CHINA AND THE UNITED STATES

In attempting to increase our understanding of the characteristics of high achievers, we posed a number of questions. How do the highly able students in the two countries regard themselves? To what do they attribute their success? Are they satisfied with their remarkable accomplishments? How do they spend their leisure time? What expectations do they hold for their future education? What are their attitudes about school in general and mathematics in particular? Do they give indications of paying a cost for their success by having higher levels of tension or greater frequencies of psychosomatic disturbances? If we are able to understand what characterises the self-evaluations, beliefs, and attitudes of these high-achieving students, we may gain a better understanding of how we might foster their development, and also improve the performance of all students.

Schools and Students

To obtain samples of students demonstrating high academic achievement, we selected schools that enrol some of the most academically successful students in each country: key schools in China and a special science and technology school in the United States. Both the Chinese key schools and the American high school for science and technology are elite schools, serving only students who have demonstrated exceptionally high academic ability. Admission to both types of schools is highly selective and many more students apply for admission each year than can actually be admitted.

Beijing. The Chinese students were 442 students enrolled in four key schools and 510 students enrolled in six regular high schools in Beijing. Beijing's role in China is much like that of the Fairfax–Washington, DC area in the United States, in that it is a political and intellectual centre for the whole country. The regular high schools were selected on the basis of the advice of Chinese colleagues as being representative of the range of Beijing high schools. Two classes were randomly selected in each of the schools and all students in these classes were included in the study.

Fairfax. The research in the United States was conducted in high schools in Fairfax County, Virginia, a suburban area outside of Washington, DC. Fairfax is not a typical American metropolitan area; it ranks first in median household income (approximately $70,000 per year) and sixth, in terms of those who hold a four-year college degree, of all counties in the United States. Five large high schools were selected by school officials to constitute a representative sample of Fairfax schools. All eleventh-grade students in attendance on the days the study was conducted were included in the study—a total of 1803 students, including 354 students from the magnet school.

Fairfax is not only considered to be among the premier school districts in the United States, it also supports the highly selective high school in science and technology. The school is a public high school, but students applying for admission must take an examination in science, mathematics, and language arts, complete application forms and essays, and participate in an interview. This school is termed a "magnet" school because it attracts highly qualified students from a broad geographic area. Annual admission of new students is limited to 400, chosen from over 2000 applicants. High-school graduates in the district have consistently received scores on college entrance tests far above the nation's average. For example, the average Scholastic Aptitude Test score in 1994 placed Fairfax seniors in the magnet school in the 97th percentile among seniors in the United States—an average reflecting remarkably high levels of ability.

The average number of years of education received by both Chinese and American parents was high; however, the average was higher for American parents than for their Chinese counterparts. Among the American fathers, the average number of years of education was 16.4 years versus 13.0 for the Chinese fathers. Among the American mothers, it was 15.3 years versus 11.8 for the Chinese mothers. In the Beijing key schools, 53% of the students were male, while in the Fairfax magnet school, 61% were male.

Mathematics achievement. We did not have results from a college entrance examination to help us to characterise the Chinese students, but we did give all of the students, both Chinese and American, a test of mathematics achievement. This test was developed on the basis of the analysis of mathematics textbooks used in the Chinese and American schools. Scores on this test proved to be highly reliable and closely related to the quantitative portion of the Scholastic Aptitude Test for the American students ($r = .87$).

The average score for the 442 Chinese students attending the key schools was 35.2; for the 354 students in the Fairfax magnet school the average score was 30.4. The average score for the regular high-school students in Beijing was 23.1; in Fairfax, 16.0. In view of the fact that the upper range of the test was quite difficult and that there were only 46 problems in the test, the average score of the students from the Chinese key schools is especially impressive. Although the scores for the Fairfax students were not as high, it seems likely, considering the educational status of the Fairfax students in the magnet school, that the average score for these Fairfax students is as high as any that would be found among public schools in the United States.

Characteristics of the elite students

We turn now to describing ways in which the students attending elite schools differed from those who were attending regular schools. The variables with which we were concerned were the following: attitudes about mathematics, the utility of effort, self-evaluations, satisfaction with their performance at school, use of time and expectations for the future, and their psychological adjustment.

Attitudes regarding school and mathematics. When comparisons were made between students in the key schools and in the regular high schools in Beijing it was found that students from the key schools were more likely to like mathematics, to think that mathematics was not hard, and to disagree that learning mathematics depends on memorisation.

Students in the Fairfax magnet school expressed attitudes similar to those of the Chinese students in several respects. Compared to the students in the regular high schools, they expressed more positive attitudes about mathematics, did not think mathematics was hard, and demonstrated a stronger tendency to believe that mathematics promotes logical thinking and to disagree that learning mathematics depends on memorisation (see Table 8.1).

Utility of effort. A number of recent studies (e.g. Hess & Azuma, 1991; Stevenson & Lee, 1990) have reported consistent differences between persons from East Asia and the West in the attributions they offer for explaining outstanding performance in academic as well as in other fields. In East Asia, the emphasis is on effort and there is relative disregard for innate abilities. According to the influential Confucian philosophy, human

TABLE 8.1
Elite and regular high-school students' attitudes about learning mathematics

| | Fairfax | | Beijing | |
	Elite School	Regular	Key Schools	Regular
1. Like math	5.1	4.2	5.0	4.5
2. Math is hard	3.0	3.8	4.3	4.5
3. Math depends on memorising	3.1	3.8	2.1	2.6
4. Math helps logical thinking	5.3	4.8	6.0	5.9

N_s = 1005–1010 (Beijing), and 1554–1656 (Fairfax). Ratings were made on 7-point scales defined by two end points (1, 7) and a midpoint (4). The anchors were labelled as follows: for item 1, "not at all", "somewhat", or "very much"; for item 2, "not at all difficult", "fairly difficult", or "very difficult"; for items 3 and 4, "strongly disagree", "neither agree nor disagree", or "strongly agree".

beings are considered to be malleable, shaped by the events of everyday life. Differences among individuals in innate abilities are recognised, but more important, according to the Confucian view, is the degree to which a person is willing to maximise these abilities through diligence and hard work.

In contrast, American and European teachers, parents, and children tend to give innate abilities a stronger role as a component of success than do persons in East Asia (Stevenson, Chen, & Lee, 1993). Western respondents recognise the importance of working hard, but they assume that the effects of hard work can be altered by differences in innate ability. According to this view, highly able students may not need to study hard in order to do well and less able students may be unable to learn, regardless of how hard they study. This is a very different interpretation from the one espoused in China that emphasises the utility of studying for the advancement of students of all levels of ability.

We evaluated the beliefs of students in both the elite and regular schools by telling them, "Here are some factors that may influence students' performance in school: having a good teacher, innate intelligence, home environment, and studying hard. Which do you think is the most important?" In line with the results of earlier studies, the majority of Chinese students in both types of school chose "studying hard", and for American students, it was "having a good teacher" (see Fig. 8.1).

Although students in both the Chinese elite and the regular high schools chose "studying hard" more frequently than did their counterparts in Fairfax, differences between the two types of high schools did not follow the same pattern in the two countries. Students in the key schools in Beijing were *less* likely to choose studying as the most important characteristic than were students in the regular schools. The opposite effect was found in Fairfax: The elite school students were *more* likely to choose "studying hard" than were the regular high-school students.

There were two other notable differences. In Fairfax, a greater percentage of students in the magnet school than in the regular high school regarded having a good teacher as the basis for doing well in school. In contrast, students in neither the key schools nor the regular high schools in Beijing often attributed success in school to having a good teacher. Rather, they assumed that a student's own efforts at studying were a more effective basis for success.

Students in the elite schools in both countries were also more willing to consider the role of innate intelligence than were their peers in the regular high schools. For these students, an emphasis on the importance of studying hard did not preclude consideration of the contribution of intelligence to academic success. The fourth alternative, " home environment", was seldom chosen by students in either city.

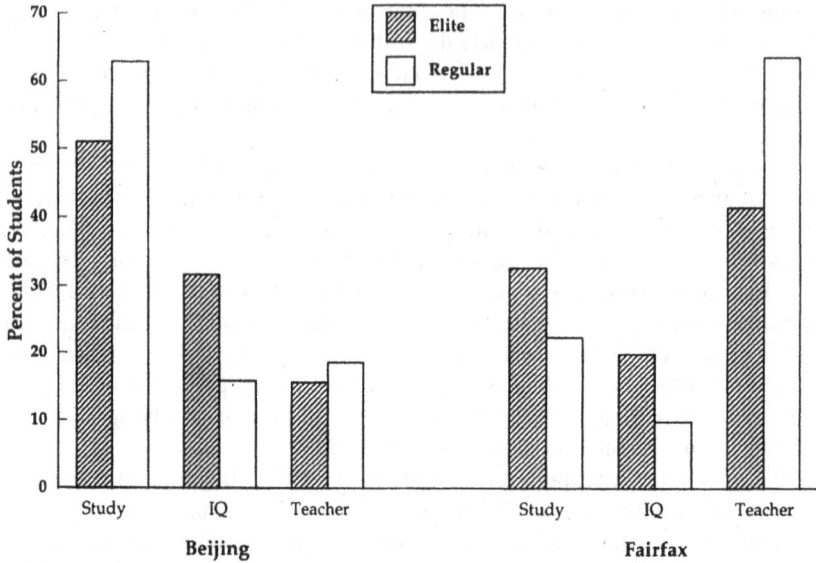

FIG. 8.1 Percentage of students in elite and regular schools offering different attributions concerning the basis of academic success in mathematics. Ns = 333 (Beijing); 777 (Fairfax). (Ns differ for different variables because time available prohibited giving every class every question in every school. Questions were therefore randomly distributed across schools.)

Perhaps the most surprising feature of these data is the degree to which the selections made by students in the elite schools followed the pattern characteristic of the cultures in which they live rather than revealing a pervasive concern about studying.

Effectiveness of schools. In Beijing, the low frequency with which the teacher was chosen as the basis for doing well in school may have been due, in part, to the students' perceptions that their teachers were not doing a good job. Half of the key school students and 19% of the regular school students in Beijing viewed the job their school was doing in educating them to be "good" or "excellent", as compared to evaluations that also included "fair" and "poor". In marked contrast, 94% of the magnet school students in Fairfax and 67% of the regular school students gave their schools a rating of "good" or "excellent".

It is also likely that the Chinese students were more critical of their schools, not because they actually thought their schools were bad, but because they assumed that, regardless of how much they were learning in school, they would have liked to be learning even more. Thus, their ratings did not reflect a condemnation of their teacher or their schools, but offer an indication that their high aspirations for academic accomplishment were not being met.

Satisfaction. The students' satisfaction with their academic achievement was evaluated by asking whether they were "satisfied", "not satisfied", or "very satisfied" with their current academic performance. A dramatic cross-cultural difference was revealed (see Fig. 8.2). A high percentage (84%) of the Chinese students, both those in key schools and in regular high schools, were dissatisfied. In sharp contrast, only a third of the Fairfax students indicated dissatisfaction with their performance, and among them, fewer in the magnet school expressed dissatisfaction than did the American students attending regular high schools.

Motivation for high achievement must depend, in part, on the degree to which the students are satisfied with their current performance. The question is how American parents and teachers can motivate students to improve their levels of academic achievement when students express such high levels of satisfaction with their current performance in school.

Self-evaluations. The failure of the Chinese students to be satisfied with their own performance was not due to their having low self-evaluations of their abilities or achievements. Both key school and regular

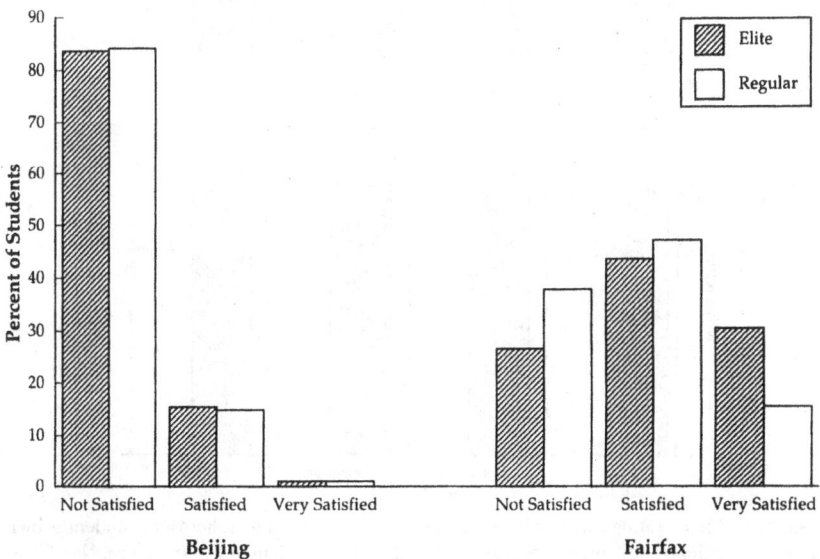

FIG. 8.2 Percentage of students in elite and regular high schools indicating various degrees of satisfaction with their academic performance. Ns = 971 (Beijing) and 1645 (Fairfax).

school students in Beijing gave themselves slightly above average ratings on characteristics such as academic achievement, intellectual ability, and their knowledge of mathematics and science; the average ratings made by students from the two types of school were very similar. This was not the case among Fairfax students. They gave themselves higher ratings than did the Chinese students, and students in the magnet school gave themselves significantly higher ratings than students in the regular high schools (see Fig. 8.3).

The highly positive self-evaluations made by the American magnet school students were primarily associated with academic and intellectual characteristics. Students in neither the magnet school in Fairfax nor the key

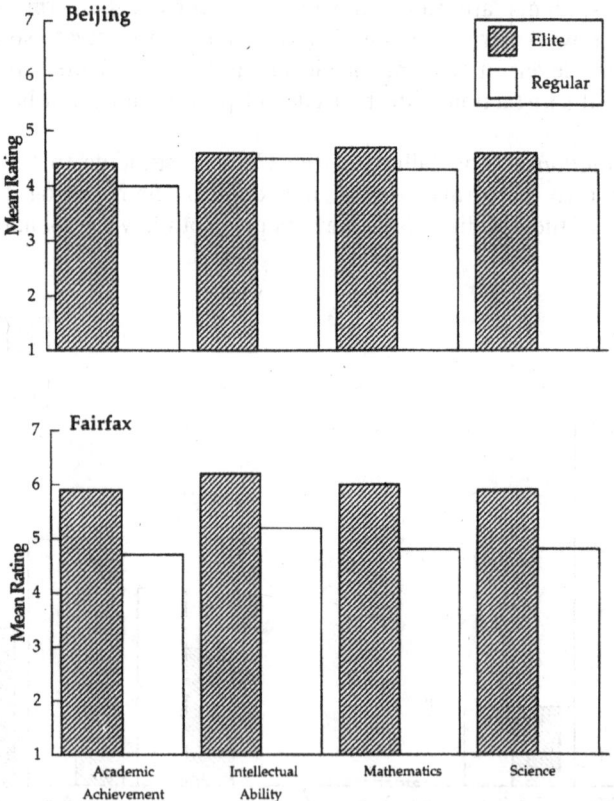

FIG. 8.3 Mean ratings by students in elite and regular high schools of student's own academic achievement, intelligence, and achievement in mathematics and science. Ns (976 to 982 (Beijing) and 1639 to 1644 (Fairfax). (1 = Much below average; 4 = Average; 7 = Much above average.)

schools of Beijing gave themselves ratings that were significantly different from those made by students in regular high schools on such non-academic activities as physical appearance, athletic skills, getting along with others, ability to solve everyday problems, or having good family relations.

Time use. An effective use of time would appear to be a critical determinant of high levels of performance. Students who have done sufficiently well in school to be admitted to some of their nation's most elite schools would be expected to spend more of their free time in activities that foster academic achievement, such as studying and reading for pleasure, than would students in regular high schools.

This was true for the American students, but not for those from Beijing (see Fig. 8.4). Students in the Fairfax magnet school spent more time studying and less time socialising with friends and watching television than did the students in the regular schools. However, in Beijing the only significant difference between students in the key schools and in the regular high schools was in the smaller amount of time the key school students spent watching television.

Expectations. The key and magnet school students held high expectations for their future education. A large majority (68%) of the Beijing students attending key schools expected to complete college, compared to 39% of the students from regular high schools. Among key school students in Beijing, 37% also expected to complete graduate or professional school, compared to 5% from the regular high schools. These remarkable findings reflect the extraordinarily high aspirations of Chinese students, for fewer than 10% of the persons of eligible ages currently attend a university. Of the Fairfax magnet school students, 74% believed they would complete post-graduate or professional school, compared to 40% of the regular school students.

These estimates are all very high. In the United States, only around a quarter of the students who have graduated from high school graduate from a four-year college. Vastly fewer complete a graduate or professional programme after their college graduation.

Adjustment. One of the most frequent questions concerning high-achieving students is whether their high achievement does not come at the cost of excessive stress and evidence of other problems of adjustment. We sought information about this matter by asking students to rate the frequency with which they experienced problems in adjustment on scales ranging from "never" to "almost every day". The scales tapped stress, depression, aggression, and psychosomatic disorders. For stress and depression, single-item scales were used. For aggression, four items, and

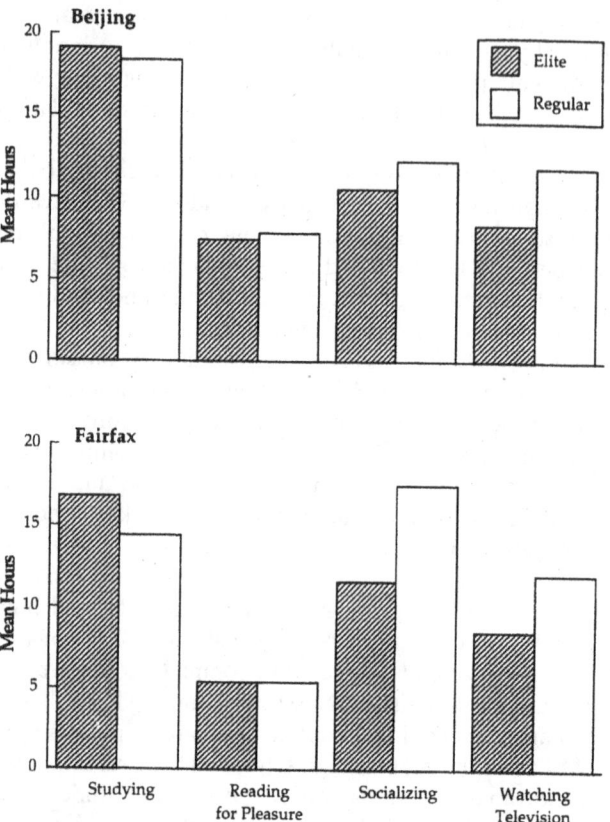

FIG. 8.4 Mean hours spent per week by elite and regular school students in out-of-school activities. Ns = 571–600 (Beijing); 1499–1551 (Fairfax).

for psychosomatic disorders, eight items were combined to form overall indexes.

Feelings of depression did not characterise either the high or average achievers, and generally, the ratings indicated a low frequency of all problems except for feelings of stress, which the Chinese students rated as occurring, on the average, between once a week and several times a week. The Americans said they felt stress even more frequently. Nor did the students in the elite schools of either Beijing or Fairfax rate themselves as having more frequent feelings of depression than did students in the regular high schools.

Only one index of potential disturbance in adjustment—psychosomatic problems—differentiated the eleventh-graders in the elite schools of both Beijing and Fairfax from their peers in regular high schools (see Table 8.2).

TABLE 8.2
Indices of adjustment

	Beijing		Fairfax	
	Key School	Regular	Elite Schools	Regular
Stress	3.3	3.4	4.2	4.0
Psychosomatic problems	1.8	1.9	2.0	2.2
Aggression	1.5	1.5	2.2	2.4
Depression	3.0	3.0	3.1	3.1

N_s = 968 (Beijing), and 1636–1637 (Fairfax). Ratings ranged from "never" (1) to "once a week" (3) to "almost every day" (5).

Students in the regular high schools in both cities described themselves as having more frequent headaches, stomach aches, and as feeling tired for no reason than did students in the elite schools. In addition, students in Fairfax's magnet school also indicated more frequent problems associated with overeating and elimination.

The students in Fairfax's magnet school also indicated less frequent feelings of stress and aggression than did the Fairfax students in the regular schools. Neither of these characteristics differentiated the students attending the key schools and regular high schools in Beijing.

The results clearly did not support the argument that the cost of high achievement is poor psychological adjustment. Rather, it was students attending regular high schools who expressed more frequent problems in adjustment. This was not the case, however, for the Fairfax magnet school students, whose self-ratings of feelings of stress were highest among both the elite and regular school students in both cities. Why this should have been the case is not clear. The most reasonable interpretation seems to be that they experience the greatest conflict about studying. Chinese students know that their parents value academic achievement over all other accomplishments during their school years and therefore they experience little conflict in carrying out what is expected of them. High achievers in American families, on the other hand, are often expected not only to do well in school, but also to have an active social life, to help with housework, possibly to have a job, and to do well in sports. Attempting to accomplish all of these goals may serve, therefore, as a source of conflict in American students' everyday lives.

CONCLUSIONS

Cross-cultural comparisons of high-achieving students offer us insights about factors associated with success that studies of a single culture might not reveal. In the case of academic achievement, contrasts between cultures as diverse as China and the United States provide a clear test of the degree to which explanations of high achievement are common across cultures. We did not find a high degree of commonality. Rather than obtaining consistent differences between students entering elite schools and those attending regular schools, we found that high levels of achievement were associated more strongly with culture than with the students' status in school.

China, emerging from decades of turmoil and upheaval in its educational system, is now producing some of the world's most able students in mathematics and science, and is therefore an especially interesting country to study. Nurtured by a system that acknowledges the importance of providing special attention and opportunities for students with exceptionally high academic abilities, students are selected for enrolment in special schools that foster high achievement. The students, propelled by a philosophical system that supports a belief in the importance of study and hard work as the basis of achievement, display an intense motivation for achievement success. This motivation to achieve is further enhanced by their self-critical attitude about their accomplishments. Accompanying high success in high school are the extraordinarily high expectations concerning the level of education they hope to attain on leaving high school. These beliefs are held commonly both by the students attending the elite school and those attending regular high schools.

Why there should have been frequent differences between the students attending the regular and elite schools in the United States but not in China is not clear. Why, for example, were the ratings made by Chinese students in the two types of schools so similar, when the differences between the two groups of American students differed consistently? Part of the explanation may be that American students in regular high schools are faced with a less demanding curriculum than are students in regular high schools in China and therefore differ more from their peers attending elite schools. Alternatively, Chinese students attending regular high schools may represent a more able group than is the case for students in regular high schools in the United States, and therefore differ less markedly from their peers in elite schools than is the case in the United States. A third interpretation is that Chinese students, both in the elite and in the regular high schools, are less likely to associate many other characteristics with high achievement than are American students.

What is clear is that it is difficult to generalise from a comparison of high and average achievers in one culture to members of another culture. This does not mean that conditions that exist in one culture cannot be transferred to another culture. It does mean that the social contexts for students' achievement behaviour differ greatly between cultures and what is commonplace in one culture is not necessarily regarded as an important factor in another culture.

We chose to study two cultures that differ greatly in many aspects. It will be of value to know the degree to which the conclusions that we have reached also characterise cultures that do not represent such extremes.

REFERENCES

Chen, C., Lee, S., & Stevenson, H.W. (1996). Academic achievement and motivation of Chinese students; A cross-national perspective. In S. Lau (Ed.), *Growing up the Chinese way: Chinese child and adolescent development* (pp. 69–92). Hong Kong: The Chinese University Press.

Hess, R., & Azuma, H. (1991). Cultural support for schooling: Contrasts between Japan and the United States. *Educational Researcher, 20,* 2–8.

Peak, L. (1996). *Pursuing excellence: A study of U.S. eighth-grade mathematics and science teaching, learning, curriculum, and achievement in international context.* Washington, DC: US Government Printing Office.

Renmin Ribao [People's Daily, Oversees Edition]. (1995, 7 July). Twisted love.

State Education Commission (1996). *Educational statistics yearbook of China: 1995.* Beijing: Author.

Stevenson, H.W., Chen, C., & Lee, S. (1993). Mathematics achievement of Chinese, Japanese and American children: Ten years later. *Science, 259,* 53–58.

Stevenson, H.W., & Lee, S. (1990). Contexts of achievement: A study of American, Chinese, and Japanese children. *Monographs of the Society for Research in Child Development. 221* (55), 1–2.

Stevenson, H.W., Lee, S., Chen, C., Lummis, M., Stigler, J.W., Liu, F., & Fang, G. (1990). Mathematics achievement of children in China and the United States. *Child Development, 61,* 1053–1066.

Stevenson, H.W., & Stigler, J.W. (1992). *The learning gap.* New York: Summit Books.

CHAPTER NINE

It's (im)possible to become a genius! The development of drawing

Werner Deutsch
Technical University of Braunschweig, Germany

INTRODUCTION

In the third year of life, the overwhelming majority of children begin to engage in activities that can be subsumed under the concept of drawing. After childhood the majority turns into a minority of grown-ups who continue drawing and painting. Why do these activities go to waste? How can a child's creativity in drawing be kept alive at later periods of development? These issues are discussed and illustrated on the basis of a longitudinal analysis of three individual cases—a normal, a rare, and an exeptional case of drawing development.

A SHORT SURVEY ABOUT DRAWING

Every year I ask the students of my introductory course in Developmental Psychology to take part in a short survey. This survey serves as a primer for a lecture and discussion on the development of drawing. It consists of two questions:

(1) Do you draw or paint?
(2) Did you draw or paint as a child?

Year after year, only a minority of not more than 15% admits that drawing and painting is part of their life. After the second question, however, the minority turns into an overwhelming majority. Over 90%

of the students in the audience remember that they had drawn or painted in the past.

I admit that my survey is not representative at all, as students are a very special population, however, I doubt that the results would be different if the two questions were answered by a representative sample of adults in Western societies. Drawing and painting are very important to children, so why does this talent go to waste when they grow up? I particularly say "go to waste" and not "disappear". If you keep questioning grown-ups about their habits then they confess that they do draw sometimes (cf. van Sommers, 1984, but also Deutsch, 1997). For example when talking on the phone or while being completely bored in a lecture, grown-ups tend to fill their notepads with geometric ornaments, doodles, and scribbles. Such graphic productions occur on the side and are to be thrown away shortly afterwards. Those drawings on a notepad resemble children's sketches during initial stages of drawing development.

Do adults draw intentionally as well? Under special circumstances they do, for example when showing someone the way. Sometimes a graphic representation can lead to a place better than a verbal description ever could. In the end adults start drawing again—involuntarily or voluntarily—when their own children or grandchildren beg them to draw a hippo, a dinosaur, a princess, a gun...

Most adults obviously have not lost the ability to draw or paint completely, it is just not as important as it used to be during childhood. When those adults were children, were they not as talented as others? Or, the other way round, those adults who still draw nowadays, were they more talented than other children when they were young? Maybe even above average? In short, is the development of drawing, the ongoing selection, connected to differences in talent? Or are other factors involved which are part of the developmental process itself?

Longitudinal studies are necessary to answer these important theoretical and practical questions. Spontaneously made drawings or paintings should then be documented. Studies like this exist, but most of them are about the development of creativity in children's drawings. They do not follow the development long enough to record the reduction of the creativity that at first increases. This reduction is not a very popular subject for studies, but I think it is a necessary one to be able to explain the continuity and discontinuity that can be found in the individual developmental processes.

THE DOCUMENTATION OF CHILDREN'S DRAWINGS

Nowadays we can find tons of children's drawings. That was not always the case—almost no original drawings were handed down from past centuries. Is the interest in children's drawings a phenomenon that varies over the centuries? Or is it also a specific cultural thing? If we look at second-hand information about the history of art (cf. Fineberg, 1995a and b), the data we find are not completely discouraging. In one of Giovanni Francesco Caroto's paintings dated 1520 a little boy can be seen who has a sheet of paper in his hands—with a drawn human being on it. When you look at the painting, it seems as if the boy is showing you his drawing. Was he the one who drew the picture? The problem is that the picture does not look as if it was made by a child. The human's legs are not attached to the head, nor are the arms which would be a typical feature of a tadpole figure. Lifelike features also cannot be found. Parallel lines are used to form arms and legs, making them unusually long. Perhaps Caroto is not representing the boy's drawing but what he thinks a child's drawing should look like. The same suspicion arises when you look at Pieter Janszoon Saeredam's painting "Interior of the Buurkerk in Utrecht" dated 1644, in which there is depiction of a trotting horse with three children on its back. The horse is supposed to look like a child's drawing, but was presumably done by an adult.

Early pioneering studies about the documentation and analysis of real children's drawings were published in 1896 by Sully in the USA, in 1913 by Luquet in France, and in 1905 by Kerschensteiner in Germany. Why does the documentation start so late, at the end of the 19th and beginning of the 20th century? Documentation is only possible if drawings and paintings can be preserved. Children in the past will have drawn—with fingers in sand, with twigs in water, or with rocks in snow—but paper was not given to them because it was too rare and expensive, as were inks and colours. So no products remained that could have been put in a safe place to be kept for later times.

One more thing was required so that children's drawings could be documented. Children had to be regarded as persons who can partly create their own development and not as (poor) miniature versions of adults. If you look at it from this perspective, children's drawings show the advantages of naivety that adult's drawings are lacking: spontaneity, vivid imagination, and pure emotions. This is not something restrictively found in only a few children or a few drawings, it is more a characteristic developmental period that appears with the beginning of school but does not survive puberty.

With the following three individual case studies I want to portray different possible stages in the development of drawing. The first case shows how normal developmental circumstances can undermine the graphic creativity that has already reached a certain level. How graphic creativity can be preserved is demonstrated by the second case—not to say that the adult's drawings deserve to be described as work of art. One of the most influential and controversial artists of our century who could not work or even live without being able to draw is introduced in the third case.

THE DEVELOPMENT OF DRAWING: THREE INDIVIDUAL CASE STUDIES

A normal case

Who collects children's drawings? Nursery-school teachers, teachers, artists, museum educationalists, paediatricians, children's psychotherapists, developmental psychologists, academics in the field of art, and—last but not least—parents. Parents in particular do a very good job of this. They do not use them for projects, do not choose special drawings for exhibitions, and do not analyse them for academic publications, but still they are the ones who keep collecting their children's drawings for years. The children themselves do not support these collections, though sometimes, years later, they might get interested in them when they are parents themselves who collect their own children's drawings.

Rose Halim, a psychology student at the Technical University in Brunswick, has been collecting her daughter Vanessa's drawings and was trusting enough to lend them to me. Most of the earlier drawings were spontaneously made and some of the later ones had to be drawn in school following the subject given by the teacher. The whole collection is ordered chronologically. Vanessa's graphic development is not unusual. All the stages that are listed in the literature (cf. Golomb, 1991) can be found in her drawings. In addition to this, Vanessa's peak regarding her graphic expression is reached in the middle of childhood, as it is for many children. On this peak Vanessa's drawings could not be more impressive. Two (originally untitled) examples will clarify my writing (Figs. 9.1 and 9.2; see also the front cover for the colours of the drawings), and to make it easier I have given them titles as I have for Figs. 9.3 and 9.4.

"A Winter Scene" is dominated by pale blue, white, brown, and black, all opaque water colours. A bird house with a symmetrical pointed roof is right in the centre of the painting coming up from the bottom. Three birds seem to be the contrast to the symmetry. All of them are given a different position—a black one opens its beak inside the bird house, another black bird flies towards it coming from the left, while another one, this time vermilion, is standing to the right, both legs in the snow. A certain dynamic is underlined by the different positions the birds have, running from the bottom upwards. Exactly the opposite way go the snowflakes, falling downwards and as big as tennis balls. What a wonderful composition! Without having intended this, a static and a dynamic side are very well balanced.

The second example "The Siblings" (Fig. 9.2) is related to the first one. Their structures are similar but their effects are completely different due to the intensive contrasts in colour in the second painting: the turquoise of the sky, the black of the siblings' hair and shoes, the pink-violet of their clothes,

FIG. 9.1 "A Winter Scene", by Vanessa, aged 7 years, watercolour, original size: 16 × 12 inches.

and the brown of their satchels. The siblings stand with their feet on solid ground. The girl's left hand touches the boy's right hand. Although they look at each other so that we can see their heads in profile, their bodies are painted from the back. Their faces have the same colour and shape but they differ in size. Looking at the mouths we come to the dynamic highlight of the picture. Using a simple technique, different states are marked—a bar for the girl's closed mouth and an angle for the boy's open mouth. After all this, how can the development of graphic creativity proceed?

At the age of 11, Vanessa's way of drawing and painting has changed completely. Formats and colours have not changed much but the depictions of humans and animals in space definitely have. A different person seems to have made the drawings shown in Figs 9.3 and 9.4.

FIG. 9.2 "The Siblings", by Vanessa, aged 8 years, watercolour, original size: 16 × 12 inches.

What has happened? Technically Vanessa's development has made good progress. "A Winter Scene" and "The Siblings" are good compositions with a very special dynamic but things are not in perspective, and neither the right proportions nor the three-dimensional aspect has been taken into account. "Two Horses" and "Three Sprinters" state the beginning of Vanessa's drawing in perspective. She chooses the brightness of the colours in such a way that the sunny yellow seems to be far away and the gaudy red, as well as the pitch-black, almost pop out of the picture. For the illusion of depth she uses the overlap of different bodyparts and lines that serve as gradients—also with or without overlap.

So what has been lost? "Two Horses" and "Three Sprinters" seem to be schematic, as if Vanessa has copied pictures for practice. Both drawings are constructions, not good for any surprises. The use of colour has changed, too. Where in the earlier paintings the colours formed the shapes,

FIG. 9.3 "Two Horses", by Vanessa, aged 11 years, colour drawing, original size: 16 × 12 inches.

FIG. 9.4 "Three Sprinters", by Vanessa, aged 11 years, colour drawing, original size: 16 × 12 inches.

in the later ones the shapes had to be coloured. Vanessa is not an exception. Many children or teenagers lose their graphic creativity during pre-puberty or puberty, when it becomes uncertain if drawing can keep its original function of expressing thoughts, imaginations, and emotions.

In 1918 (p. 186) Karl Bühler had already described this developmental trend: During ontogenetic development writing becomes more important than drawing. This process can go so far that "the whole ability of an average modern human being to express himself graphically ends in writing". If Bühler was right, the wasting away of drawing's function would have to start earlier, wouldn't it? This question can only be answered if the development of drawing and the development of writing is studied at the same time. Bühler's hypothesis of replacement is certainly an attractive one, but is definitely not the only determining factor. Other things should be taken into account, such as the way drawing is taught. Does the teacher judge drawings by certain standards as if judging a test in mathematics? Or does he or she support the individual way of expression? Finally we have to consider the possibility that children dissociate themselves from their own productions when they have reached a certain developmental level. They might not care about creativity. Their drawings would just be a leftover from developmental stages that they had passed.

A rare case

Jan Gowert Masche (JGM) belongs to the minority of adults who still draw. One example, Fig. 9.5, shows an incident that has been drawn and painted many times in many different ways over the centuries. Here the events around Christ's birth are taking place in the Department of Developmental Psychology at the Technical University in Brunswick at the end of the year 1993. Employees gather around the head of department—with moustache and halo—lying in the crib. The three wise men, very different in size, enter the picture from the left holding incense, a sausage that is typical for the area (Braunschweiger Mettwurst), and flowers in their hands. On the right-hand side of the picture there is a shepherd with three miniature sheep, a cow, and an ox in front of him (the ox is a caricature of the painter himself). Mary with a big halo is smoking, Joseph is wearing carpenter's pants, his halo being smaller than Mary's, and above them all are two angels, one of them being the cleaning lady, music coming out of her broom.

I doubt that Christ's birth has ever been represented in quite this way and blasphemy is certainly not the artist's intention. He chooses this incident to portray the persons of the department. It is a caricature where

FIG. 9.5 "The Christmas Card", by Jan Gowert Masche, aged 26 years, pencil drawing, original size: 8 × 12 inches.

the people are the important thing, not the happening itself. We used the drawing for the New Year's Eve greeting cards in 1993/94.

JGM has developed his very own way of drawing over time, he did not copy or imitate specific models. In a way it is his second personal handwriting. We can retrace its development by looking at his earlier drawings. During primary school he drew "A Schoolyard Scenario" (Fig. 9.6). A stunning stylistic continuity can be found between the christmas card and the schoolyard scenario. The contours of the persons, animals, and objects are drawn precisely. They are grouped next to each other, above and below each other. The artist wants to characterise the comical, he does not want to portray anything. It is striking that he was able to maintain his graphical individuality. He always preferred pens, only using brushes under pressure, and school was one place where he had to use brushes. There he painted the chicken shown in Fig. 9.7.

Remembering how he felt he personally comments on this picture: "Here my subversive temperament is coming through, obviously the chicken sh... on the art lesson" (Masche, personal communication, 9 April 1997). What do Jan Gowert Masche's first drawings look like? He was not born as a cartoonist. Like all children he started with scribbles, then came

FIG. 9.6 "A Schoolyard Scenario", by Jan Gowert Masche, aged 8 years, pen drawing, original size: 16 × 12 inches.

FIG. 9.7 "A Chicken", by Jan Gowert Masche, aged 12 years, watercolour, original size: 12 × 15 inches.

the tadpole figures. Nevertheless his early drawings are not quite normal, which can be seen in Fig. 9.8.

Who are the four persons? JGM remembers that the one in the centre is the birthday boy, looking like a weightlifter, bigger than all the others. His brother is on the right-hand side, smaller than the birthday boy although he is actually bigger. His parents are on the left-hand side, the mother with glasses below the father. In the top left corner the sentence: DER GOWERT HAT GEBURTSTAG... [IT IS GOWERT'S BIRTHDAY...] ends with three dots right above Gowert's head. Something seems to be wrong with this picture. The writing and drawing do not go together. Although the writing could have been done by a schoolchild, the rest of the picture looks as if a much younger child has been the artist—especially the way the people are drawn. Did two different people work on this? If we look at the result we would say yes, but the reality is a different one. JGM belongs to the tiny minority of children who taught themselves how to write and read before even going to school.

At the age of 5 JGM's writing and reading were comparable to what the majority of children learn in the second year of school. Perhaps this is how we can explain the fact that JGM was able to maintain his individuality in both means of expression. He was able to write at a very young age while the development of his drawing at that age followed the normal course.

FIG. 9.8 "Birthday", by Jan Gowert Masche, aged about 5 years, pencil drawing with colours from coloured pencils, original size: 8 × 12 inches.

What Bühler (1918) said about the development of the average human being is not right for JGM. He was able to develop his own individualistic way of drawing in the middle of childhood. This individuality was resistant to influences from the outside, for example the art lesson. His drawings may not be works of art that should be exhibited, but they show how a talent has taken its course. His christmas card, though, was definitely a much nicer surprise than the usual dull greeting card would have been!

An exceptional case

In the 20th century many artists collected children's drawings (cf. Fineberg, 1995a and b). Paul Klee included his own in his work index, but did not register those that he did during his academic years. The artist Pablo Picasso ought to have said that he wished to be able to draw like a child. What about Joseph Beuys? Like no other modern artist he kept drawing, drawing, drawing... but you have to be careful if you want to understand his way of drawing. He opened doors that had separated different artistic or creative activities. For him drawing was the prolonging of his thoughts, it was a key function—drawing means thinking, it creates something new. Beuys did not agree with the traditional view in which drawing is to portray something we have perceived.

I want to cite an excerpt from a conversation between Hans van der Grinten (G), a friend and collector of Beuys, and Beuys himself (B). They discussed the relation between drawing and spoken (or written) language. Obviously Beuys does not consider spoken or written language as more important than drawing, as Bühler did. On the contrary, drawing offers advantages that language does not have (Beuys before Beuys, 1987, p. 247): translation by Meike Watzlawik.

> G: So you think that the drawing is an improvement on the spoken or written word?
> B: Yes, improvement, or better said expansion, because here you express or try to express something for which you don't have enough words.
> G: From an artist whose work has become so extensive over the years one would like to learn something about the criteria of drawing. The drawing can be many things. It can be more than useful like many of your drawings are, it can lead to an actual artistic value. What do you think about this?
> B: Right, one aspect of drawing is that it triggers the next step in production, an action, a movement of myself or of the participants for whom the drawing was made. In the early years those drawings are schematic, to explain a principle which will later be examined or realised in plastic form. On top of this function, I think that drawing has its own autonomy which is generally a kind of language characterised by gestures and motion. I try to keep this kind of language

fluid to get beyond the usurpation of language caused by the cultural development and rationality. I want to get to another way of communication, to be able to express things that lead to deeper spheres. This expansion of language is the one I'm interested in.

G: You are not interested in graphic conventions. The graphic language is not independent of styles and fashions. The drawing mainly consists of a primary impulse and of changes in time. With your drawing you want to omit those changes?

B: That's right. I think, it's important to get in touch with elementary, let's say, evolutionary powers by drawing. I also try to portray something of this in my drawings, to show these powers. I orientate my drawings to those powers and not to the different historic styles.

Compared to written language, drawing can be an individual way of expression—as long as it does not follow conventions. I have already mentioned the art lesson. The traditional art lesson regulates drawing. Pupils are given a certain exercise and the results are judged by the teacher. The teacher's ideas, the curriculum, the aesthetic preferences of the time, or the comparison to peers all influence drawing. Beuys did not mince his words when he criticised the school or academic art lesson. Generally these lessons ignore the creative potential that every individual brings along. They do not support this potential, they more or less undermine it.

Is every human an artist? Not only in the development of drawing do we find a creative potential in almost every human being. For most of them it can be said that this potential goes to waste over time. Just a few can increase this potential to the ability of artistic expression. Beuys has been an exception; until the end of his life he was able to keep the childlike creativity alive. For him continuity and changes were not opposites but necessary circumstances for development. What might his development have looked like? Was he outstanding? Unfortunately none of his childhood drawings and only few of his youth are left. Beuys' way of combining continuity and change was to use his earliest drawings again in his later collages. Even in his drawings he did not dissociate himself from his past, he always integrated past and future. That might be the reason why only few of his drawings or paintings were produced on request—like a bunch of flowers in a vase dated 1940, painted in oil, with an old silver frame (with gold), signed by Beuys on the back. His mother had asked him for this painting. It was meant to be a gift for a couple who lived in the same house, for their silver wedding.

Beuys' development was not only special because of his talent for drawing. His energy, his curiosity, his sense of humour and variety, as well as his individuality were remarkable. He was not born to be the creator of this new understanding of art that has only just begun—development just took its course.

DEVELOPMENT AND TALENT

All humans have a creative potential. This thesis is supported by many different people. One of them is Jacob Moreno, who wanted to revive the resources of spontaneity and creativity with the help of psychodrama (cf. Moreno & Moreno, 1944). Joseph Beuys was another one. On the way to a new understanding he tried to get science, politics, economies, and society moving.

In this chapter about graphic expression I have shown how different the development of the creative potential can be. Does this way of expression become rigid under technically perfect conventions? Does drawing survive as an individualistic style preserved by the artist as a second handwriting? Or do we manage to turn the child's creativity into an artistic talent that creates the new? I have explained all three possible ways by single case studies: a normal, a rare, and an exceptional one. Extensive studies and representative samples are needed to find out how often these cases actually occur. Longitudinal case studies would be a good start to get an idea of the variety of possible developmental processes. If we look at the glossy print literature on the shelves, we mainly find studies about the most productive stages in the development of drawing. Sadly, all the other stages are not even mentioned. These unspectacular developmental stages, in which creativity and productivity fade, are especially worth studying. Only by doing so will we be able to identify conditions that influence development—either supporting or inhibiting. Talent is not an individual feature that we carry around for life like a genetic code. Talent arises under stimulating developmental conditions (cf. Mönks & Ypenburg, 1993).

ACKNOWLEDGEMENTS

Thanks go to Jan Gowert Masche and Vanessa Halim for their drawings and to Meike Watzlawik for her help with the English version of this paper.

REFERENCES

Beuys before Beuys (1987). *Frühe Arbeiten aus der Sammlung van der Grinten [Early works from the collection van der Grinten]*. Köln: Du Mont.

Bühler, K. (1918). *Die geistige Entwicklung des Kindes [The mental development of the child]*. Jena: Fischer.

Deutsch, W. (1997). Wie in der Entwicklung des Zeichnens Kreativität wächst, vergeht und—manchmal—wieder neu entsteht. [The development of drawing—how creativity grows, fades and sometimes emerges again]. In O. Kruse (Ed.), *Kreativität als Ressource für Veränderung und Wachstum [Creativity as source for change and growth]*. Tübingen: dgvt Verlag.

Fineberg, J. (1995a). *Mit dem auge des kindes. Kinderzeichnung und moderne Kunst [From a child's eye perspective. Children's drawings and modern art]*. Stuttgart: Gert Hatje.

Fineberg, J. (Ed.) (1995b). *Kinderzeichnung und die Kunst des 20. Jahrhunderts* [*Children's drawings and the art of the 20th century*]. Stuttgart: Gert Hatje.

Golomb, C. (1991). *The child's creation of a pictorial world*. Berkeley: University of California Press.

Kerschensteiner, G. (1905). *Die Entwicklung der zeichnerischen Begabung* [*The development of graphic talent*]. München: Gerber.

Luquet, G.H. (1913). *Le dessin d'un enfant* [A child's drawing]. Paris: F. Alcan.

Mönks, F.J., & Ypenburg, I.H. (1993). *Hoogbegaafde kinderen thuis en op school* [*Gifted children at home and in school*]. Assen/Maastricht: Dekker & van de Vegt.

Moreno, J.L., & Moreno, F. (1944). Spontaneity theory of child development. *Sociometry, 7*, 89–128.

Sully, J. (1896). *Studies of childhood*. New York: Appleton.

van Sommers, P. (1984). *Drawing and cognition*. Cambridge: Cambridge University Press.

PART FOUR
SUPPORTING THE DEVELOPMENT OF TALENT

CHAPTER TEN

Gifted infants: What kinds of support do they need?

J. Marianne Riksen-Walraven and Jolien Zevalkink
University of Nijmegen, The Netherlands

The main question addressed in this chapter is what kinds of experiences in the very first years of life foster the development of special talents in children. To answer this question, we cannot draw on the results of studies directly examining the effects of early experience on the development of gifted infants. These studies are simply lacking, because giftedness cannot be validly assessed in infancy. Most special talents are not yet visible in the first years of life. In many cases, special talents do not emerge before middle childhood. Signs of intellectual giftedness may be detected in the preschool years (Lewis & Louis, 1991), but research aimed at the identification of gifted infants remains a hazardous undertaking (Lewis & Michalson, 1985). Before turning to the question of whether and which experiences in infancy may possibly contribute to the development of otherwise invisible talents, we will first examine the thinking and findings in the general literature concerned with the effects of experience on the development of special talents.

THE ROLE OF EXPERIENCE IN THE DEVELOPMENT OF TALENTS

Today, no one doubts that special support and training are needed for the full development of a talent. Early identification of gifted children is considered important for precisely this reason. Once special talents have been detected, it is possible to provide the children with opportunities to further refine and develop those talents. Gifted children thus have special educational needs. When these special needs are not met, the talents of gifted children can remain undeveloped and the children end up as "mediocre" grown-ups. The value placed on both the early detection and nurturance of gifted children reflects an interactionist perspective on the "nature–nurture" debate with regard to the contribution of genes versus the environment to human development. Both genes and a supportive environment are considered important for the development of special talents. Due to genetic factors, certain children have the potential for exceptional developmental attainments. This potential can only be actualised in an environment providing the necessary support for the talent in question, however. In other words, both an individual's genetic endowment and his or her environment contribute to the development of talents. But does placement of a potentially talented child in a supportive and stimulating environment guarantee the full development of his or her talents? The answer is clearly "no".

Every counsellor working with gifted children is familiar with examples of obviously talented children attending excellent schools with special curricula, who nevertheless do not grasp the opportunities offered by these high-quality environments. Apparently, a gifted child needs more than just a stimulating environment to develop his or her talents. The child must also have an interest in the environment and be motivated to interact with it. If the child is passive or simply does not attend to the stimuli in the environment, he or she will not develop. Development can only take place when an individual actively interacts with the environment and stands open for incoming stimulation. Development is now thought to be the result of enduring reciprocal interactions between organism and environment, which actualises the organism's genetic potential. The more interactions between organism and environment, the greater the realisation of the genetic potential. Little interaction means genetic potential remaining unactualised (Bronfenbrenner & Ceci, 1994). Thus, in order to actualise their genetic potential children need not only a supportive environment which offers opportunities for growth and development but also the motivation to interact with the environment and take advantage of the opportunities provided.

It is generally recognised that motivation is necessary for the development of special talents. Some consider motivation to be an essential aspect of giftedness (Mönks & Van Boxtel, 1985; Renzulli, 1978). Others consider motivation to be a separate factor which determines the amount of energy devoted to learning activities in a given field (Gagné, 1991). We share the latter view and assume that the level of a child's motivation determines the frequency and persistence of his or her interactions with the immediate environment and thereby the actualisation of genetic potential. Given that the motivation for competence in a given field literally drives a person towards interactions that foster development, competence motivation can be considered as the primary "engine" of development.

At school, a lack of motivation for academic tasks is the most common cause of underachievement among apparently gifted pupils. Motivational differences between children are obvious to every elementary school teacher. In fact, such differences in interest and motivation can already be detected in the preschool years. And there are indications that competence motivation is strongly affected by experiences in the very first years of life. For this reason, we are convinced that early experience plays a role in the development of talents. Early experience provides the motivational base for children's interactions with the environment and thereby the actualisation of their genetic potential. In the next section, we therefore provide more evidence for this assumption and attempt to highlight the kinds of experience that appear to affect early motivational development.

A SUPPORTIVE ENVIRONMENT FOR GIFTED INFANTS IS ONE THAT FOSTERS COMPETENCE MOTIVATION

Evidence from the lives of eminent achievers

In several retrospective studies, the very early lives of eminent achievers have been considered in considerable detail. Such studies provide a rich source of hypotheses on just which experiences in infancy appear to foster the development of special talent. One of the most famous studies of this kind was conducted by Bloom (1985), whose sample consisted of young adults excelling in such skill areas as sculpting, tennis, mathematics, and neurological research. From interviews not only with the subjects themselves but also with their parents and teachers, Bloom concluded that the family climate in the early years of his subjects can generally be described as child-centred, warm, gentle, and nurturant. Parents involved their children in family activities and areas of interest, sometimes using instruction or teaching but initially in only playful ways. Disciplined training and teaching by experts was not provided until middle childhood. Robinson (1993), in a review of various other studies examining the early years of eminent persons, comes to a comparable conclusion when she characterises the early environments of these people as generally warm, affectionate, nurturant, and finely attuned to the child's needs.

These studies not only describe the early environment of gifted children but also provide information on the early behaviour and development of the subjects themselves. Once again, a relatively consistent picture emerges with motivation occupying a prominent position. Bloom (1985) concludes that his excellent subjects could be characterised in their early years as strikingly curious, energetic, and persistent in their pursuit of knowledge. Other researchers also typify gifted young children in terms of behaviours reflecting high levels of motivation, including curiosity, exploration and experimentation, persistence, enthusiasm, and pleasure in learning (cf. Lewis & Louis, 1991; Robinson, 1993). Given that these studies are retrospective and correlational in nature, it is impossible to infer a causal relationship between the early family climate of gifted children and their motivational characteristics. Nevertheless, we are strongly inclined to assume such a causal relation because the family climate described in these studies contains those characteristics that have been found in other types of studies to foster early competence motivation in children.

Evidence from intervention studies

Children's motivation to explore and effectively interact with their environment appears to be particularly vulnerable during the first years of life. Studies of institutionalised and family-reared failure-to-thrive infants have shown that deprivation of personal attention and lack of social responsiveness on the part of caregivers can lead to a loss of interest in the environment, apathy and social withdrawal already in the first months of life (Provence, 1989; Provence & Lipton; 1962; Ramey et al., 1979). Even when the quality of the care that the infants receive falls within the normal range, the interactive behaviours of their caregivers appear to influence the development of competence motivation in infants. Most convincing, of course, is evidence from intervention studies in which the quality of parents' interactive behaviour is experimentally improved. Two of these intervention studies are particularly relevant to the argument raised in this section.

In attachment theory, it is assumed that parents who sensitively respond to their infant's signals and needs foster a sense of security in their child (Bowlby, 1969) and this sense of security makes the child "free" to explore the environment. Within the framework of attachment theory, Van den Boom (1994) enhanced parental sensitive responsiveness to their 6- to 9-month-old infants and found this to promote both attachment security and the quality of the infants' exploratory behaviour. At age 1, the infants in the intervention group were not only better able to use their mothers as a secure base for exploring the environment, they also showed more "sophisticated" exploratory behaviours such as combining objects, and not just simple exploratory behaviours such as superficially touching or mouthing the objects.

An earlier intervention study by Riksen-Walraven (1978) with 100 9-month-old infants and their parents was based on the conceptual framework of "competence motivation" as defined by White (1959). In this study, it was argued that children who live in an unresponsive environment quickly learn that their behaviours have no effect. As a result of this learning, their motivation to act upon the environment will decrease, as reflected in less exploration of the environment. An enduring lack of response from caregivers will also decrease children's attentiveness to the effects of their own behaviour because effects are no longer expected. Increased parental responsiveness was therefore predicted to enhance children's competence motivation and thereby foster exploration along with the ability to detect the relation between a particular behaviour and its effect. A three-month intervention successfully enhanced parental responsiveness and thereby an increase in the children's competence motivation was also found. Those infants whose parents received the intervention showed a remarkable increase in the quality of their explorations and ability to detect behaviour–effect contingencies. Compared to infants in a non-treated control group, the intervention infants also showed a greater preference for novel over familiar stimuli, a greater variety of behaviours during the exploration of novel objects, and more quickly learned to present novel coloured slides to themselves by pushing a button than did the control infants. The children in this study were again seen when they were 7, 10, and 12 years old. Positive effects of the early intervention remained visible at all of these ages. The children and particularly the girls with parents who had been in the responsiveness programme, were characterised by their teachers as self-reliant, confident, resourceful in initiating activities, curious, and exploring (Riksen-Walraven & van Aken, 1997). These children showed increased scores for ego-resiliency (cf. Block & Block, 1980) throughout the elementary school years. Ego-resiliency evidently has a strong motivational component and according to Block and Kremen (1996, p. 351) predisposes "individuals to a positive engagement with the world, as manifested by positive affect and openness to experience." The results reviewed here show that many of the children in our intervention group retain the high level of competence motivation brought about in infancy by increased parental responsiveness. More generally, children's experiences in infancy and particularly the degree to which their parents respond sensitively to their signals and needs, appear have a significant and enduring impact on the development of their competence motivation.

Why competence motivation is particularly vulnerable in infancy

Together with Robert White (1959), we assume that all normal children are born with "competence motivation", which makes them try, from the very beginning, to interact effectively with their environment. From a biological-evolutionary point of view, it can be argued that competence motivation is vital for newborns to adapt to their environment and thus for their survival. Indeed, newborns appear to be pre-programmed to act upon their environment and to attend to the effects of their behaviour. Observing the effects of their own behaviour is assumed to bring about a pleasurable feeling of competence or efficacy which then motivates further action and exploration. Children can thus be thought of as being born with their motivational engines running at full speed. If the environment provides sufficient opportunities for effective interaction, the children will experience themselves as effective agents and thereby seek further interactions. Conversely, a repeated experience of being ineffective will slow down the child's motivational engine and thereby cause passivity and a lack of interest in what the environment has to offer.

What makes competence motivation so extremely vulnerable in the very first period of life, is simply that young infants cannot provide themselves with the efficacy experiences needed to keep their engines running. Due to their relative lack of motor competence, for example, they are simply unable to regularly elicit interesting effects from the world of things. In interactions with people, however, even weak signals and immature behaviours can elicit very remarkable and interesting effects. Caregivers tend to reward infants' attempts at interaction with often exaggerated reactions, which are also varied over the course of the interaction to keep the infant's attention. Thus, for infants, the social environment is the primary source for feelings of efficacy. The younger the children, the more dependent they are on what their caregivers are able and willing to provide.

Why early experience is as important as later experience for the development of talents

Some suggest that children's experiences in the very first years of life do not particularly influence the development of special talents. It has been proposed, for example, that mental development is highly "canalised" in infancy. That is, mental development initially follows a genetically determined course and is therefore little susceptible to environmental influences during the early years. Between the ages of 2 and 6 years, mental development becomes less canalised and hence environmental influences are assumed to become stronger and environmental effects more enduring (Lewis & Louis, 1991; McCall, 1983). The same is also hypothesised to hold for the development of talents in such areas as music or sports.

The assumption that early experience does not contribute *directly* to children's development in the specific domains of intelligence, sports, and the arts does not imply that early experience does not contribute to children's development at all. Our conclusion from the first part of this review is that children's experiences in infancy should not be considered less important for the development of their talents than their experiences in later years, when their talents have already emerged and are in need of further development and refinement via special teaching and training. The effects of early experience differ from those in later childhood in that they primarily influence children's competence motivation. Early experiences provide the motivational basis for the later development of special talents. If infants are deprived of the experiences needed to maintain a basic feeling of efficacy, there is a considerable risk of their talents simply remaining undeveloped in later years. No one may ever notice the potential giftedness of such children.

QUALITY OF SUPPORT PROVIDED BY PARENTS

Essential ingredients of adequate support

The results of the empirical studies described in the preceding section strongly suggest that the sensitivity with which parents respond to their children's signals and needs (also referred to as "warmth" or "nurturance") is the most basic ingredient of the support children need to develop their talents. This *emotional support* provides infants with a basic sense of security and competence, which motivates them to interact with the world beyond the caregiver.

Emotional support alone is not sufficient for children to develop a sense of competence in dealing with the environment. Children must also be offered opportunities to experience themselves as competent agents, which requires that parents *respect the child's autonomy*. Differences between caregivers can already be observed in interactions with their infants in the first year of life. Some parents allow their children to explore new play objects on their own and provide their children with lots of time to discover what can be done with these objects. These parents only intervene when the child needs help or when the child's attention wanes. Other parents, however, do not allow their children to discover things for themselves. They continuously interrupt their children's play with suggestions or corrections and thereby give the children little chance to experience themselves as competent agents. Enduring exposure to such an intrusive style of interaction appears to be very detrimental to children's development and functioning. For example, Egeland, Pianta, and O'Brien (1993) rated mothers' intrusiveness during play with their six-month-old infants. In the first grades of elementary school, the children of intrusive mothers were described by their teachers as emotionally unhealthy (i.e. lacking confidence and curiosity, not enjoying new experiences and challenges) and having low levels of achievement. Interestingly, the negative effects of mothers' intrusiveness proved to be independent of their affective responsiveness to the infant, which shows that respect for a child's autonomy plays a separate role in development. Respect for a child's autonomy appears to become an important element of support by the end of the first year of life when the child's capacity for object manipulation and independent exploration of the environment grows so rapidly. Respect for a child's autonomy is even more important during the second year of life, when children clearly demonstrate a growing need for autonomy.

The increased locomotor ability and need for autonomy appeal to a third supportive skill on the part of parents. During the course of the second year, it is increasingly important for parents to provide some *structure* for their children in the form of clear and consistent *limits* on their behaviour. A dramatic increase in the number of instructions from parents occurs between the ages of 12 and 18 months (Fagot & Kavanaugh, 1993). Setting consistent limits on children's behaviour or what is commonly referred to as "control" has also been shown to contribute to children's feelings of competence and particularly when provided by emotionally supportive parents (Baumrind, 1977). It should be noted that setting limits is not the converse of respecting a child's autonomy. Conceptually, the two are independent in the sense that it is possible to behave in a very intrusive and disrespectful manner without setting clear and consistent limits. It is also possible to allow a child lots of autonomy within gently but clearly defined limits.

A fourth ingredient of support which is known to foster the development of children's innate potential is *high-quality instruction* involving the provision of clear information, finely attuned to the child's needs, state, and cognitive level. Although most parents talk to their children and explain things to them from the moment they are born, the role of the parent as an instructor or teacher becomes particularly prominent in the second and third years of life, when children's linguistic and representational abilities show dramatic growth. Children can now understand simple rules and explanations. Most children obviously enjoy conversations and book reading at this time as well. A growing need for information is also evident in their endless questions at this time.

In sum, adequate support is assumed to contain four essential ingredients: (1) emotional support, (2) respect for a child's autonomy, (3) the provision of structure and limits, and (4) high-quality instruction. The first two ingredients are considered basic because they clearly foster a sense of security and competence, which then motivates further interactions with the world around. In evaluating the quality of the support provided to infants, emotional support and respect for the child's autonomy should therefore carry the most weight. In the second year of life, when informal teaching in the form of limit setting and the provision of high-quality instruction increasingly contribute to children's development, the first two ingredients of support are still of fundamental importance, because they set the stage for effective teaching. A secure and trusting relationship with a parent or teacher and feeling respected as a person generally mean a compliant and enthusiastic pupil (Matas, Arend, & Sroufe, 1978).

Quality of parental support in disadvantaged families

It has been argued so far that all children need support from people in their environment from birth onwards to develop their innate potential. In infancy, children are particularly dependent on the support provided by their parents. Most parents are, by nature, inclined to invest time and effort in their infants' health and development. Too many parents nevertheless do not succeed in providing the support for their infants needed to lay the motivational foundation for the development of potential talents in later years. In some parents, this may be caused by a lack of such personal resources as ego-resilience or intelligence. But many other parents are impeded by the poor and stressful circumstances in which they live.

A lack of parental support may explain the relative lack of children from disadvantaged backgrounds, including ethnic minority groups, in talent development programmes (Frasier, 1993; Gallagher, 1985). Children from disadvantaged backgrounds are not detected as gifted simply because their potential talents have not been actualised in earlier years. It should again be emphasised that growing up in a supportive environment is necessary for the development of special talents. The belief that children can emerge as exceptionally gifted from backgrounds that are not particularly stimulating or even disadvantageous is fallacious and not supported by facts (Radford, 1990).

In the following sections of this chapter, we will illustrate some of the arguments presented earlier with the data collected in a study of children from a cultural minority group, namely Surinamese families living in the Netherlands.

QUALITY OF PARENTAL SUPPORT AND ACHIEVEMENT OF EXCELLENCE IN SURINAMESE-DUTCH INFANTS

The children and their families

The sample considered consisted of 38 infants from Surinamese families living in the Netherlands. The children and their mothers served as a control group in an intervention study described elsewhere (Riksen-Walraven, Meij, Hubbard, & Zevalkink, 1996). All of the mothers were of Surinamese origin: two of them were born in the Netherlands; the others had immigrated from Surinam, a former Dutch colony in South America. The mean age of the mothers was 28.3 years. According to Dutch standards, the mothers' level of education was low to moderate, the highest level being four years of secondary school. The infants, 20 boys and 18 girls, were 18 months of age at the time of the study. Ten of the infants were only-children; the others had one or more siblings. Twenty children, or more than half of the sample, lived with their mothers in a single-parent household.

Surinamese-Dutch children and particularly those from less well educated families are considered at risk for academic underachievement. Although, on average, they perform better at school than children from Moroccan and Turkish immigrant families, they nevertheless perform at lower levels than indigenous Dutch children from deprived socio-economic backgrounds. They have greater grade retention than their Dutch peers and are over-represented in special education classes. This information is rather striking in light of the fact that Surinamese parents are known for the high educational aspirations and standards of achievement that they hold for their children. Despite the value they place on academic success, these parents do not appear to succeed in giving their children the support they need. This may be due to the relatively high levels of life stress to which immigrant families are often exposed. Although Surinamese families, in contrast to Moroccan and Turkish immigrant families, are generally fluent in the Dutch language, they still face the task of having to adapt to new values, customs, and living conditions. Combining parenthood with a job outside the home may also cause a lot more strain for these parents in the Netherlands than in Surinam, because less direct support is available from family members who no longer live in the neighbourhood. Although a relatively high level of life stress could be expected in our sample, an extremely high level of stress was not found because the sample contained no families with severe problems, no teenage mothers, and no mothers working outside the home for more than 20 hours a week.

Measuring the quality of support provided by the mothers

In order to assess the quality of the support provided by the mothers, they were videotaped interacting with their infants in their homes. The 25-minute interaction session consisted of seven consecutive episodes. In the first five episodes of three minutes each, the mothers were asked to let their child successively perform various tasks. They were told that they could help their child whenever they felt they needed to. The five tasks consisted of assembling a jigsaw puzzle, opening various flaps of a puzzle box, building a block tower, naming or pointing to the various body parts on a doll, and sorting objects into two groups. In the sixth episode, which lasted five minutes, the mothers were asked to read some new books with the child. Finally, the mother and child were given a five-minute period to play together freely with a set of new toys.

The quality of the support provided by the mothers for their infants was rated from the videotapes, using four 7-point rating scales developed by Erickson, Sroufe, and Egeland (1985). These scales were chosen because they represent the four basic ingredients of support highlighted earlier. The scales were labelled as follows: (1) *supportive presence* or the provision of emotional support in the form of comfort, praise, and encouragement; (2) *respect for the child's autonomy* or non-intrusiveness and active recognition of the child's individuality, motives and perspectives; (3) *structure and limit setting* or the mother effectively establishing her expectations for the child by setting clear and consistent limits on the child; and (4) *quality of instruction* or instructions that are attuned to the child's focus, stated clearly, paced at a rate that allows comprehension, and graded in logical steps for the child to understand.

Quality of support provided by Surinamese-Dutch, indigenous Dutch, and Japanese mothers: A comparison

To gain greater insight into the quality of the Surinamese-Dutch mothers' interactions with their infants, their behaviour was compared to the behaviour of mothers from two other samples; an indigenous Dutch sample and an indigenous Japanese sample. The mother–infant interaction in the latter samples was observed under the same circumstances as the mother–infant interaction in the Surinamese-Dutch group and evaluated using the same rating scales.

The Dutch sample consisted of 26 mother–infant pairs from lower-class families living in the city of Nijmegen. The group was a control group in a longitudinal intervention study and repeatedly observed between the ages of 6 and 30 months (Meij, 1992; Meij, Riksen-Walraven, & Van Lieshout, 1995). Interestingly, the educational level of the mothers in the indigenous Dutch group was exactly the same on average as the educational level of the mothers in the Surinamese-Dutch sample. Unlike the Surinamese infants, however, all of the Dutch children were firstborns and living in two-parent families. For comparison with the Surinamese-Dutch group, we used the observational data obtained at the age of 18 months. At this time, the mother–child interaction was videotaped during a visit to the lab. The session lasted 10 minutes and the mothers were asked to let their child consecutively perform three tasks, which were also used with the Surinamese-Dutch sample.

The Japanese sample consisted of 49 mothers with a 14-month-old infant living in the city of Tokyo (Vereijken, 1990; Vereijken, Riksen-Walraven, & Kondo-Ikemura, 1997). These mothers and children were seen again when the children were 24 months old, but these data are not presented here. All of the Japanese subjects lived in two-parent families. The sample consisted of both lower- and higher-educated mothers. Of the 49 mothers, 9 worked outside the home for 18 hours a week or more. The mother–infant interaction was videotaped during a home visit. The interaction session lasted 17.5 minutes and consisted of five instructional tasks with two of these also used with the Surinamese-Dutch sample. The comparison of the Surinamese-Dutch sample with the Japanese sample is particularly interesting in light of the fact that Japanese children are known for their relatively high levels of academic achievement (see Stevenson et al., this volume).

The reliability of the observations proved to be high for all three samples. The same expert, who also participated in the ratings, trained all those people rating the quality of support. In addition, a native Japanese researcher took part in the rating of the Japanese subjects.

In all three samples, the four scores reflecting the quality of support mothers give their infants were significantly interrelated (rs between .50 and .84), which means that mothers who are good at providing one kind of support are generally good at providing other kinds of support as well. The quality of maternal support proved to be remarkably stable in both the Dutch and Japanese samples where mother–child interactions were observed on different occasions. In the Japanese study, a correlation of $r = .50$ was found between the summed scores reflecting the overall quality of support at 14 and 24 months. Similarly, in the Dutch sample, the overall quality of support at 18 months correlated highly with the same scores at 12 and 30 months (rs of .85 and .70, respectively). In addition, the quality of maternal support assessed with the four scales at 18 months was found to be predicted from the mother's sensitive responsiveness towards her baby at 6 months ($r = .63$; Meij, 1992).

What might be expected regarding the quality of support provided by mothers from the three samples? In comparing the Surinamese-Dutch and indigenous Dutch samples, we expected the Surinamese-Dutch mothers to provide lower-quality support than the native Dutch mothers for several reasons. Whereas the educational levels in the two samples were equal, immigrant mothers are exposed to higher levels of life stress than native Dutch mothers. Moreover, Surinamese-Dutch children have been found to perform less well at school than their indigenous Dutch agemates with the same socio-economic background. As already observed, low-quality parental support during infancy appears to lay the foundation for later underachievement. Lower-quality support than that provided by native

Dutch mothers has already been found for Surinamese-Dutch mothers with 3- and 4-year-old children (Leseman et al., 1992) and we expected to find this difference in the interactions with 18-month-olds as well. With regard to the Japanese mothers, we expected them to be more supportive of their infants than both groups of Dutch mothers. This is because the mean level of maternal education was somewhat higher in the Japanese group than in the other groups. In addition, the relatively high levels of academic achievement generally observed among Japanese children are presumably fostered by high-quality parental support in the very first years of life.

In Table 10.1, the mean scores for the quality of support provided in the three samples are presented. All of the expected differences were indeed found, but with regard to only the first two kinds of support. The Surinamese-Dutch mothers scored significantly lower than the mothers from the other samples with regard to both supportive presence and respect for the child's autonomy. The Japanese mothers showed significantly more respect for their children's autonomy than did the native Dutch mothers, while the difference between the two groups for supportive presence was not significant. It is interesting that the expected differences between the mothers were only found for the first two kinds of support, which we consider the "basic ingredients of support" because they are assumed to foster the child's competence motivation and set the stage for effective teaching in later years. The fact that infants from cultural groups that are known to have relatively low versus high school performances are found to differ with respect to only these kinds of support, suggests once more that "teaching" in infancy is not as important for the later development of special talents as the provision of a warm and nurturant climate for the children to experience themselves as autonomous

TABLE 10.1
Quality of support provided by mothers from three samples

	Surinamese-Dutch[1] (n = 38) M (SD)	Native Dutch[2] (n = 26) M (SD)	Japanese[3] (n = 49) M (SD)	Significant contrasts
Supportive presence	3.63 (1.34)	4.31 (1.57)	4.72 (1.40)	SuD < NaD, Jap[4]
Respect for autonomy	3.84 (1.29)	4.50 (1.30)	5.10 (1.45)	SuD < NaD < Jap
Structure & limits	4.08 (1.02)	4.50 (1.45)	4.27 (1.13)	
Quality of instruction	3.92 (1.05)	4.23 (1.45)	4.18 (1.29)	

[1] Low education, children 18 months old (Riksen-Walraven et al., 1996)
[2] Low education, children 18 months old (Meij, 1992)
[3] Low to high education, children 14 months old (Vereijken, 1990)
[4] SuD = Surinamese-Dutch; NaD = Native Dutch; Jap = Japanese; t-tests, $p < .05$ (one-tailed)

and competent agents. It is nevertheless likely that differences in the parental "teaching skills" of structure and limit setting, on the one hand, and the provision of high-quality instructions, on the other hand, will become more prominent in the years beyond infancy when "teaching" increasingly contributes to children's socialisation and development.

To summarise, our lower-educated Surinamese-Dutch mothers indeed turned out to be less supportive than our native Dutch mothers with the same lower level of education. The quality of the support provided by the Surinamese-Dutch mothers was found to be low not only in a relative, but also an absolute sense. On all of the four 7-point rating scales for the quality of support, a score of 3 or less was definitely insufficient. In light of the size of the standard deviations shown in Table 10.1 and the considerable interrelatedness of the four scales, we can therefore conclude that many of the Surinamese-Dutch infants in our sample lack the basic support needed to develop their talents.

Conditions impairing parents' ability to provide adequate support to their infants

As already suggested, several factors may contribute to the relatively low quality of the support provided by the Surinamese-Dutch mothers, when compared to the indigenous Dutch mothers. A first explanation lies in culture-specific pedagogical values. The pedagogical tradition in Surinam is relatively restrictive and discipline-oriented (Jap-A-Joe & Leseman, 1994). Surinamese parents consider child obedience and respect for adults to be very important and attempt to instil these values at an early age. A high value is also placed on academic achievement, as already noted, which may also explain the controlling and interfering behaviour of many of the Surinamese-Dutch mothers (i.e. little "respect for child's autonomy"). The scores of the Japanese mothers in Table 10.1, however, demonstrate that similar values can also be pursued using a different caregiving style: Japanese parents also value obedience, respect for adults, and academic success, but tend to indulge their children and allow them to be demanding, as reflected by their relatively high scores for supportive presence and respect for autonomy when compared to the Surinamese-Dutch mothers (t-values of 3.69 and 4.28, respectively; $p < .01$).

A second possible explanation for the relatively low quality of support provided by the Surinamese-Dutch mothers may lie in the high level of life stress they are often exposed to and the relatively low level of social support they experience. In contrast to the mothers in the other samples, for example, the Surinamese-Dutch mothers belong to a cultural minority group. Most of them are immigrants facing the task of adapting to new life circumstances along with the habits and values of another society.

Particularly in the first years after immigration, the strains produced by this task may negatively affect parenting, as illustrated by the relations we found between the quality of parental support and the time since the parent's arrival in the new country. The quality of support provided by the mothers clearly increased with the number of years since immigration (correlations of .34, .25, .34 and .27 on the four scales mentioned in Table 10.1; n = 38). This relationship was found to be independent of maternal age, moreover.

Whereas the native Dutch and Japanese subjects all lived in two-parent households, more than half of the mothers in the Surinamese-Dutch sample were single parents, which may also contribute to the relatively low scores for support in this sample. Marital support is typically found to have a beneficial effect on parenting. Several studies have shown support from a spouse to influence parenting both directly and indirectly by reducing the negative impact of life stress on parenting (Belsky & Isabella, 1988; Parke & Stearns, 1993; Simons, Lorenz, Wu, & Conger, 1993).

Examination of Table 10.2 shows the mothers living in a two-parent family in our Surinamese-Dutch sample to be more supportive of their children than the single mothers in the sample. They provided significantly more emotional support than the single mothers for their infants, and their behaviour was significantly less intrusive and more respectful of the child as well. In other words, they were more effective in providing what we consider the two "basic" elements of support for this age group. Moreover, this difference between the single mothers and mothers living in a two-parent household is not explained by a difference in maternal education. In fact, the single mothers in our sample tended to be more highly educated than the mothers living with a husband. We also checked whether the two groups of mothers differed with respect to the support they received from family members living elsewhere. Single mothers received more support

TABLE 10.2
Quality of support provided by Surinamese-Dutch mothers, separately for single mothers and mothers living with a spouse

	Mothers living with spouse (n = 18)		Single mothers (n = 20)		t
	M	(SD)	M	(SD)	
Supportive presence	4.06	(1.47)	3.25	(1.12)	1.90*
Respect for automony	4.28	(1.18)	3.45	(1.28)	2.07*
Structure & limits	4.28	(1.27)	3.90	(.72)	1.11
Quality of instruction	4.22	(1.22)	3.65	(.81)	1.68

*$p < .05$, one-tailed

from their families. On the average, single mothers had family members living a significantly shorter distance from them than mothers living with a spouse; they also reported significantly more actual support from these family members (e.g. babysitting). As can be seen from Table 10.2, however, the support provided by family members did not compensate for the absence of support from a spouse.

Our data also illustrate the impact of another source of stress on the quality of support provided to the child, that is, the number of children a parent has to care for. Empirical studies have shown care for other children to occur at the cost of parental attentiveness and responsiveness to the individual child (Kendrick & Dunn, 1980). Only-children have more interactions with their parents (Lewis & Kreitzberg, 1979), and their relationships with their parents are found to be more positive and affectionate than those of children with siblings (Falbo & Polit, 1986). In our Surinamese-Dutch sample, there were 10 children without siblings, 15 with one sibling, and 13 with two or more siblings living in the same house.

As can be seen from the left-hand panel of Table 10.3, a mother's supportive presence and respect for her child's autonomy decrease as the number of siblings increases. Children with two or more siblings receive significantly less emotional support than children with only one sibling or children with no siblings (t-values 1.74 and 2.03, $p < .05$). Moreover, children with two or more siblings experienced significantly less respect for their autonomy than only-children (2.35, $p < .05$). With regard to structure and limit setting and the quality of instructions, the differences between the children with a different number of siblings were not significant. The data nevertheless show an interesting trend: a child with one (older, in all cases) sibling tends to receive somewhat better structuring and instructions than an only-child. This suggests that mothers with a second child may have learned these "teaching skills" during interactions with their firstborns. This positive effect is probably wiped out by the stress of having to care for three or more children.

The middle and right-hand panels of Table 10.3 show how the number of children within the family affects the quality of support provided by the mothers in one- and two-parent families. Due to the small numbers of subjects in the cells, statistical analyses were not undertaken. We only present the figures to highlight some interesting trends. First, it is remarkable that the aforementioned "learning effect" for the mothers with a second child is only found in two-parent families. Moreover, the data nicely illustrate the interaction between living in a one- or two-parent family and the number of siblings. Only-children and children with one sibling receive better support from their mothers when living in a two-parent versus single-parent family. For children with two or more siblings, however, the marital status of their mother does not make a difference to

TABLE 10.3

Quality of support provided by Surinamese-Dutch mothers to children with various numbers of siblings (total sample, mothers living with a spouse, single mothers)

	Total sample (n = 38)				Mothers living with spouse (n = 18)			Single mothers (n = 20)		
	No siblings (n = 10) M (SD)	One sibling (n = 15) M (SD)	Two or more (n = 13) M (SD)	Significant contrasts*	No siblings (n = 6) M (SD)	One sibling (n = 9) M (SD)	Two or more (n = 3) M (SD)	No siblings (n = 4) M (SD)	One sibling (n = 6) M (SD)	Two or more (n = 10) M (SD)
Supportive presence	4.00 (1.49)	3.93 (1.28)	3.00 (1.15)	NoSib, One > TwoM	4.33 (1.86)	4.22 (1.40)	3.00 (.00)	3.50 (.58)	3.50 (1.05)	3.00 (1.33)
Respect for autonomy	4.50 (.85)	3.73 (1.44)	3.46 (1.27)	NoSib > TwoM	4.83 (.75)	4.11 (1.45)	3.67 (.58)	4.00 (.82)	3.17 (1.33)	3.40 (1.43)
Structure & limits	4.10 (1.20)	4.27 (1.16)	3.85 (.69)		4.17 (1.47)	4.56 (1.33)	3.67 (.58)	4.00 (.82)	3.83 (.75)	3.90 (.74)
Quality of instruction	4.00 (1.15)	4.13 (1.13)	3.62 (.87)		4.17 (1.32)	4.56 (1.24)	3.33 (.58)	3.75 (.96)	3.50 (.55)	3.70 (.95)

* t-tests, $p < .05$ (one-tailed); NoSib = no siblings, TwoM = two or more siblings

the quality of the support they receive. It should be noted that the negative relation between maternal supportiveness and the number of children in the family cannot be attributed to the actual presence of or interference from siblings during the interaction sessions, as the mother and target child were observed together with no siblings present.

The preceding paragraphs have shed some light on why many Surinamese-Dutch mothers do not succeed in providing their infants with the basic support needed to fully develop their talents. Two conditions appear to be particularly detrimental. First, the need to adapt to a new culture and life setting after immigration evidently causes a lot of stress, which negatively affects the support mothers are able to provide their infants. Second, many Surinamese-Dutch mothers are single mothers and thus lack the support of a husband, which can mitigate the effects of life stress, promote their well-being, and thereby have a beneficial effect on the quality of the mothers' interactions with their infants.

Five excellently achieving Surinamese-Dutch infants

In addition to observing the Surinamese-Dutch infants in interactions with their mothers, we also assessed the children's level of mental development using the Dutch version of the Bayley (1969) Mental Scale of Infant Development. Remarkably, this "disadvantaged" sample contained five infants with excellent performance on the Mental Development scale when compared not only to the other Surinamese-Dutch children, but also to the norm group of native Dutch agemates described in the test manual (Van der Meulen & Smrkovsky, 1983). We defined "excellent" performance as a Mental Developmental Index of 125 or higher (i.e. scores lying more than one and a half standard deviations above the population mean of 100). The five excellent Surinamese-Dutch infants, two girls and three boys, had scores of 127, 129, 131, 136, and 137, respectively. We were curious as to whether these five subjects would stand out against the rest of the sample in other respects as well. In light of the insights presented earlier in this chapter, we expected these excellently performing youngsters to have received high-quality support from their mothers, particularly with regard to the basic ingredients of emotional support and respect for the child's autonomy. Given that these elements of support are assumed to foster a sense of security and competence in infants, clear indications of a secure relationship with the mother and signs of high competence motivation were also expected. With regard to the living conditions of the families of our five outstanding infants, the question was whether the conditions would be relatively favourable or whether excellent performers can be found in families having to cope with relatively high levels of life stress.

Table 10.4 contains a comparison of our five excelling Surinamese-Dutch subjects with the other infants in the Surinamese-Dutch sample. A comparison of the family characteristics yielded no differences between the two groups with regard to the mother's age, the number of years since immigration to the Netherlands, or the amount of contact maintained with the family. It should be noted, however, that none of the mothers in the excellent group appeared to be particularly at risk. No mother was very young or very old, no one had immigrated very recently, and no one had less than average contact with her family. Four of the five mothers with excellent infants lived together with a husband, which is favourable in comparison with the rest of the sample where almost 60% of the mothers were single parents. Finally, four of the five infants in the excellent group had one (older) sibling, while the other child in the excellent group was an only-child. Although the difference between the mean number of siblings in the two groups did not reach significance, the situation appears somewhat more favourable in the excellent group where none of the subjects had more than one sibling. One of the excellent subjects (subject 2) had a combination of two "risk factors", which might undermine her mother's supportiveness: she was the child of a single mother also caring for another child. As shown in Table 10.3, children with this combination receive very low-quality support from their mothers when compared to other children.

The quality of support provided by the mothers of excelling children proved to be very high when compared to the rest of the sample. The four mean support scores for the excellent group were not only significantly higher than those for the non-excellent subjects, they were also high in absolute terms (i.e. all mean scores were 5 or higher). The mean level of supportive presence or emotional support provided for the excelling infants was particularly impressive and found to be more than two points higher than the mean level of emotional support for the other children in the sample. Inspection of the scores for the individual infants shows that no one of the children received low-quality of support on any of the four scales. Scores of 3 or lower simply did not occur in the excellent group, while many of the subjects in the remainder of the sample were found to score below three on one or more of the scales.

Table 10.4 also contains scores for mother "hostility" during the 25-minute interaction episode with the child. Hostility was scored using a 7-point rating scale developed by Erickson et al. (1985). A score of 1 shows no irritation or anger towards the child during the entire interaction episode; a score of 2 indicates slight signs of irritation or annoyance with the child; and higher scores indicate increasing expressions of irritation, anger, and hostility by the mother. It should be noted that high scores on this scale are rare because parents tend to conceal hostile feelings towards their children

TABLE 10.4
Five excellent Surinamese-Dutch 18-month-olds compared to their Surinamese-Dutch agemates

Variables	Excellently achieving infants					Exc. ach. infants (n = 5)		Other infants (n = 33)		t-test
	1	2	3	4	5	M	(SD)	M	(SD)	
Gender	Girl	Girl	Boy	Boy	Boy					
Bayley MDI	127	129	131	136	137	132.0	(4.36)	102.33	(12.40)	10.20**
Family characteristics										
Age of mother	30	27	28	26	28	27.80	(1.48)	28.48	(5.32)	ns
Years since M's immigration	22	14	27	6	11	15.60	(8.79)	15.12	(6.27)	ns
M living with spouse	yes	no	yes	yes	yes					
Contact with M's family[1]	4	4	5	3	4	4.00	(.71)	3.79	(.93)	ns
Number of siblings	1	1	0	1	1	.80	(.45)	1.27	(1.07)	ns
Quality of support[2]										
Supportive Presence	6	5	6	5	6	5.60	(.55)	3.33	(1.16)	4.25**
Respect for Autonomy	6	5	5	4	5	5.00	(.71)	3.67	(1.27)	2.28*
Structure & Limits	6	4	5	5	6	5.20	(.84)	3.91	(.95)	2.87**
Quality of Instruction	6	4	5	4	6	5.00	(1.00)	3.77	(.97)	2.66**
M's Hostility	1	1	1	1	1	1.00	(.00)	1.55	(.75)	4.16**
Child interactive behaviour[2]										
Negativity	1	4	1	2	1	1.80	(1.30)	3.30	(1.47)	-2.16*
Avoidance	1	3	1	2	1	1.60	(.89)	4.06	(1.66)	-3.22**
Compliance	7	4	5	6	6	5.60	(1.14)	3.79	(1.47)	2.62*
Affection	6	3	4	4	6	4.60	(1.34)	2.52	(1.09)	3.87**
Child competence motivation[2]										
Persistence	6	6	6	5	6	5.80	(.45)	4.33	(1.47)	4.51**
Enthusiasm	5	5	7	5	6	5.60	(.89)	4.55	(1.50)	2.21*

* $p < .05$, ** $p < .01$: two-tailed   [1] 5-point scale; 1 = no contact, 5 = daily contact   [2] 7-point rating scales

in front of a camera. Despite the low mean scores for the two groups, the level of hostility shown by the mothers in the excellent group proved to be significantly lower than that in the other group. In fact, none of these five mothers showed the slightest sign of irritation towards her child.

The quality of the infants' behaviour towards their mothers was also judged on the basis of the videotaped mother–child interaction sessions. Four 7-point rating scales (Erickson et al., 1985) were used to assess the quality of the children's interactive behaviour. High scores on the first two scales, negativity (i.e. expressions of anger, dislike and hostility towards the mother) and avoidance (i.e. a tendency to avoid interaction with the mother), reflect negative feelings towards the mother and an insecure attachment relationship. High scores on the scales for compliance and affection indicate a willingness to cooperate with the mother and to follow her suggestions, along with the expression of positive affect towards the mother. Both compliance with the mother and expressions of positive affect characterise children securely attached to their mother (Matas et al., 1978). Comparison of the mean scores for the excelling and remainder of the subjects showed significant and impressive differences between the groups on all four scales. The individual score patterns for four out of the five excelling children show very low scores (1 or 2) for negativity and avoidance on the one hand, and above-average to high scores for compliance and affection. This pattern reflects a genuinely positive orientation towards the mother. One of the children, however, clearly expressed anger towards her mother and exhibited a slight tendency to avoid interaction with her. This child was also the least compliant of the children in the excellent group and also expressed relatively little affection towards her mother. It should be noted that this girl was indeed the daughter of the mother with the stress of being a single mother with two children.

Finally, we assessed the children's competence motivation, or the persistence and enthusiasm with which they performed the tasks presented in the interaction session. Task persistence and task pleasure are considered key indicators of competence motivation in studies with young children (Barrett, Morgan, & Maslin-Cole, 1993). In the present study, we rated the children's task behaviour using two 7-point rating scales (Erickson et al., 1985). As can be seen from Table 10.4, the excellently achieving subjects, without exception, exhibited high levels of competence motivation. They were clearly and significantly more persistent and enthusiastic on average than the other infants in the Surinamese-Dutch sample.

When the evidence presented in Table 10.4 is considered as a whole, the picture that emerges of our excelling infants bears a remarkable resemblance to that which has been found for the early lives and development of gifted individuals. First, the family climate of our five infants can be described as very supportive. The climate is warm and nurturant; there is a high level of emotional support, a lack of annoyance and hostility in the mothers' behaviour, and obvious respect for the child as a person. Second, our excellent subjects all exhibited high levels of competence motivation, which is one of the most outstanding characteristics of gifted preschoolers. Finally, very young gifted children have been described as functioning well in social interchanges and exceptionally able to get and hold the attention of adults in socially acceptable ways (White, 1985). Given the quality of their interactive behaviour, our excelling infants can certainly be characterised as conspicuously competent in dealing with their caregivers.

The question now is whether this means that our excelling subjects are gifted children who will develop special talents in later years. This conclusion cannot be drawn. What we can say is that these five children would not have performed at this high level if they had lived in a less supportive environment. The high levels of competence motivation fostered by excellent parental support have allowed them to actualise much more of their genetic potential than their agemates living in less favourable circumstances. Such eminent performance at this age, however, tells us little about the potential talents of these children. They may or may not demonstrate special talents in later years. Other children, not classified as "excellent" in our sample, may also have the innate potential to become later an eminent achiever. The only thing that we can say at this point is that our excelling 18-month-olds have a much better chance of developing whatever talents they may have than their less well functioning agemates. First, the talents of excelling 18-month-olds are more likely to be detected as they tend to have sensitive and involved parents with a keen eye for the states and needs of their child. These parents are also more inclined to seek such stimulating environments as high-quality schools and teachers for their children. In addition, the excelling children themselves are much better prepared than their agemates to take advantage of the opportunities they are offered. The style of interaction they have developed with their parents along with their basic sense of security make them more easy and pleasant for teachers to interact with than other children (Motti, 1986). And last, but not least, the high levels of competence motivation that characterise these children increase their chances of effective interaction with the environment and thereby further development of their innate potential.

CONCLUSIONS: BACK TO THE BEGINNING

The answer to the question of the kinds of support needed by gifted infants should, by now, be clear. As infants, gifted children do not need special treatment. Their needs are the same as for infants with the genetic potential for less excellent achievement. To make the best of whatever potential they are born with, children should already receive support from their parents or primary caregivers in infancy. Two elements of support are of particular importance in the very first years of life: a warm and nurturant climate with sensitive responding to the children's needs, and the provision of ample opportunities for the children to experience themselves as effective agents, which means little intrusion with their behaviour and otherwise respecting their autonomy as a person. These two elements of support are considered basic for the development of competence motivation, which drives children towards further interaction with the environment and thereby the actualisation of their genetic potential. No specific stimulation, training, or teaching is needed in infancy, although the imposition of clear and consistent limits and guidelines along with the provision of clear explanations and instructions attuned to the child's needs and level of comprehension are increasingly important during the second year of life.

We consider adequate parental support in infancy to be a necessary but not sufficient condition for the development of special talents in later years. Children who experience high-quality support as infants are well prepared to develop special talents, provided they have these talents and receive adequate support at later ages. Infants growing up in an unsupportive environment simply lack the opportunities to build up the competence motivation and socio-emotional skills needed to develop the special talents they may have. In many cases, these talents may even go undiscovered.

Whether or not parents are able to provide proper support for their children largely depends on such personal resources as resilience and intelligence. High levels of life stress have also been found to affect the quality of parents' behaviour in interactions with their infants and may actually explain why relatively few children from disadvantaged and ethnic minority groups are identified as "gifted". The mean level of support provided for infants in these groups is generally quite low and therefore not sufficient to provide a foundation for the development of special talents at later ages.

Unfortunately for children in disadvantaged families, the quality of support provided by parents tends to be very stable throughout the infancy period. Unless they experience dramatic improvements in their living conditions, unsupportive parents are likely to remain unsupportive. In a sample of 26 lower-class Dutch families, the quality of support measured using the four scales described earlier in this chapter proved to be remarkably stable between the ages of 12 months and 30 months. A correlation as high as .85 was found between overall quality of parental support at 12 months and 18 months, with stability coefficient of .70 between the assessments at 18 months and 30 months. Part of this stability can, of course, be explained by the continued levels of life stress and relative lack of social support experienced by the parents. The developing infants can also be seen to contribute to the stability of their parents' behaviour. Infants of unsupportive parents tend to develop such "unpleasant" or "difficult" behaviours as a tendency to avoid or resist contact with their parents and non-compliance to the suggestions or commands of their parents. Such unpleasant behaviours make it even more difficult for parents to interact with their children in a nurturant and respectful manner and not show irritation or hostility. In other words, unsupportive parents and their infants run the risk of getting caught in a downward spiral with decreased parental support as a result. This was indeed found in the lower-class Dutch sample just described. A significant decrease in the overall quality of parental support was observed between the ages of 18 months and 30 months along with increased parental hostility.

These findings do not imply that trying to increase parents' supportiveness for their infants is hopeless. If parents are provided with proper support at the proper time, remarkable increases in the quality of the support they give can be observed. Three successful programmes illustrate what we mean by "proper support at the proper time" for parents with infants. Two of the intervention studies described earlier in this chapter (Riksen-Walraven, 1978; Van den Boom, 1994) have shown the effectiveness of support programmes for parents with infants in the first year of life. Van den Boom's programme for Dutch lower-class mothers with irritable infants started when the children were six months old, i.e. at the age at which the quality of mother–infant interaction in this particular group is known to start deteriorating. The content and intensity of the intervention were properly geared to the characteristics of the target group as assessed in an earlier study. Riksen-Walraven's (1978) intervention programme for Dutch lower-class mothers with a first-born infant started later in the infant's first year. This programme was also less intense and included fewer home visits than van den Boom's programme. Such lower-level intervention nevertheless proved to be effective, in part because the target group was less at risk than van den Boom's group and did not require an earlier or more intensive intervention. In our intervention study with Surinamese-Dutch families, a 16-week intervention programme started when the infants were 13 months old (Riksen-Walraven et al., 1996). Intervention before the infants' first birthdays was not deemed necessary because the strains and problems in the interactions between the mothers and children in our target group tend to arise during the second year. During 16 home visits, specially trained Surinamese-Dutch women taught and encouraged the mothers to initiate and maintain supportive interactions with their infants. The programme proved to have a positive effect on both the quality of the mothers' interactive behaviours measured using the four support scales discussed earlier and the infants' performance on the Bayley Mental Scale. Although the latter sample did not contain families with severe problems, the intervention studies certainly show that it is indeed possible to provide children from disadvantaged families with the support they need and thereby lay the foundation for the development of any potential talents in the future.

The actualisation of talent is important for not only for the well-being of the gifted individual but also society at large. Talents that remain undiscovered, undeveloped, or unused may certainly be considered a social waste. Considerable concern has been expressed about the waste of talent among children from disadvantaged and culturally different backgrounds in particular. Children from these groups are clearly under-represented in talent-development programmes and the special curricula for gifted pupils. It is generally assumed that this is due to under-identification, and considerable effort is therefore being devoted to adaptation of identification instruments and development of culturally specific checklists for gifted children from "different" backgrounds (Frasier, 1993). No doubt this will help reduce the waste of talent among these groups, but we think it is not enough. Poor assessment methods are not the only reason why so few disadvantaged children are identified as gifted. It should also be recognised that there may simply be less talent in such disadvantaged as opposed to more privileged groups. In this chapter, we have argued that children receiving insufficient support in infancy lack the motivational and socio-emotional foundation for full actualisation of their innate potential. Their talents do not become visible and thus are not detected. In other words, the provision of sufficient support in infancy is needed to reduce the waste of talent among disadvantaged children.

REFERENCES

Barrett, K.C., Morgan, G.A., & Maslin-Cole, C. (1993). Three studies on the development of mastery motivation in infancy and toddlerhood. In D. Messer (Ed.), *Mastery motivation in early childhood: Development, measurement and social processes* (pp. 83–109). London: Routledge.

Baumrind, D. (1977). *Socialization determinants of personal agency*. Paper presented at the biennial meeting of the Society for Research in Child Development, New Orleans.

Bayley, N. (1969). *Bayley Scales of Infant Development*. New York: Psychological Corporation.

Belsky, J., & Isabella, R. (1988). Maternal, infant, and social-contextual determinants of attachment security. In J. Belsky & T. Nezworski (Eds.), *Clinical implications of attachment* (pp. 41–95). Hillsdale, NJ: Lawrence Erlbaum Associates Inc.

Block, J., & Kremen, A.M. (1996). IQ and ego-resiliency: Conceptual and empirical connections and separateness. *Journal of Personality and Social Psychology*, 70, 349–361.

Block, J.H., & Block, J. (1980). The role of ego-control and ego-resiliency in the organization of behavior. In W.A. Collins (Ed.), *The Minnesota Symposia on Child Psychology, Volume 13*, (pp. 39–101). Hillsdale, NJ: Lawrence Erlbaum Associates Inc.

Bloom, B.S. (Ed.) (1985). *Developing talent in young people*. New York: Ballantine.
Bowlby, J. (1969). *Attachment and loss (Vol. 1). Attachment* [2nd ed. 1982]. New York: Basic Books.
Bronfenbrenner, U., & Ceci, S.J. (1994). Nature–nurture reconceptualized in developmental perspective: A bioecological model. *Psychological Review, 101*, 568–586.
Egeland, B., Pianta, R., & O'Brien, M.A. (1993). Maternal intrusiveness in infancy and child maladaptation in early school years. *Development and Psychopathology, 5*, 359–370.
Erickson, M.F., Sroufe, L.A., & Egeland, B. (1985). The relationship between quality of attachment and behavior problems in preschool in a high-risk sample. In I. Bretherton & E. Waters (Eds.), *Growing points of attachment theory and research. Monographs of the Society for Research in Child Development, 50*, 147–166.
Fagot, B., & Kavanaugh, K. (1993). Parenting during the second year: Effects of children's age, sex and attachment classification. *Child Development, 64*, 258–271.
Falbo, T., & Polit, D. (1986). A quantitative review of the only child literature: Research evidence and theory development. *Psychological Bulletin, 100*, 176–189.
Frasier, M.M. (1993). Issues, problems and programs in nurturing the disadvantaged and culturally different talented. In J. Freeman (Ed.), *The psychology of gifted children: Perspectives on development and education* (pp. 685–693). New York: Wiley.
Gallagher, J.J. (1985). *Teaching the gifted child* (3rd ed). Boston: Allyn & Bacon.
Gagné, F. (1991). *Toward a differentiated model of giftedness and talent*. In N. Colangelo & G. A. Davis (Eds.), *Handbook of gifted education* (pp. 65–81). Boston: Allyn & Bacon.
Jap-a-Joe, S.R., & Leseman, P.P.M. (1994). *Surinaamse opvoedingstradities. Behoud en verandering na migratie: een aanzet tot beschrijving en analyse* [Surinamese pedagogical traditions. Retention and change after migration]. Rotterdam: RISBO.
Kendrick, C., & Dunn, J. (1980). Caring for a second baby: Effects on interaction between mother and firstborn. *Developmental Psychology, 16*, 303–311.
Leseman, P.P.M., Vergeer, M.M., Sijsling, F.F., Jap-a-Joe, S.R., & Sahin, S. (1992). *Amount, content and quality of parent–child interactions and the development of language and cognition*. Paper presented at the XXV International Congress of Psychology, Brussels, 19–24 July.
Lewis, M., & Kreitzberg, V.S. (1979). Effects of birth order and spacing on mother–infant interactions. *Developmental Psychology, 15*, 617–625.
Lewis, M., & Louis, B. (1991). Young gifted children. In N. Colangelo & G. A. Davis (Eds.), *Handbook of gifted education* (pp. 365–382). Boston: Allyn & Bacon.
Lewis, M., & Michalson, L. (1985). The gifted infant. In J. Freeman (Ed.), *The psychology of gifted children: Perspectives on development and education* (pp. 35–59). New York: Wiley.
Matas, L., Arend, R., & Sroufe, L.A. (1978). Continuity of adaptation in the second year: The relationship between quality of attachment and later competence. *Child Development, 49*, 547–556.
McCall, R.B. (1983). A conceptual approach to early mental development. In M. Lewis (Ed.), *Origins of intelligence: Infancy and early childhood* (2nd ed., pp. 107–133). New York: Wiley.
Meij, J.Th., Riksen-Walraven, J.M.A., & Van Lieshout, C.F.M. (1995). *Patterns of change and consistency in parental support as related to children's competence motivation*. Paper presented at the Academy Colloquium 'Early mother-child interaction and attachment: Old and new approaches' Amsterdam, 30 May–2 June.
Meij, J.Th.H. (1992). *Sociale ondersteuning, gehechtheidskwaliteit en vroegkinderlijke competentie-ontwikkeling* [Social support, attachment, and competence]. Nijmegen: Catholic University (Doctoral dissertation).
Mönks, F.J., & Van Boxtel, H.W. (1985). Gifted adolescents: A developmental perspective. In J. Freeman (Ed.), *The psychology of gifted children: Perspectives on development and education* (pp. 275–297). New York: Wiley.

Motti, E. (1986). *Patterns of behaviors of preschool teachers with children of varying developmental history.* Unpublished predoctoral dissertation. University of Minnesota.
Parke, R.D., & Stearns, P. (1993). Fathers and child rearing: A historical analysis. In G. Elder Jr., J. Modell, & R.D. Parke (Eds.), *Children in time and place: Developmental and historical insights.* New York: Cambridge University Press.
Provence, S. (1989). Infants in institutions revisited. *Zero to Three, 9,* 1–4.
Provence, S., & Lipton, R. (1962). *Infants in institutions.* New York: International Universities Press.
Radford, J. (1990). *Child prodigies and exceptional early achievers.* New York: Harvester Wheatsheaf.
Ramey, C.T., Starr, R., Pallas, J., Whitten, C., & Reed, V. (1979). Nutrition, response-contingent stimulation, and the maternal deprivation syndrome: Results of an early intervention program. *Merrill-Palmer Quarterly, 21,* 45–54.
Renzulli, J.S. (1978). What makes giftedness? Reexamining a definition. *Phi Delta Kappa, 60,* 180–184, 216.
Riksen-Walraven, J.M.A. (1978). Effects of caregiver behavior on habituation rate and self-efficacy in infants. *International Journal of Behavioral Development, 1,* 105–130.
Riksen-Walraven, J.M.A., Meij, J.Th., Hubbard, F.O., & Zevalkink, J. (1996). Intervention in lower-class Surinam-Dutch families: Effects on mothers and infants. *International Journal of Behavioral Development, 19* (4), 739–756.
Riksen-Walraven, J.M.A. & van Aken, M.A.G. (1997). Effects of two mother–infant intervention programs upon children's development at 7, 10, and 12 years. In W. Koops, J.B. Hoeksma, & D.C. van den Boom (Eds.), *Development of interaction and attachment: Traditional and non-traditional approaches* (pp. 79–93). Amsterdam: North-Holland.
Robinson, N.M. (1993). Identifying and nurturing gifted, very young children. In K.A. Heller, F.J. Mönks, & A.H. Passow (Eds.), *International handbook of giftedness and talent* (pp. 507–525). Oxford: Pergamon.
Simons, R.L., Lorenz, F.O., Wu, C., & Conger, R.D. (1993). Social network and marital support as mediators and moderators of the impact of stress and depression on parental behavior. *Developmental Psychology, 29,* 368–381.
Van den Boom, D.C. (1994). The influence of temperament and mothering on attachment and exploration: An experimental manipulation of sensitive responsiveness among lower-class mothers with irritable infants. *Child Development, 65,* 1457–1477.
Van der Meulen, B.F. & Smrkovsky, M. (1983). *BOS 2–30 Bayley Ontwikkelingsschalen.* Lisse: Swets & Zeitlinger.
Vereijken, C.M.J.L. (1990). Attachment to mother in Japanese children: Comparison with the Netherlands. *Research Reports of the Matsushita International foundation, 2,* 17–19.
Vereijken, C.M.J.L., Riksen-Walraven, J.M.A., & Kondo-Ikemura, K. (1997). Maternal sensitivity and infant attachment security in Japan: A longitudinal study. *International Journal of Behavioral Development, 21*(1), 35–49.
White, B. (1985). Competence and giftedness. In J. Freeman (Ed.), *The psychology of gifted children: Perspectives on development and education* (pp. 59–74). New York: Wiley.
White, R.W. (1959). Motivation reconsidered: The concept of competence. *Psychological Review, 66,* 297–323.

CHAPTER ELEVEN

Teaching for talent: Lessons from the research

Joan Freeman
Middlesex University, London

PROBLEMS OF DEFINITIONS

In order to provide appropriately for teaching the talented it is essential to know who they are and how they function. However, there is considerable disagreement among experts on what talent is, and which features can reliably be used to distinguish talented children. Nevertheless, schemes of special education continue to be devised for them, often with considerable claims for success. The author's survey of international research (Freeman, 1998) has been aimed at finding out some of the best ways to educate pupils who have the potential to make a creative and valuable contribution to knowledge and the arts, and so possibly to affect the way people think and act.

The description "talented" is chosen here as preferable to the more commonly used term "gifted". This is because of the many problems surrounding the concept of "giftedness", such as the implication of relatively fixed abilities identifiable by high-level achievement, and also because the general tenor of work in this area is moving away from that term. Indeed, the new outlook is nicely summed up by the Americans Treffinger and Feldhusen (1996), who after very many years of school-based research in this area, now describe the blanket term "gifted" as "indefensible". Talent is taken here to mean either the demonstration of exceptionally high-level performance, whether across a range of endeavours or in a limited field, or the potential for excellence which has not yet been recognised by either tests or experts. There is a distinction between the recognised abilities of children and those of adolescents and adults. The children's are usually seen in precociousness in comparison with others of the same age, and the adults' are in productions based on many years of dedication to the chosen domain.

Distinguishing high-level potential—as distinct from measurable production—is particularly difficult because the true potential of talented children, who are "merely" working at above average level is easily missed. Research shows that such children are not a homogeneous group, whether in terms of learning style, creativity, speed of development, personality, or social behaviour. Consequently, there are dozens of definitions of "giftedness" around, almost all of which refer to children's precocity, either in psychological constructs, such as intelligence and creativity, or by teachers more usually in terms of high marks in school subjects (Hany, 1997). This use of precocity as the prime identifying feature is probably responsible for the children's later apparent return to a more normal level, often called "burn out", which is usually due to the others catching up. In formal school education, however, social or business talents are rarely considered, and physical and artistic prowess is frequently seen as inborn potential which can be developed to excellence by coaching and practice. To some extent, the way a talented child is defined depends on what is being looked for, whether it is academic excellence for formal education, innovation for creative commerce, or solving paper-and-pencil puzzles for an IQ club.

So often it seems that it is political and social attitudes, rather than the availability of resources, which are more influential in the recognition of the needs and consequent educational provision for the talented. In some richer countries such as Sweden and Denmark, it is *not* generally acceptable to recognise and provide for outstanding potential, although in line with current trends, this is now on the point of changing (Persson, 1998; Tirri, 1997). In other poorer countries, such as China and the former USSR, educational emphasis has for many years been placed on practical provision for the promotion of excellence, largely via specialist schools, which have produced so many outstanding achievers in sports and mathematics. In the West, however, fear of elitism appears to have inhibited specialist provision, even though there has been a steady growth in the development of theories and models, mostly American.

The research and educational schemes presented here have been chosen to represent an overview of the evidence on the teaching of the most able, whether statistically presented or demonstrable, but it is certain that not everyone will agree, either with the selection or the conclusions.

SOME SPECIFIC RESEARCH CONCERNS

Serious scientific study of the exceptionally able began about 150 years ago with Galton in England (1869). He investigated the examination results of 180 mathematics graduates at Cambridge University, and even though he knew little else about their lives, he concluded that "men" are not born equal in ability. Although research methodology has improved considerably since then, the quality of work in this area still varies widely and is not always generalisable. The subject also attracts enthusiastic self-styled "experts" who have little understanding of scientific evidence, but who may have strong feelings about what to do for children at the top end of the ability range. Greater scientific rigour is needed in studying the talented, to improve the value of the efforts and money spent. This should include case-studies, surveys, experimental education, and follow-up studies.

Research in this area of child development is not straightforward. It brings some quite specific problems, which not only affect the outcomes but also possible educational provision. For example, a summer school for very able children may well increase their knowledge, which the organisers perceive as highly satisfactory; but only comparison both with other programmes and non-specialist summer schools could tell us that the programme would be the best choice for those or any other children, and this is never done.

Most children defined as gifted for special programmes are identified by conventional intelligence tests resulting in an IQ, such as the Stanford-Binet or the Wechsler, particularly in the USA. But both tests are decidedly influenced by learned material, and so to some extent they are measures of achievement based on age norms. The tests cannot distinguish learning and thinking processes, nor predict high-level creative production (Cropley, 1995). What is more, they are not a sensitive measure of talent because of the "ceiling effect", the upper limit of the tests being too low to differentiate satisfactorily between the top few percent. Is there really a difference in potential between IQ 180 and IQ 200? So much current research is indicating that intelligence, however defined and measured, is only part of the complex dynamics of exceptionally high-level performance, which must combine both opportunity and motivation. The discussion as to what talent is and the identification of talented children is destined to run and run.

The high-IQ highly achieving student has been found to have considerable problems in producing original insightful ideas (Sternberg & Lubart, 1995). Using Sternberg's Triarchic Theory of Intelligence, students were divided into "high analytics", "high creatives", and "high practicals".

Each of these groups was compared with balanced-gifted group (equally high in all three areas) and a balanced above-average control group on a challenging college-level psychology course. Afterwards they were assessed for basic recall, analysis, and creative and practical use of the new information. The "high analytics", those who had often been identified as gifted by IQ, did worst of all the groups on the creativity tests. The authors concluded that these students had rarely been asked to make a creative effort, but had learned to conform to expectations of being good scholars by using memory to gain high grades.

Some researchers favour the case-study approach because they say a talented child is unique and so cannot be compared with any other children, whereas to others the talented are normal children with some exceptional aptitudes. A case-study can be vividly illustrative, but in order to be most effective and rigorous it has to be set in a wider social context to justify generalisations. It is certain, for example, that without a violin, tuition, and family support Yehudi Menuhin would not have become a great violinist; but then if one were to give other children the same upbringing, would they also grow up to be virtuosi? Howe, Davidson, and Sloboda (1998) argue that almost any child could play just as well, given Menuhin's circumstances.

Many experimental samples are made up only of children who are *already* highly achieving. This makes it difficult to measure how much of their subsequent improvement is due to any special treatment, and how much to the fact that the best predictor of future success is present success. However, many educational programmes for the talented, especially those run by parent-backed organisations, do not have *any* research to support them—they proceed on faith.

So many studies, especially retrospective ones, do not make comparisons with any other children, not even of siblings in the same family when family influences are concluded as being strongly influential (e.g. Bloom, 1985). Although it is generally accepted that parental influence and provision is paramount in promoting talent, many parents do work extremely hard at encouraging their children to reach great accomplishments—without success—and others—such as the musician Leonard Bernstein's father, who sold the piano because his son practised too much—actually discourage their talented children.

Even often-referenced studies may have tiny samples that are possibly unrepresentative. In Australia, Gross (1993) used the contentious IQ of 200 to select just three "profoundly gifted" young children. They were described as exhibiting the "typical" gifted symptoms of emotional disturbance, such as school-refusal and friendlessness, because for them, Gross wrote (p. 475), being with normal children was the same as interacting "solely with children who are profoundly intellectually handicapped." But are the described heavy emotional problems really typical of frustrated future world-changers in a mixed-ability class, or could they be because of subtle messages from home that the child is "too clever" and thus too sensitive to fit in socially?

Longitudinal studies are particularly valuable in child development. The best known and still continuing one in this area, which unfortunately reflects the methodological problems of its time, is that of Terman (1925–1929) which began in the 1920s. He examined a sample of IQ 140+ children, mostly of the university staff in California, failing to recognise, however, that they had experienced superior physical and educational nourishment to that of the general population who he used for comparison. He concluded that his "geniuses" were clearly above-average in every possible way, including physique and leadership. However, the most recent report shows that, quite regardless of their IQ scores, the subjects were not noticeably more successful in their adult careers than if they had been randomly selected from the same social and economic backgrounds (Holahan & Sears, 1995). In a review of 14 follow-up studies, Arnold and Subotnik (1994) point to an "inextricable link" between the identification of potential and timing due to age-related stages of development, so that accuracy in predicting achievement increases with the cohort's age.

A unique study in California began with 130 one-year-olds of unknown potential (Gottfried, Gottfried, Bathurst, & Guerin, 1994). Various measures of intellectual, physical, and social development were made regularly until they were 9 years old. Those with an IQ 130 or more on the Wechsler Intelligence test were designated gifted and compared with the others. The researchers concluded that giftedness is a developmental phenomenon, which can rise—and fall—over time: "late bloomers" do exist and can be missed in a single testing. Accordingly, for the greatest reliability, information should be collected at different points in an individual's life, most reliably within specific subject areas in which the child shows promise. Although school performance has not been found reliable as a long-term indicator of outstanding careers (Subotnik, Kassan, Summers, & Wasser, 1993), the child's own interests appear to be an excellent and often neglected indicator of adult attainment (Hany, 1996; Milgram & Hong, 1997).

Looking back at the lives of eminent adults (e.g. Albert, 1992; Goertzel, Goertzel, & Goertzel, 1978; Radford, 1990), also presents problems of interpretation, such as unreliability of memory, the perception of early experiences in terms of later achievements and the different outlooks of those times. Biographical work has also shown how so many who became outstanding in later life were not talented as children. In his investigations into great people of this century, such as Freud, Einstein, and Virginia Woolf, Gardner (1993, 1997), found that by the age of 20 only Picasso's work had been so outstanding that his world stature could have been predicted. In truth, though, we have to recognise that we can never identify and measure the full context of anyone's life, even in the present, and interpretation of data can only be as well informed as possible.

In China, "Hundreds of talented children" have been compared on many tests, in different forms of education, then followed up (Zha, 1993). The identification procedures were designed to look at the whole child, including measures of creativity and personality in the test, as well as teacher opinions. More than 50 schools and 10 universities have been involved in special programmes. These have been based on learning procedures, such as compacting, discussion, research by the children, self-regulation, and self-actualisation. The results so far show that great strides in the children's achievements can be made using these techniques. The Chinese have also found, in common with so many others, that the earlier the start the better the outcome.

HOW THE TALENTED ARE DIFFERENT

Talent or giftedness in children is often recognised through their advancement in one or more areas of education, usually attributed to high intelligence. Advancement, however, is the product of many factors, notably opportunity and encouragement, as well as the coordination of potential with the culture (Sternberg, 1985). Children without those supports will be handicapped in the development of their learning and coping skills (Freeman, 1992a). But in many Pacific Rim countries all success is largely attributed to effort (Hess & Azuma, 1991). Flynn (1991) argues that it is the culture of hard work that enables many American Asians with lower IQs than their classmates to be more highly achieving. Research with people in creative work (e.g. Simonton, 1994) indicates that above a certain high level, personal characteristics such as independence may contribute *more* than intelligence to reaching the highest levels. An exceptionally high intelligence is not, then, the only precursor of a gifted performance.

Gender

Being talented is different for girls and boys (Freeman, 1996). Gender has emerged as the strongest single variable across many studies of talent: girls and boys respond differently to knowledge of their measured abilities as well as to educational experiences. Girls are more likely to dismiss their success as due to luck, for example (Heller & Ziegler, 1996). Talented girls are much more like boys in their intellectual interests and behaviour, but more like other girls in their social-emotional reactions (Stapf, 1990), such as in underestimating their abilities (Reiss & Callahan, 1989). Additionally, parents may actually inhibit talented girls' ambitions, which also affects their self-confidence, especially in mathematics (Jacobs & Weisz, 1994).

Benbow and Lubinski (1993) found that although in the USA talented girls do significantly better than boys in mental arithmetic and general mathematics at school, they much less frequently take it to a higher level. They concluded that there is a genetic mathematical bias in favour of boys—which apparently does not show itself until *after* school. The situation is similar in Britain (as in many other countries). Girls are now scoring more highly than boys at all levels of mathematics while at school, but do not go on to study the subject at university in anything like the same proportions (Arnot, Gray, Ruddock, with Duveen, 1998). The causes of this discrepancy in the USA are either the outcome of social expectations, or else at about the age of 18 girls' genes for mathematics go into self-destruct!

Emotion

The 14-year study by Freeman (1991) compared recognised talented and non-recognised talented children and a random control group (initially aged 5 to 14) across Britain. In-depth interviews were conducted with all the subjects and their families in their own homes, and the teachers in the schools. The children were also given a wide variety of tests, and their environmental circumstances rated. A major aim was to find out why some were seen as talented, while others—of identical measured ability—were not. It became clear that those who had been labelled "talented" or gifted (whether they actually were so or not), had significantly more behaviour problems than those of *equal ability* who were not so labelled. However, the possession of a Stanford-Binet IQ of 140 or more was not found to be independently related to emotional problems. Any emotional problems in the children, whether talented or not, had come from other difficulties in their lives, even though the talent often got the blame.

In fact, most studies of high achievers of all ages have found them to be emotionally stronger than others, with higher productivity, higher motivation and drive, and lower levels of anxiety (Czechlik & Rost, 1988; Olszewski-Kubilius, Kulieke, & Krasney, 1988). As children, however, the talented may be subjected to extra pressure from parents and teachers to be continually successful. This problem was specifically mentioned in a follow-up of 1964–68 Presidential Scholars in America (Kaufman, 1992). Although the ex-scholars continued to do well, they often described how as adults they still relied on academic memory skills to provide them with an identity. In school, there may be stress from the unrelenting pressure of teachers, who expect a high level of absorption and reproduction of information, leaving the talented feeling intellectually unexercised. No one can perform at a high level all the time; fear of failure and feelings of failure and of disappointing the parents will inevitably occur, with possible poor emotional consequences for life.

The talented also suffer from widely different stereotyping and its expectations; the spectrum of expectations runs from emotional handicap to perfection. Problems can arise because a child's talents produce reactions in others that may be too difficult for the child to adjust to. Abilities may develop at different and extreme rates, which can bring difficulties of developmental coordination (Terassier, 1985; Zha, 1993). The parents of highly able children can themselves have resulting emotional problems, either feeling inadequate, or trying to gain social advantage from living vicariously through their child. Whatever problems already exist in the family, these can be intensified when there is an unusual child present (Freeman, 1993). The talented are at least as emotionally strong as any other children, but sometimes suffer from these specific pressures. School counsellors and teachers should be aware of this and be given guidelines on how to help these pupils.

EDUCATING FOR THE DEVELOPMENT OF TALENT

High-level achievers appears to think and learn differently from others. They have been found to use self-regulatory learning strategies more often and more effectively. They are also better able to transfer these skills to novel tasks, to such an extent that measures of autonomous learning could even indicate talent (Risemberg & Zimmerman, 1992; Shore & Kanevsky, 1993). Both their less able age-peers and older youngsters need more external regulation by the teacher (Span, 1995). Research with young children has also found an extra quality of playfulness among the talented learners (Kanevsky, 1992). Because of such differences in learning ability and style, it is important to teach talented pupils appropriately. There are quite a number of new techniques that can help, such as child-initiated learning, peer tutoring, guided dialogue. Such techniques have been found to be particularly useful for deprived bright children (Ari & Rich, 1992).

The degree to which talent can be strengthened and mobilised depends on the acquisition of the meta-activities needed for autonomy in learning. This not only means involving the metacognitive "overview" and the direction of one's own thought processes, but also encouraging the mixture of attitudes, including curiosity, persistence, and confidence, as well as the efficient use of learning strategies, such as planning, monitoring, and evaluation. Differences in problem-solving strategies between high and average school performers were investigated by Shore, Coleman, and Moss (1992), who audio-taped and analysed the young pupils' thinking-aloud comments. They concluded that the performance of the more successful learners was closer to that of experts, in that they made more reference to prior knowledge rather than to information only presented in the problems. Knowledge is, of course, vital to outstanding performance: individuals who know a great deal about something will be better at it than those who do not (Elshout, 1995). But this knowledge must be flexibly organised for both accurate fast processing, and deeper more considered processing.

Teacher recognition

Teachers do not always recognise and encourage the skills of their potentially talented pupils, often because they lack confidence in their own ability to identify them (Treffinger & Feldhusen, 1996). There is evidence of a wide difference in teacher identification and attitudes towards the talented, which can vary from an unwillingness to recognise them at all (Ojanen & Freeman, 1994) to all-round overestimation (Carr & Kurtz-Costes, 1994). But teachers have been found to judge the talented consistently, in that they will continue to pick the same kind of children (Hany, 1993). Hany (1997) found that teacher judgements usually depended on their sources of information, and that they often kept a mental image of a gifted pupil who would have exceptionally good logical reasoning, quick comprehension, and intellectual curiosity—in combination with good school grades. It is to be expected that the definitions and special facilities provided by educational authorities would have some effect on teachers' choices.

Check-lists of the supposed characteristics of talented pupils vary considerably, and some of the items can be confusing and socio-cultural. For example, a child asking a lot of questions can either be seen as gifted or as attention-seeking, or perhaps lives in a home where questioning is encouraged rather then one where children are encouraged to work things out for themselves. One list may ask the teacher to look out for dedicated seriousness, while another suggests a keen sense of humour—although in a rare survey of experimental work, humour has not been found to have any relationship with creativity or intelligence (Galloway, 1994). Other lists point to perfectionism and introversion as typical features of the high-IQ child, although there is no reliable evidence of any personality features being associated with IQ. Others suggest that the teacher looks for solitary friendlessness in children as a sign of giftedness.

Very able children who do not speak the language of the test-makers or who think in different ways are less likely to be recognised as having high potential. In an overview of 20 research-based international papers on the gifted disadvantaged across all five continents, Wallace and Adams (1993) concluded that it is not only culture that can cut such children out of recognition and special provision, but poverty. There is, they wrote

(p. 446), "the equation, in reality, of wealth with giftedness, special educational provision and giftedness."

When pupils move to more challenging work, both teacher and pupil expectations are increased (Good, 1996). What is more, a report of the British Schools' Inspectorate (DES, 1992) found that where the highly able were given special attention, the effects often spread so as to raise the teachers' expectations for all pupils, sometimes even with an improvement in the school's overall examination results.

However, adult success resulting from specially designed educational programmes for the talented is not promising. In fact, none of a sample of 210 New York children selected for the Hunter College Elementary School their high IQ scores (mean IQ 157) and provided with a dedicated rich education, had reached eminence by the ages of 40 to 50 (Subotnik et al., 1993). But, this approach to educating the talented may have been handicapped by using the IQ as a criterion for identification, especially as we now know that other aspects of the child may be at least as important to adult success. Much knowledge has accumulated since then and the future of education for the very able is undergoing major changes in outlook, which may well bring improved results.

Programmes for the talented have been widely investigated, and found to be variable in educational value, although they do consistently provide the very positive benefits of opportunities for interaction with equally able and motivated peers, as well as improving home–school relations (Cox, Daniel, & Boston, 1985). However, recent well controlled work, which separated academic and other aspects of self-concept, found that special classes for the talented reduced the level of academic self-concept, while leaving all other forms of self-concept untouched (Marsh, Chessor, Craven, & Roche, 1995). The long-term benefits of early programmes for the talented are particularly unsure, although many have been in action for a quarter of a century. In spite of an initial higher measured achievement, the advantages of extra tuition have been found to disappear over three years (White, 1992).

Boredom is sometimes a problem for a child with a curious mind in a dull classroom (Feldhusen & Kroll, 1991; Freeman, 1992b). It can become a bad habit, especially when developed early, with consequent lowering of motivation for learning. To relieve this unpleasant experience, youngsters may escape into daydreams or deliberately provoke disturbance. The talented often develop their own strategies for coping with boredom, such as the writer's discovery of the "Three Times Problem" (Freeman, 1991). In this manoeuvre, to avoid the boredom of listening to teacher's repetitions—usually three in number—quick learners develop a technique of mentally switching-off at repeats two and three, then switching on again for the next new point—involving considerable mental skill in several domains. However, until this technique is running smoothly, they may miss parts of the lessons, so that teachers may be confused about their abilities. As with all habits, this one tends to persist, so that even as adults the talented may not listen carefully to what other people say, apparently distracted by higher thoughts—the absent-minded professor syndrome.

CURRENT TRENDS IN DEVELOPING TALENT

In their various forms, the two most frequently used methods in schools that aim to provide special help for the talented pupil are accelerating the learning of children, either by moving them up to an older age-group or compacting the material they have to learn, and enrichment, rounding out and deepening the material to be learned. These procedures are not discussed here, other than to point out that the success of acceleration is very dependent on the context in which it is done, e.g. the flexibility of the system, how many others in a school are accelerated, the child's level of maturation, and the emotional support received (see Southern & Jones, 1991). Enrichment is certainly enjoyable for the talented as well as other pupils, but unless it is focused it does not appear to lead to exceptionally high-level adult achievement (Subotnik et al., 1993).

Instead, a newer approach that is emerging from the research is considered here, the dynamics being child-driven. This movement away from identification and provision towards the dynamic development of talent has been partly inspired by the work of Vygotsky in the 1920s (Wertsch, 1990). It is suggested here that given the opportunity and with some adult guidance, children of high potential and motivation should be able to select themselves to work in any area at a more advanced or deeper level. Such an interactive approach, considering aptitude and provision together, places less emphasis on school-type achievement, and instead seeks to find and provide for strengths and talents of all kinds. Researchers are in agreement that the very able cannot make progress without the means to learn.

To accommodate to this new flexible approach in finding the potentially talented, special educational techniques are needed, which are different from the conventional route (at least in the USA) of an IQ test followed by a gifted programme which is often simply more school-type teaching. Treffinger and Feldhusen (1996) suggest that there should be considerable involvement by the pupils in their own identification as they come to understand their own potentials and decide their own goals. This does not mean a one-off self-selection, but should be continuous over the school years, resulting in a flexible open-ended talent profile that is regularly added to by all those involved, especially the pupil.

All the evidence indicates that specific provision within subject areas is by far the most effective in promoting talent, rather than general enrichment without identified goals. This might be, for example, a journalism class for sharp writers or photography for the visually talented. It is helpful to observe children in rich and varied educational settings; perhaps a dancer in a serious dance class, or future programmers with access to good-quality computers. Without high-level learning opportunities it is hardly possible for most high-level potential to be seen. Eighteen years after secondary school, 48 of the original 159 subjects from a high school in Tel Aviv, Israel, were surveyed on their occupational accomplishments and outstanding career achievements, and with few exceptions were seen to have focused on a single domain of endeavour (Milgram & Hong, 1997). Focus is particularly important because unevenness in gifts is more likely than being superb at everything.

A form of self-selection can be seen in action in China in the Children's Palaces, where a highly successful combination of encouragement and provision is offered to primary school children (visited by the author). The scheme relies on the children's own motivation and interest for its success. Each "palace" is simply a large house with rooms crammed with activities. Whole schools of mixed-ability children come at one time and are let loose. Some run right through into the playground while others head for the calligraphy, puppet theatre, stationary bicycles, science labs, music rooms etc. The children are not tested for aptitude, but many are stimulated by the novelty of what they discover there to want to learn more. The rules are simple. Those who want to take their chosen subject further must make a contract to come for a specified number of lessons. If they do not attend them all (without good reason) they cannot continue. Some come for years and reach breathtaking standards in their chosen field. Normal teachers are paid extra for this work, which they say they greatly enjoy.

Recent work is beginning to reflect the outcomes from this wider and more child-directed approach. At the Szold Institute in Jerusalem, Zorman (1997) is working on experimental education, termed *Eureka*, which takes special education for the highly able away from the medical model of "diagnose and treat", and uses instead a dynamic approach looking at the outcomes of exposing children to opportunity in the visual arts and sciences. It is based on a seven-year follow-up of 60 talented pupils. The model is now implemented in 56 schools and includes all the country's religions. The assessment process uses teacher ratings of pupils' behaviour, professional evaluation of portfolios, and task performance. The research also uses self-report questionnaires both inside and outside school, including the children's social behaviour. Voluntary out-of-school enrichment activities are available, and children's talents are also assessed from their learning there. Hence the assessment net is flung widely. Although the pupils are generally above average, it has been found that the most important predictor of their success is their high motivation within the chosen subject area. There are also indications that pupils' reading comprehension has been improved, and that their interests have been extended beyond the visual arts and sciences.

Another Israeli example of self-selection through provision is at The Technological Centre for the Galilee, which is dedicated to the study of ecology (Brumbaugh, 1994). The centre works in concert with the local comprehensive school, from which teenage boys and girls have been invited over the past 18 years to work on their own projects under supervision. They are not pre-selected in any way. The centre has the specific aim of developing scientific thinking, using projects such as the effects of magnesium on plants, or cultivating wild mushrooms, or the effects of hormones on fish reproduction. At the laboratory, youngsters design and conduct work on original problems for which there are no existing answers nor (often) methods, then continue to work with the data back at school. The teenager has to prepare and write a research proposal, which is discussed with the laboratory supervisor, and submitted to the Ministry of Education for approval, then he or she can begin, either alone or in a group. Each participant has to be able to work on a computer, eventually to provide a bound dissertation. The Centre displays the youngsters' work, which is sometimes of master's degree standard. The cost is low and largely supported by the state.

The sports approach

Excellence in some abilities is more acceptable than others in all cultures. In many parts of the world, for example, local education authorities encourage keen talented footballers to benefit from extra tuition outside school hours, provide them with equipment (possibly including clothing), arrange transport for them to meet and engage with others at roughly the same level as themselves—and pay for it all. Although there is some provision around for other subjects, notably music, and there are mathematics contests and extra-curricular activities, such as art classes in museums, the idea of opening up the school laboratories for a Saturday morning chemistry session is rare, if it exists at all. It is not difficult or expensive to find out what interests and motivates pupils via questionnaires, interest tests—or simply by asking them. And the facilities are already largely in place to provide excellent support for talents other than football.

Freeman (1995) has proposed that given the opportunity, and with some guidance, the talented (and motivated) should be able to select themselves to work at any subject at a more advanced and broader level. She terms this the "Sports Approach". In the same way as those who are talented and motivated can select themselves for extra tuition and practice in sports, they could opt for extra foreign languages or physics. This would mean, of course, that such facilities must be available to all, as sport is, rather than only to those pre-selected by tests, experts, or money. This is neither an expensive route, nor does it risk emotional distress to the children by removing them from the company of their friends. It makes use of research-based understanding of the very able, notably the benefit of focusing on a defined area of the pupil's interest, as well as providing each one with what they need to learn with and make progress.

But to practice the sports approach, teachers will need more training in differentiated teaching methods, in addition to a variety of specific techniques for bringing out high-level potential. For example, there would have to be some training in helping pupils to collect information for a portfolio. But most importantly there would have to be some unification of approaches within a school or authority. The recognition of talent in this way would also include some form of recognition of the provision to which the pupils had access. This could be done by a simple rating scale so that children who were excelling within their context would be seen to be doing so and not penalised because they had less provision than others to teaching and to material to learn with. To sum up the sports approach, the development of talent through provision:

- Development should be process-based and continuous.
- Identification should be by multiple criteria, including provision for learning and outcome.
- Indicators should be validated for each course of action and provision.
- The pupil's abilities should be presented as a profile rather than a single figure.
- Increasingly sharper criteria should be employed at subsequent learning stages.
- Recognition should be given to attitudes possibly affected by outside influences such as culture and gender.
- The pupils must be involved in educational decision making, notably in areas of their own interest.

CONCLUSIONS

It is clear from the evidence that excellence does not emerge without appropriate help: using measured achievement as the basic means of recognition misses much undeveloped potential. To reach an exceptionally high standard in any area, potentially talented children need the means to learn, which includes material to work with and focused challenging tuition, and sometimes a higher standard and variety of educational provision than is usually provided in normal schools. Every school should have a clear policy for the encouragement of high-level performance in both pupils and teachers (see Freeman, 1995). Not only should such a statement provide an indication of how the school attends to the different educational requirements of all its children, but it must also have the commitment of the principal and a whole-school approach.

High-level potential can be developed in schools through the two somewhat overlapping routes of differentiation—the appropriate match between the curriculum, the content, and the characteristics of the pupil and individualisation—where the pupil has greater responsibility for the content and pace of his or her own educational progress. Hence, rather than continuing the search for definitions, it would be more productive to look at the dynamic interaction between individuals and their opportunities for learning throughout life. Without that dynamic element, we return to the old ideas of fixed abilities, most notably of intelligence. What is needed to develop every child's potential is often already available, at least in the developed world. Using the example of school sport—the Sports Approach—less popular subjects, such as chemistry, French, or business studies could be supported with similar generosity. By such means the proportions of those we now consider to be talented could be considerably increased to the greater benefit of all concerned.

REFERENCES

Albert, R.S. (Ed.) (1992). *Genius and eminence: The social psychology of creativity and exceptional achievement* (2nd ed.). Oxford: Pergamon Press.

Ari, B.A., & Rich, Y. (1992). Meeting the educational needs of all students in the heterogeneous class. In P.S. Klein & A.J. Tannenbaum (Eds.), *To be young and gifted*. New Jersey: Ablex.

Arnold, K.D., & Subotnik, R.F. (1994). Lessons from contemporary longitudinal studies. In R.F. Subotnik & K.D. Arnold, (Eds.), *Beyond Terman: Contemporary longitudinal studies of giftedness and talent*. New Jersey: Ablex.

Arnot, M., Gray, J., Rudduck, J., with Duveen, G. (1998). *Recent Research on Gender and Educational Performance*. London: The Stationery Office.

Benbow, C.P., & Lubinski, D. (1993). Psychological profiles of the mathematically talented: Some sex differences and evidence supporting their biological basis. In G.R. Bock & K.A. Ackrill (Eds.), *The origins and development of high ability* (Ciba Foundation Symposium). Chichester, UK: Wiley.

Bloom, B.S. (1985). *Developing talent in young people*. New York: Ballantine Books.

Brumbaugh, K., Marchaim, U., & Litto, F.M. (1994). How should Developing Countries plan for and implement educational technology: one example. Conference proceedings, *11th International Conference on Technology and Education*, London, March 27–30. pp. 43–45.

Carr, M., & Kurtz-Costes, B.E. (1994). Is being smart everything? The influence of student achievement on teachers' perceptions, *British Journal of Educational Psychology, 64*, 263–276.

Cox, J., Daniel, N., & Boston, B.A. (1985). *Educating able learners: Programs and promising practices*. Austin: University of Texas Press.

Cropley, A.J. (1995). Creative intelligence: A concept of "true" giftedness. In J. Freeman, P. Span, & H. Wagner (Eds.), *Actualizing talent: A lifelong challenge*. London: Cassell.

Czeschlik, T., & Rost, D.H. (1988). Hochbegabte und irehe peers. *Zeitschrift für Pedagogische Psychologie, 2*, 1–23.

DES [Department for Education] (1993). *Exceptionally able children*. London: Department for Education.

Elshout, J. (1995). Talent: the ability to become an expert. In J. Freeman, P. Span, & H. Wagner (Eds.), *Actualizing talent: A lifelong challenge*. London: Cassell.

Feldhusen, J.F., & Kroll, M.D. (1991). Boredom or challenge for the academically talented in school. *Gifted Education International, 7*, 80–81.

Flynn, J.R. (1991). *Asian Americans: Achievement beyond IQ*. Hove, Hillsdale, NJ: Erlbaum.

Freeman, J. (1991). *Gifted children growing up*. London: Cassell. Portsmouth, NH: Heinemann Educational.

Freeman, J. (1992a). *Quality education: The development of competence*. Geneva: UNESCO.

Freeman, J. (1992b). Boredom, high ability and underachievement. In V. Varma (Ed.), *How and why children fail*. London: Jessica Kingsley.

Freeman, J. (1993). Parents and families in nurturing giftedness and talent. In K.A. Heller, F.J. Mönks & A. H. Passow (Eds.), *International handbook for research on giftedness and talent*. Oxford: Pergamon Press.

Freeman, J. (1995). Towards a policy for actualizing talent. In J. Freeman, P. Span, & H. Wagner (Eds.) *Actualizing talent: A lifelong challenge*. London: Cassell.

Freeman, J. (1995). Where talent begins. In J. Freeman, P. Span & H. Wagner (Eds.). *Actualizing talent: A lifelong challenge*. London: Cassell.

Freeman, J. (1996). *Highly able girls and boys*. London: Department for Education and Employment.

Freeman, J. (1998). *The education of the very able: Current international research*. London: The Stationery Office.

Galloway, G. (1994). Psychological studies of the relationship of sense of humor to creativity and intelligence: A review. *European Journal for High Ability, 5*, 133–144.

Galton, F. (1869). *Hereditary genius*. London: Macmillan.

Gardner, H. (1993). *Creating minds: An anatomy of creativity seen through the lives of Freud, Einstein, Picasso, Stravinsky, Elliot, Graham, and Gandhi*. New York: Basic Books.

Gardner. H. (1997). *Extraordinary minds*. London: Weidenfeld & Nicolson.

Goertzel, M.G., Goertzel, V., & Goertzel, T.G. (1978). *300 eminent personalities*. San Francisco: Jossey Bass.

Good, T.L. (1996). Teacher expectations. In E. de Corte & F.E. Weinert (Eds.), *International encyclopedia of developmental and instructional psychology*. Oxford: Pergamon.

Gottfried, A.W., Gottfried, A.E., Bathurst, K., & Guerin, D.W. (1994). *Gifted IQ; Early developmental aspects*. New York: Plenum.

Gross, M.U.M. (1993). Nurturing the talents of exceptionally gifted individuals. In K.A. Heller, F.J. Mönks, & A.H. Passow (Eds.), *International handbook of research and development of giftedness and talent*. Oxford: Pergamon Press.

Hany, E.A. (1993). How teachers identify gifted students: Feature processing or concept based classification. *European Journal for High Ability, 4*, 196–211.

Hany, E.A. (1996). How leisure activities correspond to the development of creative achievement: Insights from a study of highly intelligent individuals. *High Ability Studies, 7*, 65–82.

Hany, E. A. (1997). Modelling teachers' judgements of giftedness: A methodological inquiry of judgement bias. *High Ability Studies, 8*, 157–176.

Heller, K.A., & Ziegler, A. (1996). Gender differences in mathematics and natural sciences; Can attributional retraining improve the low performance of gifted females? *Gifted Child Quarterly, 40,* 200–210.

Holahan, C.K., & Sears, R.R. (1995). *The gifted group in later maturity.* Stanford, CA: Stanford University Press.

Howe, M.J.A., Davidson, J.W., & Sloboda, J.A. (1998). Innate talents; Reality or myth? *Behavioral and Brain Sciences, 21,* 399–442.

Jacobs, J.E., & Weisz, V. (1994). Gender stereotypes: Implications for gifted education. *Roeper Review, 16,* 152–155.

Kanevsky, L. (1992). Gifted children and the learning process: Insights on both from the research. In F. Mönks & W. Peters (Eds.), *Talent for the future.* Assen: Van Gorcum.

Kaufman, F.A. (1992). What educators can learn from gifted adults. In F.J. Mönks & W. Peters (Eds.), *Talent for the future.* Assen: Van Gorcum.

Marsh, H.W., Chessor, D., Craven, R., & Roche, L. (1995). The effect of gifted and talented programs on academic self-concept: The big fish strikes again. *American Educational Research Journal, 32,* 285–319.

Milgram, R.M., & Hong, E. (1997). Leisure activities and career development in intellectually gifted Israeli adolescents. In B. Bain, H. Janzen, J. Paterson, L. Stewin, & A. Yu (Eds.), *Psychology and education in the 21st century.* Edmonton: ICP Press.

Ojanen, S., & Freeman, J. (1994). *The attitudes and experiences of headteachers, classteachers, and highly able pupils towards the education of the highly able in Finland and Britain.* Savonlinna: University of Joensuu.

Olszewski-Kubilius, P.M., Kulieke, M, & Krasney, N. (1988). Personality dimensions of gifted adolescents: a review of the empirical literature. *Gifted Child Quarterly, 2,* 347–352.

Persson, R.S. (1998). Paragons of virtue: Teachers' conceptual understanding of high ability in an egalitarian school system. *High Ability Studies, 9,* 181–196.

Radford, J. (1990). *Child prodigies and exceptional early achievers.* London: Harvester Wheatsheaf.

Reiss, S.M., & Callahan, C.M. (1989). Gifted females: They've come a long way—or have they? *Journal for the Education of the Gifted, 12,* 99–117.

Risemberg, R., & Zimmerman, B.J. (1992). Self-regulated learning in gifted students. *Roeper Review, 15,* 98–100.

Shore, B.M., Coleman, E.B., & Moss, E. (1992). Cognitive psychology and the use of protocols in the understanding of giftedness and high level thinking. In F. Mönks & W. Peters (Eds.), *Talent for the future.* Assen: Van Gorcum.

Shore, B.M., & Kanevsky, L.S. (1993). Thinking processes: Being and becoming gifted. In K.A. Heller, F.J. Mönks, & H.A. Passow (Eds.), *International handbook of research and development of giftedness and talent.* Oxford: Pergamon Press.

Simonton, D.K. (1994). *Greatness: Who makes history and why.* New York: The Guilford Press.

Southern, W.T. & Jones, E.D. (Eds.) (1991). *The academic acceleration of gifted children.* New York: Teachers College Press.

Span, P. (1995). Self-regulated learning by highly able children. In J. Freeman, P. Span, & H. Wagner (Eds.), *Actualizing talent: A lifelong challenge.* London: Cassell.

Stapf, A. (1990). Hochbegabte Madchen: Entwicklung, Identifikation und Beratung, insbesondere im Vorschualter [Highly able girls: Development, identification and counselling, especially at pre-school age]. In W. Wieczerkowski & T.M. Prado (Eds.), *Hochbegabte Madchen.* Bad Honnef: K.H. Bock.

Stephenson, H.W. (1998). Cultural interpretations of giftedness: the case of East Asia (61–77). In R. Friedman & K.B. Rogers (Eds.), *Talent in context: Historical and social perspectives on giftedness.* Washington: American Psychological Association.

Sternberg, R.J. (1985). *Beyond IQ: A triarchic theory of human intelligence.* Cambridge: Cambridge University Press.
Sternberg, R.J., & Lubart, T.I. (1995). *Defying the crowd: Cultivating creativity in a culture of conformity.* New York: Free Press.
Subotnik, R., Kassan, L., Summers, E., & Wasser, A. (1993). *Genius revisited: High IQ children grow up.* New Jersey: Ablex.
Terassier, J-C. (1985). Dysynchrony: Uneven development. In J. Freeman (Ed.), *The psychology of gifted children.* Chichester, UK: John Wiley.
Terman, L.M. (1925–1929). *Genetic studies of genius,* Vols. I–V. Stanford, CA: Stanford University Press.
Tirri, K. (1997). How Finland meets the needs of gifted and talented pupils. *High Ability Studies, 8,* 211–220.
Treffinger, D.J., & Feldhusen, J.F. (1996). Talent recognition and development: Successor to gifted education. *Journal for the Education of the Gifted, 19,* 181–193.
Wallace, B., & Adams H.B. (Eds.) (1993). *Worldwide perspectives on the gifted disadvantaged.* Bicester, UK: AB Academic Publishers.
Wertsch, J.D. (1990). *Voices of the mind: A sociocultural approach to mediated action.* London: Harvester Wheatsheaf.
White, K.R. (1992). The relation between socio-economic status and academic achievement. *Psychological Bulletin, 91,* 461–481.
Zha, Z. (1993). Programs and practices for identifying and nurturing giftedness and talent in the people's republic of China. In K.A. Heller, F.J. Mönks, & A.H. Passow (Eds.), *International handbook of research and development of giftedness and talent.* Oxford: Pergamon Press.
Zorman, R. (1997). Eureka: the cross-cultural model for identification of hidden talent through enrichment. *Roeper Review, 20,* 54–61.

CHAPTER TWELVE

The Juilliard model for developing young adolescent performers: An educational prototype

Rena F. Subotnik
Hunter College, New York, USA

INTRODUCTION: THE JUILLIARD SCHOOL

Juilliard is America's most prestigious conservatory for classical music, boasting students like Itzhak Perlman, Emmanuel Ax, Van Cliburn, James Levine, Leontyne Price, Wynton Marsalis, Yo-Yo Ma, and Pinchas Zukerman. The study of a special environment like Juilliard allows us to explore the confluence of great, emerging musical talent, an instructional tradition honed over the ages, and a curriculum delivered by teachers at the pinnacle of expertise.

According to Zuckerman (1977), American Nobel laureates attended a small number of elite institutions of higher education. The selection dynamic was interactive, in that the most talented students wanted to enrol in departments with renowned scientists, while the finest scientists, including Nobel laureates, sought out gifted protégés as students. The same pattern appears to fit the Juilliard School (Conservatory), as well as its academy for young musicians, the Pre-College programme (JPC). Through socialisation and direct instruction from expert teachers, gifted musicians learn styles and methods of working, as well as values and attitudes held in the classical music world. At Juilliard, students understand that exposure to the highest standards assures them they are capable of great performance (Ochse, 1990).

Juilliard always maintained a separate division for younger students. When the Conservatory moved in the 1960s to its current location at

Lincoln Center in New York City, only those children with a serious interest in pursuing a professional career in music were accepted into the Pre-College Division. Currently there are 330 students enrolled in the programme, with 75–80 students graduating every year. The average age at admission is 12–15 years old, however, some of the "tinies", the string players, may start as early as age 7 or 8, and may participate in the programme for up to 10 years. The students in Juilliard's Pre-College programme, are not novices. They have already had the benefit of one or more teachers who introduced them to the rudiments of the instrument and who nourished their love of music. By the time they arrive at the campus, they are primed to refine technique and their unique interaction with the music.

Of 67 JPC faculty members, 49 did some part of their training at Juilliard—either in the Pre-College, Conservatory, or Graduate School. Most are recruited from the Conservatory or Graduate faculty, or through word of mouth. All are highly experienced in performance on a national and international level, having been protégés of the most renowned teachers of the twentieth century. Teachers at Juilliard serve as role models for their pupils. Not only is their instruction purposeful, but so is the socialisation they offer in behaviour, style, attitudes, and habits. According to Sosniak (1985), master teachers love their music at least as much as their pupils, and students of the same teacher tend to become both comrades and competitors.

The Juilliard Pre-College programme fits the definition of a "cultural organism" (Feldman, 1993, pp. 232–233) in that it is designed to "enhance the possibilities for discovery, development, and optimal expression of human talent in various domains ... and also serve as a repository of knowledge and wisdom about how to select, preserve, and enhance the qualities of the domain itself." Music is a domain of human ability that, when properly guided, engages the comprehension and abilities of children to the degree that they may find their life's direction through it (Walters & Gardner, 1986). As music is intrinsically appealing to children and is organised around a rule-governed structure, highly able children are able to intuit the regularities and integrate them with ease and pleasure (Winner, 1996). Further, music falls into the category of domains in which giftedness is revealed early, making a pre-college programme of rigorous study essential to career development. Because the level of competition and challenge is so high at the Juilliard School and Pre-College, it can serve as a "grand edifice" (Feldman, 1993, p. 246) within the cultural organism, the place where the accumulated efforts and expanse of all the developmental levels of music learning and talent identification can be gathered and celebrated (Feldman, 1986, 1993).

STRUCTURE OF THE STUDY

Objectives

Two sets of variables were explored in this study. One set I call "explicit" because these variables were more easily accessible, including the programme's philosophy and goals, sources of applicants, the audition process, and the curriculum. The second "more implicit" set was derived exclusively from interviews with key members of the Juilliard community. These variables included: beliefs held by faculty about sources of musical talent, the role of competition and drive, tacit knowledge shared by teachers with students, support available for the most gifted and the least successful students, student attributions of status, and recommendations for change within the institution. These variables are offered in contrast to the environment available to American adolescents with equivalent talent in the academic subjects.

Subjects

Three groups of study subjects were contacted for interviews. One group included six currently enrolled students representing varying instruments, ages, degrees of involvement with the composition programme, and years of experience at the Pre-College. Two student subjects are string players, one is a brass performer, and the other three are primarily pianists. Three students identified themselves as composers as well as performers.

The six faculty interviewees consisted of two solfege (ear training) teachers, one theory teacher, and one member each from the wind, piano, and string faculties. Representing administration, the Director of the programme, Dr Andrew Thomas, and the Director of the Music Advancement programme (see later description) were interviewed as well.

The third group of interviewees included six alumni of the JPC programme. Three are recent graduates and three completed their studies several years ago. Four of the alumni are currently enrolled in the Conservatory—two at the undergraduate level and two at the graduate level. The two graduate students also serve as faculty in the Pre-College, one in strings and the other in solfege. The two alumni who are not attending the Juilliard Conservatory have continued with their music, but at liberal arts institutions, where they can study both music and another discipline.

Interviews

The interviews were conducted by phone or in person. Each of the subjects was posed a standard set of questions to ensure triangulation of data. Students and alumni were asked about:

- How their families first heard about the Juilliard Pre-College programme.
- How their teacher was selected.
- What the audition process was like for them.
- What they determined the philosophy of the JPC to be.
- Their Saturday schedule.
- The kinds of tacit knowledge they received from teachers.
- Whether they would have preferred a full-time programme.
- Experiences with concerto competitions and recitals.
- On what basis friendships were formed at JPC.
- Favourite aspects of the programme.
- Recommendations for change.
- Advice for future students.

In the course of conversation, all the subjects interjected additional information including the importance of summer music camps, the pressures of integrating practice into a rigorous academic study schedule, changing dreams of performance careers, and the thrill of being part of the Juilliard environment.

Faculty (including selected alumni on the faculty) and administration perspectives on the following topics were solicited in order to complement student responses to various facets of the JPC talent development process:

- Their background and training.
- Philosophies and goals for instruction.
- How they recognise talent and their ideas about the sources of talent.
- How they plan for individual students.
- Counselling of most and least successful pupils.
- Opinions on the notion of prodigies.
- Opinions on special full-time schools of music.
- Experiences with tacit knowledge.
- Thoughts on how students form peer groups at JPC.
- Addressing changes in student aspirations (e.g. from performer to doctor).

EXPLICIT TALENT-DEVELOPMENT VARIABLES

Philosophy and goals

According to the faculty and administration of the JPC, the goal of the programme is to serve children who have "been caught" by classical music, and want to think about music as their life and career. Although the faculty members believe that all children can learn music well enough to benefit from the discipline and cognitive growth that comes from learning an instrument, all of them recognise that those students with deep interests and commitment need a different level of instruction, and the Pre-College faculty are uniquely placed to offer this special form of talent development.

Although the JPC prepares most students, particularly those in strings and piano, for solo careers, the curriculum includes an immersion in ensemble and orchestral work. The faculty is also sensitive to the fact that many of the JPC students will choose other professions by the time they graduate from the programme. Some of those who leave the music career trajectory will find their way back. Others will serve as knowledgeable supporters of classical music in their communities.

Academically, the goals of the JPC are: (a) to offer individualised lessons that are responsive to each students' unique characteristics; (b) to help students learn to solve musical problems in listening, composing, aesthetics, and historical analysis:

> I keep a fairly intense and high standard so that I give my students the opportunity to continue as a performer by the time they graduate. Also there's a tremendous value in learning anything in depth that requires physical, mental, and emotional discipline, and has cultural and spiritual overtones. What one learns from music can be transposed into other areas with tremendous success. Kids know that saying they went through our program enhances their college applications and other things they're applying to do. Fundamentally, my main goal is to develop an enriched human being musically, intellectually, and culturally. We're training our audiences and cultural citizens of the future.... But at a certain point, some students realize they love practicing and want to enter competitions. They want to learn the entire repertoire. Then you try to help them go in that more highly intensive performance direction. [*Faculty*]

> How best can I bring out the talent and ability of my students? I think it is one of the most fascinating and challenging professions on earth because you have to encompass an awful lot of areas even beyond your instrument. You have to hope you have talented students, those with musicality, and also very relaxed with their instrument. You have to try quickly to have a sense of your students and what they're about and how you can best get through to them. On the one hand I treat my students with love and compassion, and on the other, depending on what kind of person they are, I have to get the most out of them. To get your ideas across to a student, you have to strike a strong balance between teaching the craft without temporarily taking away their innate musicianship. [*Faculty*]

> I believe that everyone deserves the best you've got. Those who go further, you end up teaching at a much higher level, and of course then you're going to give them all the preparation you can for the possibility of a career...

> They are going to have to work a great deal harder, and practice a great deal more. You have to see to it that they do. My feeling is that they should be developed in every area of music because they shouldn't be told they're going to be one of the top concert artists of the age and that's all they prepare for. They need experience with theory, ensembles, orchestras, because you just don't know what will happen with a career, especially as they go through adolescence. [*Faculty*]

Another goal is to expand students' repertoire in 20th century Western music written in the classical tradition:

> The limited concert repertoire is gone from the musical world that our students will inherit when they're out of college. It's vital to bring the school up to date and more assertively involved in the music world that is out there today.
> The curriculum remains Western and European. Nobody is teaching Balinese music, for example. We focus on the Western concert tradition. We are trying to locate symphonic works from Japanese, Chinese, and Korean composers who compose in the Western tradition, since we have such a large component of students from those countries. I want them to have a sense that there are composers from their own countries that are contributing to the literature. Unfortunately, what I've seen so far is too difficult ... although a small, select group of kids in the contemporary music ensemble is doing really fabulously at handling very challenging work. [*Director*].

In the affective domain, faculty and administration are committed to balancing pressures for excellence in performance with a healthful involvement with music and musical peers. They recognise that for many students, the most important component of the JPC is providing opportunities for young, gifted musicians to socialise with others who share their same passions and interests.

Sources of applicants

Over 80% of the JPC students auditioned with a JPC faculty member in anticipation of applying for admission. A network of regional, national, and even international instrumental teachers serves as a feeder system that directs prospective students to those JPC teachers. Families without access to that network rely on the biographies listed in the catalogue. The minority of students who audition for the JPC without having made a connection with a standing faculty member do so because of the prestige of the programme, more specifically its reputation as the finest pre-college programme in the United States.

The ratio of applicants to admittees varies from 3:1 to 14:1 depending on the instrument and the year. The prestige instruments, those that elicit the greatest competition for admission, include piano, violin, and cello, followed by flute and clarinet. During certain years, for example, when a number of pianists will graduate, the admissions quota for pianists may be larger. According to Dr Thomas, the Director, ratios are smaller than expected because so much self-selection is taking place before the auditions. Most of the applicants, as mentioned earlier, come recommended by an elite group of teachers who form a pipeline for excellent candidates. Also, some families are not prepared to sacrifice the money for tuition, and others live too far away to make a once-a-week programme seem worthwhile.

Approximately half of the students are Asian nationals or Asian-Americans. In fact, one-third of the JPC student body is Korean. The next largest group of Asian students are Japanese, followed by Taiwanese. The ethnic composition of the student body has changed over time due to historical patterns of immigration as well as the draw of various conservatories in other parts of the world. For example, according to Dr Thomas, more European students are choosing to stay in Europe for their musical training than was true in former years. He also believes that the Shanghai Conservatory will soon attract larger number of candidates from the region to receive the level of training available at Juilliard.

Another notable source of students is MAP (Music Advancement Program), also housed at Juilliard's Lincoln Center site. Established in 1991 by Juilliard's President Joseph Polisi, the programme was designed to counteract the disappearance of music performance and appreciation classes from the local public schools, as well as to address the need for a larger and more diverse audience for classical music. Consequently, approximately 500 Black and Latino New York City Public School students apply and 35 are admitted to MAP each year. According to MAP's Director, Edward Lawrence, applicants need not have more than six months of previous training on an instrument before they can audition. Once admitted, students experience an intensive weekly program that mirrors the JPC, including individual lessons, music history, theory, ear training, ensemble work, and recitals. Teachers for the programme come from the Conservatory or word of mouth through the Conservatory grapevine. Five of the MAP students, based on their teachers' recommendation, applied for the JPC in 1997, and two were offered admission. Due to outreach efforts on the part of the MAP staff, larger numbers of students are applying and, according to Edward Lawrence, the quality of the enrolled student body is increasing exponentially.

Audition process

Clearly, without a level of knowledge about and access to the current faculty at the JPC, one's chances for admission are diminished. Most students audition for or even study with a member of the faculty before the audition, as preparation for their application to the programme. Performance fields, especially highly developed ones like music, tend to channel promising youngsters through a series of teachers that eventually places them in the hands of the great master teachers of the day (Feldman, 1986; Sosniak, 1985). Given the JPC's reputation as a repository of international teaching talent, it makes sense that families who enter the "pipeline" know how to best position their child for the audition process:

> The school is world famous. Even the kids in Korea have a good sense of who are the teachers of the moment. Some teachers are known for getting their kids into high level careers, others are known for getting students into good colleges or winning concerto competitions, etc. Faculty members can become competitive for a good student. [*Director*]

There are no minimum age requirements for application to the JPC. Anyone with sufficient preparation can audition in front of a faculty jury. Students are expected to perform their pieces for the audition from memory, except those on wind instruments, brass, and percussion. In addition, each applicant must sit for a placement examination in music theory and ear training. According to the Juilliard Pre-College Division Catalogue, 1997–98, a sample basic repertoire for applicants to the highly competitive violin department who are under the age of 11 includes:

> Major and minor scales and arpeggios in two octaves.
> An etude on the level of Lamoureaux, Wohlfarht, Mazas, or Kayser.
> A slow and fast movement from a Baroque concerto or sonata by a composer such as Vivaldi, Corelli, Telemann, or Handel.
> A contrasting piece by a Romantic or contemporary composer.

The youngest applicants are string players, followed by pianists. Some as young as age 5 or 6 may audition for the violin faculty. Many of the string players who audition have been immersed in the Suzuki method for several years before moving to an individual teacher. In other words, those who audition are seasoned instrumentalists with a wide repertoire and array of skills in hand. Students who apply for wind instrument, voice, or composition openings tend to be older, given the more advanced physical and cognitive developmental levels required for high-quality performance in these areas.

During the 15-minute to half-hour audition, instrumentalists choose a piece from their repertoire to play, perform another piece on demand, and also may be asked to demonstrate scales or other skills. Composers bring copies of their scores to discuss. They may also be asked about their musical background, favourite composers, interests and goals, and the process by which they compose. None of these requests comes as a surprise, as typically a candidate will have worked with a member of the faculty as a student for at least a year in preparation for this audition:

> There were about five faculty members sitting behind a long table about 10–15 feet from the piano. They asked what you'd like to start with. They stop you somewhere and you play a little bit of each selection that you've prepared. The whole thing takes about 10–15 minutes. It's common knowledge what standard auditions are, because they're basically the same anywhere you go to audition, whether it's a school or competition. They require a piece out of the four style periods. It wasn't more or less challenging than anywhere else. The challenge is in what pieces you pick or your teacher picks for you. And there's a huge selection to choose from. [*Alumnus*]

Admission also affects the placement of students with specific teachers. Each faculty member has responsibility for approximately 8–10 students. Each candidate has the opportunity to request a teacher, and if that teacher has room in his or her schedule and wants that candidate, that student will be placed accordingly.

The degree of stress associated with the audition varied by instrument and age. Those who were older and applying for a spot in the prestige departments were most likely to feel anxious about the audition:

> A month or two before, there was all this planning about my future and what I was going to do. I had to practice about 3 or 4 hours a day. That's the least someone can do in order to prepare for an audition. That made it sound as if the audition was pretty hard and it was. When I was 9, I didn't have that much school work so I could devote after school time to practice.
>
> There was a lot of stress associated with the audition, more than even there would be in a solo concert because to me it basically meant all my future. I guess that's pretty important! I'm sure everyone gets nervous because it's just you and a panel of judges who can decide whether they want you in the school or not. My teacher was one of the judges. I didn't know the other judges. It lasted about 15 minutes. I had to wait about a month to find out if I'd been accepted. I felt like I did the best I could and now it was out of my hands. [*13-year-old student*]

All of the faculty members interviewed for this study identified a candidate's degree of musicality as the key criterion for admission. Technique could be improved in the course of study, but musicality was viewed as innate and essential to the level of potential associated with a student. The faculty members rate each student on scoring sheets (see Fig. 12.1). When the forms are completed, they are delivered to the Director who conducts the selection process based on the faculty's recommendations and his own judgements.

The Juilliard School
Pre-College Division
Entrance Audition Examination Form 1997–98

                        Student Information
                                Do not write in this space

Name: _____ Admit: _____ Reject: _____

Age: _____   Scholarship

Decision: _____

Major: _____ Major

Teacher: _____

Years of prior instruction: _____

Audition Evaluation:

Please evaluate the applicant using the categories listed below:

	Exceptional	Superior	Very Good	Good	Fair/Poor
OVERALL RATING					
Technique					
Tone					
Musicality					
Rhythm					
Memory					
Intonation					
POTENTIAL					

Would you accept this student into your schedule? Should the applicant be encouraged to re-apply if not admitted?

Yes _____ Possibly _____ No _____   Yes _____ No _____

Additional Comments:

Signed: _____ Date: _____

FIG. 12.1 Entrance audition examination form.

Curriculum

Classes are held on Saturdays. Occasionally, individual lessons may be conducted on other days if a student lives in the New York City metropolitan area. In addition to individual lessons and master class with all of a teacher's pupils, students are required to take a core curriculum that includes theory, solfege (ear training), orchestra and chamber music (for those majoring in orchestral instruments), or chorus and chamber chorus (for those majoring in a keyboard instrument or composition). Electives include contemporary ensemble (by audition) and a secondary major such as another instrument or composition. Composition majors can take courses in counterpoint and twentieth-century theory. In theory classes, students learn to analyse music in light of history and aesthetic styles. The skills taught in solfege include recognising harmonic, melodic, and rhythmic structures, as well as score reading and transposition (basic rudiments of composition). Placement in theory and solfege classes is based on examinations given every year.

Some resistance was expressed by students to taking time away from practice and lessons to attend theory and solfege classes, although these two courses are regular offerings in all serious music programmes. According to Scripp and Davidson (1994), 80% of conservatory students come in without deep understanding of the structure of music, and tonal and notational knowledge only come with training. As one faculty member explained:

> In ear training and chorus, my philosophy is that the pianists need ensemble experience. They need experience with Pythagorean tuning which they don't get on the piano. We do orchestral works with them so they can get the ear development of the instruments and see that people playing the instruments know the ranges and pitch.
>
> In the choral program, the composers are all required to do some conducting. They all have to conduct their pieces at some point in their life. A composer has to be able to perform anything that he or she writes. So they have to be able to sight sing. I put a lot of emphasis on words since they don't get any training in this area except with vocal music. We learn poetry and how we maintain vowels. We learn the international phonetic alphabet. They can sing in Chinese and Japanese.
>
> In ear training, they have to learn to hear, repeat, and use the materials aurally. We also include sight reading, sight singing, and rhythmic reading. All of these skills are more easily learned before puberty. Before seven is even easier. It's all coordination. The hand, ear, eye, all related muscles have to be coordinated. We do dozens of exercises that target those muscles in a developmental way. So we have a sequence of courses in ear training and choral work that builds into greater and greater expertise. We teach in a spiral. We repeat skills using different music. By the time they graduate, some kids have had 11 years' experience. [*Faculty*]

Such understandings are designed to transform the child musician's conception of music as high-level imitation to one of artistic maturity (Bamberger, 1991; Bastian, 1994). Noted Beaux Arts Trio cellist Bernard Greenhouse made these comments (Delbanco, 1985, p. 62) on theory and solfege training:

> The concentration should be on musical ideas rather than on the instrument as such. When I perform today, I find that I am not even aware of the cello in front of me. My concentration is entirely on something else. I sing the phrase before it's produced. I hear it in my mind and I get ideas for how to perform that phrase before it comes out of the instrument.

MORE IMPLICIT TALENT-DEVELOPMENT VARIABLES

Sources of musical talent

Faculty members were asked to reflect on the sources of their students' talents. Their responses ranged from factors that were almost totally trainable to those they consider to be almost entirely innate.

Physique. Having a particular body type and structure can lead parents and early teachers to match students with certain instruments. For example, a tuba or bass may go to a big or tall child whereas flute or piccolo may be assigned to a smaller child. More subtle stereotyping can happen based on lung and hand size. According to faculty members, most physical contributions to performance quality can be compensated for through training. In other words, within reason, a student's physique should not have to be a barrier to great performance. The most important physical attribute is sense of touch.

Aesthetic sense. Faculty agreed that this variable was teachable. Every aspect of the curriculum addresses the question of what makes music beautiful. Participation in lessons and ensembles gives students the opportunity to experience the beauty of music both physically and emotionally. The topic of aesthetics is addressed intellectually in solfege and theory classes, especially with composition students.

Technique. According to the faculty, of all the components of talent, technique is the most trainable. Technique is a central focus of the individual lessons and master classes, particularly in the earlier years of the programme. Each teacher has a unique method for teaching technique, but each is aimed at preparing students for a range of career and competition opportunities.

Coordination. The faculty agreed that a minimal threshold of physical coordination was necessary for potential talent to be transformed into great performance. Coordination is built up slowly and with great deliberation during lessons on technique, and in solfege through such activities as sight singing and harmonising.

Musicality. The one variable that is necessary and sufficient to identify performance talent is musicality. According to faculty members, musicality is a personal quality of communication which shows intense love of music and a drive to express it. The consensus of the interviewees was that although it could be assisted by early exposure to music, musicality was innate, and consequently difficult or impossible to transmit from teacher to pupil.

Intelligence. Another element in the constellation of talent is musical intelligence, which includes high-speed understanding of the concepts being taught. The faculty believes that while musical intelligence is innate, it is not a primary variable in the making of a great performer. In other words, a minimal threshold is required, but high levels are not essential.

Personality. Faculty members identified drive and having a "thick skin" as personality characteristics that enhanced or diminished potential talent. The latter served as protection from the constant criticism that performers experience in the course of their careers:

> If you don't think you're terribly good, you probably don't have a thick enough skin to be able to deal with the many disappointments you're going to have in the field, because you're going to have them, no matter how good you are. If you want it so much that you can put up with it even though it hurts, then you'll be OK. If you're going to be thrown by every disappointment, then you probably can't make it. But I think that's true in any field, isn't it? You have to be a strong person to take the disappointments that life throws at you. Some people who go into these kinds of fields have a very strong need for admiration. If their need is strong enough, they may make it. But they still have to be able to take the criticism. That drive is very important. [*Faculty*]

Competition and drive

Competition. Scholarships are awarded on the basis of juried competition as a recognition of outstanding talent. Concerto competitions are held every year for solo performances in the prestige instruments. Participation is voluntary, but these events provide several important benefits to students: (a) reward for practice, (b) attention and recognition, and (c) feedback on what needs to be worked on next (Sosniak, 1985). As students listen to others play, they can judge how they would like to hear themselves performing the same piece. Of course, competitions have their down side too:

> There's an enormous amount of competition and comparison among the students because they are so career oriented. It can be unhealthy. It's hard to avoid it because we have these concerto competitions. And there's an enormous amount of prestige for winning one of these competitions, although, I must say that sometimes it's really the parents who are most upset if a child doesn't win. For many, there are great sacrifices made to send their child to the program, including financial burdens. [*Administration*]

The three JPC orchestras designate placement by age. Within each orchestra, however, auditions are held for instrument seating:

> Orchestra recitals are competitive, but only the teachers attend. Everyone gets a chance. If you perform with the orchestra one year, then you're not allowed to perform the next year. For each concert we do one symphony and two concertos. If you sit first for symphony, then you sit second for the two concertos. But you audition for a place in second or a place in first. The concert master is the first chair in the first violin section. If there's a solo section in the symphony, then the concert master or mistress plays that. I don't care much about seating because we're all playing the same music so I don't know why it matters where you sit other than for the concert master. [*12-year-old first year student*]

> It isn't necessarily beneficial for a child to spend 12 years in the same orchestra. They needed to learn a different kind of repertoire. The idea was to have the early music, the classics in the younger orchestras. In the symphony you would look forward to the Romantics and the contemporary at a slightly less exhausting level than the Orchestra. If we couldn't fill a section in the top two orchestras with members of the student body, we'd fill them in with students from the College. That way we kept up the standards of performance. [*Faculty*]

> I'm in the first orchestra because it's done by age group. When I turn 14, I'll be in the middle one. They determine positions by auditioning the piece they're playing. At first everyone sits wherever they want. They play the piece and get used to it. They go home and practice and practice. In a couple of weeks, the conductor auditions people on the piece, and the conductor determines who will be concertmaster and who will be assistant concertmaster. [*13-year-old first year student*]

> Every time you did a concert, the next week you'd come in and there'd be a whole new seating chart, so you never knew if you were going to be at the bottom or the top. The written music is the same, but the first chair is the one

who'll get to play the solo. The conductor expected us to come to the first rehearsal already very familiar with the piece and ready to play any of the horn parts. Not perfect, but very familiar. At first I didn't know that kids were taking the parts home over the summer and preparing them. From then on I was very anal about preparing. [*Alumnus*]

All students are required to perform a senior recital in order to graduate. However, the size and nature of the audience depends on the status of the student:

Here I was in Paul Hall in Lincoln Center. My parents provided the audience. I felt that in some ways it really mattered how I played, and in others it didn't. My private teacher was there and others stopped in to see how I was doing. The attendance at recitals seemed to be selective. If someone was considered not so good, then recitals would be skipped by the other students. You were expected to attend the recitals of the elite group. I wanted certain people to be there who didn't come. I realized it's because they didn't consider that I was up to their musical standard. They are so used to being around professional musicians and their idea of what they sound like. To go to a friend's recital was not appealing. [*Alumnus*]

Senior recital was a bit more difficult for me as a composer since I had to depend on other people to perform for me. I don't have the luxury of being a good enough pianist to program a composition for myself to play. I am so grateful that these excellent musicians put themselves into my pieces and seemed to enjoy themselves. It was difficult, though. One of the pieces I wrote for my recital was for ten people. Looking back it was insane. I thought it would be no big deal to organize ten people's schedules for rehearsals. I realized that everyone had completely conflicting schedules and I had to rearrange the piece for a string quartet instead of for a chamber group. It took me all year to get the rehearsals organized. [*Alumnus*]

Socially and academically there's pressure to perform. That does lead to comparison and competition. My advice would be to not be competitive. Just absorb what they're doing and how it can benefit you in any way possible. That's maturity. This attitude is essential to surviving in a competitive environment. Otherwise you'll stifle your creativity. [*Alumnus*]

Drive. Although most individuals seem to seek leisure as a reward for carrying out their responsibilities, those with great talent are often driven to spend their time further honing their skills. In spite of the disappointments arising from competition, immersing oneself fully in the world of a talent domain can stave off a haunting regret that a dream was not pursued (Csikszentmihalyi, Rathunde, & Whalen, 1997).

For the individual who is both self-confident and self-critical, disappointment spurs the desire to prove that next time will be better

(Bastian, 1994). According to Ochse (1990), this "I'll show you" response to failure or disappointment is a major source of motivation for great performance and creativity. Enormous drive and motivation are needed to maintain a commitment to art, especially when no more than 1 in 2500 can survive financially as a working artist (Csikszentmihalyi et al., 1997).

By the time a student enters a serious music programme like Juilliard's Pre-College, they have built much of their life around music. A day will hardly go by without practice, no matter what else comes up. This prioritisation may be based on habit or on a determination to prove something to oneself or to others (Sosniak, 1985). In spite of the enormous talent and commitment exhibited by JPC students, there still exists variation in amounts of enthusiasm for practice and preparation:

> In JPC, you should not only be talented, but you have to work hard. It's not going to come to you without any work. But the work really pays off. You know if you've worked hard enough. Your teacher can tell too. You feel the music when you practice hard and concentrate. [*12-year-old student*]

> Some students go on Saturdays out of routine, or their parents are pushing them. There was a problem this year with attendance in orchestra. People would come in late or skip a lot. I think it's the responsibility of both the students and the teachers. The school could have a stricter attendance policy. It's better now. But it's still a problem. In orchestra it's true that people attend and pay more attention when they like the piece, when it's challenging and fun. A piece with a lot of character and energy. Also the difficulty of the piece has to be spread out among the orchestra to keep everyone involved. For example, in Mozart, the winds and violins get a lot, and the cello gets nothing, so it's harder to get excited. [*Student, in programme for eight years*]

The motivation to practise for hours a day follows a developmental feedback loop of practice, success, and further commitment (Bastian, 1994). Following such a regimen over the course of at least 10 years requires persistence, hard work, and support from family and teachers. Further, making a routine of practising a certain number of hours a day is not sufficient. The regimen must be focused on improving one's current level of performance, and that is best determined by an expert teacher (Ericsson, Krampe, & Tesch-Römer, 1993).

Support mechanisms

Faculty members were asked how the exceptional students in this already selective population were counselled by the institution. In the course of adolescence, students' priorities may shift and they may not be willing to put in the effort and concentration needed to fulfil their potential:

> I get the feeling that those students who really want a career in music are completely focused in a way that's different from those who want to be doctors, etc. Their attitude about music, class work, and their instrument is very different. There's a natural draw to those students who are really interested in their instrument and in their art. If I see a student who's really talented and working very hard, I find myself being more encouraging because they seem more serious. They are drawn into more adult relationships and conversations with the faculty. I'm not sure that it's intentional or something natural. [*Faculty*]

> With the most successful students you have to be very specific about what's out there, what the opportunities are, and when to go for them. With the least successful, I'm generally supportive and I don't try to be discouraging. Most of them discover soon enough, at 15 or so, they have other interests or plans. They start to think about studying harder and practicing less. [*Faculty*]

Poor performance is differentiated according to the domain of underachievement. If it takes place in theory or solfege classes, a student might be held back from advancing to the next level, or parents may be asked to hire a tutor to help with catching up. If students come irregularly or are under-prepared for lessons or orchestra, the policy is to talk with the student, and if necessary involve the parents in finding a solution:

> As for the students not doing so well, that's a sensitive issue. We don't want to make them feel like they're not as strong as others. We usually have a class or two that goes a little more slowly. Students are never counseled out of the Pre-College based on performance in solfege. It may happen in the instrument domain. Although I may feel it would be best sometimes, it's not my place to tell students to leave. I take responsibility for taking the time to win over the student or to help him or her learn. I believe everyone can learn solfege. [*Faculty*]

Some of the students are clearly stars, standing out even among their talented peers. Within that subset exists a small number of youngsters who could be categorised as prodigies, competing on the concert stage with adult musicians. Stars tend to choose specific teachers among the faculty renowned for the tacit knowledge and connections they offer their pupils. These faculty members are especially well versed in the mechanisms that will advance their students' careers beyond the curriculum offered in the programme. As a support, theory and solfege faculty may offer make-up lessons to those who may have fallen behind after going on tour.

The faculty witnessed the "burnout" of a few prodigies in the programme. They attributed this to the child's competing interests and to changing expectations. According to Bamberger (1986, p. 393), young gifted musicians learn by "feel", which she describes as a sophisticated form of imitation. Over time a musician becomes more reflective and self-conscious about all the components that go into his or her playing. She quotes a 16-year-old in her study (1986, p. 410) as saying, "It's easy to feel like your playing has gotten worse because now you're listening and hearing so much more." If a young prodigy can view the disequilibrium they are experiencing as a passage into a deeper level of understanding, then the transition can be rewarding. Expert guidance through this developmental process is no doubt a hallmark of a teacher who works with young gifted musicians:

> When I was in school, the big name was Midori. You'd think, wow, there she is. Her pictures all over the place. Now that I'm teaching, I see how star children are treated. They are capable of handling the pressure and they are willing to learn. You sometimes end up spending extra time with them, to brief them on what they've missed. They get a lot of homework when they're away from ear training. [*Faculty and alumnus*]

Young students are matched with older students in their department when they enter the programme. Beyond that, however, no other institutional efforts are made to encourage student socialising. Relationships tend to be created through the shared experience of music learning and making. Mostly students seemed to handle stress privately:

> The students are taught to be pretty self-reliant. Whenever I was feeling upset, I realized that it was implicitly considered a "crime" to show it. I was very lucky to have one conductor take me under his wing and give me a lot of support and encouragement. On a couple of different occasions I would go to him for some extra help. Even though he was a clarinet player, he would take his lunch hour and sit there with me and critique my rhythm and tuning. I really appreciated the help. When I thanked him at graduation he said that every year there was someone who needed a little extra push and I was that year's project. [*Alumnus*]

Student attributions of status

Having a peer group made up of talented individuals who share a passion for music is an essential component of an ideal talent-development institution. Discussion, criticism, suggestions, and humour coming from classmates help refine one's goals and form one's identity (Davidson & Scripp, 1994). Asking for help from one's peers is often less threatening than requesting assistance from even well meaning adults.

In adolescence, many gifted musicians begin to question the motivation for their playing, and efforts designed to please parents and teachers may be viewed as a reason to drop out (Bamberger, 1986). Having a peer group committed to musical performance no doubt helps to neutralise this rebellion. Saturdays are viewed by most Pre-College students as the most important day of their week. Unless they have a lesson with their teacher on another day, Saturday is the time for demonstrating the results of their practice efforts, and being around other students who share the same lifestyle and commitments (Kogan, 1987).

All subjects of this study were asked about how student social groups were formed. The following factors were mentioned: instrument, ability, level of motivation, where one lived, and language groups. The factor mentioned most frequently was instrument. Students in the same instrumental department may share orchestra, solfege and theory, chamber music, and even master class together. Beyond that arrangement however, students do sort themselves by other variables. For example, foreign students feel comfortable communicating in their native language, others may form groups with those who attend the same high school or commute from the same neighbourhood.

The most interesting and unique responses however, concerned the role of motivation and ability in the formation of both friendship groups and attributions of status. Some students are highly motivated, taking all aspects of the programme very seriously, including library work. They are most likely to take second majors, and to participate in as many electives as they can squeeze in. Others are focused almost exclusively on their instrument-related classes and lessons, and less committed to theory, solfege, and other electives. Finally, a third group is generally focused on peer group socialising, and might choose a long lunch over needed practice:

> I honestly didn't like the PC socially, especially my third and fourth years. I got the impression that people were not really interested in going into music. They were just doing it for their Harvard application. People really didn't want to make an effort in orchestra. They didn't take things seriously, or being intent on working. More than 50% of the students were like that, and it cut across instruments. I don't know how you can screen them out. It would be nice to have more serious students there, people who took orchestra and classes seriously. After a while it sucked the motivation out of me. All of them were talented, but the level of their performance and motivation was not as high as I would have expected from a top music school. [*Alumnus*]

> The students were divided by focus. If you were very interested in learning, that was where I was, you were interested in getting as much as you could out of the program. We were the nerds. We'd stay after hours and talk to teachers and go to the library. Then there were those who were goof offs. This is all relative since you can't be a total goof off and be there, but compared to the rest in the program they were. They weren't necessarily interested in learning. They were there because their parents made them. [*Alumnus*]

> There definitely is a clear recognition of who works and who doesn't, who's interested and who's not. It does affect the morale of the class. Those who are not really interested are looked down upon as, "why are you here?" That's not to say that everyone is enthusiastic about everything going on, but there tends to be a certain level of expectation of performance in all areas, even if you're disinterested. [*Faculty*]

Contrary to what might be found in more typical school environments, those JPC students who are most renowned for their talent are viewed with admiration instead of contempt or disparagement. When students were asked to elaborate on this phenomenon, it appeared that the talent exhibited by their "star" peers was viewed as a source of challenge:

> It was somewhat of a relief to meet other students with the same passions and interests. But it was also a little shocking because you go along thinking you're one of the best. And then you go there and realize you're one of many. It's both a relief and also a glimpse of what the real world is like. During my first few years at Juilliard, there was very little competition. We didn't have the repertoire for the competitions. It was just knowing that some brilliant players were there that gave you a shock. The orchestra for the youngest children has rotating seats. On occasion, the other two orchestras have ranking for seats. You get a bad seat, you work harder for the next time. [*18-year-old student*]

Composers as a unique group. Most children become concerned with singing songs correctly by the time they are 5, thereby limiting the amount of spontaneous improvisation they indulge in. Musically gifted children are more likely to continue transposing and improvising, although composing from scratch will not usually happen before adolescence (Winner, 1996). JPC offers a composition major that attracts bright and creative adolescents. Most of the faculty and students interviewed saw the youthful composers as separate and unique from the instrumental students:

> Very, very different. Composers tend to be very inwardly focused. They tend to be introverts, to be a little more academically and scholarly inclined. They are very serious and focused about their studies. Instrumentalists are only interested in their instrument, and the performance end of it. Most are not interested at all in theory, history, or any other aspect of the art. Most instrumentalists see theory as something they have to get through because it's part of the curriculum. If they had their choice, they wouldn't take those classes. Composers would seek them out. [*Faculty*]

> Composition majors are admired and disrespected at the same time. They're admired because most of the students in the Pre-College could not sit down and write a symphony. The way they're disrespected is that we have com-

poser readings and from those composer readings a decision is made as to whose compositions will be performed for a concert. That's a very prestigious award. The orchestra doesn't take time to warm up when it's composer reading. It seems like there's such a lack of awe for what's sitting before them. The student composer gets one shot for it to be read through and for it to sound decent. If it were one of the instrumentalists' concerto, they'd expect everyone in the room to be attentive. [*Alumnus*]

The relationship between composers and instrumentalists is challenging because composers depend on their fellow students to perform their pieces:

Here performing is more valued, even though composing might be considered more creative. Performing is also creative. For me, I have to almost write the piece again in order to perform it. So composing is breaking the next barrier. During orchestral composition readings, some people take it like a morning off, or like a substitute teacher. The orchestra is forced to take on these student compositions. It's a classic story about performers being resistant to composers. But too many composers don't help that. They don't always have a good attitude toward performers. I think it works better when people are both. [*17-year-old student*]

Tacit knowledge offered by teachers

Teachers can help moderate the effects of negative personality characteristics. They can provide relaxation techniques to reduce stress and inflexibility and help students by providing relevant tacit knowledge. Tacit knowledge is important advice offered to novices or protégés that exists outside the formal curriculum. The general purpose of tacit knowledge is to help the one receiving it to be more successful in meeting his or her goals. This is done in two ways: (a) by exposure to networks of power, including gatekeepers and renowned mentors, and (b) by learning to capitalise on one's unique strengths (Sternberg & Wagner, 1986):

If you're a good teacher you can work within the constraints of a student's personality, physical attributes, musicality etc. The gray areas which are terribly important are their own motivation, their own degree of relaxation, and their own musicality. The degree of these are terribly important. The ones to rise to the top have those qualities. [*Faculty*]

Three pieces of tacit knowledge emerged from the interviews:

True Commitment. Do not ask your teacher or mentor if you should pursue a musical career. Asking implies that you can survive as a non-performer. To make it in music you need to want to be a performer or "die":

What do you I tell someone when he or she asks, "Am I good enough?" It depends on why that counsel is being asked. To: " Am I good enough to be a great concert violinist?" usually I say very simply, " I don't know whether you can make it. There are in the field probably a half a dozen people who make a living just from being a concert artist, and from what I see now I don't think you're one of those. If music is important to you however, go for it. If you feel 'I have to have it whether I'm wonderful or not. I have to live a life in music', then go for it and you can do it. If you're asking me if you should be a professional musician, the fact that you're not sure yourself says to me that you shouldn't be. You have to have a calling for it. It's what you want to do and nothing else." That's what I usually say. It's up to you and how badly you want it. [*Faculty*]

The importance of teacher selection. Some teachers are more focused on providing mentoring, tacit knowledge, and access to career opportunities than others. Selecting the right teacher is crucial to one's musical development:

My teacher really looked after me. She loaned me a violin and bow at one point. She attended every concert I gave, even if it were out of town. She would drive me there and take her little tape recorder. She'd give me the tape afterwards. After I'd listen to the tape, we'd discuss our reactions. She gave me excellent support and guidance. I think she was doing the same for all of her students. [*Alumnus*]

There was a real professionalism in the school. They were really preparing us for the harsh reality that there weren't many spots out there, and that not everyone could be special, so only the best will shine, so it's your job to make yourself the best. That included advice on recital preparation and concert attire. We would give concerts in black tie dress. We learned about bowing, how to come out on stage, and where you were supposed to gaze during different parts of the concert. I'd never been exposed to such a serious atmosphere about how you do music. Other types of music were considered rather taboo. Classical music was the supreme art. Good jazz was borderline acceptable but nothing else. [*Alumnus*]

My teacher covered the territory. The foremost was the presentation itself—what is a good performance, how to bring out the character and beauty of the music, and how to make the audience feel connected. She talked about how you walk on stage. She held weekly master classes in which we played for our peers. Once I made a mistake and said, "whoops!" I remember everyone laughed and my teacher told me after class how to deal with mistakes so you don't lose concentration and dwell on what has already passed. She would sit down with me and work out programming with me, including what pieces to play and in what order. I was very excited about learning to be a fine performer. She made sure that I built a well-rounded repertoire list. In the first couple of years we went through a lot of pieces. [*Alumnus*]

Developing an artistic identity. At some point, a performer or composer establishes an artistic identity. Along with that identity comes some engaging mythology about one's history and source of talent. Most faculty members feel strongly that it is too early for JPC students to be dealing with this aspect of professional life:

> We talk a lot about artists' myths and legends, but we don't spend a lot of time talking about creating their own, because I try to make the artistic world more realistic for them. If they aspire to a professional career, they need to understand that artists are real people. As for their own legends, I'm not sure I believe in it for this age. There is a course in the college division called the Colloquium, where they begin to think about artistic identity and whom they wish to be as an artist. The JPC kids are too busy getting through their real lives as adolescents to be bothered yet with the creation of a mythological life. [*Faculty*]

> This is a completely implicit lesson. But studying with someone like Mr T, who is a professional composer, or Mr B, you see that is their life and you have a contrast with the mythical figures you read about. And I can see that there are people in my life who are making worthwhile music. The most encouraging thing to me is seeing role models like Mr B or Mr T who compose, make a living, get commissions, who do what they do. They write commercial music, write film scores. Not only is it possible, it's not even crazy. It may be a golden age for composers. I've come to see that through my contact through my teachers. [*Alumnus*]

Overall, the environment appears to focus on serious consideration of students' futures, whether in the music world or in other domains:

> I don't think the Juilliard program is given enough credit for how it changes the lives of its students. The focus and direction that it gives youngsters who come in with the high school mentality of, "I'll worry about that later", is tremendous. This program hammers home that you have to take control of your own future. You have to start practicing now, to start focusing on your art and refining it now, so that later on you can achieve your goals. [*Alumnus*]

Recommendations for change

In order to accommodate the Music Advancement Program, performance and practice space that had been solely used by the JPC now had to be shared, breeding some resentment on the part of students and parents. However, as time passes and more people forget how much space was available before the advent of MAP, and more MAP students are admitted to the JPC, the administration hopes these concerns will be allayed.

All the interviewees complained about lack of time. Faculty members felt that there was too little time to individualise, or to enrich classes as they would like. Students found that cramming all the classes into one day was exhausting. However, when students were asked whether the Russian model of full-time specialty schools, like a junior conservatory, would be appealing, the response was mixed:

> I like music on Saturdays. It gives me something to look forward to. It's not every day. It gives you time to practice and do your homework. Because music lessons are not checked every day it feels less like spoon feeding. You have to really think for yourself because you don't have your teacher there all the time. [*12-year-old student*]

> What would be ideal is my school for academics and a more intense music studies department. I would like my weekdays to be more like Saturdays, but with academics. That would be wonderful. I don't actually envision a career as a performer. I'd like to do it as a second hobby. I'd like to be a plastic surgeon or archeologist. [*12-year-old student*]

> I know that the American reaction is, how can you limit these kids to music so exclusively? But you get unbelievably good products from the full-time model. There's one student here whom I admire and respect because he exudes love of music. He attended the Russian conservatory school. But I don't know how it would work for me since there are other activities I'm really interested in as well, like baseball. Then again, perhaps that's a very American way of looking at things. Maybe the way I've done it is not the best way, but I've got to keep reassuring myself that it is, or else I'll be really unhappy! [*17-year-old student, at JPC for three years*]

Solfege and theory faculty are concerned about time to individualise lessons for their students. These classes have grown larger, and in spite of placement tests, the range of acquired knowledge within classes remains large. Also, more attention could be paid to student compositions. Solfege and theory teachers also wished that the curriculum would be more standardised among faculty so that teachers were assured that specific developmental concepts had been covered at each level.

Some faculty members complained that the audition process was a popularity contest, although all acknowledged that the process was consistent with how admission was conducted in most pre-college programmes.

Some students wanted more opportunities to perform. They also wanted more challenging and experienced conductors, and stricter solfege and theory teachers who would control unruly students. In orchestra they wanted a wider repertoire and fewer composer's readings.

CONCLUSIONS

It is unrealistic to suppose that, in the foreseeable future, secondary schools will adapt the kind of focused commitment to talent development exhibited by the Juilliard Pre-College programme. However, if we are to avoid the tragic waste of creative ability that exists in every school today, we must turn our attention to studying the ideal circumstances under which elite-level talent is nurtured.

The Juilliard Pre-College programme is supported by tuition and has none of the constraints that result from receiving public funding. Further, attendance is only required once a week. How useful, then are the comparisons we can make with what is offered to our most talented young scientists, mathematicians, historians, and writers? I would argue that looking at the ideal circumstances for talent development in one domain can shed light on what improvements we can make to publicly funded opportunities made available to the academically gifted.

The key differences between the two environments are indicated in Table 12.1. Most publicly funded programmes for the academically gifted focus on a well-rounded education, and despite a burgeoning literature on domain-specific talent, students are expected to do their best in all subjects. Specialisation is discouraged. Also, at least in the United States, much effort has been expended to include a wide range of topics and

TABLE 12.1
Contrasting the JPC and academic gifted programme for gifted students

Variable	Juilliard Pre-College	Academic programme
Philosophy and goals	Specialised and narrow	Broad and inclusive
Admissions	Self-selection and audition	Standardised tests
Curriculum	Press for individualisation	Press for heterogeneity
Beliefs about talent	No hesitation to recognise contributions of innate talent Belief that one builds on innate musicality with expert instruction and disciplined practice	Hesitation to admit to contributions of innate talent because that is considered elitist Concerned about early specialisation
Peers	Macho about practice and revere most talented	Admire those who are successful with the least effort expended
Tacit knowledge	Derived from master teacher	Derived haphazardly from teacher or parent

perspectives to make the curriculum more inviting to its diverse school population. In contrast, the philosophy of the Juilliard Pre-College programme is simple and clear: excellence in performance and composition of music in the Western European classical tradition. Once a limited and specific goal is agreed on and acknowledged as legitimate, assessment, instruction, and curriculum development is far less prone to conflict.

Publicly funded programmes for academically gifted adolescents are expected to conduct extensive outreach efforts. Ideally, no stone should be left unturned in searching for a potentially able student. At Juilliard, the outreach is limited almost exclusively to a network of outstanding teachers who serve much like talent scouts in their respective communities. Most of the selection takes place even before the audition process.

Admission to academic gifted programmes tend to be based on a cut-off score on a test, the items of which are not available for public perusal. Although other variables such as teacher recommendations are sometimes included, nearly universal dependence is placed on some kind of standardised evaluation. The admissions process for the JPC is exclusively based on audition. The requirements are clearly connected to the curriculum and expectations for the programme. The basic criteria for the audition are publicly available, allowing potential applicants to prepare or to self-select out of the process.

Current reform movements in the United States involve increasing heterogeneity in the classroom. Most elementary schools have, at least overtly, eliminated streaming or ability grouping except for within-class reading and mathematics. Separate gifted programmes are not popular options for young children in most communities. On the secondary level, the move towards "de-tracking" has been less successful, but there are definite shifts towards greater inclusivity—offering more children a high-level curriculum. Because the JPC is highly selective, and has no pressure being placed on it to be less so, the focus of curriculum improvement can remain on individualisation for talent development.

Support for exceptional students seems consistent in both environments. That is to say, those students who are strongest and those students who are weakest get more individual attention than those in the middle. The variability within the group, however, is much smaller in the JPC group than in a typical academic situation devised for academically gifted students.

Teachers in programmes for the academically gifted tend to hold beliefs that at least some component of ability is innate, yet are reluctant to express this in a climate that finds such views elitist. Faculty at JPC had no problem coming to agreement on which components of performance talent were innate, which were trainable given a certain threshold of talent, and what combinations of components were necessary and sufficient or insufficient to fulfilment of potential.

The differences between values held by peer groups in the typical academic environment with those in the JPC are dramatic. Academic programmes tend to value performance in the social and athletic domains over purely academic acuity, and studiousness is looked upon with some suspicion. In contrast, Juilliard students are known to brag about the amount of time they practise, and the most talented among them are the most revered.

At schools where a teacher is responsible for at least 50 students' progress, opportunities for sharing tacit knowledge are more haphazard. Most of the networking a student might benefit from is acquired from parents or from participation in summer programmes. At JPC, one's instrument teacher is the main connection to careers and general performance opportunities, the person through whom connections are made, and who generally socialises you into the music business.

The most promising adaptations from the conservatory world to the realm of programmes for the academically gifted appear to be a clear and limited goal for the programme, authentic evaluation for admission with publicly available criteria to work towards, more opportunities for individualisation, and the master class model for sharing tacit knowledge. The time is ripe for change in the way that talent in academics is developed. With increased rigour, individualisation, and socialisation into the world of scholarship, academically gifted students could better enjoy the fruits of their labours, have more opportunities for recognition, and plant the seeds for possible contribution to the beauty or well-being of our world.

NOTE

This chapter was presented earlier as a paper at the 12th World Conference of the World Council for Gifted and Talented Children. Seattle, Washington, USA. July 31, 1997.

REFERENCES

Bamberger, J. (1986). Cognitive issues in the development of musically gifted children. In R. Sternberg & J. Davidson (Eds.), *Conceptions of giftedness* (pp. 388–413). Cambridge: Cambridge University Press.

Bamberger, J. (1991). *The mind behind the musical ear.* Cambridge, MA: Harvard University Press.

Bastian, H.B. (1994). From the everyday world and the musical way of life of highly talented young instrumentalists: Some findings from a biographical study of national winners of the competition JUGEND MUSIZIERT. In K.A. Heller & E.A. Hany (Eds.), *Competence and responsibility: Vol 2* (pp. 153–163). Seattle, WA: Hogrefe & Huber.

Csikszentmihalyi, M., Rathunde, K., & Whalen, S. (1997). *Talented teenagers: The roots of success and failure.* Cambridge: Cambridge University Press.

Davidson, L., & Scripp, L. (1994). Conditions of giftedness: Musical development in the preschool and elementary years. In R.F. Subotnik & K.D. Arnold (Eds.), *Beyond Terman:*

Contemporary longitudinal studies of giftedness and talent (pp. 155–185). Norwood, NJ: Ablex.

Delbanco, N. (1985). *The Beaux Arts Trio: A portrait*. New York: William Morris.

Ericsson, K.A., Krampe, R.T., & Tesch-Römer, C. (1993). The role of deliberate practice in the acquisition of expert performance. *Psychological Review, 100,* 363–406.

Feldman, D.H. (1986). *Nature's gambit: Child prodigies and the development of human potential.* New York: Basic Books.

Feldman, D.H. (1993). Cultural organisms in the development of great potential: Referees, termites, and the Aspen Music Festival. In R.H. Wozniak & K.W. Fischer (Eds.), *Development in context: Acting and thinking in specific environments* (pp. 225–251). Hillsdale, NJ: Lawrence Erlbaum Associates Inc.

Kogan, J. (1987). *Nothing but the best: The struggle for perfection at the Juilliard School.* New York: Random House.

Ochse, R. (1990). *Before the gates of excellence: Determinants of creative genius.* Cambridge: Cambridge University Press.

Perkins, D.N. (1988). The possibility of invention. In R.J. Sternberg (Ed.), *The nature of creativity* (pp. 362–385). New York: Cambridge University Press.

Scripp, L., & Davidson, L. (1994). Giftedness and professional training: The impact of music reading skills on musical development. In R.F. Subotnik & K.D. Arnold (Eds.), *Beyond Terman: Contemporary longitudinal studies of giftedness and talent* (pp. 186–211). Norwood, NJ: Ablex.

Sosniak, L. (1985). Learning to be a concert pianist. In B. Bloom (Ed.), *Developing talent in young people* (pp. 19–67). New York: Ballantine.

Sternberg, R.J., & Wagner, R.K. (Eds.) (1986). *Practical intelligence: Nature and origins of competence in the everyday world.* New York: Cambridge University Press.

Walters, J., & Gardner, H. (1986). The crystallizing experience: Discovering an intellectual gift. In R.J. Sternberg & J.E. Davidson (Eds.), *Conceptions of giftedness* (pp. 306–331). New York: Cambridge University Press.

Winner, E. (1996). *Gifted children: Myths and realities.* New York: Basic Books.

Zuckerman, H. (1977). *Scientific elite: Nobel laureates in the United States.* New York: Free Press.

CHAPTER THIRTEEN

Talent and self-narrative: The survival of an underachieving adolescent

Hubert J.M. Hermans
University of Nijmegen, The Netherlands

Margreet F. Poulie
Private clinician, Nijmegen, The Netherlands

The focus of this chapter is on the relationship between talent and self. It is our premise that talent should be a constitutive part of one's self-reflection, so that talented people are aware, as soon as possible in their personal development, of the existence of exceptional qualities and of the performance areas in which these qualities can most productively be applied. This should include awareness not only of the existence of specific qualities and their facilitating environments, but also of the obstacles, in their own selves and in the situation, that prevent the realisation of these qualities.

In the discussion of talent and its facilitating or inhibiting environments, it makes sense to make a distinction between processes and performance areas. Renzulli (1978) proposed ability, creativity, and motivation to be the three main processes which, in their interaction, form the core of talent. In his view, these processes can be applied to a great variety of general performance areas (e.g. mathematics, visual arts, music, linguistic arts, philosophy) or specific performance areas (e.g. statistics, biography, poetry, electronic music, jewellery design). In Renzulli's view, ability is not necessarily of a superior level but it is rather above average; his emphasis lies much more on the mutually fertilising influence between ability, creativity, and motivation (or task commitment) than on the exceptional ability itself.

As Mönks (1996) has recently argued, special attention is required for talented underachievers. There are at least two reasons for underachievement in talented students. First, there is the paradoxical finding that a talented individual may lack ability. A specific learning problem or handicap (e.g. dyslexia) may hinder the development of talent although general ability may be high or even very high. In another case, the student may never have acquired the basic skills necessary for productive learning (e.g. reading). Second, the lack of positive self-experience may cause underachievement. This may be observed in those students who, as a result of bad performance, lower their self-esteem, with the outcome that low self-esteem itself, often in combination with other factors, becomes the cause of underachievement. If the environment does not offer adequate opportunities to compensate for these negative experiences, the process of deterioration in self-esteem may result in a sense of general incompetence. Although some authors (e.g. Butler-Por, 1993) see great difficulties in overcoming underachievement, adequate counselling programmes are required to restore the students' self-confidence and motivation to learn (Mönks, 1996).

THE TEMPORAL ORGANISATION OF SELF-NARRATIVE

Since James' (1890) founding work, the psychology of the self has become a specific field within our discipline (for a review see Rosenberg, 1979). In the past decades we have witnessed an upsurge of studies of the self. Many of these new developments have criticised earlier approaches as over-simplistic and static (e.g. characterising the self as positive or negative *in toto*), and instead emphasise the self as a dynamic multiplicity of elements. The self has been described and analysed as a complexity of images (Rhodewalt & Morf, 1995), mental representations (Kihlstrom & Cantor, 1984), facets (Marsh, 1986), goals (Brandstädter & Rothermund, 1994), tasks (Sheldon & Emmons, 1995), possible selves (Markus & Nurius, 1986), private, public, and collective selves (Triandis, 1989), or actual, ought, and ideal selves (Higgins, 1987). These concepts represent what Pratkanis and Greenwald (1985) have called the organisation of knowledge metaphor and, as such, they are appropriate for dealing with the ways in which the component elements of the self are organised.

A recent development in the psychology of the self is the so-called "narrative approach" which considers the self from the perspective of a story. The basic assumption is that each person has a story to tell about him- or herself and that the events of one's life receive meaning as parts of a narrative structure (Bruner, 1986; Cohler, 1982; Gergen & Gergen, 1988; Hermans, 1996; McAdams, 1993; Sarbin, 1986; Thomae, 1988). The narrative approach and the organisation of knowledge approach have in common that they both emphasise the self as a dynamic multiplicity of elements. More specifically, the advocates of a narrative approach have in common an emphasis on time. Events in the life of a person are, like historical events, temporally organised. Sarbin (1986), for example, considers narrative to be a way of organising episodes, actions, and accounts of actions in time and space, and as an achievement that brings together mundane facts and fantastic creations. Our fantasies and daydreams are unvoiced stories; our plans and memories and even our loves and hates, are guided by narrative plots.

It is our view that the narrative approach is particularly appropriate for the investigation of the selves of talented individuals. It allows us to study the achievements, creations, failures, problems, and plans of talented people as significant events which receive meaning in the context of their evolving personal history. As part of a temporally ordered self-narrative, not only their experiences in the past, but also their concerns in the present, and their goals, doubts, and aspirations regarding the future can be taken into account. Moreover, the multiplicity of performance areas in which the individual's ability, creativity, and motivation are applied, can be reflected in the multiplicity of personal events and circumstances that receive their personal meaning as parts of the individual's self-narrative. In other words, when a talented individual succeeds in realising his or her ability, creativity, and motivation in one or more performance areas or, on the contrary, is not able to do so as a result of obstacles, the resulting achievements or failures are understood as positively or negatively experienced events in an organised self-narrative.

The central part of our contribution is a case study in which the self-narrative of a talented, underachieving adolescent, Leo, is described and analysed as it evolves during a period of five months. We will give an impression of his situation, his main achievements and disappointments, and the challenges he faces during this period. Particular attention will be given to the constancies and changes in his evolving narrative. In keeping with the preceding theoretical considerations, we will elaborate on the dynamic multiplicity and on the temporal organisation of his story in such a way that the reader may understand the nature of his struggle.

The purpose of this idiographic study is twofold. First, we wish to illustrate how the events that are associated with Leo's talent receive personal meaning as part of an organised self-narrative. Second, we present a particular method, the self-confrontation method, which allows people to tell and retell significant events of their life-stories as part of an extensive self-investigation. In illustrating the method we will show how talent, in its positive and negative aspects, is represented in the self of an exceptional person. Let us start with a description of the theory on which the self-confrontation method is based.

VALUATION THEORY: SELF AS AN ORGANISED PROCESS

Valuation theory (Hermans, 1987a,b, 1988, 1989; Hermans & Hermans-Jansen, 1995; Hermans & Van Gilst, 1991) is devised for the study of significant events in one's life, their ordering into a meaning system, and the development of this meaning system across time and space. The theory, inspired by the philosophical thinking of James (1890) and Merleau-Ponty (1945), conceives the self as an *organised process of valuation*. The "process" aspect of the self refers to the narrative-historical nature of human experience, and implies a spatio-temporal perspective: The person tells the events in his or her life from a specific point in space (the "here") and a specific point in time (the "now"). The "organisational" aspect of the self refers to the composite whole that is created when experiences, associated with different positions in time and space, receive a narrative order in the process of telling and self-reflection.

The central concept, valuation, includes anything people find to be of importance when talking about their life history and situation. A valuation is any unit of meaning associated with positive (pleasant), negative (unpleasant), or ambivalent (both pleasant and unpleasant) affect for the individual. A valuation can include a broad range of phenomena: a dear memory, a difficult problem, the contact with an inspiring person, a fantasy figure, a creative achievement, an unreachable goal, an anticipated failure, and so forth. Through the process of telling and self-reflection, divergent and even contrasting valuations referring to the past, present, and future are organised into a self-narrative (Crites, 1986; Sarbin, 1986). Different valuations also emerge as a result of the individual's changing orientation in time and space.

A central assumption is that each valuation has an *affective connotation*, which corresponds to James' (1890) notion of "self-feelings". More specifically, each valuation implies a particular pattern of affect or an affective modality. When we know which types of affect are implied by a particular valuation, we know something about the valuation itself. Affect is not considered a direct "result" of cognitive or unconscious processing but is inherent in the valuation itself.

Latent–manifest distinction

More insight into the organisation of the valuation system can be gained by introducing the *latent–manifest distinction*. It is assumed that a small set of basic motives are latent in the affective component of the valuation system. These motives, moreover, are assumed to be similar across individuals and to be continuously active within each individual. At the manifest level, however, valuations vary phenomenologically not only across individuals but also within a single individual across time and space.

Special attention has been given to two motives: the striving for self-enhancement (the S-motive), that is, self-maintenance and self-expansion, and the longing for contact and union with the other (the O-motive). A number of psychologists have discussed the basic duality of human experience: Bakan (1966) viewed agency and communion as fundamental dynamic principles; Angyal (1965) proposed the concepts of autonomy (self-determination) and homonomy (self-surrender); and Klages (1948) considered *Bindung* (solidification) and *Lösung* (dissolution) as basic motives of human character. Within a narrative context, McAdams (1985) has elaborated on the distinction between power and intimacy.

When a person values something, he or she always feels something about it and in these feelings the basic motives are reflected. A valuation (e.g. "I got high grades for that examination by studying hard") can function as a gratification of the S-motive. Feelings of strength and pride experienced in connection with the valuation are indicators of this motive. Similarly, a valuation (e.g. "I like to listen to my son's playing of his instrument") may represent a gratification of the O-motive, and in that case the person experiences feelings of tenderness and intimacy in connection with the valuation. The general idea is this: The motivational base on the latent level is represented in the affective component of the valuation system on the manifest level.

Generalisation and idealisation

Two concepts, generalisation and idealisation, particularly represent the dynamic nature of valuation theory and play a central role in the methodology presented in the following section. The more a particular valuation *generalises* as part of the system, the more it determines the "general feeling" of a person. When one asks somebody how he or she feels in general, it is likely that particular experiences colour this general feeling more than others. Suppose that a talented, underachieving student perceives the bad judgements he receives in school as "injustice". In that case there is a good chance that the feelings associated with these judgements are more determining of the student's general feeling in this period than, for example, the good contact with his mates at the sports club. In other words, not all valuations are equally influential in the system. The more generalising power a valuation has, the more influential the affective component of this valuation is in colouring the person's general feeling in a certain period of life.

Valuations may also differ in the extent of *idealisation*. The basic idea is that certain valuations fit more with the way an individual ideally would like to feel. When people are actually going through a period in which they are faced with personal problems that affect their selves to a significant degree, the valuations that influence the general feeling are often different from those that colour the ideal feeling. In such cases the ideal feeling typically has an affective modality that is in contrast to the affective modality of the general feeling.

THE SELF-CONFRONTATION METHOD: AFFECTIVE ORGANISATION OF MEANING UNITS

The self-confrontation method is an idiographic, dynamic assessment procedure based on valuation theory. The method is designed to study the relation between valuations and types of affect, and the way in which these variables become organised and reorganised over time (Hermans & Hermans-Jansen, 1995). The procedure involves elicitation of a set of valuations and then association of these valuations with a standardised set of affect terms. The result is an individualised matrix in which each cell represents the extent to which a specific affect is characteristic of a specific valuation (see Table 13.1).

Valuation construction phase

The valuations (i.e. rows in the matrix) are elicited with a series of open-ended questions. For present purposes we have used an adolescent version of the self-confrontation method. The main questions are outlined in Table 13.2 and devised to bring out important units of meaning for the past, the present, and the future. The questions invite individuals to reflect on their life situations in such a way that they feel free to mention those concerns that are most relevant from the perspective of the present situation. The subjects are free to interpret the questions in any way they want. The subjects are also encouraged to phrase the valuations in their own terms so that the formulations are as much as possible in agreement with what they intend to say. The typical form of expression is the sentence (i.e. the basic unit of text). In a sentence the subject brings together those events that the person feels belong together as elements of a personal unit of meaning. In the case of a complex unit of meaning, the subject is permitted to use several sentences for its expression. A quick response is not required, and there is no one-to-one relation between question and answer. The individual is encouraged to mention all valuations that come to mind and, typically, each question leads to more than one valuation. At the end of the interview subjects are explicitly asked whether the survey contains all of the experiences they want to include in the self-investigation. If something important is missing, they can add this. At the end of the procedure the number of valuations varies greatly but in most cases it is between 20 and

TABLE 13.1
Matrix of Valuation × Affect

	Affect Term																							
	1	2	3	4	5	6	7	8	9	10	11	12	13	14	15	16	17	18	19	20	21	22	23	24
	P	N	S	N	P	S	N	P	O	O	N	O	N	S	N	P	N	O	P	N	S	P	P	P
Val. no.																								
1	4	0	4	0	4	1	0	4	4	4	0	3	0	4	0	5	0	4	4	0	3	3	4	5
2	0	5	0	2	0	1	2	2	0	0	0	5	5	3	2	0	0	0	0	5	2	2	2	0
3	5	0	5	0	5	5	0	4	5	5	0	5	0	4	1	4	0	5	4	2	2	5	4	4
4	0	5	4	4	2	2	0	0	5	4	0	5	0	3	5	5	4	5	5	4	4	3	5	5
5	0	5	4	1	0	2	0	0	5	0	5	0	0	0	5	0	4	0	0	5	5	5	2	0
6	5	0	5	0	5	5	0	5	5	5	0	5	0	5	0	5	0	5	5	0	4	5	5	4
7	0	5	3	0	0	4	0	0	0	0	2	1	0	5	0	0	0	0	0	5	2	2	2	2
8	0	5	3	0	0	0	0	0	0	0	2	2	0	0	0	0	3	0	0	5	2	2	2	2
9	5	0	5	0	5	5	0	5	2	2	0	0	0	5	0	3	0	0	2	0	5	5	5	5
10	5	0	5	0	5	2	0	5	4	5	4	3	0	5	2	5	2	3	0	0	5	5	5	5
GF	2	4	5	2	2	2	2	4	4	5	0	5	3	3	2	2	4	3	0	4	2	3	2	4
IF	5	0	5	0	5	5	0	5	5	5	0	5	0	5	0	5	0	5	5	0	5	5	5	5

Rows represent valuations and columns represent affect terms used for the indices S, O, P, and N, where S = affect referring to self-enhancement, O = affect referring to contact with the other, P = positive affect, and N = negative affect. GF = general feeling; and IF = ideal feeling.
Affect terms: 1 = glad (P); 2 = powerless (N); 3 = competent (S); 4 = scared (N); 5 = happy (P); 6 = strong (S); 7 = disappointed (N); 8 = enjoying (P); 9 = united (O); 10 = loving (O); 11 = alienated (N); 12 = sympathetic (O); 13 = guilty (N); 14 = self-confident (S); 15 = lonely (N); 16 = trusting (P); 17 = inferior (N); 18 = together (O); 19 = safe (P); 20 = angry (N); 21 = proud (S); 22 = energetic (P); 23 = calm (P); 24 = free (P).

TABLE 13.2
Questions from the adolescence version of the self-confrontation method used to elicit valuations

Set 1: The Past
Do you sometimes think about something that happened in your past?
- Perhaps an important event, or contact with a particular person?
- Something which influenced your life and still plays an important role? It may be something pleasant or something unpleasant.

Set 2: The Present
(a) School
- When you think about your contact with your schoolmates, what comes to mind? What do you find important?
- When you think about your contact with your teachers, what comes to mind? What do you find important?
- When you think about the subjects which you learn at school, and about your homework, what comes to mind?
- Are there other things which relate to you, your school, or your study and which you see as relevant?

(b) Home
- In what respects are your parents as you would like them to be?
- In what respects are your parents not as you would like them to be?
- When you think about your home situation, is there something you find important? (Concerning your brothers and sisters, your place at home, a pet, some members of your family?)

(c) Peers
- Is there somebody who you get on with very well?
- When you think about your contact with friends, what comes to mind? What does it mean to you?
- Perhaps you have a relationship with somebody? What does it mean to you to have a boy-friend or girl-friend?
- Is there somebody you don't like? What does this person mean to you?

(d) Yourself
- In what respects do you see yourself as competent?
- Is there something which you would like to improve?
- What do you find really important to develop in yourself?

Set 3: The Future
When you think about your future, what concerns you?
- Perhaps you have some notion of the direction you want to take.
- Perhaps about the person you really don't want to become.
- Is there somebody who wants to decide for you what you should become?

40. Each valuation is written by the interviewer on a separate card and in this form is available for the second part of the investigation.

Affective rating phase

In the second part of the investigation, a standard list of affect terms (columns in the matrix) is presented to the subject. Concentrating on the first valuation, the subject indicates on a 0–5 scale the extent to which he or she experiences each affect in relation to the valuation (0 = *not at all*, 1 = *very little*, 2 = *to some extent*, 3 = *quite a lot*, 4 = *much*, and 5 = *very much*). The subject, working alone now, rates each valuation with the same list of affect terms, and the different valuations can then be compared according to their affective profiles. The list of affect terms used in the present investigation is an adolescent version of the list presented by Hermans and Hermans-Jansen (1995, p. 277). On the basis of the affective ratings for the different valuations, a number of indices can be calculated that in their combination represent the affective organisation of the valuation system.

(1) Index S is the sum of the scores for four affect terms expressing self-enhancement: Numbers 3, 6, 14, and 21 in Table 13.1.

(2) Index O is the sum of the scores for four affect terms expressing contact and union with the other: Numbers 9, 10, 12, and 18 in Table 13.1. For each valuation, moreover, the S–O difference can be determined. When the experience of self-enhancement is stronger than the experience of contact with the other, S > O. When the feeling of contact with the other prevails, O > S. When both kinds of experiences coexist, S = O.

(3) Index P is the sum of the scores for eight positive affect terms: Numbers 1, 5, 8, 16, 19, 22, 23, and 24.

(4) Index N is the sum of the scores for eight negative affect terms: Numbers 2, 4, 7, 11, 13, 15, 17, and 20. For each valuation, again, the P–N difference can be studied. This indicates the degree of well-being the person experiences in relation to a specific valuation. Well-being is positive when P > N, negative when N > P, and ambivalent when P = N. (Note that the scores for S and O range from 0 to 20 and for P and N from 0 to 40 for each valuation.) In summary, the degree of S and O affect indicates the extent of realisation of the basic motives, whereas the degree of positive and negative affect reflects the extent to which these motives meet superable or insuperable obstacles.

(5) The extent of *generalisation* (G) of a valuation within the system is assessed by using the following question at the end of the valuation construction phase: "How do I generally feel these days?" This question does not ask for a specific valuation but is devised to assess the "general

feeling". The person answers directly with the list of affect terms that was used for the characterisation of the valuations. The product–moment correlation between the pattern of affect that belongs to a specific valuation and the pattern of affect that belongs to the general feeling is a measure of the extent of the generalisation of this valuation. The more positive the correlation, the more this valuation is supposed to generalise within the system. For example, when a person is worrying all the time about his or her studies, it is expected that a valuation referring to this problem (e.g. "Wherever I am, I always worry about failing in my studies"), has a high degree of generalisation in the system. In that case the correlation between the affective profile belonging to this valuation and the affective profile belonging to the general feeling is expected to be high. (Note that the correlation between the affective profiles of any two valuations can be used in order to explore their common affective meaning.)

(6) The assessment of the *idealisation* (I) of a valuation is determined by using the question: "How would I like to feel?" The correlation between the affective profile belonging to a specific valuation and the affective profile belonging to the ideal feeling indicates the ideal quality of this valuation. The height of the correlation indicates the extent of the idealisation of the valuation. The more positive the correlation, the higher the idealisation. When a valuation has an affective profile that contrasts with the ideal feeling, this is expressed in a negative (minus) correlation. (General feeling [GF] and ideal feeling [IF] represent the last rows in the matrix, see Table 13.1.) (For reliability and validity data of the indices presented so far, see Hermans, 1987b; for the discussion of the data with the client see Hermans & Hermans-Jansen, 1995.)

A second (and sometimes a third and a fourth) self-investigation usually follows, typically after some months. In this case, however, the subjects do not start "from scratch". Instead, they are confronted with the statements they constructed in the first (or previous) investigation. The interviewer reads the original questions and, after each question, produces the statements that the person provided in the preceding self-investigation. The subjects are instructed to consider, for each statement separately, whether they still go along with it; that is, would they still come up with the same response to the question? When this is not the case, the interviewer explains that there are various options available: An old valuation may be reformulated (modification); replaced (substitution); discarded altogether (elimination); or a new response may be added (supplementation). In this way the subjects have considerable freedom to point to the constant and changing elements in their own valuation systems.

LEO'S STORY: FROM THE COLD ROAD TO THE ROAD OF FIRE

Leo was born in South America but was adopted by Dutch parents when he was a few months old. His parents described him as a "very active, ingenious child", and as "very sensitive" to their reactions and attitudes. Leo remembers that he first faced serious problems during his first year of elementary school. The teacher frequently punished him by locking him in the broom cupboard, a punishment that she also meted out to other children. Leo experienced her behaviour as extremely threatening and as contrasting with the safety that he felt with his parents, who did not hear about the teacher's behaviour until more than six months later. This experience formed the basis of Leo's subsequent distrust of every other teacher. He later described his period in elementary school as a time of "total confusion" because he could not work out which rules applied in which social situations. This period, moreover, was a prelude to one of the main themes in his later self-narrative: taking hold of the reins so that he was less dependent on the arbitrariness of his teachers and trainers. His problems were made worse by his dyslexia, which was not recognised by his environment as a specific learning problem, but instead explained as a general inability. He remembers that in school he was simply regarded and labelled as "stupid" or "lazy". He responded to this situation by trying very hard to take control of his own life. Later, during his high-school period, a psychiatrist wrote a report on him in which he was classified as "developmentally disturbed". Finally, Leo became so frustrated with school that he decided to drop out. At the same time, however, he felt the urge to continue his education, but in his own way. Leo was able to do this after a psychiatrist made an official statement allowing him to deviate from the compulsory school attendance law. As soon as he was on his own, he decided, with the support of his parents, to "build his own school". He decided himself to visit several official schools in order to gather information about the contents of their curricula, and he explained his situation to the teachers. Borrowing elements from the school curricula, he devised his own curriculum, which ran parallel to the official programme. In order to obtain adequate feedback, he asked several school teachers to provide him with their examinations and to give him marks for his performances. He continued his systematic independent study between the ages of 14 and 19, and progressively reached higher levels of high-school programmes. Finally, he returned to school in order to participate in the class that would prepare him for university. However, being in the official school again, a strong sense of anxiety prevented him from passing the final examination that would give him entrance to the university. For this reason he contacted a counsellor (the second author), who offered him the opportunity to conduct a self-investigation.

There are three reasons to consider Leo a talented student. First, he exhibited very strong motivation: Instead of simply dropping out of school, he continued his education on his own initiative and, in an independent way, he did this over a long period of time (between the ages of 14 and 19), fighting against the disadvantage of his dyslexia and, as a consequence of this, the lack of understanding from his school environment. Second, he was very creative in compensating for his handicaps. He not only developed his own curriculum, adapted to his own personal abilities, but he also compensated for his inability to organise and recall sequentially presented auditory information (a consequence of his dyslexia). He did this by converting this information into a great variety of visual diagrams and colour systems, allowing a simultaneous overview. Third, there were signs that Leo, despite his handicaps, was of above average intellectual ability. Although his verbal memory was below average (Wisc-R), he was above average in logical reasoning and nonverbal intelligence (Raven's Progressive Matrices).

Leo carried out two self-investigations. In the first investigation he explored his problems in the context of his self-narrative and in the second, five months later, he retold his narrative, taking into account what he had learned about himself and his environment in the meantime. In the interval between the two investigations, Leo had two sessions with the second author, in which he discussed with her his daily experiences.

First self-investigation

In his first self-investigation Leo formulated 36 valuations according to the described procedure. Most of his valuations (75%) belonged to the following three categories: (a) low S, low O, low P, and high N (failing to achieve self-enhancement and contact and union with the other); (b) high S, low O, high P, and low N (achieving self-enhancement); (c) high S, high O, high P, and low N (achieving a combination of self-enhancement and contact and union). From each category some examples are selected and presented on the left side of Table 13.3. The following observations can be made with regard to the content and affective organisation of his valuation system.

- Valuations 1–2, referring to some of his negative experiences, have the highest generalisation (see column G in Table 13.3) of all valuations in his system at Investigation 1. Although these events took place in the past, they continue to influence his general feeling in the present.

- Valuations 4–8 are positive (P > N) and seem to form a firm counterpoise against his negative experiences; but these valuations, however positive they may be, have no generalising power in this period of his life.
- Most of the valuations show a preponderance of self-enhancement (S) affect over affect referring to contact with the other (O). This corresponds well with the high S score and low O score for his ideal feeling. This suggests that Leo is so focused on his survival and self-maintenance that he seems to eschew experiences of contact and union, in spite of the fact that he reports high levels of O affect both in his relationship with his grandfather (valuation 5) and in his relationship with the girl with whom he felt in love (valuation 10). These parts of the valuation system reveal a discrepancy between his ideal and actual feeling, which creates a considerable tension in the system (see also the discrepancy between his ideal and general feeling).

An organising theme in Leo's self-narrative: "Taking hold of the reins"

With the self-confrontation method it is possible to detect one or more organising themes in a person's self-narrative. This is done by selecting a particular valuation as a pivot and calculating the correlations of this valuation with all other valuations in the system. In Leo's case the psychologist considered valuation 6 as pivotal and decided to take it as a starting point for correlation with all other valuations (see the column marked 6 in Table 13.3). This valuation was selected because it seemed to refer to a guiding principle in Leo's life and represented an affective experience that was dominant in his valuation system as a whole (high S, low O, high P, and low N). The psychologist then offers the pivotal valuation and the highest correlating valuation (no. 7 or 8 in Leo's case) to the client and invites him to say what these two valuations have in common. The same procedure is followed with valuations that show the next highest correlation with the pivotal valuation (no. 4 is the next highest correlating valuation in Leo's case). Here are his interpretations:

Valuation 6 with 7: r = .79
"In playing with Lego I have everything in hand; nothing can disturb you, you have freedom in everything you are doing ... the blocks don't lose confidence, but people sometimes do."

Valuation 6 with 8: r = .79
"In sport I take hold of the reins; I can be confident that it will all go well, and then I can loosen the reins, but still continue to have influence."

TABLE 13.3
Valuations of Leo's first and second self-investigation and their scores on the affective indices

Valuations at self-investigation 1	S	O	Affect P	N	G	6	Valuations at self-investigation 2	S	O	Affect P	N	G
1. My dyslexia became worse and worse; the teachers didn't understand me and called me lazy.	2	0	1	23	.56	-.32	[Same formulation as in Investigation 1.]	1	0	1	26	-.29
2. After a long time I was frustrated and wanted to stop my studies for ever; I was fed up; I retreated, tired of fighting.	5	0	5	36	.59	-.25	[Same formulation as in Investigation 1.]	0	0	0	21	-.08
3. I've always looked for the faults in myself, comparing myself with "normal people", so that I could prove that I'm fairly normal too.	7	0	14	24	.10	.55	My cold water aggression (convincing other people that they are wrong and proving this) drives me, like a lonely beast of prey focused only on one thing: winning and achieving the highest marks.	11	0	12	14	.10
4. When I found out that I had made progress, for example by receiving a high score on an intelligence test or high marks for maths in high school, this made up for the stigma.	18	0	39	8	.12	.73	[Same formulation as in Investigation 1.]	16	0	23	0	.65
5. I could listen to my grandpa for hours on end: I enjoy learning about things which are worth knowing, for example, genetics.	18	18	38	0	-.43	.58	[Same formulation as in Investigation 1.]	16	7	39	0	.48

	S	O	P	N			S	O	P	N	
6. I want to keep all the strings in my hand and I'm afraid that it will go wrong if I let them loose.	14	0	23	0	-.04	—	6	0	4	0	.04
7. When I'm playing with Lego, I'm doing two things at the same time: I'm building in my head a few steps ahead of what I am building at the moment. I don't actually have the blocks.	18	0	29	6	.07	.79	17	0	29	0	.64
														[Same formulation as in Investigation 1.]											
														It's typical of me to think a few steps ahead, before actually undertaking something (as I did with block building).											
8. In sports I can excel; sport is a way of letting off steam; I play hockey.	16	3	26	0	-.12	.79	18	4	24	5	.49
														In sports I can excel; sport is a release, and gives me the confidence to try out new things: learning to play with fire.											
9. I would like to know where my ceiling is, so that I don't bump my head when I try to make progress.	3	0	4	15	.25	-.12	11	0	24	0	.66
														My ceiling is where I MYSELF put it and I'm allowing MYSELF to decide to stop.											
10. I'm in love with Carla, because of her sharp mind.	17	19	38	0	-.45	.51	5	16	22	5	.07
														[Same formulation as in Investigation 1.]											
11. [New valuation]. As a result of my self-investigation I discovered that I've also another side to develop; I'm looking for a way to recognise this side: the road of fire (the way of becoming happy and a broader perspective).							10	0	20	3	.70
General feeling	4	0	15	22	—	-.04	13	3	24	9	—
Ideal feeling	16	3	37	0	-.13	.81	20	8	40	0	.63

S = affect referring to self-enhancement; O = affect referring to contact; P = positive affect; N = negative affect; G = generalisation; 6 = valuation that is correlated with all other valuations.

Valuation 6 with 4: r = .73
"The test result gave me a 'string of confidence' in myself, that it was not right to label me as 'lazy' and 'dumb'; it is like a tug of war: what is true? who is right?"

After a few more interpretations, Leo was asked if he could say what his conclusion was, taking all his interpretations into account. He responded in this way:

"*At this moment I have the feeling that I'm left with only this string* [taking a hold of the reins]... *I think that, in order to make progress, I need more strings...*" At this moment Leo could not be more specific; he just had the feeling that there should be more but he could not tell what it was.

In summary, we can make two observations that are central to the process of self-investigation (which apply not only to Leo's self-investigation but also to many others). First, by exploring the affective commonalities between the pivotal valuation and the other valuations that most highly correlate, Leo increases his awareness of the existence of a main theme in his self-narrative which he metaphorically describes as "taking hold of the reins". Second, by becoming aware of the pervasive influence of this theme in his story, Leo wonders if there is or should be more. Although he is not yet able to formulate what he is lacking in any specific way, he will be able to do so in the second investigation as a result of his self-reflections and experiences since the first investigation.

Second self-investigation

The valuations of Leo's second self-investigation are presented on the right side of Table 13.3. The following observations reflect some significant features of his valuation system:

- Leo changes the formulation of some valuations (nos. 3, 7, 8, and 9) and keeps other formulations constant (nos. 1, 2, 4, 5, 6, and 10). This indicates the coexistence of constancy and change.
- As a result of his self-reflection, Leo introduces an entirely new valuation (no. 11) in which he describes "the road of fire" which contrasts with the "cold water aggression" in valuation 3. The polarity between "hot" and "cold" and the specific meanings associated with these metaphorical qualifications, represent an extension and reorganisation of his self-narrative. At the end of the first investigation he felt that there was more than "having that one string" but was unable to specify what this "more" included. In the second investigation however, the explicit introduction of the hot–cold polarity not only extended his self-narrative but also reorganised it, with a new direction in his future orientation as a result.

- The new valuation (no. 11) and other positive valuations (nos. 4, 7, and 9) strongly generalise in the system (note that there were positive valuations in the first investigation but they did not generalise). The implication is that, in contrast with the first investigation, the general feeling has more positive than negative affect.
- Despite the clarifications and changes in valuations 3 and 11 and the strong generalisation of positive valuations (nos. 4, 7, and 9), there is a remarkable continuity from the perspective of the latent level of organisation. As in the first self-investigation, most valuations in the second investigation are associated more with self-enhancement (S) affect than with affect referring to contact and union with the other (O). This constancy is also reflected by the low level of O affect in contrast with the high level of S affect for the ideal feeling. This suggests that, although there is a convincing reorganisation of the valuation system on the manifest level, there is a remarkable constancy on the latent level.
- This constancy at the latent level was formulated by Leo in a striking way at the end of the second self-investigation, when he was talking about valuation 9:

> When you ask where my ceiling is, then I have been aware of this in the past. In my first period of high school they showed me my ceiling. When I later discovered that I was able to follow a higher level curriculum, I discovered that the earlier ceiling was a false one. Therefore, I become quite wary of possible new ceilings ... as in examinations. However, as long as you go on, you will not be beaten. When you permit yourself to decide when to stop, you will not be beaten. *The ice road and the fire road thus have the same goal: not being beaten.* The ice road: winning at any price; the fire road: becoming happy, conquering the wild bull within myself.

In other words, Leo discovered a new direction (the "fire road") in the course of his self-exploration, but he realised that both roads served the same basic goal: survival in an intimidating (external or internal) situation.

In summary, Leo's case sheds some light on the ways in which significant aspects of the person–situation interaction are organised and reorganised as parts of a self-narrative. The component parts of this narrative are organised around one or more narrative themes. For Leo the main theme was metaphorically expressed in "taking hold of the reins". Becoming aware of the pervasive influence of this theme in his self-investigation, Leo extended his self by including the polarity between the "ice road" (fighting against others) and the "fire road" (becoming happy by keeping his internal forces under control). Despite all these changes on the manifest level, there was a striking constancy on the latent level of self-functioning (survival).

THE RELEVANCE OF BECOMING AWARE OF ONE'S TALENT

We started this study with the assumption that talent can be conceived of in terms of processes and performance areas. The processes of creativity, motivation, and ability can be applied to a great variety of performance areas. We argued that it is important that talented individuals become aware of the strengths and weaknesses in their own personalities and of the possibilities and obstacles in their environment. Therefore, the relationship between talent and self functions as a central axis in the development of individuals who have the potential to contribute to the societies to which they belong and to enhance their personal value. This view requires a particular conception of the self that promotes the development of talent. We argued that recent developments in psychology emphasise the self as a dynamic multiplicity of component elements, which corresponds with talent as a multiplicity of processes and performance areas. We presented the concept of self-narrative as particularly appropriate for exploring the self as a dynamic multiplicity of events. As parts of a narrative structure, events are combined and related under the organising influence of themes. Studying the self of a talented person in terms of a narrative has, moreover, the advantage of studying past achievements and failures, present concerns, and goals and doubts related to the future as interrelated phenomena. The examination of past, present, and future as interconnected orientations makes it possible to study not only the organisation of the self but also its reorganisation (e.g. the setting of new goals as a result of learning from the past).

Some specific guidelines for future self-investigations

We have presented a method of self-investigation based on a theory in which the self is considered to be an organised process of valuation. The concept of valuation, which gives meaning to the events of one's life, is part of a valuation system that is organised around one or more themes. The method enables us to study the self as a dynamic multiplicity of valuations referring to past, present, and future, and to investigate the constancies and changes of the valuation system over time.

The use of the method was illustrated by describing and analysing the valuation system of a talented but underachieving adolescent. In our analysis we focused not only on the content (formulation) of the valuations but also on their affective organisation. In order to elaborate on the organised nature of the self-narrative, we focused on one of the central themes in Leo's story. It was assumed that the assessment of the guiding theme would increase the insight into the relationship between the several parts of the self-narrative. We found that this insight was particularly useful to Leo because it helped him to see his problems as parts of an encompassing structure and to explore a new direction in his life (the "road of fire").

More specifically, we advise giving special attention to the following phenomena when researchers or practitioners apply the self-confrontation method to talented people:

(a) It is important that personal qualities and obstacles are represented as explicit elements of the individual's self-narrative and self-reflection, so that individuals become aware of their specific abilities, creative potentials, and commitments, and the performance areas to which these processes can be applied. In the application of the self-confrontation method people are invited to formulate in their own words the nature of qualities and obstacles in terms of personal valuations.

(b) The affective properties of qualities and obstacles give insight into their personal meaning and into their interrelation as parts of a more encompassing valuation system. Valuations with a high level of self-enhancement affect and a high level of positive affect are particularly relevant to talent because they are a useful indication of successful performance on the basis of personal qualities (Hermans & Hermans-Jansen, 1995).

(c) A well differentiated study of the organisation of the self requires attention to the generalisation of valuations referring to qualities and obstacles. When a person is able to cope with obstacles and effectively to realise his or her qualities, there is a good chance that positive valuations referring to these processes will have a strong generalising potential in the self-system. On the other hand, when obstacles are felt to be insurmountable, negative valuations may generalise in the system with a negative general feeling as a result. Between these opposite possibilities, one may find that there are specific obstacles that arouse negative feelings, but that the valuations referring to these obstacles do not generalise in the system, so that their influence is rather limited.

(d) For the study of changes in the self it is worthwhile to take the latent–manifest distinction into account. Reformulation of valuations, affective restructuring, and changes in the generalising influence of particular valuations may all take place on the manifest level only. Deeper changes become visible when they take place on the latent level. An example of such a change is when none of the valuations in the first self-investigation has a high level of self-enhancement affect, whereas in the second investigation, after influential successful experiences, the person introduces a new subsystem of valuations with high self-enhancement affect. Another example of this would be a situation in which a person with many self-enhancing valuations and a complete lack of valuations referring to contact and union in the first investigation, introduces a significant amount of valuations of the latter type as part of the second investigation. Such changes reflect more fundamental transformations of the self-narrative, and require special attention from a developmental point of view.

Assessment, process promotion, and evaluation

Is the method that we have presented devised for the psychologist or for the client? The best answer is: for both. It is useful to the psychologist who wishes to obtain information and insight into the content and organisation/ reorganisation of the person's self-narrative. From the client's point of view, the method provides the opportunity to perform a thorough self-investigation, in which they face the ways in which they interact with themselves and their environments. They do this in the context of what happened in the past and what they want for the future. Along these lines the method functions as part of a collaborative relationship between psychologist and client.

The presented method has three functions: assessment, process promotion, and evaluation. The assessment function aims at an overview of valuations and associated affect as they manifest in a particular period of life. The process promotion function aims to give self-investigators the opportunity to reorganise their self-narratives as a response to new experiences in everyday life and to the cognitive or behavioural consequences of the process of self-reflection (for an example see valuation 11 in Table 13.3). Finally, the evaluative function aims to provide information about the nature of new experiences or insights by studying them as parts of the total valuation system in the second self-investigation. When the three functions of the method are combined, we have an active self-investigator who is involved in a process of self-reflection. Productive self-reflection requires a certain sensitivity to experiences and a certain degree of self-awareness. At the same time, the method stimulates and increases this sensitivity and awareness. Talented people are also challenged to apply their special qualities to the process of self-investigation.

ACKNOWLEDGEMENT

The authors thank Sue Houston for her editorial remarks.

REFERENCES

Angyal, A. (1965). *Neurosis and treatment: A holistic theory*. New York: Wiley.
Bakan, D. (1966). *The duality of human existence*. Chicago: Rand-McNally.
Brandstädter, J., & Rothermund, K. (1994). Self-percepts of control in middle and later adulthood: Buffering losses by rescaling goals. *Psychology and Aging, 9*, 265–273.

Bruner, J.S. (1986). *Actual minds, possible worlds.* Cambridge, MA: Harvard University Press.
Butler-Por, N. (1993). Underachieving gifted students. In K.A. Heller, F.J. Mönks, & A.H. Passow (Eds.), *International handbook of research and development of giftedness and talent* (pp. 649–668). Oxford: Pergamon.
Cohler, B.J. (1982). Personal narrative and life course. In P.B. Baltes & O.G. Brim (Eds.), *Life-span development and behavior* (Vol. 2, pp. 205–241). New York: Academic Press.
Crites, S. (1986). Storytime: Recollecting the past and projecting the future. In Th.R. Sarbin (Ed.), *Narrative psychology: The storied nature of human conduct* (pp. 152–173). New York: Praeger.
Gergen, K.J., & Gergen, M.M. (1988). Narrative and the self as relationship. *Advances in Experimental Social Psychology, 21,* 17–56.
Hermans, H.J.M. (1987a). Self as organized system of valuations: Toward a dialogue with the person. *Journal of Counseling Psychology, 34,* 10–19.
Hermans, H.J.M. (1987b). The dream in the process of valuation: A method of interpretation. *Journal of Personality and Social Psychology, 53,* 163–175.
Hermans, H.J.M. (1988). On the integration of idiographic and nomothetic research method in the study of personal meaning. *Journal of Personality, 56,* 785–812.
Hermans, H.J.M. (1989). The meaning of life as an organized process. *Psychotherapy, 26* (1), 11–22.
Hermans, H.J.M. (1996). Voicing the self: From information processing to dialogical interchange. *Psychological Bulletin, 119,* 31–50.
Hermans, H.J.M., & Hermans-Jansen, E. (1995). *Self-narratives: The construction of meaning in psychotherapy.* New York: Guilford Press.
Hermans, H.J.M., & Van Gilst, W. (1991). Self-narrative and collective myth: An analysis of the Narcissus story. *Canadian Journal of Behavioural Science, 23,* 423–440.
Higgins, E.T. (1987). Self-discrepance: A theory relating self and affect. *Psychological Review, 94,* 319–340.
James, W. (1890). *The principles of psychology.* (Vol. 1). London: Macmillan.
Kihlstrom, J.F., & Cantor, N. (1984). Mental representations of the self. *Advances in Experimental Social Psychology, 17,*1–47.
Klages, L. (1948). *Charakterkunde [Characterology].* Zürich, Switzerland: Hirzel.
Markus, H.R., & Nurius, P. (1986). Possible selves. *American Psychologist, 41,* 954–969.
Marsh, H.W. (1986). Global self-esteem: Its relation to specific facets of self-concept and their importance. *Journal of Personality and Social Psychology, 51*(6), 1224–1236.
McAdams, D.P. (1985). *Power, intimacy, and the life story: Personological inquiries into identity.* Chicago: Dorsey Press. [Reprinted by Guilford Press].
McAdams, D.P. (1993). *The stories we live by: Personal myths and the making of the self.* New York: William Morrow.
Merleau-Ponty, M. (1945). *Phénoménologie de la perception [Phenomenology of perception].* Paris: Gallimard. [Trans. to English by Colin Smith (1962), *Phenomenology of perception.* London: Routledge & Kegan Paul.]
Mönks, F.J. (1996). High ability: Self-concept and underachieving. In U. Munandar & C. Semiawan (Eds.), *Optimizing excellence in human resource development* (pp. 43–57). Jakarta: University of Indonesia Press.
Pratkanis, A.R., & Greenwald, A.G. (1985). How shall the self be conceived? *Journal for the Theory of Social Behaviour, 15,* 311–329.
Renzulli, J.S. (1978). What makes giftedness? Reexamining a definition. *Phi Delta Kappan, 60,* 180–184.
Rhodewalt, F., & Morf, C.C. (1995). Self and interpersonal correlates of the Narcissistic Personality Inventory: A review and new findings. *Journal of Research in Personality, 29,* 1–23.
Rosenberg, M. (1979). *Conceiving the self.* New York: Basic Books.

Sarbin, Th.R. (1986). The narrative as a root methaphor for psychology. In Th.R. Sarbin (Ed.), *Narrative psychology: The storied nature of human conduct* (pp. 3–21). New York: Praeger.
Sheldon, K.M., & Emmons, R.A. (1995). Comparing differentiation and integration within personal goal systems. *Personality and Individual Differences, 18,* 39–46.
Thomae, H. (1988). *Das Individuum und Seine Welt* [*The individual and his world*] (2nd ed.). Göttingen: Hogrefe.
Triandis, H.C. (1989). The self and social behavior in differing cultural contexts. *Psychological Review, 96,* 506–520.

CHAPTER FOURTEEN

Support for university students: Individual and social factors

Kurt A. Heller and Petra Viek
University of Munich, Germany

INTRODUCTION

Gifted education has attracted increasing attention, particularly within universities, over the last few years (Fraser, 1995; Herrnstein & Murray, 1994; Jacoby & Glauberman, 1995; Mönks, 1996; Sternberg et al., 1995). In Germany and many other European countries, this discussion became intense as the current rate of economic innovation and, at the same time, an increase in unemployment demanded appropriate means for their remediation. Despite the occasional controversial views that are expressed regarding the causes of such conditions, insight into the urgency for achievement-based funding and support of the elite is finding ever more supporters. For many experts, the answer to this problem lies in the act of nurturing the talented—instead of "punishing" excellent achievement (Henry, 1995). In order to activate human resources, one expects substantial contributions from the most able university students. Therefore, questions must be asked regarding the efficiency level of current practices used to identify and support gifted individuals in the university sector, as well as to support innovation more generally.

This study of highly gifted scholarship holders is based on a dynamic concept of talent which attempts to build a bridge to action-oriented models of talent. Excellence of performance is here postulated to be a product of internal cognitive and motivational dispositions in the sense of individual giftedness potentials and social stimulating conditions of the learning environment. Characteristic of this model is the postulation of multiple interaction and compensation processes. The intrapersonal antecedent conditions of exceptional performance are thereby interpreted as the boundary posts of a remarkable talent. This chapter seeks answers to the following questions:

(1) What sorts of personality characteristics are relevant in the selection of talented students?
(2) Using these selection criteria, can one differentiate between students who received scholarship support and those who did not?
(3) What sorts of individual and social determinants are favourable for the development of academic excellent achievement?

The most important results of the research are presented here and their consequences for the promotion of highly gifted students at university level are discussed.

CURRENT FINDINGS ON RESEARCH INTO TALENT AND EXCELLENT PERFORMANCE IN HIGHER EDUCATION

When nurturing highly talented students, the question of reliable and valid identification procedures arises. Although traditionally exceptional talent has been seen as a general performance disposition, in the past few years this view has been modified. Research findings consisting of relatively low correlations between *general* achievement predictors and career success have contributed to this development (see Siegler & Kotovsky, 1986). Ghiselli (1966) reported average correlation coefficients of .20 in a survey of over 100 studies. This result is, for the most part, to be explained by two causes: First, there is variation in the predictors of excellent achievement in the various segments of one's life. For example Csikszentmihalyi (1990) could show that graduates of an art academy whose troubleshooting abilities were above average, were extremely successful, whereas 18 years later the quality of the troubleshooting played an insignificant role in the prediction of career success. This could be better predicted by social abilities and practical intelligence (see also Sternberg, 1994, this volume). Second, next to the cognitive abilities of a person, the non-cognitive or personality characteristics represent a vital requirement for excellent achievement and indicate the motivational aspects associated with performance *readiness*. For success in scientific matters, Trost and Siegler (1992) (also Trost, 1993) could demonstrate that highly gifted scientists differ from scientists with average talents with respect to motivational characteristics, especially concerning the drive to solve problems, initiative, leadership, concentration ability, and tenacity. Nichols and Astin (1966) stressed the importance of non-cognitive factors in the prediction of academic performance (Cattell & Butcher, 1968; Dweck, 1986, 1996; Khan, 1969; Lavin, 1965; Steinkamp & Maehr, 1983). No one disputes the fact that persons with extreme talents, in the sense of high levels of intelligence, perform better at the beginning of their scholastic career than those who are less gifted. However, in addition to cognitive, perceptual, and motor-based talent factors, an increasing significance is being accorded to motivational factors in the development of expertise. As exceptional achievements can only be attained through continual, and occasionally tiring, dealings with a domain, a large degree of specific motivation (Ericsson, Krampe, & Tesch-Römer, 1993) and a positive attitude towards achievement are indispensable (Gruber, Weber, & Ziegler, 1996). Without an active learning environment supported by internal motivational (dealing with success/failure, motivation to achieve, etc.) and suitable environmental signs, the talent itself cannot develop optimally (Ziegler & Perleth, 1997).

In summary, exceptional talent presents a causal system in the form of a multifaceted net in which cognitive, perceptual, and motor-based abilities as well as specific forms of previous knowledge, internal characteristics, and environmental factors must be considered. However, a pure ex-post facto definition in which persons who are considered to be highly talented demonstrate this talent in excellent performance (although practicable and plausible), proves to be theoretically and practically unsatisfying. Hence, Trost (1985) formulated the following theses:

- The identification of high talent aims to predict future excellent achievement which can subsequently be empirically validated.
- Cognitive abilities considered to be well above average are a necessary although not a sufficient condition for exceptional achievement. One certainly also has to consider interest, attitude, motivation, and learning habits.
- Previous outstanding achievements are one of the most important indicators for expected future excellence (the Matthew effect according to Merton, 1968).
- For the identification of high talent among students, a combined multi-level diagnostic approach appears to be necessary to obtain reliable and valid results. A suitable combination would include (a) an evaluation of previous achievements, (b) the investigation of cognitive performance dispositions through means of diagnostic instruments initialised by the analysis of differential ability constructs in the university sector, and (c) the review of relevant personality characteristics and social behavioural patterns in the form of interviews or group discussions.

Identification problems and evaluation demands

The selection of grant recipients is of practical interest during academic and/or excellent career performance, and in this sense the appropriateness of supporting an individual has to be predicted. One hopes to be able to identify candidates who are especially engaging and who, based on their previous achievements, can be expected to perform outstandingly in the future. In this sense it is very important to make clear which motivational "early indicators", aside from cognitive predictors, make strong predictions about the likelihood of achieving in the adult years. Here various factors have proved to have different levels of relevance. Under personality characteristics we find academic (and general) self-concept, causal attributions, learning style, achievement motivation (success vs. failure motivation), general fear as well as fear of tests, stress and stress management, belief in one's own efficacy, etc. to be particularly important (Arnold, 1994; Ericsson et al., 1993; Franks & Dolan, 1982; Mansfield & Busse, 1981; Mönks, van Boxtel, Roelofs & Sanders, 1986; Renzulli, 1978; Subotnik & Steiner, 1994).

A good prediction of achievement cannot just rely on standard measuring practices of cognitive achievement capabilities (test intelligence). Rather, one must also collect information regarding motivational and other personality characteristics—the so called mediator variables—as well as concerning the social environment. Accordingly, it is expected that support measures will only be of assistance during the course of the achiever's development, when they sufficiently take into consideration the multifaceted individual configurations of the person to be supported.

As one illuminates the current state of talent identification in the university sector, the following deficits come to light: A lack of conceptual dealings with a differential concept of talent in the area of university education, as well as a considerable deficit of valid diagnostic instruments for identifying domain-specific study aptitudes. Apart from a few exceptions (Trost, 1986, 1993; Trost & Siegler, 1992) in which students on college preparatory tracks and other students who were chosen on the basis of future career plans were investigated, previous diagnostic instruments focusing on exceptional talent have chiefly been limited to younger students and children. Therefore, there exists not just a deficit in prognostically valid identification methods for talent in future career areas (Lamers, 1991), but rather a general deficit of empirical psychological research on identification and education of the gifted in the vocational area (Manstetten, 1996). A survey of the predictive power of psychometric prognosis processes for the identification of later excellent achievement is given by Subotnik and Arnold (1993).

There are very few investigations that empirically compare the predictive power of various identification methods. Among the few exceptions is the study by Albert and Runco (1986) and the evaluation study made by the Studienstiftung des Deutschen Volkes (German Educational Foundation; Laagland, 1978; Trost, 1985). Trost (1985, 1993) retrospectively evaluated, with a multistep selection process consisting of a series of standardised tests, interviews, and scholastic observations, the predictive power of the selection instruments with respect to specific academic achievement and satisfaction criteria. It could be demonstrated that the test-analyses of the selection tests of the German Educational Foundation provided satisfactory reliability values. The objectivity (or agreement between the interviewers) was $r = .55$. The correlation coefficients between the interviewer ratings and the behaviour observations averaged $r = .48$. The intercorrelation of the individual diagnosis with the instruments fluctuated between $r = .20$ and $.30$.

A good model for the diagnosis of exceptional talent and the analysis of developmental processes, is to be found in the Munich Dynamic Giftedness Model (Ziegler & Perleth, 1997). The model unifies antecedent and constraining conditions of exceptional achievements conceived as the realisation of talent in an active learning process (Fig. 14.1). From this viewpoint one has a solid basis for the evaluation of the prognostic validity of the antecedent factors postulated for exceptional achievement.

Individual potential or internal talent factors are postulated as antecedent conditions of exceptional achievement. In accordance with patterns developed by Ackerman (1988), cognitive, perceptual, and motor-based performance dispositions are differentiated. Additionally, the significance of specific previous knowledge is stressed. The actualisation of individual internal talent factors requires the existence of conducive environmental conditions. Without active learning processes, which are supported through one's internal motivational (coping with success/failure, achievement motivation) and suitable environmental conditions, exceptional talent cannot develop optimally. Exceptional achievement is accordingly seen as a product of the interaction of one's internal cognitive achievement dispositions or, in another sense, motivational characteristics and environmental conditions. Among these three factor groups, multiple interactive and compensatory processes take place.

Forming the goals of a retrospective explorative study[1]

The investigation reported here concerns the questions of (1) the existence of differences in selection-relevant personality characteristics between students who did and did not receive scholarships, and (2) to what extent

---

[1] This study was supported by the Federal Ministry of Education and Science (BMBF) in Bonn (Grant number M 1323.006).

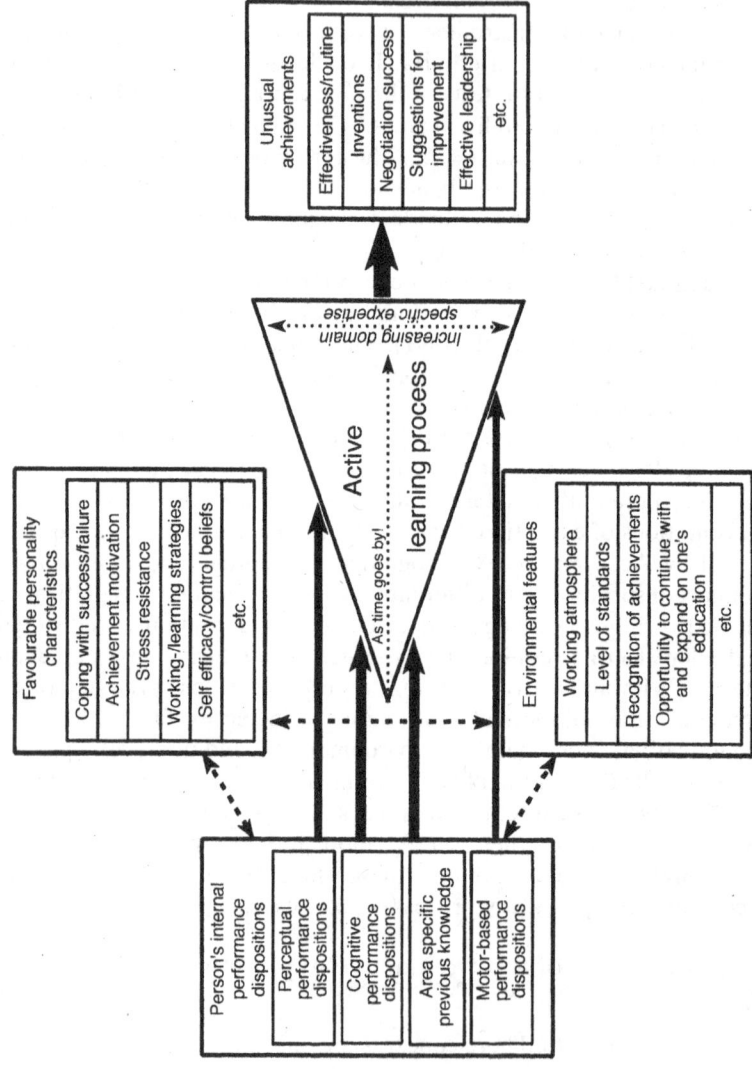

FIG. 14.1 The Munich Dynamic Giftedness Model (according to Ziegler & Perleth, 1997).

an analogy with respect to these differences exists between former grant recipients and former students who did not receive scholarships. A pragmatic approach was followed to identify possibly relevant characteristics of grant recipients. Accordingly, an attempt was made to identify every principle employed by the grant-giving foundations, which included not only intellectual but also personality characteristics and value assessments. A priori, it was assumed that with respect to support of talented students, differing personality characteristics for identical competency levels were not necessarily similarly demanded. In the selection process the entire range of characteristic combinations must be represented. This defined the differences in the target populations of the various grant foundations. It was also expected that the ideal support package would be made available over the course of the grant period.

A few serious limitations were created due to the fact that the study could not be conducted in longitudinal format. One was that, with the design used, no definite statements could be made about the antecedent conditions of a successful promotion. Also no assessment of the interplay between individual talent and performance development with respect to specific promotional measures could be conducted. Furthermore, one cannot determine whether through interventions of specific grant foundations specific characteristics were developed in specific ways. Answers to such questions can be expected from a planned longitudinal study designed as a combined longitudinal and cross-sectional study (1999–2001). The questions relevant for the present investigation (conceived as a cross-sectional study) can be summarised as follows:

- What sorts of goals do the promoters of talented students in the university sector have in common? What sorts of personality characteristics are relevant in the selection of talented students?
- Can one, with respect to these selection criteria, differentiate between students who receive scholarship support and those who do not?
- What sorts of individual and social determinants are favourable for the development of academic excellent achievement?

Hence two main *hypotheses* for the investigation could be expounded:

(1) It is expected that scholarship recipients should differentiate themselves from students not receiving scholarship support with reference to unusual achievements.
(2) The postulated achievement differences mainly result from the interaction of favourable personality characteristics and environmental features, the latter consisting primarily of being selected for a scholarship and being supported.

One would expect promotion (i.e. the award of a scholarship) to demonstrate an influence on the development of excellent achievement. One would further expect that the noncognitive characteristics are mediators for the development of excellent academic achievement.

THE PROGRAMME EVALUATION STUDY: METHOD

Sample and design

The aim of this programme evaluation study was to investigate the development of excellent academic achievement in the framework of education at the university level. Consequently, scholarship recipients and a selected group of students (non-scholarship holders), as well as groups of former scholarship recipients and former students (non-scholarship holders) who displayed parallel levels of achievement, were investigated. The scholarship recipients and former scholarship recipients were recruited through 10 foundations providing scholarship support for the gifted and talented on the basis of the identification model in Fig. 14.2. The funding for most of these programmes was provided by the German Ministry for Education, Science, Research, and Technology in Bonn. The comparison between promoted and non-promoted students should provide information on the nature of the selection processes. A similar comparison between the selected students and the former students should also offer insights into the development of academic excellence when considering individual and social conditions.

This set of analyses involved 770 persons (45.1% women, 54.9% men) divided into various target groups (TG) and comparison groups (CG): grant recipients (TG1) and former grant recipients (TG2) from 10 foundations promoting the gifted and talented were placed into the target groups. One of the comparison groups consisted of students who were classified as being gifted but had never received promotion in the form of scholarship grants (CG1), while the other comparison group consisted of former students who were parallel for the most part with respect to subject major, academic grade, and gender, to the former scholarship recipients, although they had never received such support (CG2). Table 14.1 gives an overview of the organisation of the sample.

The subjects in the target groups were recruited by 10 scholarship foundations. The group of gifted but never promoted students (CG1) were recruited from various universities in the southern part of Germany and were all nominated by their professors. The professors were requested to pass the questionnaires on to the students they considered to be their best 1–2%, and who never had received scholarship funding.

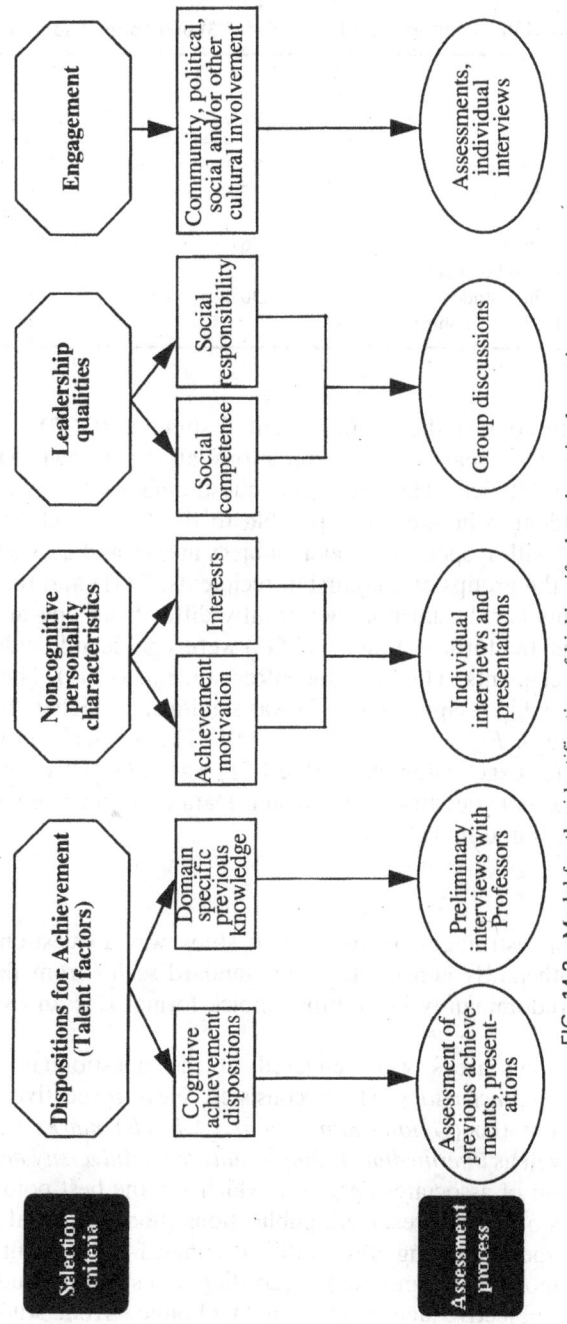

FIG. 14.2   Model for the identification of highly gifted students in the tertiary area.

TABLE 14.1
Composition of the samples, split into target (TG) and comparison groups (CG)

Groups	Group-N N	Age Means	SD	Sex (%) Female	Male
TG1: Scholarship recipients	348	25.35	3.62	46.6	53.4
TG2: Former scholarship recipients	275	35.38	3.11	45.9	54.1
CG1: Talented students (never applied for scholarship)	54	26.00	3.40	33.3	66.7
CG2: Talented former students (never applied for scholarship)	93	30.09	3.29	45.2	54.8

In order to contact the former talented students (CG2), support was sought from the Boards of Examinations at the Ludwig-Maximilians University in Munich. They sent the questionnaires to an appropriate group of students who were comparable to the former scholarship recipients (TG2) with respect to gender, subject major, and academic grades.

Although the groups of scholarship recipients (TG1) and the especially gifted students (CG1) did not significantly differ from one another with respect to age, the former students (CG2) were significantly older than the scholarship recipients (TG1) and the gifted students (CG1). The age of the former scholarship recipients, (TG2) was significantly higher than that for all other groups, $F_{(3,665)} = 362.73$, $p < .001$. The gender composition for each group (for exact values see Table 14.1) was not exactly equal, but the difference was not statistically significant. Data on gender and age of each group can be found in Table 14.1.

Measures

The principal instrument in the present study was a questionnaire consisting of both newly constructed and standard scales from the research literature, predominantly in multiple choice format (for an overview see Table 14.2).

The following areas were covered in the questionnaire: *objective achievement characteristics* which consisted of retrospective self-report estimates about the *(Gymnasium) abitur (A-levels) marks* (grade point average) as well as *intermediate testing results from university achievements* (the equivalent of associates degree in which 1 is the best point and 6 the worst), prizes or awards received, publications (books, journal articles) as well as time spent studying abroad (0 = no time; 1 = 1–3 months; 2 = 4–6 months; 3 = more than 6 months). According to a study by Ludwig (1984) self-reported objective achievement data obtained from students in an

TABLE 14.2
Instruments that form the questionnaire for the evaluation of talent promotion in the tertiary area

Author and year published	Test name	Dimensions assessed
Heller & Viek (1997)	Ascertainment of biographic data	Socio-demographic statements, previous scholastic achievements, extra-curricular university activities, social status
Funke, Krais, Hartung, & Nuthmann (1986)*	Questionnaire regarding the educational history and career status of former grant recipients	Educational and career course, satisfaction with promotion received, university entrance goals
Jerusalem (1986)	Perceived intelligence	Self-estimations of own intelligence within the assessment of other self-related cognitions
Kuhl & Fuhrmann (1995)*	Performance motivation	Self-related attentiveness, positive self-motivation, planning ability, failure coping skills, initiative, volitional self-trust, self-discipline, effort avoidance
Hörmann (1986)* German translation of Marsh & O'Neill (1984)	Self-description questionnaire for high-school and university students	General self-concept, academic self-concept, creativity, and problem solving ability
Lotz (1984)*	Social competence questionnaire	Verbal expression competence, prudence, poise
Seifert & Bergmann (1983)	Questionnaire to assess career values—orientations	Career-related values in the sense of goals, effects, and concomitant circumstances that a person would see as worthwhile and would actively try to attain
Krampen & Wünsche (1984)*	Trier inventory of political participation	Various aspects of political engagement are assessed
Heller & Viek (1997)	Questionnaire for the assessment of subjective promotion needs among students, grant recipients, doctoral recipients, and former grant recipients	Need for promotion, promotion deficits, satisfaction

*Scales and items were extracted from the instruments named.

anonymous format are for the most part valid measurements. Furthermore, in order to obtain information about the *subject's perception of her/his own achievement level*, questions were posed involving the subjective estimation of one's own achievement abilities, social competence, and political involvement.

Self concept. An actual German version of the questionnaire written by Marsh and O'Neill (1984) was used, the *Selbstbeschreibungsfragebogen für Schüler und Studenten* (Self-description questionnaire for high school and university students) developed by Hörmann (1986). The 5-point format offered a concrete measurement of the general and academic self-concepts as well as self-belief in one's creative and problem-solving skills. Analyses of internal consistency suggested the scales to be of adequate reliability (Cronbach's alpha: *general self concept* = .87; *academic self concept* = .79; *creativity* = .79).

Social competence. Different aspects of social competence were registered with the *Fragebogen zur sozialen Kompetenz* (Questionnaire on social competence) developed by Lotz (1984) with three scales. With a 5-point format, the scales of social competence referred to communicative competence, interactive competence, and self-security. Reliability analyses indicated the scales had good internal consistency (Cronbach's alpha: *verbal competence* = .85; *level-headedness* = .84; *composure* = .89).

Motivation. In order to obtain information about motivational aspects the Volitional Components Questionnaire developed by Kuhl and Fuhrmann (1995) was used. The questionnaire provides information about the volitional aspects of motivation. Eight different scales were used, all of them having a 5-point format. All scales had good internal consistency (Cronbach's alpha: *goal orientation* = .77; *positive self-motivation* = .74; *planning ability* = .74; *coping with failure* = .72; *initiative* = .76; *self-trust* = .79; *self-discipline* = .69; *stress-avoidance* = .75).

Political involvement. Information about the subject's political involvement was registered through the use of the *Trierer Inventar zur politischen Partizipation* (Trier inventory for political participation) by Krampen and Wünsche (1984). Various aspects of political involvement were measured with scales covering "public political participation", "conventional political participation", "political participation at the university level", as well as "political activities with respect to private affairs". Analyses of internal consistency suggested that all scales had adequate reliability (Cronbach's alpha: *public political participation* = .85; *conventional political participation* = .58; *political participation at the university level* = .80; *political activities with respect to private affairs* = .54).

RESULTS

Comparison of antecedent characteristics between the groups

In order to answer the question of whether the scholarship recipients differ from students not receiving scholarship support with respect to unusual achievements, a comparison with regard to the following characteristics was undertaken.

Abitur (A-levels) and intermediate testing scores. In order to measure achievement characteristics the *abitur* (A-levels) scores and intermediate testing results of subjects in all groups were obtained through self-report. In selecting scholarship recipients, *abitur* (A-levels) scores are an important criterion for grant agencies. By contrast, the intermediate testing scores could be seen as an objective achievement index, which cannot have played a role in the selection.

Table 14.3 shows that the average value for the scholarship recipients ($M = 1.71$) was the lowest (most successful) and that the subjects in CG1 had the highest average value of 2.13. The former scholarship recipients (TG2) had an average *abitur* (A-levels) score of 1.85, better than the former non-promoted talented students of CG2 whose average score was 2.05. A two-way ANOVA with type of group (target vs. comparison group) and cohort (present vs. former group) was performed. The *abitur* (A-levels) scores were significantly different between groups, $F_{(1653)} = 27.50$, $p < .001$, but not between cohorts.

The intermediate testing scores for the scholarship recipients and the former scholarship recipients showed average values of 1.88 and 1.86, respectively, while the members of CG1 had an almost identical value of 1.92. Only the members of CG2 were above all groups with an average

TABLE 14.3
Scores: Means and standard deviations

	Abitur (A-levels) score		Intermediate testing score	
	Means	SD	Means	SD
Scholarship recipients (TG1)	1.71	0.59	1.88	0.67
Talented students (CG1)	2.13	0.72	1.92	0.63
Former scholarship recipients (TG2)	1.85	0.62	1.86	0.69
Former students (CG2)	2.05	0.57	2.25	0.72

Means and standard deviations of *abitur* (A-levels) and intermediate testing scores for scholarship recipients (TG1), non-promoted talented students (CG1), former scholarship recipients (TG2), and former non-promoted talented students (CG2). (1 = high score, 6 = very low score).

score of 2.25. A two-way ANOVA was performed and showed significant relations for the intermediate testing scores with group, $F_{(1,432)} = 3.74$, $p < .001$, and cohort, $F_{(1,432)} = 4.31$, $p < .05$. There was also significant cohort × group interaction, $F_{(1,432)} = 5.00$, $p < .05$.

In addition, there was confirmation of the moderate predictive power of *abitur* (A-levels) scores towards intermediate testing scores. The correlation between *abitur* (A-levels) scores and intermediate testing scores in this study was moderate: this is in agreement with results from other research studies reporting a range between .40 and .48 (Schuler, Funke & Baron-Boldt, 1990; Stumpf & Nauels, 1990).

Group differences with respect to selected criteria

Publication of articles/books, prizes awarded, and university studies abroad. The participants were asked if they already had articles or books published. One would expect that the former scholarship recipients and former students would have more success here than the members of the other two groups, as the probability for publication increases with age. Figure 14.3 shows the group distribution for the publication of articles and books as well as the award of prizes.

With respect to publication of books and articles, more scholarship recipients had credits to their names than the group of selected students. However, the differences were not significant. Clearly, all differences between the former scholarship recipients and the former students with respect to the three achievement areas were significant $\chi^2(2) = 24.62$, $p < .001$; $\chi^2(2) = 12.99$, $p < .002$; $\chi^2(2) = 7.21$, $p < .027$. The differences between the scholarship recipients and the students were only significant with respect to the award of prizes, although both groups of scholarship recipients were superior to all other groups, $\chi^2(6) = 33.97$, $p < .001$.

The participants were also asked if they had studied at a university outside of Germany, and for how long. In Table 14.4 the means and

TABLE 14.4
Study time outside Germany

	Means	SD
Scholarship recipients (TG1)	0.98	1.27
Non-promoted talented students (CG1)	0.48	1.00
Former scholarship recipients (TG2)	1.24	1.33
Former non-promoted talented students (CG2)	0.62	1.13

Means and standard deviations of time studying at a university outside Germany for scholarship recipients (TG1), non-promoted talented students (CG1), former scholarship recipients (TG2), and former non-promoted talented students (CG2).

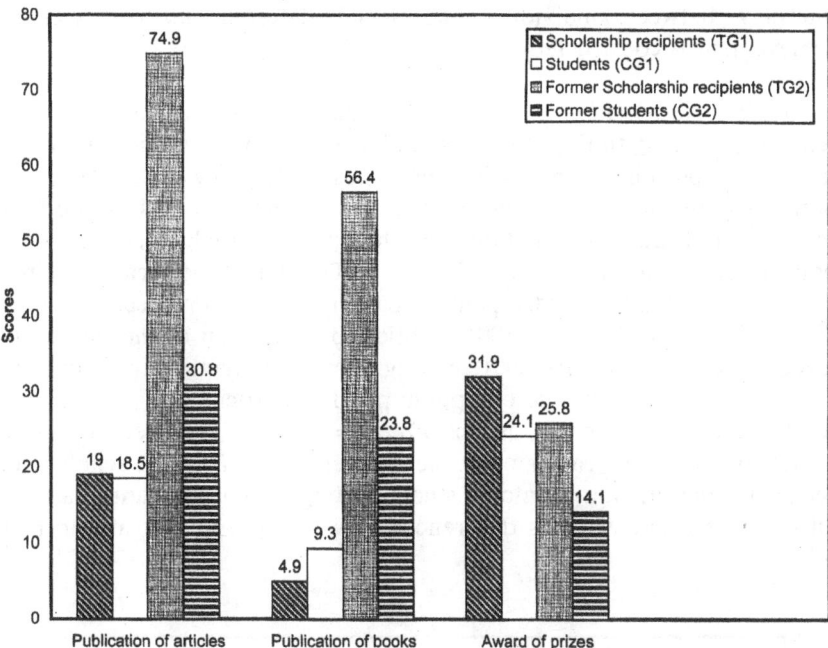

FIG. 14.3 Percentage of group members indicating publication of books or articles as well as the award of prizes for scholarship recipients (TG1), non-promoted talented students (CG1), former scholarship recipients (TG2), and former non-promoted talented students (CG2).

standard deviations are presented. Here, as expected, the scholarship recipients demonstrated significantly higher rates than the non-promoted talented students, and the former scholarship recipients significantly higher rates than the former non-promoted talented students. The univariate test of the two-way ANOVA showed a significant relationship between time spent at a foreign university and group, $F_{(1,658)} = 21.06$, $p < .001$. There were no significant cohort differences.

With respect to objective achievement characteristics one can conclude that the scholarship recipients differ consistently in all characteristic areas from the non-scholarship students. Referring to the achievement differences, there were significant cohort effects. By looking at the differences between the present and former students, one can say, in a somewhat limited fashion, that the differences between the groups increased in a cumulative manner. The results indicated that the achievement differences between highly gifted and gifted students became larger over the course of time *and as result of* experiences. It is especially relevant to obtain information about how the differences between the scholarship recipients and the selected students develop over the long term, as this is where the interplay between individual and social determinants of excellent achievement is constructed.

Political participation. In addition to achievement parameters, many scholarship foundations put interest and involvement in political activities in a central position in their selection processes. A two-way ANOVA was performed and showed significant relationships between each of the four scales of political participation and the groups variable: conventional political participation, $F_{(2,662)} = 39.89$, $p < .001$; public political participation, $F_{(2,662)} = 15.38$, $p < .001$; political participation with respect to private affairs, $F_{(2,662)} = 21.75$, $p < .001$; political participation at the university level, $F_{(2,262)} = 21.18$, $p < .001$. No significant interactions of group by cohort was found, with one exception: political participation with respect to private affairs: cohort × groups, $F_{(1,661)} = 9.45$, $p < .005$ (see Fig. 14.4).

Summarising, one can say that the differences between the scholarship recipients and the non-promoted student group were significant in almost all characteristics, whereas differences between the present and former

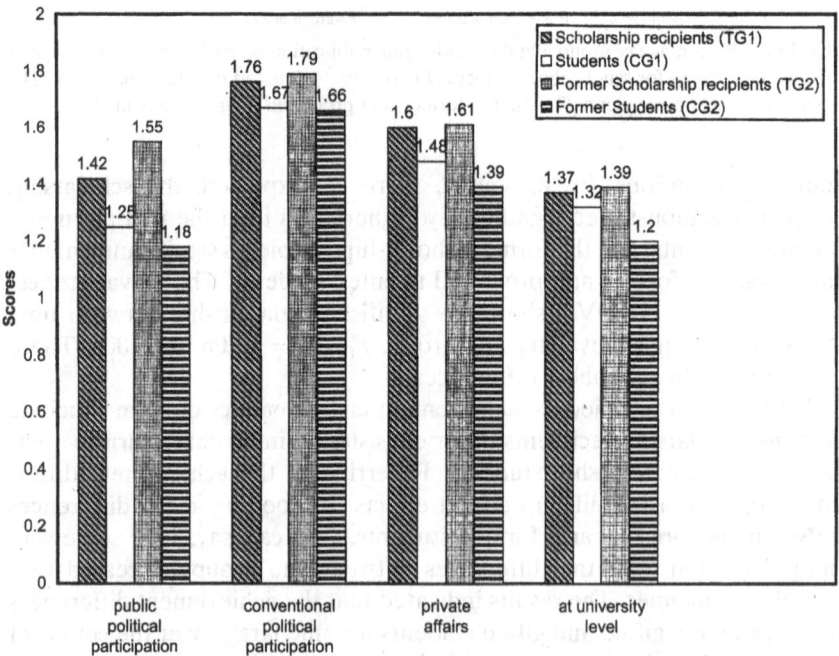

FIG. 14.4 Means of the scales for political engagement among the scholarship recipients (TG1), students, i.e. non-promoted talented students (CG1), former scholarship recipients (TG2), and former non-promoted talented students (CG2).

students were only found in the *abitur* (A-levels) score and in a single aspect of political participation. The differences between the scholarship recipients and non-scholarship students conformed to our expectation that the interplay between promotional measures and non-cognitive personality characteristics gives rise to cumulative effects that affect achievement. The scholarship recipients consistently proved themselves to be more involved and more achievement-oriented than those students who were not the beneficiaries of promotional efforts. The systematic differences between the scholarship recipients and the students lead one to suspect that, especially during the promotion period, after the lower-level university course period, changes that were relevant to achievement took place. It can be concluded that these changes were influenced by individual (noncognitive personality characteristics) and social (promotional environment) determinants.

Predicting excellent achievement in higher education

In order to answer the question of whether the postulated achievement differences mainly resulted from the interaction of favourable personality characteristics and environmental features, or rather from the fact that the student was selected for a scholarship and supported, a linear regression was computed.

The issue of which noncognitive variables can be considered as suitable for the prediction of excellent academic achievement must be addressed at this point. As a criterion of excellent academic achievement one aggregate value was constructed based on the z-scores of the *abitur* (A-levels) scores and intermediate testing scores. As predictors, social competence, volitional aspects of motivation, and self-concept were used (for descriptions see earlier method section). Results of the linear regression showed that scholastic and academic achievement could be predicted by the self-concept and by aspects of achievement motivation. The explained variance was low with $R^2 = .10$, but significant ($p < .001$). This indicated that a high academic and general self-concept as well as a high degree of goal-oriented attention lead to better scores.

DISCUSSION

In considering scholarship aid for highly gifted students in the university sector, one is confronted with a varied and flexible system of requirements, offers, and incentives. One can assume that developmental potential can be systematically guided and goal-oriented. However, as very little is known about the requirements and developmental conditions for later achievements, it is difficult to select goal-oriented, individualised, realistic support measures. Weinert (1990) warned that promotion of the highly talented cannot consist of a perfect diagnosis system and a rigid obedience to types of special organisations. Due to the inherent variety in talent constellations and the variability of the developmental processes, support systems for the gifted should consist of a rich choice of attractive goals, models, and readily available help, avoiding those attitudes that foster negativity and retarding influences.

Numerous hindering circumstances seem to be the rule, as Subotnik and Arnold (1993) point out in their survey. Performance excellence is not just the product of cognitive abilities. Rather it is also dependent on contextual and situational conditions, and is bound to personality factors. These include favourable success and failure attributions which positively influence the self-concept of one's capabilities and support motivation towards achievement. Tolerance for failure, veridicality of one's estimation of own abilities, individual performance motives, willingness to apply effort over the long haul, competitive spirit, clarity with respect to goal orientation, and perseverance are also among the relevant personality factors. Morkel (1987, p. 87) adds here that, in order for talents to unfold and exceptional achievements to be accomplished, there is a need for demanding practice, environmental encouragement, and correct timing, along with disciplined work under the guidance of a teacher who is seen as a role model. (See also Subotnik, this volume.)

Most importantly, the interaction of intellectual abilities, non-cognitive (motivational) characteristics in the sense of moderating or mediating variables, general and situational specific contextual conditions, and excellent achievement, is given too little attention. Intellectual giftedness alone is not sufficient to bring about high levels of performance. Individual, person-specific performance conditions need to be considered and must be promoted so that the transfer from abilities into achievements can be made more easily. This means that, in addition to general intellectual stimulation, which contributes to the promotion of excellent achievement, learning requirements must be constructed which serve to form a state of achievement *readiness*. In addition it is important, in the sense of an *individual* promotion as intended by the funding foundations, to focus on a specific theme and to support personal (achievement) motivation towards specific goals.

Consequences for the promotion of highly gifted students attending universities

(1) Faced with the enormous complexity of the conditional structure of excellent achievement in the early adult years, it is hardly surprising that the spectacular effects brought about by individual promotional measures

are difficult to identify. Our hypothesis of a *cumulative promotional effect* was supported in this study: We observed (large) differences in achievement between groups of previously promoted individuals (former grant recipients) and those not having received promotional assistance (already occupationally active). Similar but smaller differences were observed between students currently enjoying grant support versus non-promoted students.

(2) The findings confirmed a *developmental dynamic* among the extremely gifted or talented, as demonstrated by Zuckerman (1967, 1992) in her biographical analysis of American Nobel prize-winners, as well as in other studies dealing with the concept of creativity research. The development of excellence (Simonton, 1988, 1991) can be stimulated by "creative" learning environments and well balanced group dynamics (Amabile, 1983; Weinert, 1990). Also stimulating is mutually beneficial personal contact with one's peers and mentors (e.g. placing the grant recipients under the care of a faculty advisor or a representative of the grant foundation). However, random factors also have an influence. From the start, "perfect" predictions of academic and career success among those considered extremely gifted or talented are difficult. Therefore, a warning should be sounded against exaggerated expectations of prognostic validity in the selection of grant recipients. Nevertheless, the validation values presented here were well within the range of values for other findings referenced (Subotnik & Arnold, 1993, 1994; Trost, 1986, 1993). Despite this variability, efforts towards further improvements in selection procedures should continue. Such efforts are necessary to improve the legitimacy of measures taken with respect to candidates rejected for promotion.

(3) To improve the promotion of the highly talented in academic fields, the relationship between teacher and student has to be elaborated, not only quantitatively but also qualitatively. One way in which this could be realised is by inviting highly gifted and talented university students to participate in the teaching profession (for example as student mentors) or in the scientific field. Thus, important learning facilities are offered which allow independent and self-responsible practice and consequently support motivation for studying as well as interest in science. Longitudinal studies of excellent achievement have frequently shown that during early stages of talent development motivation and interest for a subject or a domain are of prime importance, whereas later instructional methods or the standard of university teaching become more significant (e.g. Arnold, 1994; Subotnik & Steiner, 1994). To promote excellent achievement effectively, next to exceptional cognitive abilities and motivational preconditions, a sufficiently stimulating "creative" environment is necessary. Referring to the results of the present study, this factor—the creation of a satisfying,

individually challenging environment—was especially important for the most able university students.

According to research in expertise (cf. Ericsson et al., 1993; Schneider, 1993), the quality of deliberate practice seems to be more important than mere quantity. Whether, and in what way, these learning facilities are being utilised depends entirely on the individual readiness to get involved. Thus the interdependence of individual and social factors that contribute to the development of extraordinary talent and excellent achievement in university students has again been confirmed. It is increasingly obvious that the role of social settings in the development of the highly gifted and talented should be studied both theoretically and empirically (cf. Mönks, 1986, 1992; Mönks et al., 1986; Mönks, Katzko, & Boxtel, 1992).

REFERENCES

Ackerman, P.L. (1988). Determinants of individual differences during skill acquisition: Cognitive abilities and information processing. *Journal of Experimental Psychology: General, 117*, 288-318.

Albert, R.S., & Runco, M.A. (1986). The achievement of eminence: A model based on a longitudinal study of exceptionally gifted boys and their families. In R.J. Sternberg & J.E. Davidson (Eds.), *Conceptions of giftedness* (pp. 332-357). Cambridge: Cambridge University Press.

Amabile, T.M. (1983). *The social psychology of creativity.* New York: Springer.

Arnold, K.D. (1994). The Illinois Valedictorian Project: Early adult careers of academically talented male high school students. In R.F. Subotnik & K.D. Arnold (Eds.), *Beyond Terman: contemporary longitudinal studies of giftedness and talent* (pp. 24-51). Norwood, NJ: Ablex.

Cattell, R.B., & Butcher, H.J. (1968). *The prediction of achievement and creativity.* Indianapolis/New York: Bobbs-Merrill.

Csikszentmihalyi, M. (1990). Theories of creativity. In M. Runco & R.S. Albert (Eds.), *The domain of creativity* (pp. 190-212). Newbury Park, CA: Sage.

Dweck, C.S. (1986). Motivational processes affecting learning. *American Psychologist, 41*(10), 1040-1048.

Dweck, C.S. (1996). Implicit theories as organizers of goals and behaviour. In P.M. Gollwitzer & J.A. Bargh (Eds.), *The psychology of action: Linking cognition and motivation of behaviour* (pp. 69-90). New York: Guilford.

Ericsson, K.A., Krampe, R.T., & Tesch-Römer, C. (1993). The role of deliberate practice in the acquisition of expert performance. *Psychological Review, 100*(3), 363-406.

Franks, S.B., & Dolan, L. (1982). Affective characteristics of gifted children: Educational implications. *Gifted Child Quarterly, 26*, 172-178.

Fraser, S. (1995). *The bell curve wars: Race, intelligence, and the future of America.* New York: Basic Books, Inc.

Funke, A., Hartung, D., Krais, B., & Nuthmann, R. (1986). *Karrieren außer der Reihe. Bildungswege und Berufserfolg von Stipendiaten der gewerkschaftlichen Studienförderung.* Köln: Bund-Verlag.

Ghiselli, E. (1966). *The validity of occupational aptitude tests.* New York: Wiley.

Gruber, H., Weber, A., & Ziegler, A. (1996). Einsatzmöglichkeiten retrospektiver Befragungen bei der Untersuchung des Expertiserwerbs. In H. Gruber & A. Ziegler (Eds.), *Expertiseforschung* (pp. 169-190). Opladen: Westdeutscher Verlag.

Heller, K.A., & Viek, P. (1997). *Explorationsstudie zur Begabtenförderung im Tertiärbereich.* Final report to the BMBF in Bonn. München LMU, Fak 11.
Henry, W.A. (1995). *In defense of elitism.* New York: Doubleday.
Herrnstein, R.J., & Murray, C.A. (1994). *The bell curve: Intelligence and class structure in American life.* Cambridge: Free Press.
Hörmann, H.-J. (1986). Selbstbeschreibungsfragebogen für Schüler und Studenten. In R. Schwarzer (Ed.), *Skalen zur Befindlichkeit und Persönlichkeit (Forschungsbericht 5)* (pp. 51–68). Berlin: Freie Universität Berlin, Institut für Psychologie.
Jacoby, R., & Glauberman, N. (1995). *The bell curve debate.* New York: Times Books.
Jerusalem, M. (1986). Perzipierte Intelligenz. In R. Schwarzer (Ed.), *Skalen zur Befindlichkeit und Persönlichkeit. Forschungsbericht 5* (pp. 43–46), Berlin: Freie Universität, Institut für Psychologie.
Khan, S.B. (1969). Affective correlates of academic achievement. *Journal of Educational Psychology, 60,* 216–221.
Krampen, G., & Wünsche, P. (1984). Konstrukte und Indikatoren politischen Engagements: Literaturübersicht und Experimentalversion des Trierer Inventars zur politischen Partizipation (TIPP). *Trierer Psychologische Berichte, 11 (7),* p. 7.
Kuhl, J., & Fuhrmann, A. (1995). *Kurzmanual für den VCQ (Volitional Components Questionnaire).* Osnabrück: Universität Osnabrück.
Laagland, E. (1978). *Evaluierung eines Auswahlverfahrens für die Ermittlung der Studierbefähigung. Nacherhebung zur Oberprimanerauswahl der Studienstiftung des Deutschen Volkes.* München: Minerva-Publikation.
Lamers, H. (1991). Zur Problematik der Identifikation von besonders Begabten. In R. Manstetten & G. Albrecht (Eds.), *Begabungsforschung und Begabtenförderung in der Berufsbildung* (pp. 31–36). Frankfurt/Main: Lang.
Lavin, D.E. (1965). *The prediction of academic performance. A theoretical analysis and review of research.* New York: Sage.
Lotz, G. (1984). *Streß, Bewältigung und soziale Kompetenz bei Schülern.* Frankfurt: Lang.
Ludwig, S. (1984). *Stressbewaeltigung im Hochschulstudium. Eine motivationspsychologische Analyse person- und situationsspezifischer Faktoren.* Unpublished Habilitationsschrift. München: LMU, Fak. 11.
Mansfield, R.S., & Busse, T.V. (1981). *The psychology of creativity and discovery.* Chicago: Nelson Hall.
Manstetten, R. (1996). *Begabtenförderung in der beruflichen Bildung.* Göttingen: Hogrefe.
Marsh, H.W., & O'Neill, R. (1984). Self-Description Questionnaire III (SDQ III): The construct validity of multidimensional self-concept ratings by late-adolescents. *Journal of Educational Measurement, 21,* 153–174.
Merton, R.K. (1968). The Matthew effect in science. *Science, 159,* 156–163.
Mönks, F.J. (1986). Hochbegabung und Studiengewohnheiten: Persönlicher Lebensstil, bevorzugte Instruktionsmethode und Verarbeitung von Lernstoff. In M. Amelang (Ed.), *Bericht über den 35. Kongreß der Deutschen Gesellschaft für Psychologie in Heidelberg 1986,* Bd. I (p. 259). Göttingen: Hogrefe.
Mönks, F.J. (1992). Ein interaktionales Model der Hochbegabung. In E.A. Hany & H. Nickel (Eds.), *Begabung und Hochbegabung. Theoretische Konzepte—Empirische Befunde—Praktische Konsequenzen* (p. 17–22). Bern: Hans Huber.
Mönks, F.J. (1996). Elite-Debatte im Scheinwerfer. *Psychologie in Erziehung und Unterricht, 43,* 225–230.
Mönks, F.J., Katzko, M.W., & Boxtel, v. H.W. (Eds.) (1992). *Education of the gifted in Europe: Theoretical and research issues.* Amsterdam/Lisse: Swets & Zeitlinger.
Mönks, F.J., van Boxtel, H.W., Roelofs, J.J.W., & Sanders, M.P.M. (1986). The identification of gifted children in secondary education and description of their situation in Holland. In K.A. Heller & J.F. Feldhusen (Eds.), *Identifying and nurturing the gifted. An international perspective* (pp. 39–65). Toronto: Huber.

Morkel, A. (1987). Hochbegabtenförderung an den Hochschulen im Bereich der Geisteswissenschaften. In F.E. Weinert & H. Wagner (Eds.), *Die Förderung Hochbegabter in der Bundesrepublik Deutschland: Probleme, Positionen, Perspektiven* (pp. 84–93). Bad Honnef: Bock.
Nichols, R.C., & Astin, A.W. (1966). Progress of the merit scholar: An eight-year follow-up. *Personnel and Guidance Journal, 44*, 673–681.
Renzulli, J.S. (1978). What makes giftedness? Reexamining a definition. *Phi Delta Kappa, 60*, 180–184, 261.
Schneider, W. (1993). Acquiring expertise: Determinants of exceptional performance. In K.A. Heller, F.J. Mönks, & A.H. Passow (Eds.), *International handbook of research and development of giftedness and talent* (pp. 311–324). Oxford: Pergamon.
Schuler, H., Funke, U., & Baron-Boldt J. (1990). Predictive validity of school grades—A metaanalysis. *Applied Psychology: An International Review, 39(1)*, 89–103.
Seifert, K.H., & Bergmann, C.H. (1983). Deutschsprachige Rekonstruktion des Work Values Inventory von D.E. Super: Ergebnisse bei Gymnasiasten und Berufstätigen. *Psychologie und Praxis, 27*, 160–172.
Siegler, R.S., & Kotovsky, K. (1986). Two levels of giftedness: Shall ever the twain meet? In R.J. Sternberg & J.E. Davidson (Eds.), *Conceptions of giftedness* (pp. 417–435). Cambridge: Cambridge University Press.
Simonton, D.K. (1988). *Scientific genius. A psychology of science.* Cambridge: Cambridge University Press.
Simonton, D.K. (1991). Career landmarks in science: Individual differences and interdisciplinary contrasts. *Developmental Psychology, 27*, 119–130.
Steinkamp, M.-W., & Maehr, M.-L. (1983). Affect, ability, and science achievement: A quantitative synthesis of correlational research. *Review of Educational Research, 53* (3), 369–396.
Sternberg, R.J. (1994). Triarchic theory applied to student instruction and assessment methods. *General Psychology, 30*, 42–48.
Sternberg, R.J., Callahan, C., Burns, D., Gubbins, E.J., Purcell, J., Reiss, S.M., Renzulli, J.S., & Westberg, K. (1995). Return gift to sender: A review of The Bell Curve. *Gifted Child Quarterly, 39*, 177–179.
Stumpf, H., & Nauels, H.U. (1990). Zur prognostischen Validität des "Tests für medizinische Studiengänge" (TMS) im Studiengang Humanmedizin. *Diagnostika, 36* (1), 16–32.
Subotnik, R.F., & Arnold, K.D. (1993). Longitudinal studies of giftedness: Investigating the fulfillment of promise. In K.A. Heller, F.J. Mönks, & A.H. Passow (Eds.), *International handbook of research and development of giftedness and talent* (pp. 149–160). Oxford: Pergamon.
Subotnik, R.F., & Steiner, C.L. (1994). Problem finding, problem solving, and creativity. In M.A. Runco (Ed.), *Problem identification in academic research: A longitudinal study from adolescence to young adulthood.* Norwood, NJ: Ablex.
Trost, G. (1985). Pädagogische Diagnostik beim Hochschulzugang, dargestellt am Beispiel der Zulassung zu medizinischen Studiengängen. In R.S. Jäger, R. Horn, & K.H. Ingenkamp (Eds.), *Test und Trends 4* (pp. 41–83). Weinheim: Beltz.
Trost, G. (1986). Identification of highly gifted adolescents—methods and experiences. In K.A. Heller & J.F. Feldhusen (Eds.), *Identifying and nurturing the gifted. An international perspective* (pp. 83–91). Toronto, Huber.
Trost, G. (1993). Prediction of excellence in school, university, and work. In K.A. Heller, F.J. Mönks, & A.H. Passow (Eds.), *International handbook of research and development of giftedness and talent* (pp. 325–336). Oxford: Pergamon.
Trost, G., & Siegler, J. (1992). Biographische Indikatoren herausragender beruflicher Leistungen. In E.A. Hany, & H. Nickel (Eds.), *Begabung und Hochbegabung. Theoretische Konzepte—Empirische Befunde—Praktische Konsequenzen* (pp. 95–104). Bern: Huber.

Weinert, F.E. (1990). Der aktuelle Stand der psychologischen Kreativitätsforschung. In P.H. Hofschneider, & K.U. Mayer (Eds.), *Generationsdynamik und Innovation in der Grundlagenforschung*, Vol. 3, (pp. 21–44). München: MPG.

Ziegler, A. & Perleth, Ch. (1997). Schafft es Sisyphos, den Stein den Berg hinaufzurollen? Eine kritische Bestandsaufnahme der Diagnose- und Fördermöglichkeiten von Begabten in der beruflichen Bildung vor dem Hintergrund des Münchner BegabungsProzeßModells. *Psychologie in Erziehung und Unterricht, 44,* 152–163.

Zuckerman, H. (1967). The sociology of the Nobel prizes, *Scientific American, 217(5)*, 25–33.

Zuckerman, H. (1992). The scientific elite: Nobel Laureates' mutual influences. In R.S. Albert (Ed.), *Genius and eminence* (2nd ed., pp. 157–169). Oxford: Pergamon.

Author Index

Ackerman, P.L., 303
Adams, H.B., 239
Albert, R.S., 235, 303
Amabile, T.M., 317
Ambrose, D., 7
American Psychological Association, 93
Angyal, A., 281
Arend, R., 211, 223
Ari, B.A., 238
Arnold, K.D., 95, 235, 302, 316, 317
Arnot, M., 237
Ash, M.G., 77
Astin, A.W., 72
Astin, H.S., 301
Azuma, H., 174, 236

Baillargeon, R., 21
Bakan, D., 112, 281
Baltes, P.B., 37, 157
Bamberger, J., 260, 265, 266

Bandura, A., 72
Baron-Boldt, J., 312
Barrett, K.C., 127, 223
Bastian, H.B., 260, 264
Bathurst, K., 235
Baumrind, D., 210
Bayley, N., 220
Behrman, J.R., 75
Belskey, J., 217
Benbow, C.P., 237
Benigni, L., 24
Berg, K., 75
Bergmann, C.H., 309
Berlin, I., 141
Bernstein, M., 46, 48
Berry, J.W., 46
Beuys before Beuys, 196
Binet, A., 43, 45, 67
Blau, P.M., 70
Block, J., 104, 105, 106, 207
Block, J.H., 104, 105, 106, 207
Block, N., 94

Bloom, B.S., 205
Blythe, D.A., 119
Blythe, T., 58
Boom, J., 128, 234
Bornstein, M., 12
Bosman, A.N.Th., 34
Boston, B.A., 240
Bowlby, J., 206
Boxtel, V.H.W., 318
Brandstädter, J., 278
Breilinger, K., 21
Bronfenbrenner, U., 30, 204
Brooks, L., 72
Brown, D., 71, 74
Brugman, D., 127
Brumbaugh, K., 243
Bruner, J.S., 12, 278
Bühler, K., 192, 196
Bukowski, W.M., 118
Burggraf, S.A., 142
Burns, D., 299
Busse, T.V., 302
Butcher, H.J., 301
Butler-Por, N., 278

AUTHOR INDEX

Callahan, C.M., 236, 299
Campos, J.J., 127
Campos, R.G., 127
Cantor, N., 278
Capron, C., 94
Cardon, L.R., 89
Carr, M., 239
Carroll, J.B., 46
Caspi, A., 104, 106, 109
Cattell, R.B., 301
Ceci, S.J., 30, 204
Chen, C., 171, 175
Chessor, R., 240
Cillessen, A.H.N., 112, 116, 118
Clinkenbeard, P., 59
Cloninger, C.R., 103
Cohen, L.M., 7
Cohler, B.J., 278
Colby, A., 125, 128, 129, 145
Cole, M., 10, 13, 46
Coleman, E.B., 238
Collins, J., 13
Conger, R.D., 217
Conway, B.E., 46, 48
Corey, L.A., 75
Costa, P.T., 103
Cox, J., 240
Craven, R., 240
Crick,.N.R., 120
Crites, S., 280
Cropley, A.J., 233
Csikszentmihalyi, M., 6, 10, 12, 14, 263, 264, 300
Czeschlik, T., 237

Damon, W., 125, 129, 145
Daniel, N., 240
Daniels, D., 152
Davidson, J., 156
Davidson, J.E., 50
Davidson, J.W., 18, 234

Davidson, L., 259, 266
de Raad, B., 104
De Waal, F.B.M., 120
DeFries, J.C., 75
Delbanco, N., 260
Dent-Read, C., 19
DES (Department for Education), 240
Detterman, D.K., 44, 89
Deutsch, W., 186
Dias, M.G., 127
Doise, W., 112
Dolan, L., 302
Donaldson, G., 83
Dörfert, J., 69, 77, 84
Dostoevsky, F.M., 132
Duncan, O.D.E., 70
Dunn, J., 218
Duveen, G., 237
Dweck, C.S., 301

Earles, J.A., 56, 70, 94
Eaves, E.J., 75
Eddy, A.S., 57
Edelman, G.M., 26
Egeland, B., 209, 213, 221, 223
Elias, N., 23
Elshout, J., 239
Emmons, R.A., 278
Erickson, M.F., 213, 221, 223
Ericsson, K.A., 72, 93, 264, 301, 302, 318

Fagot, B., 210
Falbo, T., 218
Falconer, D.S., 89
Fang, G., 171
Feldhusen, J.F., 6, 231, 239, 240, 241
Feldman, D.H., 4, 5, 6, 7, 8, 9, 10, 11, 12, 13, 14, 250, 256
Ferguson, T.J., 141, 142

Ferrari, M., 59
Fineberg, J., 187, 196
Fisher, D.M., 25
Flanagan, O., 128
Flavell, J., 20
Flynn, J.R., 236
Fogel, A., 19, 27, 28, 30
Forsythe, G.B., 44, 52
Frank, A., 157
Frankena, W.K., 146
Franks, S.B., 302
Fraser, B.J., 70, 94
Fraser, S., 299
Frasier, M.M., 5, 211, 227,
Freeman, J., 231, 236, 237, 238, 239, 240, 243, 245
Frijda, N., 127, 161
Fuhrmann, A., 309, 310
Fulker, D.W., 75
Funke, A., 309
Funke, U., 312
Futterweit, L., 157

Gagné, F., 5, 7, 11, 204
Gallagher, J.J., 211
Galloway, G., 239
Galton, F., 233
Ganzeboom, H.B.G., 72
Gardner, H., 6, 9, 10, 12, 13, 14, 44, 46, 58, 235, 250
Gardner, H.I., 58
Gardner, M.K., 49
Garner, W.R., 54
Gastel J., 50
Gay, J., 46
Gelman, R., 36
Geppert, U., 77
Gergen, K.J., 278
Gergen, M.M., 278
Ghiselli, E., 300
Gibson, E.J., 19
Gibson, J.J., 23, 30, 32

AUTHOR INDEX   325

Gilligan C., 72, 119, 120, 131
Glauberman, N., 299
Glick, J., 46
Goertzel, M.G., 235
Goertzel, T.G., 235
Goertzel, V., 235
Goldberg, L.R., 103, 104
Golomb, C., 188
Good, T.L., 240
Gooding, R.Z., 70, 74
Goodman, N., 50
Gottfredson, L.S., 72
Gottfried, A.E., 235
Gottfried, A.W., 235
Gottlieb, G., 18, 19, 23, 26
Gottschaldt, K., 76, 77
Graham, S., 142
Gray, J., 237
Greenfield, P.M., 46
Greenwald, A.G., 278
Greller, M.M., 72
Griffin, R., 25
Grigorenko, E.L., 44, 59
Gross, M.U.M., 234
Grotpeter, J.K., 120
Gruber, H., 301
Gubbins, E.J., 299
Guerin, D.W., 235
Guyote, M.J., 49

Haertel, G.D., 93
Haidt, J., 127
Hampson, N.H., 136, 137, 140
Hany, E.A., 232, 235, 239
Hartung, D., 309
Haselager, G.J.T., 104, 106, 112, 116
Hattie, J.A., 70, 94
Hauser, R.M., 70
Heath, A.C., 75

Hedlund, J., 44
Heft, H., 32
Heil, J., 153
Heller, K.A. 236, 309
Henry, W.A., 299
Hermans, H.J.M., 278, 280, 282, 285, 286, 295
Hermans-Jansen, E., 280, 282, 285, 286, 295
Herrnstein, R.J., 55, 70, 299
Hershberger, S.L., 75, 94
Hess, R., 174, 236
Heymans., P., 152, 154, 155
Higgins, E.T., 278
Hofstee, W.K., 104
Holahan, C.K., 235
Hong, E., 235, 242
Hörmann, H.-J., 309, 310
Horn, J.L., 83
Horvath, J., 44
Horvath, J.A., 52, 54
Howe, M., 156
Howe, M.J.A., 18, 234
Hubbard, F.O., 211, 216, 226
Hudley, C., 142
Hunter, J.E., 56
Hunter, J.W., 70

Isabella, L., 92
Isabella, R., 217

Jackson, A., 58
Jacobs, J.E., 237
Jacobson, K., 21
Jacoby, R., 299
James, W., 278, 280
Jap-a-Joe, S.R., 215, 216
Jencks, C., 74
Jensen, A.R., 48, 56

Jerusalem, M., 309
John, O.P., 106, 109
Johnston, T.D., 23, 26
Jones, E.D., 241

Kalinowski, A.G., 17
Kanevsky, L.S., 238
Karmiloff-Smith, A., 165
Kassan, L., 235, 240, 241
Katzko, M.W., 318
Kaufman, F.A., 237
Kavanaugh, K., 210
Kelso, J.A.S., 28
Kendrick, C., 218
Kerschensteiner, G., 187
Ketron, J.L., 46, 48
Khan, S.B., 301
Kihlstrom, J.F., 278
Kinsella-Shaw, J., 153
Kirsch, M., 70, 74
Klages, L., 281
Kliegl, R., 79
Kogan, J., 267
Kohlberg, L., 128
Koller, S.H., 127
Kondo-Ikemura, K., 214
Kornhaber, M.L., 46
Kotovsky, K., 300
Krais, B., 309
Krampe, R.T., 264, 301, 302, 318
Krampen, G., 309, 310
Krasnegor, N., 12
Krasney, N., 237
Krechevsky, M., 58
Kreitzberg, V.S., 218
Kremen, A.M., 207
Kroll, M.D., 240
Kugler, P., 153
Kuhl, J., 309, 310
Kulieke, M., 237
Kurtz-Costes, B.E., 239

AUTHOR INDEX

Laagland, E., 303
Laboratory of Comparative Human Cognition, 46
Lamers, H., 302
Lavin, D.E., 301
Lee, S., 171, 174, 175
Lerner, R.M., 71, 72
Leseman, P.P.M., 215, 216
Lewis, M., 203, 206, 208, 218
Li, J., 58
Lichtenstein, P., 75, 94
Lindenberger, U., 79
Lipton, R., 206
Liu, F., 171
Loehlin, J.C., 103
Lorenz, F.O., 217
Lotz, G., 309, 310
Louis, B., 203, 206, 208
Lubart, T.I., 49, 51, 233
Lubinski, D., 237
Ludwig, S., 308
Luiten, A., 142
Lummis, M., 171
Luquet, G.H., 187
Luria, A., 27, 34

Macomber, J., 21
Maehr, M.-L., 301
Magnus, P., 75
Malatesta, C.Z., 142
Mansfield, R.S., 302
Manstetten, R., 302
Markus, H.R., 278
Marsh, H.W., 240, 278, 309, 310
Maslin-Cole, C., 223
Mason, E.J., 3, 5, 6, 13
Masten, A.S., 114
Matas, L., 211, 223
Mayer, K.U., 70, 71, 93
Mayr, U., 79
McAdams, D.P., 278, 281

McCall, R.B., 208
McCartney, K., 26, 70
McClearn, G.E., 75
McCrae, R.R., 103
McNally, J., 52
McNamara, G., 106
Meij, J.Th., 211, 213, 214, 215, 226
Melamed, T., 93
Mele, A., 153
Meltzoff, A., 165
Merleau-Ponty, M., 280
Merton, R.K., 301
Meulemann, H., 73
Michalson, L., 203
Milgram, R.M., 235, 242
Miller, E.R., 142
Miller, P.A., 20
Miller, S., 20
Miller-Tiedeman, A., 72
Moffitt, T.E., 106
Mönks, F.J., 3, 5, 6, 7, 13, 14, 69, 95, 125, 128, 198, 204, 277, 278, 299, 302, 318
Morelock, M.J., 3, 4, 6, 7, 14
Moreno, F., 198
Moreno, J.L., 198
Morf, C.C., 278
Morgan, G.A., 223
Mori, M., 48
Morison, P., 114
Morkel, A., 316
Moss, E., 238
Motti, E., 224
Murray, C., 55, 70, 299

Nance, W.E., 75
Nauels, H.U., 312
Neale, M.C., 89
Newcomb, A.F., 118
Nichols, R.C., 301
Noe, R.A., 70, 74

Nurius, P., 278
Nuthmann, R., 309

O'Brien, M.A., 209
Ochse, R., 249, 264
Ojanen, S., 239
Okagaki, L., 46, 54, 58
Olsen, M.E., 142
Olszewski-Kubilius, P.M., 237
Olthof, T., 127, 128, 141, 142
O'Neill, R., 309, 310
Ornstein, S., 92
Osipow, S.H., 72
Oyama, S., 26

Pallas, J., 206
Parke, R.D., 217
Parmelee, L., 158
Passow, A.H., 5
Pattee, L., 118
Peak, L., 167
Pedersen, N.L., 75, 94
Pellegrini, D.S., 114
Perleth, Ch., 301, 303, 304
Persson, R.S., 232
Piaget, J., 27, 45
Pianta, R., 209
Plomin, R., 69, 75, 89, 152
Polit, D., 218
Port, R.F., 28
Powell, J.S., 49
Pratkanis, A.R., 278
Provence, S., 206
Purcell, J., 299
Puyn, R., 159

Radford, J., 211, 235
Ramey, C.T., 206
Rathunde, K., 263, 264
Ree, M.J., 56, 70, 94
Reed, E.S., 30
Reed, V., 206

Reiss, S.M., 236, 299
Renmin Ribao, 168
Renzulli, J.S., 7, 12, 204, 277, 299, 302
Rest, J.R., 128
Rhodewalt, F., 278
Rich, Y., 238
Ridley-Johnson, R., 25
Riksen-Walraven, J.M., 106, 206, 207, 211, 213, 214, 215, 226
Risemberg, R., 238
Robins, R.W., 106, 109
Robinson, N.M., 205, 206
Roche, L., 240
Roelofs, J.J.W., 302, 318
Rogoff, B., 27, 31
Rosenberg, M., 278
Ross, P.O., 5, 6, 14
Rost, D.H., 237
Roth, M., 158
Rothermund, K., 278
Roubertoux, P.L., 94
Rudduck, J., 237
Rudé, G., 136, 137, 139
Ruff, H., 157
Rule, B.G., 141, 142
Runco, M.A., 303

Sahin, S., 215
Sameroff, A.J., 23, 29
Sanders, M.P.M., 302, 318
Sarbin, Th.R., 278, 279, 280
Scarr, S., 26, 70, 95, 152
Schama, S., 136, 137
Scheuch, E.K., 79, 81, 85
Schmidt, F.L., 56, 70
Schmitt, N., 70, 74
Schneider, W., 17, 69, 318

Scholte, R.H.J., 108, 109, 113, 114, 116
Schulenberg, J.E., 71, 72
Schuler, H., 312
Scripp, L., 259, 266, R.R., 70, 235
Seifert, K.H., 309
Seiffge-Krenke, I., 158
Sewell, W.H., 70
Sharp, D.W., 46
Shaw, R., 153
Sheldon, K.M., 278
Shore, B.M., 238
Siegel, L.S., 68
Siegler, R.S., 11, 300, 302
Sijsling, F.F., 215
Simmons, R.G., 119
Simon, T., 43, 45, 67
Simons, R.L., 217
Simonton, D.K., 14, 236, 317
Sloan, K.D., 17
Sloboda, J.A., 18, 156, 234
Smith, L.B., 19, 20, 21, 24, 28
Smitsman, A.W., 33, 34, 36
Smrkovsky, M., 220
Snook, S., 44
Solaas, M.H., 75
Sosniak, L.A., 17, 20, 21, 250, 256, 262, 264
Southern, W.T., 241
Span, P., 238
Spelke, E.S., 21, 36
Sroufe, L.A., 211, 213, 221, 223
Stadler, M., 77
Starkey, P., 36
Starr, R., 206
State Education Commission, 169, 170

Stearns, P., 217
Stefanek, J., 84, H., 142
Steiner, C.L., 302, 317
Steinkamp, M.-W., 301
Sternberg, R.J., 12, 43, 44, 45, 46, 47, 48, 49, 50, 51, 52, 54, 55, 57, 58, 59, 60, 69, 93, 233, 236, 269, 299, 300
Stevenson, H.W., 171, 174, 175
Stigler, J.W., 171
Stroh, R.J., 72
Stumpf, H., 312
Subotnik, R.F., 95, 235, 240, 241, 302, 316, 317
Sully, J., 187
Summers, E., 235, 240, 241
Sundet, J.M., 75
Super, D.E., 72, 73
Sweeney, P., 52

Tambs, K., 75
Tangney, J.P., 142
Tannenbaum, A., 7
Taubman, P., 75
ten Brink, P.W.M., 118
Terassier, J-C., 238
Terman, L.M., 235
Tesch-Römer, C., 264, 301, 302, 318
Tetewsky, S.J., 50
Thelan, E., 19, 20, 21, 24, 25, 28
Thissen-Pennings, M.C.E., 118
Thomae, H., 153, 278, L.A., 89
Tiedeman, D.V., 72
Tirri, K., 232
Treffinger, D.J., 4, 5, 231, 239, 241
Treiman, D.J., 72

Triandis, H.C., 278
Trost, G., 300, 301, 302, 303, 317
Tsai, S., 70
Turiel, E., 120
Turner, M.E., 49

Ulrich, B.D., 25
Ultee, W.C., 72

Vaccaro, D., 108
Valsiner, G., 24
van Aken, M.A.G., 106, 108, 109, 114, 116, 207
Van Boxtel, H.W., 204, 302, 318
Van den Boom, D.C., 206, 226
Van der Meulen, B.F., 220
Van Geert, P., 11, 19, 153
Van Gelder, T., 28
Van Gilst, W., 280
Van het Reve, K., 145
Van Leeuwen, C., 33
Van Leeuwen, L., 33
van Lieshout, C.F.M., 104, 106, 108, 109, 112, 114, 116, 213
Van Loosbroek, E., 36
van Sommers, P., 186

Vereijken, C.M.J.L., 214, 216
Vergeer, M.M., 215
Vernon, P.A., 48, P., 77, 309
Vincente, K., 153
Vogler, G.P., 75
Vondracek, F.W., 71, 72
Vygotsky, L., 27, 34

Wagner, P.E., 142
Wagner, R.K., 12, 44, 46, 48, 52, 54, 55, 57, 58, 269
Wake, W.K., 46
Walberg, H.J., 70, 93, 94
Wallace, B., 239
Walters, J., 250
Wasser, A., 235, 240, 241
Wattendorf, J., 52
Weber, A., 301
Wechsler, D., 68, 79
Weil, E.M., 49
Weinberg, R.A., 95
Weinert, F.E., 69, 77, 84, 316, 317
Weinstein, T., 93
Weisz, V., 237
Welch, W.W., 70, 94
Wertsch, J.D., 241

Wertsch, J.V., 23, 33
Westberg, K., 299
Whalen, S., 263, 264
White, B., 224
White, K.R., 240
White, N., 58
White, R.W., 206, 207
Whitten, C., 206
Wigdor, A.K., 54
Williams, E., 142
Williams, W.M., 44, 45, 52, 54, 58
Wills, T.A., 108
Wilson, A., 142
Winner, E., 250, 268
Wober, M., 46
Wu, C., 217
Wünsche, P., 309, 310
Wynn, K., 36

Yang, S.Y., 47
Ypenberg, I.H., 198

Zevalkink, J., 211, 216, 226
Zha, Z., 236, 238
Ziegler, A., 236, 301, 303, 304
Zimmerman, B.J., 238
Zorman, R., 242
Zuckerman, H., 249, 317
Zukow-Goldring, P., 19

Subject Index

Ability, lack of, 278
Academic achievement, 167–183, 299–321
 expectations of, 179
 prediction, 300–301, 302–303, 315
 satisfaction with, 177
 time use, 179, 180
Achievement approach, 4
Adaptation, 12, 44
Addictive behaviour, 109, 110
Adjustment, 109, 110–111, 115, 179–181
Adolescent resilience, 108–121
 agentic, 112–121
 communal, 109, 112–121
Adversities, 157–158
Affordances, 32
Aggression, 141
Agreeableness, 104, 106–107, 109, 112, 121
Analytical ability, 47–49
Anger, 141–142
Antisocial behaviour, 109, 110
Arima model, 161–163
Art, *see* Drawing

Attributions of status, 266–269

Bayley Mental Scale, 220
Behavioural constraints, 27–28
Behavioural interaction 206–207, 223, 224
Big Five personality model, 104–112
Boredom, 240–241
Bullying, 109, 111
"Burn out", 232, 265
Business management, 54–56

Capabilities, 29–32
 enhancement by tool use 32–37
 plasticity 29–30
Case study approach, 234
Cell differentiation, 25
Change, 24
Chess, 13
Child-driven education 241–244
Children
 autonomy of, 209–210, 225
 number in family, 218–220
 "popular", 116, 117, 118
Children's Palaces, 242

330   SUBJECT INDEX

Chinese education system, 168–171, 242
Cognition, 20
Componential analysis, 48–49
Competence motivation, 205–209, 215, 223
Competition, 261–263
Composers, 268–269
Conceptual-project problems, 50
Confucian doctrine, 174–175
Conscientiousness, 104, 106–107, 112
Creative potential, 197, 198
Creativity, 49–51, 187, 192
Cross-cultural comparisons
  concept of intelligence, 46–47
  mathematics achievement, 167–183
  parental support, 213–216
Crystallised intelligence, 69, 83

Developmental domains, 8–10
Developmental narrative, 156
Developmental nexus, 153–158
Developmental theory, 7–8
Dichotomies, 23
Disadvantaged families, 211, 225
Discontinuity, 24–25, 34
Domains, developmental, 8–10
Drawing, 185–199
  by adults, 185–186, 192–193
  case studies, 188–197
  by children, 185, 186–187
  development of, 186, 188–198
  individuality of, 193, 196
  lessons, 197
  stylistic continuity, 193
Drive, 263–264
Dynamic relationships, 23–24

Education, 231, 232, 299
  child-driven approach, 241–244
  expectations of, 179
  higher education, 299–321
  "Sports Approach", 243–244
  teacher recognition of talent, 239–241
  teaching methods, 58–62, 231, 232, 238–239, 241–244

Effort, 174–176, 236
Ego-control/resilience, 104–106, *see also* Resilience
Embryology, 25, 26
Emergent properties, 31
Emotion, 161, 237–238
Emotional stability, 104, 106–107, 112, 119, 121
Emotional support, 209
Employment
  job performance, 54–56, 58
  promotion within, 52, 53
  satisfaction with, 73, 85, 88
  status, 71, 75, 81, 85–86, 87, 89–92
  see also Occupational development
Enrichment, 241
Environment, 28–32, 204, 205–209, 317–318
  organism-environment system 23–28
Evolution, 12
Exchange, 24–28
Experience, 203–205
Expertise, levels of, 9
Extraversion, 104, 106–107, 112, 119

Family climate, 205, 206, 223–224, 225, *see also* Parental support; Parents
  disadvantaged families, 211, 225
Fischer, Bobby, 13
Fluid intelligence, 69, 83

Gender differences
  mathematics ability, 237
  in personality resilience, 108, 119–120, 121
  in talent, 236–237
"General intelligence" measures, 12
Generalisation, 281, 285–286
Genetic factors
  educational attainment, 74–75
  intelligence, 69–70, 89–92
  mathematics ability, 237
  occupational achievement, 75, 89–92, 94–95
  personality, 103

Genetic potential, 204
"Gifted achievement", 4
"Gifted child", 3–4
Gifted personality, 103–123
Giftedness
  categories, 6–7
  defined, 5–6, 232
  misidentification of, 43
  misuse of the term, 231
  recognition, 239–241, 301–303
  see also Talent
GOLD study, 75–82
Graduate Record Examination (GRE), 45
Guilt, 141, 142

Heritability, see Genetic factors
"Hidden core" hypothesis, 21–22
High schools, 172–173
Higher education, 299–321

Idealisation, 281–282, 286
Incantation Theory, 152, 154–155, 163
Individual differences in intelligence, 69, 83–84
Individuality, 10–11, 193, 196
Inheritance, see Genetic factors
Innate abilities, 174–176
Insight, 50–51
Intelligence, 67–70
  crystallised, 69, 83
  cultural variations in concept of, 46–47
  fluid, 69, 83
  genetic factors, 69–70, 89–92
  individual differences, 69, 83–84
  life-span development, 83–84, 87
  measures, 12, 45, 233
Intelligence, successful, 43–65
  components of, 47–58
  defined, 44
Interactive behaviour, 206–207, 223, 224
Intervention programmes, 206–207, 226–227
IQ measures, 12, 233

Javits program, 5
Job performance, 54–56, 58
Job promotion, 52, 53
Job satisfaction, 73, 85, 88
Juilliard School, 249–276

Key schools, 170

Leadership, 44
Life skills, 45
Life-span development, 83–84, 87, 92
Life stress, 212, 214, 216–217, 225
Longitudinal study approach, 235–236
Love, 131–133

Managerial performance, 54–56
Marland Report, 6
Mathematics, attitude to, 174
Mathematics achievement, 167–183
  and gender/genetics, 237
"Matthew principle", 70
Mental causation, 153
Metacomponents, 48
Meta-moral perspective, 143–147
Moral absolutism, 139–140, 143
Moral actions, 127
Moral dilemmas, 128
Moral emotions, 127, 141
Moral excellence, 127–133, 142–147
Moral exemplars, 129–130
Moral giftedness, 125, 128
Moral perspective, 126–127, 143, 146
Morality, 125–149
  controversial, 130–131
  and love, 131–133
Mothers, hostility of, 221, 223
Motivation, 177, 204–209, 215, 223, 264, 300–301, 310, 315
Motives, latent/manifest, 280–281
Munich Dynamic Giftedness Model, 303, 304
Music/musicians
  auditions, 255–258
  competition, 261–263
  composers, 268–269
  drive, 263–264

SUBJECT INDEX

Juilliard School, 249–276
musicality, 22, 261
personality, 261
physical coordination, 261
physique, 260
pianists, 17, 32
technique, 260

Narrative approach, 278–279
Non-universal theory, 7–12, 14

Occupation
job performance, 54–56, 58
promotion within, 52, 53
satisfaction with, 73, 85, 88
status, 71, 75, 81, 85–86, 87, 89–92
Occupational development, 70–95
genetic factors, 75, 89–92, 94–95
phases, 92
prediction, 85–89
Only children, 218, 219
Openness, 104, 106–107, 119
Organism-environment system, 23–32
Overcontrol, 105, 107, 109, 110–111

Paradigm shifting, 4–5
Parental support, 209–227, 234
cross-cultural comparisons, 213–216
essential ingredients of, 209–211, 225
improvement, 226
measurement, 212–213
stability, 225–226
Parents, 234
cultural variations in concept of intelligence, 46–47
hostility towards children, 221, 223
limit setting by, 210
recognition of child's autonomy, 209–210, 225
responsiveness of, 206–207
teaching role of, 210
Peer group
importance of, 266–269
reputation within, 109, 111, 114–115
Persistence, 24

Person-centred approach, 104
Personal goals, 47
Personality, 103–104, 300–301, 302, 316
Big Five model, 104–112
and gender, 108, 119–120, 121
genetic factors, 103
resilience, 104–121
Pianists, 17, 32, *see also* Music/musicians
Plasticity, 29–30
Play, parental intrusiveness into, 209–210
Political involvement, 310, 314
Popularity, 116, 117, 118
Practical abilities, 51–58
Practical Intelligence for Schools, 58
Precocity, 232
Preformism, 22–23
Problem-solving, 48–49
Prodigies, 265–266
Promotion at work, 52, 53
Psychosocial adjustment, 109, 110–111, 115, 179–181
Psychosomatic problems, 180–181
Puberty, 119–120, 192

Reading, 48
Reasoning, 48–49
Relational support, 109, 110, 112–114, 116, 117, 118, *see also* Parental support
Religion, 145–146
Research methodology, 233–236
Resilience, 104–121
agentic, 112–121
communal, 109, 112–121
and gender, 108, 119–120, 121
Robespierre, Maximilien, 133–141

School, attitude towards, 174
Scientists, 300–301
Selective encoding, 50
Self-concept, 310, 315
Self-confrontation method, 279, 282–286, 289, 295–296
Self-enhancement, 295–296

Self-esteem, 278
Self-evaluation, 177–179
Self-investigation, 286, 288–293, 294–296
Self-narrative, 278–279
Self-reflection, 296
Self-selection, 241–242, 243–244
Sex differences, *see* Gender differences
Shaping, 44
Siblings, number of, 218–220
Single mothers, 217–218
Social competence, 310
Sociometric status, 116, 117, 118
Speech, 196–197
"Sports Approach", 243–244
Stepping reflex, 25
Stereotyping, 238
Stress, 212, 214, 216–217, 225
Successful intelligence, 43–65
   components of, 47–58
   defined, 44
Symbolic media, 35–37

Tacit knowledge, 51–58, 269–271
Talent
   categories, 6–7
   contract, 155–156
   development of, 4, 6, 17–40, 198
   for development, 152, 164, 165–166
   "hidden core" hypothesis, 21–22
   recognition, 239–241, 301–303
   and self, 277
   spatial aspects, 18–19
   temporal aspects, 18
   see also Giftedness
Teacher recognition of talent, 239–241
Teaching methods, 58–62, 231, 232, 238–239, 241–244
   art lessons, 197
   child-driven, 241–244
   "Sports Approach", 243–244
"Three Times Problem", 240–241
Time use, 179, 180
Tool use, 32–37
Transformational narrative, 163–164
Transformational symbols, 155, 163, 164–165
Twin studies, 76–82
Tyranny, 136–137

Underachievers, 277–278
Undercontrol, 105, 107, 109, 110–111
Universal to unique continuum, 8–10

Valuation theory, 280–282
Variable-centred approach, 104

Word comprehension, 49
Work, *see* Employment
Writing, 192, 195, 196–197